Developments in British Politics 7

Related titles

Laura Cram, Desmond Dinan and Neill Nugent (eds)
DEVELOPMENTS IN THE EUROPEAN UNION

Peter A. Hall, Jack Hayward and Howard Machin (eds)
DEVELOPMENTS IN FRENCH POLITICS (Revised edition)

Ian Holliday, Andrew Gamble and Geraint Parry (eds)
FUNDAMENTALS IN BRITISH POLITICS

Gillian Peele, Christopher Bailey, Bruce Cain and B. Guy Peters (eds)
DEVELOPMENTS IN AMERICAN POLITICS 3

Martin Rhodes, Paul Heywood and Vincent Wright (eds)
DEVELOPMENTS IN WEST EUROPEAN POLITICS

Gordon Smith, William E. Paterson and Stephen Padgett (eds)
DEVELOPMENTS IN GERMAN POLITICS 2

Stephen White, Judy Batt and Paul Lewis (eds)
DEVELOPMENTS IN CENTRAL AND EAST EUROPEAN POLITICS 3

Stephen White, Alex Pravda and Zvi Gitelman (eds)
DEVELOPMENTS IN RUSSIAN POLITICS 4

Developments in British Politics 7

Edited by

Patrick Dunleavy

Andrew Gamble

Richard Heffernan

and

Gillian Peele

palgrave
macmillan

Editorial matter, selection and Chapter 1 © Patrick Dunleavy, Andrew Gamble, Richard Heffernan and Gillian Peele 2003

Individual chapters (in order) © Andrew Gamble, Richard Heffernan, Ben Rosamond, Martin J. Smith, Geoffrey Evans, John Curtice, Richard Heffernan, Raymond Kuhn, James Mitchell, Jonathan Tonge, Gillian Peele, Vernon Bogdanor, Paul Kelly, Wyn Grant, Andrew Denham, Mathew Humphrey, Caroline Kennedy-Pipe and Rhiannon Vickers, Patrick Dunleavy 2003

First published 2003 by
PALGRAVE MACMILLAN
Houndmills, Basingstoke, Hampshire RG21 6XS and
175 Fifth Avenue, New York, N.Y. 10010
Companies and representatives throughout the world

PALGRAVE MACMILLAN is the global academic imprint of the Palgrave Macmillan division of St. Martin's Press, LLC and of Palgrave Macmillan Ltd. Macmillan® is a registered trademark in the United States, United Kingdom and other countries. Palgrave is a registered trademark in the European Union and other countries.

ISBN 0–333–98704–7 hardback
ISBN 0–333–98705–5 paperback

This book is printed on paper suitable for recycling and made from fully managed and sustained forest sources.

A catalogue record for this book is available from the British Library.

Library of Congress Catalog Card Number: 2003050931.

10	9	8	7	6	5	4	3	2
12	11	10	09	08	07	06	05	04

Typeset by Cambrian Typesetters, Frimley, Camberley, Surrey

Printed and bound in Great Britain by Creative Print & Design (Wales) Ebbw Vale

This book is a direct replacement for *Developments in British Politics 6*, published 2000

To the memory of
Henry Drucker
(1942–2002)

Henry developed the original conception, philosophy and framework of the *Developments in British Politics* series. He was the lead editor for the first two *Developments* volumes (and revised editions of each) from the inception of the series in 1983 up to 1990. In 1987 he had left political science academia for a new career as a fundraiser as the first-ever Director of Development for Oxford University, where he directed the £340m Campaign for Oxford. He later set up and ran his own consultancy company for non-profit organizations, Oxford Philanthropic.

An inspirational teacher and innovator in the analysis of British politics, Henry's contribution to *Developments* has long outlasted the editions in which he was directly involved. A good friend to all of us, he will be sadly missed.

Contents

List of Figures, Tables and Boxes   xiii

Acknowledgements   xv

Notes on the Contributors   xvi

1   Introduction: Transformations in British Politics   1
    Patrick Dunleavy, Andrew Gamble, Richard Heffernan
    and Gillian Peele

    The 2001 election: the repeat-on-auto-pilot poll   2
    Politics beyond Britain: the impacts of the international
        arena   7
    Changing the political rules: the remaking of the UK
        political system   9
    Public policy: new threats   12
    Conclusion   16

2   Remaking the Constitution   18
    Andrew Gamble

    The nature of the Constitution   21
    Parliament: House of Commons   24
    Parliament: House of Lords   28
    The Monarchy   31
    The judiciary: accountability and transparency   34
    Conclusion   36

3   The Europeanization of British Politics   39
    Ben Rosamond

    Europeanization and British debates about the EU   41
    The Europeanization of governance   44
    Enforced Europeanization?   47
    Europeanization and national adaptation   50
    Ideational Europeanization   52
    Europeanization as feedback   54
    Conclusion   59

4   **The Core Executive and the Modernization of Central Government**   60
Martin J. Smith

Understanding the core executive   62
From personalism to institutionalism in central
    government   65
The modernization of Whitehall: changing relations
    between ministers and civil servants   69
The limits of Prime Ministerial power   76
Conclusion   81

5   **Political Culture and Voting Participation**   82
Geoffrey Evans

Participation and political culture   83
Explaining participation   84
A declining culture of participation?   85
Participatory culture and (non)-voting   87
Why bother? Voting and the character of party
    competition   89
Social inclusion   91
Britain in comparative perspective   94
Conclusion   97

6   **Changing Voting Systems**   100
John Curtice

Varieties of electoral systems   101
The level and quality of electoral participation   103
The role of elections   108
Representation   115
Conclusion   118

7   **Political Parties and the Party System**   119
Richard Heffernan

Electoral change and its impacts: the fragmentation of the
    British party system   120
Organizational change: the emergence of the modern
    British political party   125
Intra-party politics: privileging the party in public office   128
Leadership predominance, political collegiality and the
    party in public office   131

Political realignment within the reworked British party
    system 134
The end of traditional party politics? 138

8   **The Media and Politics** 140
   Raymond Kuhn

The political communications media 140
Public relations politics 143
Labour and news management 149
Government and the news media: differences and
    disagreements 151
Spin as problem, not solution? How can government
    manage news management? 157
Conclusion 159

9   **Politics in Scotland** 161
   James Mitchell

A Scottish political system? 162
Scottish institutions and policies pre-devolution 164
Public opinion and parties pre-devolution 167
Why devolution? 168
Scottish institutions and policies after devolution 173
Public opinion and parties after devolution 176
Conclusion 178

10   **Politics in Northern Ireland** 181
   Jonathan Tonge

The Good Friday Agreement: a new consociational
    democracy? 182
Practical and theoretical problems with the Good
    Friday Agreement 187
Ethic bloc politics: the party system in Northern Ireland 191
Nationalist and republican politics 193
Unionist and loyalist politics 197
Defending a consociational deal 200

11   **Politics in England and Wales** 203
   Gillian Peele

Devolution and decentralization 203
Regionalism 205
London 208
Local government 210

Local democracy   215
Control of local government by central government   217
Conclusion   221

12   **Asymmetric Devolution: Toward a Quasi-Federal
     Constitution?**   222
     Vernon Bogdanor

     Devolution and the United Kingdom   222
     Devolution and the Westminster Parliament   225
     Devolution for England?   230
     Beyond the unitary state: devolution and its impacts   234
     Britain as a multi-national state   238
     Conclusion   240

13   **Ideas and Policy Agendas in Contemporary Politics**   242
     Paul Kelly

     Ideological disaggregation and modern politics   244
     Policy agendas and the language of progressive politics   246
     Policy agendas, think tanks and ideological entrepreneurs   248
     Third Way thinking in action: social justice   251
     Disaggregation and new thinking: the Conservatives   255
     Conclusion   259

14   **Economic Policy**   261
     Wyn Grant

     From Old to New Labour via Thatcherism   262
     Globalization, regionalism and the European Union   264
     Explaining depoliticization   267
     Attempts to depoliticize fiscal policy   271
     Labour's first term restraint on expenditure   273
     Getting and spending: the 2002 budget   275
     Britain and the single currency: the case for and against
       Euro membership   276
     Can the government win a referendum on entering the
       Euro?   280
     Conclusion   281

15   **Public Services**   282
     Andrew Denham

     The road to 1997   283
     Reforming public services   287
     Welfare policy   293

The Private Finance Initiative 299
Conclusion 301

16 **Environmental Policy** **302**
Mathew Humphrey

The history of the environment as a policy issue 303
New Labour and environmentalism 305
The structure of environmental governance under Labour 308
New Labour's record on key environmental issues 310
New Labour, international governance and the
    environment 316
The critique of New Labour 317
Conclusion 319

17 **Britain in the International Arena** **321**
Caroline Kennedy-Pipe and Rhiannon Vickers

Clear and present dangers 321
Globalization and internationalization 327
The international moralism of New Labour: arms
    sales to Indonesia, Sierra Leone and Zimbabwe 330
Conclusion: a presidential foreign policy? 335

18 **Analysing Political Power** **338**
Patrick Dunleavy

Power in the Cabinet Committee system 342
Thinking about power using rational choice models 351
Conclusion 359

Guide to Further Reading 360

Bibliography 366

Index 391

List of Figures, Tables and Boxes

Figures

1.1	Declines in turnout across 3 consecutive general elections in the UK, and 11 other liberal democracies since 1945	3
1.2	How much survey respondents' liked or disliked the main parties in June 2001	4
1.3	The most important issues in the 2001 general election	5
1.4	How survey respondents rated Labour's handling of different issues, 2001 general election	6
3.1	Enforced Europeanization	48
3.2	Europeanization through national adaptation	50
3.3	Ideational Europeanization	53
3.4	Europeanization as feedback	57
4.1	No. 10 organization chart	67
4.2	The hollowed out state under Labour	80
5.1	Voters' perceptions of political efficacy and trust in government	86
5.2	Voters' interest in politics and perceptions of a civic duty to vote	87
5.3	The decline of party identification	88
5.4	Turnout levels in 1997 and 2001 by age group	93
18.1	The Cabinet Committee System in May 2001	345
18.2	Two measures of Cabinet ministers' positional influence in May 2001, and changes in the positions of major Cabinet posts, 1992–2001	348
18.3	The UK core executive budget process 1	353
18.4	The UK core executive budget process 2	354
18.5	The UK core executive budget process 3	355
18.6	The UK core executive budget process 4	356

Tables

2.1	Labour's constitutional reform plans, 1997	19
4.1	The resources of the Prime Minister, ministers and officials	63
5.1	Reported political action, 1986–2000	96

6.1   Turnout at elections in Britain, 1997–2001   105
6.2   How turnout in 2001 varied by the marginality of seats
       and by the party holding the seat   106
6.3   How changes from the 2001 pattern of votes under
       SMPS would affect Labour and Conservatives   111
6.4   Seats and votes in recent PR elections   114
7.1   Vote and seat share, 1979 and 2001 general elections
       compared   124
7.2   Contrasting party membership, 1953 to 2002   127
7.3   MPs' voting in the Conservative leadership race, 2001   132
9.1   Results of Scottish devolution referendum, 1997   173
10.1   Northern Ireland Assembly prior to suspension, 2002   186
10.2   The Good Friday Agreement referendums, 1998   187
10.3   Election results in Northern Ireland, 1992–2001   189
10.4   Preferred long-term policy for Northern Ireland, 2001   200
11.1   The constitutions of local authorities in England   214
11.2   Council results England and Wales, 2002   217
14.1   Unemployment and inflation, 1992–2001   261
14.2   Relative labour productivity levels   262
14.3   Real average annual increase in taxation and spending   274
18.1   How the PM's and the Chancellor's blocs matched up
       in 1992 and 2001   350

Boxes

2.1   The Norton Commission to strengthen Parliament, 2000   27
2.2   Stage 2 of House of Lords reform   30
3.1   Britain and European integration: landmarks since 1997   41
3.2   The Maastricht convergence criteria   49
3.3   Gordon Brown's five economic tests for entering the Euro   54
7.1   Party system development since 1945   121
7.2   The modern electoral professional party   126
7.3   The parliamentary party as key leadership resource   134
7.4   Key features of the modern British political party   138
10.1   Main political and paramilitary organizations in
       Northern Ireland   184
12.1   Social attitudes survey, 1997 and 1999   231
16.1   Key UK environmental policy since 1997   303
16.2   UK institutions of environmental governance   309

Acknowledgements

From this seventh edition of *Developments in British Politics*, Ian Holliday has left the team and we would like to thank him for his splendid past contributions. Richard Heffernan replaces him. As ever, our list of authors is entirely new. As the name of the series suggests, *Developments* focuses its attention on up-to-date, cutting-edge developments in British politics and we are enormously grateful to all our contributors for their expertise and their efforts. We are particularly indebted to them for meeting exacting deadlines that fell in a busy time in the academic year. Thanks also to Keith Povey and Barbara Collinge for first-class copy-editing and for managing the book's production.

As always, however, we must especially thank our publisher, Steven Kennedy, the 'fifth editor', for his customary drive, enthusiasm and encouragement, and not least for his numerous informed editorial insights.

Patrick Dunleavy
Andrew Gamble
Richard Heffernan
Gillian Peele

Notes on the Contributors

Vernon Bogdanor is Professor of Politics and Government at Brasenose College, University of Oxford. Recent publications include *The Monarchy and the Constitution, Power and the People: A Guide to Constitutional Reform* and *Devolution in the United Kingdom*.

John Curtice is Professor of Politics at the University of Strathclyde, co-Director of the British General Election Study from 1983 to 1997 and Deputy Director of CREST, the Centre for Research into Elections and Social Trends since 1994. He is co-author of *How Britain, Understanding Political Change*, and *On Message*, and also co-editor of *Labour's Last Chance* and of annual British Social Attitudes reports since 1994.

Andrew Denham is Reader in Politics at the University of Nottingham. His research interests include contemporary political theory, British public policy and the politics of the welfare state. His main publications include *Think Tanks of the New Right, British Think Tanks and the Climate of Opinion* (with M. Garnett) and *Think Tanks Across Nations: A Comparative Approach* (edited with D. Stone and M. Garnett) and *Keith Joseph* (with M. Garnett).

Patrick Dunleavy is Professor of Political Science and Public Policy at the London School of Economics and Chair of the LSE Public Policy Group. He has published *Democracy, Bureaucracy and Public Choice* among many other books and papers, and he is also Executive Editor of the journal *Political Studies*.

Geoffrey Evans is Official Fellow in Politics, Nuffield College, and Professor of the Sociology of Politics, University of Oxford. A member of the British Election Study team for many years, he is joint editor of the journal *Electoral Studies* and has published numerous works on social structure, political attitudes and political behaviour. He has also conducted studies of social and political change in Eastern Europe and Northern Ireland. Recent books include *The End of Class Politics?* and (with Pippa Norris) *Critical Elections*.

Andrew Gamble is Professor of Politics and Director of the Political Economy Research Centre at the University of Sheffield. Previous books include *The Free Economy and the Strong State: The Politics of Thatcherism* and *Politics and Fate* and he has just completed a book on the future of British politics (forthcoming). He is the co-editor of the journal *Political Quarterly*.

Wyn Grant is Professor of Politics at the University of Warwick and is Chair of the Political Studies Association of the UK, 2002–5. His principal research area is comparative public policy with special reference to economic and trade policy, agricultural policy and environmental policy. He is the author of *Economic Policy in Britain*.

Richard Heffernan is Lecturer in Government and Politics at The Open University. He has published widely on many aspects of British politics, and recent publications include *New Labour and Thatcherism: Political Change in Britain* and *The Labour Party: A Centenary History*.

Mathew Humphrey is Lecturer in Political Theory at the University of Nottingham. His publications include *Political Theory and the Environment: a Reassessment* (ed.) and *Preservation versus the People? Nature Humanity, and Political Philosophy*.

Paul Kelly is Senior Lecturer in Political Theory at the London School of Economics. He has published on a variety of issues in Political Theory and Philosophy. He has edited and contributed to *Multiculturalism Reconsidered* and co-edited *Political Thinkers* and he is one of the editors of the journal *Political Studies*.

Caroline Kennedy-Pipe is Professor of International Relations in the Department of Politics at the University of Sheffield. She has written a number of books and articles on the making of foreign policy and is working on security policy after September 11, 2001.

Raymond Kuhn is Senior Lecturer in the Department of Politics at Queen Mary, University of London. He has published widely on the politics of the media in both Britain and France. He is co-editor with Erik Neveu, of *Political Journalism: New Challenges, New Practices*.

James Mitchell is Professor of Politics at the University of Strathclyde. He is author of *Conservatives and the Union; Strategies for Self-Government* and co-author of *Politics and Public Policy in Scotland, How Scotland Votes*, and *Scotland Votes: The Devolution Issue and the 1997 Referendum*.

Gillian Peele is Fellow and Tutor in Politics at Lady Margaret Hall, University of Oxford. She is the author of *Governing the UK* and the co-editor of *Developments in American Politics 4*.

Ben Rosamond is Reader in Politics and International Studies at the University of Warwick and co-editor of the journal *Comparative European Politics*. His books include *Theories of European Integration*, *Politics: An Introduction*, 2nd edition (co-author), and *New Regionalisms in the Global Political Economy* (co-editor). His next book is to be entitled *Globalization and the European Union*.

Martin J. Smith is Professor of Politics and Head of Department at the University of Sheffield. He has published widely on the Labour Party, central government and public policy. His publications include *The Core Executive in Britain, Changing Patterns of Governance* (with David Marsh and David Richards) and *Governance and Public Policy in the United Kingdom* (with David Richards).

Jonathan Tonge is Professor of Politics and Director of the Centre of Irish Studies at the University of Salford. His books on Irish politics include *Northern Ireland: Conflict and Change, Peace or War? Understanding the Peace Process in Northern Ireland*, edited with Chris Gilligan and *The SDLP and Sinn Fein 1970–2001: From Alienation to Participation*, with Gerard Murray (forthcoming).

Rhiannon Vickers is Lecturer in International Politics at the University of Sheffield. She is the author of *Manipulating Hegemony: State Power, Labour and the Marshall Plan in Britain*. She has published on the Labour government's handling of the Kosovo crisis and on New Labour's foreign policy. She is completing a two-volume book on the political history of the Labour Party's foreign policy.

Chapter 1

Introduction: Transformations in British Politics

PATRICK DUNLEAVY, ANDREW GAMBLE,
RICHARD HEFFERNAN and GILLIAN PEELE

In 1992, the Conservative Party seemed so dominant that a senior political scientist could claim, 'Britain no longer has two major political
parties. It has one major political party, the Conservatives, one minor
party, Labour, and one peripheral party, the Liberal Democrats' (King
1992: 224). Ten years on, however, the picture is very different. The
2001 election seemed to offer an almost exact mirror image of Labour
predominance, repeating almost exactly the 1997 pattern of giving
Labour a landslide Commons majority on just 42 per cent of the vote.
It seemed to set British politics in a pattern to which no serious
commentator could see any definite end in prospect. Despite a string of
troublesome crises for individual ministers (such as the A levels exam
scandal in summer 2002, which helped precipitate the resignation of
Estelle Morris as the Education Secretary) and once or twice for the
government as a whole, Labour's opinion poll lead continued unbroken
into its second term.

By 2003 the Conservatives had been flatlining in almost every voting
intention survey for a full decade, and to compound their misery they
began coming within a few per cent of the rising Liberal Democrat
ratings in some polls. Ever since the autumn 1992 crisis which forced
sterling out of the then European Exchange Rate Mechanism, the Tories
have run at best in the low 30 per cents in virtually all opinion polls –
fully 10 to 15 per cent below their twentieth-century average of 44 per
cent of the vote in general elections.

Following his predecessors John Major and William Hague, Iain
Duncan Smith became the third uncharismatic Tory leader in a row to
confront damaging evidence of divisions in his party. Long before his
promised 'reforms' in Tory policies had yielded any easily perceptible
results, the semi-public lack of faith in his leadership in the parliamentary party provoked Duncan Smith to call an extraordinary impromptu
press conference in November 2002, where he publicly urged his party

1

to 'Unite or Die' in the bluntest terms. A month later the *Sun* decided to award him the 'dead parrot' accolade, and his future seemed anything but rescued by his earlier *coup de theatre*. The continuing government insulation from electoral damage, plus the Tories' agonies, seemed to confirm that the British political system had switched wholesale, from 13 years of almost undisturbed Conservative hegemony (1979–92) to a period of apparently almost unshakeable Labour predominance (1992 onwards), with no intervening period of close electoral competition. We first trace the lineaments of this transition by analysing some key features of the 2001 election, and then seek the origins of Labour's success in its chequered policy record in office.

The 2001 election: the repeat-on-auto-pilot poll

Never in Britain's democratic history have two elections been so similar in the party vote shares and their constituency consequences as 1997 and 2001. Only 13 out of 659 seats changed hands (that is, less than 2 per cent), far fewer over four years than in the two elections held in the same year in 1974 or the 1950 and 1951 elections. But 2001 also charted another first – the lowest general election turnout ever under universal suffrage. In raw numerical terms the 1918 turnout was marginally lower, but we must remember that at that time many UK troops had not returned from the First World War, the electoral register was imperfect, and a broadening of eligibility criteria meant a majority of people had never voted before, so the whole context of the election was not comparable. In 1992 turnout surged a bit to 77 per cent, but from that small peak it first fell back to a more normal 71 per cent in 1997 and then collapsed to just 59 per cent in 2001.

Figure 1.1 shows that the UK's decline in turnout is 18 per cent across three consecutive general elections. It is far greater than the largest declines across three consecutive elections experienced in other established liberal democracies in Europe, North America or the Commonwealth since 1945.

The nearest parallel to a change of this magnitude is France's experience during the constitutional crisis and collapse of the Fourth Republic and the birth of de Gaulle's Fifth Republic at the end of the 1950s. The next nearest is Canada under the current hegemony of the Liberals: another Westminster-style system with single member plurality rule elections just like Britain, and where the leading party has triumphed over an under-represented opposition fragmented between multiple parties. Britain's exceptionalism here reflects the fact that turnout in most countries bobs up and down quite a lot, even in those countries which have

Figure 1.1   *Declines in turnout across three consecutive general elections in the UK and 11 other liberal democracies since 1945*

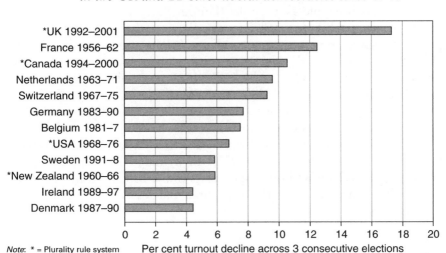

Note: * = Plurality rule system   Per cent turnout decline across 3 consecutive elections

seen dramatic long-run falls in turnout over several decades, such as Switzerland where voting fell from 66 to 36 per cent from the 1970s to now, or the USA where it declined from 63 to 49 per cent between the late 1950s and early 1970s, before bobbing up slightly. The largest other declines across three consecutive elections in the UK were 6 per cent in 1950–5 and 4 per cent in 1959–66, so the post 1992 change is a dramatic one in British terms as well.

The worry must be that further falls could bring the proportion of people voting down to US levels, just above 50 per cent – a barrier already passed in one 2001 Liverpool constituency where turnout reached just 39 per cent. And the decline in voting has been across the board, affecting all forms of election: parliamentary, local and European. However, the proportion of people voting at the 2002 local elections increased a little on its previous depressed state, partly because of government experiments to make participation easier, suggesting that a small bounce-back is also still feasible. A fierce academic and practitioner debate continues to rage about how serious the 2001 decline in turnout is, how it should be interpreted and how it might be reversed.

The most optimistic view of 2001 sees the slump in turnout as conjunctural, produced by a one-off coincidence of a strong government and a weak opposition, which made the election look like a walkover from the start. The Labour Party was in a determined 'catch-all' mode, its centrist conservative policies not enthusing its previously most loyal supporters amongst manual workers and voters in Labour safe seats. Blair proclaimed in 1997 that 'Labour is the political arm of none other than the British people as a whole' (Labour Party 1997), and the party under his leadership focused its campaign on the economy and the public services, eschewing any publicity for its modest redistributive efforts and completely avoiding any class-related appeals. The Conservatives meanwhile, led by William Hague, failed to look a credible alternative government, did not shake off the unsuccessful taint of John Major's previous Conservative government, and did not mobilize the many partial critics of the government's record.

A key basis for the parties' differing fortunes in 2001 seems to have been a rather generalized appraisal of their image and reputations by voters. Figure 1.2 shows how respondents to the British Election Studies cross-section survey rated the top three parties on an eleven-point like/dislike scale.

Figure 1.2   *How much survey respondents' liked or disliked the main parties in June 2001*

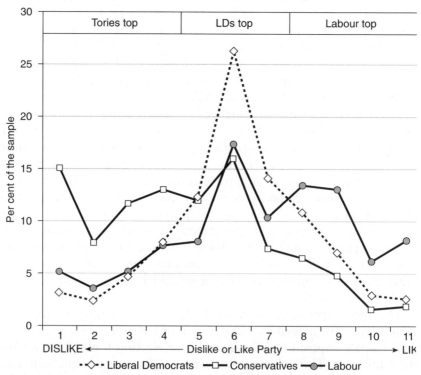

Source: British Elections Study 2001

More than one in seven people rated the Conservatives on the 'maximum dislike' point and the party was far more disliked (and less positively liked also) than its two rivals. Respondents' feelings about the Liberal Democrats showed a strong peak around the neutral point – the party energized few voters, not attracting strong feelings either way. By contrast, Labour was much more clearly liked than the other two parties, easily predominating amongst nominations at the positively liked end of the scale.

Labour also successfully set the agenda for the election around public service issues, although as we shall see the electorate was also critical of aspects of government performance here. Figure 1.3 shows that the NHS dominated the election when people were asked to nominate the most important issue involved, followed by educational standards running third.

Economic issues (inflation, unemployment, the economy generally, taxation, etc.) were the fifth ranking issue, and Britain and the EU (on which William Hague had focused much of his appeal) trailed in sixth. Notice that the second place in Figure 1.3 is occupied by the one in six respondents who either did not know what the most important issue was or else proclaimed that there was none. And the fourth rank is occupied by a miscellaneous category involving more than 250 other suggestions that did not fit neatly into the pollsters' categories. More than a quarter of the electorate thus either could not name the most important issue, or named one of their own devising, falling outside the main partisan agendas. When people were asked to nominate the party best equipped to tackle the most important issues as they saw it, Labour

Figure 1.3 *The most important issues in the 2001 general election*

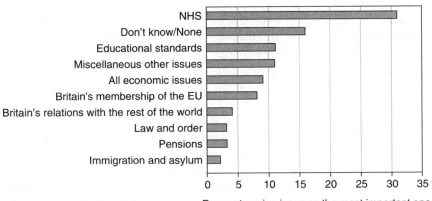

Source: 2001 British Elections Study

Per cent seeing issue as the most important one

Figure 1.4   *How survey respondents rated Labour's handling of different issues, 2001 general election*

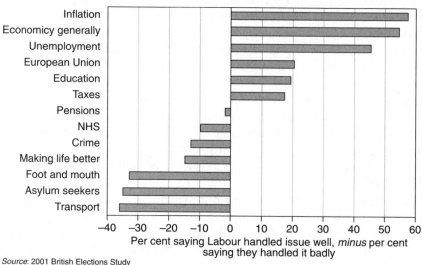

Per cent saying Labour handled issue well, *minus* per cent saying they handled it badly

Source: 2001 British Elections Study

was nominated by 41 per cent (almost as much as their actual vote), the Conservatives by 13 per cent (almost a third of their actual vote), the Liberal Democrats by 7 per cent and the Greens by 2 per cent. The SNP in Scotland and Plaid Cymru in Wales fared about as well as the Liberal Democrats within their respective countries.

Surprisingly perhaps, the public services were not generally strong issues for Labour in the election. Figure 1.4 shows that while a majority of the public saw Labour as having handled education well rather than badly, the balances of opinion on other public service issues were negative – moderately so on the NHS and crime, but strongly negative on transport.

The government also fared badly in the public's view on its handling of two acute policy crises in 2000–1, over the foot and mouth epidemic and on asylum seekers. Labour's real strengths were almost exclusively on economic issues, with strong approval of the government's inflation record, general handling of the economy and unemployment, and even its handling of taxation attracting a positive balance. In other words if credit were to be allocated amongst ministers, primary responsibility for Labour's big vote-winning achievements lay with the Chancellor of the Exchequer, Gordon Brown. Arguably much of Labour's success stemmed from his initial decision (within days of assuming office) to vest the Bank of England with control over interest rates policy. Apart from the economy and the Prime Minister's proclaimed priority of education, the only other substantially positive issue for Labour in Figure 1.4 is its handling of European Union issues. Blair successfully ended the discreditable tradition of British isolation in EU decision making. But the Blair-Brown split over entry to the Euro created a complex Labour stance of triggering a referendum only when the government determined it was in Britain's economic interest (and Labour's political interest) to join. In electoral terms, Figure 1.4 shows that this stance was a modest positive success in 2001. The maxim 'It's the economy, stupid!' is a key reminder that it was the Chancellor's success which has crucially underpinned Labour's electoral and political fortunes.

Politics beyond Britain: the impacts of the international arena

While a contested notion, the debate on globalization and its impacts reflects an ever more interdependent world, one born of the exchange of capital, goods and services (if not yet labour) across ever more open national borders. Now further encouraged by previously unimaginable international flows of information resulting from technological innovation, the global marketplace has become a twenty-first century reality. Although the interdependent world lacks an integrated global community, the global economy limits the powers of national actors to manage their 'own' economies, driving out punitive tax regimes and regulated labour markets.

Because globalization prompts an internationalization of decision making, the phenomenon of Europeanization is an acknowledgement that by themselves 'individual states alone can no longer be conceived of as the appropriate political units for either resolving key policy problems or managing effectively a broad range of public functions' (Held and McGrew 2000: 13). Several factors promote 'ever closer union' between EU member states, and the Europeanization of national politics is prompted by deepening economic internationalism or globalization, functional integration and growing supra-national co-operation, and, to a much lesser extent, Euro-federalist aspirations. In addition, national interests, the belief that Britain is well served by membership of the EU, also explains UK Europeanization, particularly when the state acknowledges that expanding transnational forces reduce the national control they can exercise over their domestic market.

Thus Labour is strongly supportive of EU enlargement, which will create a single market with more consumers than the United States and Japan combined. The impact on Britain's economy alone is potentially enormous, even if the ten new applicants in 2004, while adding 23 per cent to the EU's land area and 20 per cent to its population, adds just 4 per cent to its GDP. However, ministers are more cautious over the current EU Constitutional Convention, presently chaired by the former French President Giscard d'Estaing, opposing all arguments in favour of a federal Europe, even ones that are suggested simply by a name change or by the creation of a European citizenship. Instead, Britain wants merely to simplify the existing treaties without changing their content while examining the EU's institutional architecture of the EU – such changes being agreed not by the Convention, but by EU governments acting by unanimous agreement at an Inter-Governmental Conference.

Naturally, under Labour, an instinctively pro-European government, Britain's relationship with its EU partners has vastly improved, particularly when compared with the record of its Conservative predecessors. Yet the Blair government still prioritizes Britain's 'national' interests over its 'European' interests, something starkly evidenced in its attitude to European Monetary Union. Like Denmark and Sweden, Britain met the conditions of euro membership, but chose to stay out, reserving the right to join (or not to join) at a future date.

While the Conservatives, divided on all things European, oppose joining the single currency, Labour is in favour of entry in principle, although it has adopted a 'wait and see' stance. Committed to a national referendum on entry, expected to be held some time in the 2001 Parliament, ministers support joining 'when the time is right', providing certain economic tests are met and it is in Britain's 'national interest'. Without yet declaring his unequivocal support, Tony Blair favours entry, but the Chancellor of the Exchequer, Gordon Brown, is cautious, describing his position as one of 'pro-euro realism'. Provided entry does not damage Britain's economy, that macroeconomic stability is enhanced, and entry is politically beneficial, or at the very least not harmful, to Labour, the government will recommend entry. It will do so, if only because monetary union is seen to be inevitable and Britain has therefore to join for geo-political, pro-European, reasons. Foremost among Labour's current thinking on the Euro is the need for the government to win any referendum it calls. To support entry but be rebuffed in a national poll would be deemed a disaster, a scenario Labour ministers (none more so than the Prime Minister) are determined to avoid.

Foreign policy has been dominated by the events arising from September 11 and the indefinite 'war on terrorism' waged by the USA with the active participation of Britain. Having supported military intervention in Afghanistan, Tony Blair endorsed US efforts to get tough with Iraq. In March 2003, having failed to persuade the UN Security Council to support a war in Iraq, thanks in large part to the tabling of a French veto, the USA and Britain launched their military strike to overthrow Saddam. Blair's stance drew much criticism, prompting three ministerial resignations, including Robin Cook, the former Foreign Secretary, and provoking a huge parliamentary rebellion, which saw 139 Labour MPs, one in three of the Parliamentary Labour Party, vote against the war. Although the war produced both the largest public demonstration in British history and the biggest parliamentary revolt ever, Blair sent British troops to Iraq to free the Iraqi people from Saddam's rule and protect the world from the consequences of a rogue state with the capacity to use weapons of mass destruction.

Under Blair new life has been breathed into the US–British 'special relationship'. While supportive of a multilateral world order based on institutions such as the UN, the IMF, the World Bank and the WTO, Britain is prepared to support US leadership, even in the face of opposition from within the UN and the EU. Taking action against rogue states by multilateral action, if possible, but by unilateral means, if necessary, seems to be the geo-political watchword. Military action has previously been conducted under a broad international coalition but, as the war with Iraq demonstrates, a new phase may be opening where Britain endorses US-led pre-emptive action against designated enemies of the 'international community' deemed to offer a 'clear and present danger'.

Changing the political rules: the remaking of the UK political system

Since 1997, the seamless, incremental development of the political rules and regulations defining how the British state operates has been impacted by a series of disparate (if interlinked) constitutional reforms. Together, Scottish and Welsh devolution, the Northern Ireland peace process, electoral reform (but not for the House of Commons), reform of the House of Lords, and the enactment of the Human Rights Act have offered a programme of change more radical than any previous set of constitutional proposals (Blackburn and Plant 1999). Such reforms did not feature as an issue in the 2001 ballot, indicating that voters and opposition parties alike had come to accept the reforms Labour had introduced since 1997. They have, however, in tandem with the ongoing internationalization of politics, steadily transformed the institutional structures within which British politics is enacted. While these changes owe much to the policy and practices of the Labour government, they also reflect much deeper historical factors.

Foremost among the constitutional innovations introduced by Labour has been devolution, the creation of the Scottish Parliament and the Welsh Assembly (and the Northern Ireland Legislative Assembly), and the granting to them of wide legislative powers in respect to key areas of domestic policy. Before the 2003 elections, coalition administrations embrace Labour and the Liberal Democrats in both Scotland and Wales (both nations where Labour enjoys a commanding lead in Westminster elections), something which demonstrates a shift in political culture, away from the tradition of single party government. Such a qualification of one of the key features of Britain's majoritarian political system (Lijphart 1999) is itself very significant, and it owes much to electoral reform in Scotland and Wales, and the adoption of the Additional Member System (AMS) in preference to the non-proportional Single Member Plurality System (SMPS).

Although it is still too early to be certain, the cumulative effect of Labour's constitutional reforms may well be the remaking of the United Kingdom. As a result of devolution, Scotland and Wales have now begun to forge new and separate political systems, which are also multiparty systems, again thanks to electoral reform. Northern Ireland remains very much an exceptional case given the historical nature of the ethno-national conflict long waged there. Certainly, devolution has prompted a quasi-federalization of the political parties, and both Westminster and Whitehall have had to adapt their practices to fit changed circumstances. While Labour at Westminster intends devolution to progress no further, demands exist within both Scotland and Wales for further reforms granting the devolved assemblies increased powers. In addition, tensions between the Westminster centre and the Scottish and Welsh periphery over financial matters and public policy differences have begun to arise. New machinery, probably a Constitutional Court, will be needed to resolve these. If these differences are not sorted out, with the result that parties eager to extend devolution increase their support, Labour's political base at Westminster could shrink.

Echoes of the Westminster model remain and the localization of the UK needs to be put in some perspective: of the UK total population of 59 million, 49 million, 83.6 per cent, live in England, where, ongoing discussions about regionalization aside, power has not been devolved. Scotland claims only 8.6 per cent of the UK population, Wales 4.9 per cent and Northern Ireland 2.9 per cent. With 84 per cent still falling exclusively under the remit of Westminster, only 16 per cent of the population benefit from the establishment of new political institutions. In addition, while domestic policy competences have been devolved, 'high politics', economic management, revenue-raising, foreign policy, European matters and constitutional affairs remain at Westminster, which continues to exert a considerable influence over governance in Britain. The constitutional reform agenda remains inconsistent, because, although power has been devolved to Scotland and Wales, it has not so far been devolved to England, and the government has also continued the trend towards centralization of power in Downing Street. The Westminster club ethos, the domination of the political game by the two major parties, still does not value pluralism and political diversity, two things from which Blair-led Labour, as do all governments, all too often instinctively recoils.

At Westminster itself, other constitutional changes aside (particularly the enactment of the Human Rights Act and the first stage of House of Lords reform), politics largely continues much as before. Although Labour's resurgence, accompanied by the eclipse of the Conservatives, has had its impacts, the majoritarian system remains in place, despite the dispersion of power evidenced through devolution. At the Westminster centre, Britain retains a centralized government, even if it is now less of a unitary state. The executive form remains a single party government; executive–legislative relations are characterized by executive dominance; and, Lords reform notwithstanding, legislative arrangements still involve an asymmetrical bicameralism, one where the elected House of Commons enjoys great supremacy over the unelected House of Lords (Lijphart 1999).

Such constitutional reforms affecting Westminster as have been introduced (especially in relation to the House of Commons) have been designed to maintain the government's freedom of manoeuvre and avoid strengthening parliament's ability to call the government to account. Although Labour remains loosely committed to further consideration of the issue, electoral reform for the House of Commons has been essentially ruled out for this very reason. Government MPs are invariably content to remain bricks in the buttress protecting the executive from having its powers and prerogatives encroached upon.

The same is true of Lords reform: having introduced the first stage of Lords reform, the removal of all but 92 of the hereditary peers in 1999, the government is now proceeding to stage two, remaking the Lords, with some combination of elected and appointed members, while ensuring the continued primacy of the House of Commons. The last thing the government wants is a democratic – and therefore legitimate – second chamber. Limited election and an appointed chamber is what is on offer; Tony Blair created 248 peers in his first four years, compared with Margaret Thatcher's 216 in eleven years. But the Government's hand may be forced, since a largely appointed House did not command a majority in the Commons in February 2003, but nor did a largely elected House either. The most likely current outcome is perhaps a chamber with 50 or 60 per cent elected members, adding either a new regional list system of proportional representation or another additional member system to the catalogue of alternative electoral systems in Britain. The probable consequence of such a change, should it happen, is that further changes in the legislative process will take place, with some considerable accretion of legitimacy for the second chamber's views. Alternatively, given the absense of a consensus on Lords reform, the government might just well kick the topic into touch.

A more developed system of institutional checks and balances might thus come into being by the second half of the current decade, to add to the existing changes following through on the Human Rights Act 1999. Yet, constitutional reforms that seriously enhance the checks and balances on the executive, do not find favour with Labour. A remaining prime dynamic of the UK's majoritarian political system is the means by which the single member plurality system converts votes cast for parties into Commons seats held by parties, substantial deviation from proportionality resulting, granting the largest minority party in terms of votes the largest majority of House of Commons seats.

Public policy: new threats

In his 2001 budget, which established NHS improvements as the leitmotif of new Labour's second term, Gordon Brown made provision for a large increase in public spending in the period up to 2005 (the presumed date of the next general election), chiefly as a counter-cyclical move, to help avert a downturn in the economy turning into full-scale recession. In the event the downturn in UK and world stock markets following the failure of the 'dot.com' boom was more severe in 2002 than Treasury forecasts had predicted. Stock markets slumped and economic growth was significantly lower than anticipated, so tax receipts were much less buoyant. Although the Chancellor put a brave face upon these developments, declaring no need for substantial tax rises thanks to his past prudence and lower national debt making extra borrowing sustainable, the UK's run of consistent economic luck under Labour was perhaps played out.

In addition, by early 2003 the government faced a concatenation of recession-related policy issues which perhaps held a potential to cumulate and inter-link more than almost any other set of economic issues had done previously for Labour. The announcement of large increases in health and education spending along with other public services coincided with the end of a long period from the mid 1990s onwards when public sector pay and conditions lagged behind wages in the private sector. A correction to re-equilibrate the position of public sector workers was always likely, especially in expanding services (like the NHS and the schools sector), where attracting sufficient qualified personnel emerged as a key aspect of improving service improvements. In the NHS there was little evidence of improved labour productivity or increases in the throughput of patients. Instead much of the extra monies seemed to get absorbed in restoring salary comparabilities and rectifying anomalous situations created in the years of acute spending constraint from 1996 to 2000.

The most out-of-control aspects of the economic situation for Gordon Brown became the house prices boom, which roared ahead by over 20 per cent across all regions of the country during 2002, in a period when overall inflation was close to 2.5 per cent and the Bank of England's official interest rate was 4 per cent. Partly this boom reflected the low costs of borrowing, partly the collapse of stock market growth expectations after the dot.com slump, which led investors with spare assets to pile into the domestic property market in search of the returns previously earned from equities. In one way the growth of mortgage lending supported the economy in a period when it might have slumped, as people withdrew some of the rising value of their houses to spend on consumption goods. But it also made the problems of finding affordable accommodation much more acute for lower income people, especially public sector workers on small salaries in London and the south-east.

By autumn 2002 the rising prices of houses directly fuelled public sector trade unions' increasing militancy, with widespread day strikes in the capital over London allowances by education unions, and a succession of disputes on the railways and the Tube. The Fire Brigades Union submitted a pay claim of 40 per cent and called its first national strike for more than 25 years, with pressure from London and the south-east fuelling much of its militancy. Details of numerous multi-year wages deals emerged across much of the public sector, linking pay increases at above-the-trend inflation rate to modernization and job reduction changes. The government could still argue that industrial disputes were at a low ebb compared with even the mid 1990s. Yet the possibility of an explosion of large public sector wage claims undermining Brown's economic strategy and generating renewed inflationary pressure in the economy generally moved from a remote contingency to a more substantial possibility.

A second front in the trade unions distancing themselves from Labour opened up over the Private Finance Initiative (PFI). First introduced by the Conservative Chancellor Norman Lamont in the early 1990s, the programme was seized upon and greatly expanded by Gordon Brown as a means of financing capital expenditure without including it in government borrowing. A huge programme of school and hospital building as well as prison and transport projects were begun using the PFI mechanism in the first term. Critics argued that these projects were not value-for-money because the finance for them could be raised more cheaply by conventional public sector borrowing, and that where facilities' operation was included in PFIs they created a two-tier labour market. No real risk transferred to the private sector, because the government always stood ready to bail projects out, and additional costs were loaded onto future generations of taxpayers, because many of the contracts ran for up to thirty years. The Treasury insisted that these projects were value-for-money because risk was being transferred to the private sector, and by comparison with conventional public sector capital projects PFI schemes were more likely to be delivered to time and on-budget, especially for construction schemes.

Tony Blair declared in a speech to the Labour Party Conference in 2002, that using PFIs involved no issues of principle: 'The ends, universal provision, remain the same. The means of delivery, a partnership between public, private and voluntary sectors, and between state and citizen.' For instance, in regard to new hospitals, citizens 'don't care who builds them, so long as they're built. I don't care who builds them. So long as they're on cost, on budget, and helping to deliver a better NHS and better state schools for the people' (Blair 2002). Such reforms are designed to end the failing ' "one size fits all", mass production public service'. However, ministers' rhetoric stressing that PFIs are not creeping privatization often seems to conflict with government practice. The policy's big union opponents still forced a motion critical of PFIs through the Labour Conference, calling for an examination of whether PFIs delivered value for money, a demand which ministers immediately indicated that they would ignore. With Tony Blair and Gordon Brown for once united in defending PFIs, their future seems assured, although they may be used more sparingly in future.

Meanwhile the direct privatization of state-owned or public service operations remains much more controversial and problematic. The railway infrastructure company Railtrack (privatized by the Conservatives only in 1996) acrimoniously collapsed back into public ownership in summer 2002, after signally failing to maintain basic rail safety and becoming unable to finance new investment when its shares depreciated. The National Air Traffic Control Service, where 46 per cent of the equity was sold to a consortium of airlines in 2000 against the opposition of many Labour MPs, ran into problems when air traffic declined after 11 September and it had to be bailed out with extra government funds. The privatized nuclear power company British Energy producing 30 per cent of the UK's power almost went bankrupt in 2002, and was promised hundreds of million of pounds in government support, whose legality was then contested by Greenpeace. The longer run future of the London Tube under a 'public–private partnership' (PPP) which would effectively part-privatize it, also remained fiercely disputed between the central government and Ken Livingstone, the London Mayor. Livingstone threatened legal action involving the European Court of Justice, imperilling the financial future of some PPP companies, while ministers propped up the firms and threatened not to hand over the Tube system to the mayor's control as planned until the legal action threat was lifted. In all these cases it became apparent that involving private companies integrally in the provision of essential public services introduces an extra risk element if their financial prospects are called in question for any reason.

In emphasizing public services issues, the 2001 election clearly marked a watershed in the evolution of new Labour's policymaking. Instead of significantly raising spending on public services as soon as it was elected, the first Blair government stuck doggedly to the very severe spending limits inherited from the Conservatives. Almost paradoxically, public spending as a proportion of GDP was actually lower under the first Blair government than it was under the Major government (Mullard 2001; Glyn and Wood 2001). Labour tried to anticipate this by promising very little before the 1997 election, but expectations still soared once it was in government and what promises it did make proved hard to deliver. After 1999, when Labour did start increasing public spending, department allocations were regularly underspent, partly because of the time it took to negotiate agreement on changes to working practices before extra resources were released.

By 2001 Labour ministers began publicly acknowledging that the pace of change had been very slow, and that very few citizens had experienced any substantial improvements in public services. In some cases, particularly transport, voters clearly perceived that services had deteriorated (see Figure 1.4). Labour's holding rhetoric at the general election stressed that its first priority in government had been to rectify the public finances, and that only now was it able to plan incremental and sustainable investment in the resources devoted to public services. So the need to deliver on key touchstone issues such as health, education, transport and crime by pushing through public sector reforms to improve service delivery, became the mission of Labour's second term. Public services are to be user-led, not producer-led, so continuing the Conservative policy of devolving responsibility to frontline staff and encouraging efficiency through competition.

The high risk elements of Labour's public services strategy are obvious. Even if some of the reforms work, and the extra resources are applied to increasing the number of teachers and doctors rather than the pay of the existing ones, it is still unclear that improvements in public services could be demonstrated in a clear and unambiguous way. A sceptical news media, keen to publicize local failings in services, has meant that so far opinion surveys find most people are satisfied with the service they get from the schools and hospitals in their area, but still believe that the NHS and the education service nationally were poor or getting worse. The education crisis over A levels marking in the summer of 2002 also showed how quickly even those public services where voters previously acknowledged government achievements could be tarnished by adverse developments.

Conclusion

No longer of and for the working class, Labour has long sought votes from all classes and social interests, championing its 'national' credentials. The culmination of this strategy, perhaps first evidenced as far back as 1955–9, came in the general election of 1997. Then, rather than articulate the interests of a core Labour constituency, union members, the organized (and disorganized) working class, women and ethnic minorities, Blair-led Labour targeted disaffected Conservative voters with an ever more moderated appeal. In fact, New Labour successfully recast itself as nothing less than a 'One Nation' party, a label only the Conservatives had previously proudly attached to themselves. To this appeal, the Conservatives have cast around in vain for a workable alternative appeal of their own.

While empowered by the Westminster club ethos, once in office British governments normally age quickly, accreting problems and fiascos, tiring intellectually at the centre, often losing their edge. New Labour in power has worked through (and under media pressure ejected) quite a few people in top ministerial offices, including those like Peter Mandelson, Stephen Byers and Estelle Morris, all of whom were very close to the Prime Minister. Many policies enunciated early on have been scrapped, from the incessant 'churning' of Public Service Agreement targets supposed to bind the spending departments to do what Brown's Treasury orders, to John Prescott's national transport strategy, which was buried in all but name at the end of 2002. But the essentials of Brown's economic strategy seem to have held up well into the government's second term, and Blair's leadership and willingness to promote public service change and modernization have not seemed to flag much.

Within Labour's ranks the simmering Blair–Brown dispute may

continue to trigger serious tensions that could eventually erode Labour's credibility, as conflicts amongst the Prime Minister, the Chancellor and the Foreign Secretary did for the Thatcher and Major governments. The duopoly of power at new Labour's heart has been a unique one in British government, with the Chancellor on some measures being in an unusually strong position vis-à-vis the Prime Minister. The test for the future will be both the management of the Blair–Brown succession, if there is ever to be one while Labour is in office. This is something which is closely associated with the upcoming decision on Britain's possible entry into the Euro, where Blair remains profoundly in favour of entry, whereas Brown is far more cautious.

Whatever the future personal prospects of Blair or Brown, the inclusive politics practised by Labour has thus far compressed the centre ground of British politics. With Labour's electoral support presently a mile wide, if in places an inch deep, it remains to be seen if any party can mount a short term robust challenge sufficient to unseat Labour from the commanding position it has established in British politics. To this end, after selecting three low key, uncharismatic and anti-European leaders in a row, the Conservative party may finally choose to dump Iain Duncan Smith as a lost cause before the expected 2005 general election, and opt instead for a major figure like Kenneth Clarke or Michael Portillo who can perhaps strike more chunks off the Labour record and extend their appeal more widely in the electorate. Even a new 'continuity' candidate, like David Davis, could gain the Tories a chance to get back in the race that they have so conspicuously been losing for ten years now. The wrecker in the wings for the recovery potential of even such drastic pre-election surgery remain the Liberal Democrats, whose dream of displacing the Conservatives as the second party in England no longer looks as futile as it once did.

By 2002 Labour found itself in a strong and commanding position in British politics, more dominant politically than the Conservatives had been ten years before. Yet, falling turnout hardly suggested that the government inspired great loyalty or affection. The inability of the Conservatives to recover support even in the mid-term of parliaments, in sharp contrast to all previous oppositions, puzzled many commentators, but the resurgence of opposition to Labour – be it from the Conservatives or the Liberal Democrats – surely cannot be too far away. Such events cannot be predicted in advance, nor can changes within the parties themselves be easily foreseen, but when they come they do change the political weather, and with this dramatically alter the fortunes of parties.

Chapter 2

Remaking the Constitution

ANDREW GAMBLE

In 2001 the first phase of Labour's constitutional revolution was complete, but there were many loose ends, and many issues still to be addressed. The Government elected in 1997 had embarked upon the most far-reaching programme of constitutional reform since 1832 and, some argue, since 1688 (Barnett 1997; Hitchens 1999). The Blair Government is likely to be remembered for its constitutional reforms in the same way that the Thatcher Government is remembered for its economic reforms. The proposals of the Labour and Liberal Democrat Joint Consultative Committee on Constitutional Reform shaped Labour's 1997 manifesto and in its first term Labour pushed through no fewer than 12 major bills on the Constitution. Six new Cabinet Committees were created to plan the legislation (Hazell 2001). Many of the changes, such as the reform of the House of Lords, had been stalled for a hundred years.

The reforms have been hailed by radicals and condemned by traditionalists, but both at least agree that taken together they mark a watershed in British constitutional development (Sutherland 2000). The only dissentient seems to be the British Government, which has done its utmost to avoid the impression that there is a coherent programme of reform or to claim credit for it. Despite constant urging from the constitutional reform lobby, the Government declined to make any major statement about the Constitution, still less draw up a new constitutional document, announce a Constitutional Convention, or even set out its plans in a White Paper. No new administrative machinery to oversee the changes was introduced, so that the work had to be split between eight Departments. Tony Blair has rarely mentioned constitutional reforms in his speeches, and has never devoted a whole speech to the subject. The major speech on the Constitution planned for the first term was shelved.

There are several reasons for this caution. The Constitution is seen as an issue with limited political appeal, popular amongst a vocal section of the political class, but largely regarded with bemusement by the rest of the electorate. Secondly, constitutional reform became a major part of Labour's programme under the leadership of John Smith. It never had

Table 2.1   *Labour's constitutional reform plans 1997*

Labour Manifesto 1997	Progress Report 2002
Reform of the House of Lords	Stage 1 completed
	House of Lords Act 1999
	Stage 2 under discussion
Modernization of the House of Commons	Modernization Committee Proposals
Controls on Party Funding	Electoral Commission
	Political Parties, Elections and Referendums Bill 2000
Referendum on Electoral Reform for Commons	Not held
Freedom of Information Act	Enacted 1999
Scottish Parliament	Enacted 1998
Welsh Assembly	Enacted 1998
More Accountable Local Government	Elected Mayors
Strategic Authority for London	Establishment of GLA
Regional Assemblies for England and Wales	White Paper 2002
Incorporation of the European Convention on Human Rights into UK Law	Human Rights Act 1998
Devolution in Northern Ireland	Good Friday Agreement 1999

Source: Hazell (2001)

the same priority for Tony Blair, but many of the commitments, particularly those on devolution, were impossible to abandon, and the party fought the 1997 election on a far-reaching programme of constitutional reform (see Table 2.1). In government, however, the Blair Government, like all Labour Governments before it, proved cautious in the way it implemented the programme, often choosing the least radical option, and disappointing the high hopes of the reformers.

If constitutions are looked at comparatively across democratic political systems, the big divide is between those which concentrate power and those which disperse it. Constitutions can be mapped on two dimensions, the federal/unitary dimension and the executives/parties dimension (Lijphart 1999). When this is done, the Westminster model of the UK as it existed in the mid 1990s appeared an outlier in comparative terms (Lijphart 1999, p.14.2) because of the extent to which its constitution promoted the dominance of the executive and allowed few countervailing powers. The Westminster model is characterized by executive supremacy upheld by single party majority governments, a disproportional electoral system, a subordinate legislature with a weak second chamber, an adversarial political culture, and a subordinate judiciary and Central Bank. The constitution in such a system is 'flexible' rather than 'rigid', meaning that it can be adjusted by simple majorities in Parliament, rather than having to meet more stringent criteria, such as a two-thirds majority, as well as independent judicial review. The Westminster model has long been unashamedly majoritarian and flexible. Winner takes all in this system, and the winner is always the executive. The constitutional reform movement which arose in the 1980s challenged the Westminster model, seeking changes that would make Britain more like other democracies, by decentralizing and redistributing the powers of the executive. The key to achieving this has been seen as transforming the unitary state through devolution, and altering the balance of power between the executive, Parliament and the judiciary.

There are three broad views on the constitutional reform programme as it has unfolded under the Blair Government:

- The *constitutional modernizers*, well represented in the leaderships of the two main parties, think there is need for some change, but argue that this is best accomplished in a gradual way, so that the changes can preserve institutional continuity and disturb as little as possible the way the constitution works, in particular the supremacy of the executive. From this perspective many of the reforms are cosmetic, and unlikely to lead to fundamental change. After all the fuss, the Constitution so lovingly described by Walter Bagehot one hundred and fifty years ago (Bagehot 1963), will still be recognizably the same animal, although brought up to date. There will have been no constitutional revolution, no founding of a new constitutional order, no new Glorious Revolution, no new Republic. Some critics allege that the Blair Government is just the latest band of reformers to be absorbed and domesticated within the majestic orb of the Constitution. The *ancien régime* lives on (Nairn 2000).
- *Constitutional radicals*, however, (strongly represented in the Labour party and the Liberal Democratic party) are optimistic that despite the Government's caution, more fundamental change is under way. They argue that even if there has been no constitutional revolution since 1997, there has been a significant constitutional *evolution*, both in legal and political terms. As the separate changes unfold, so problems emerge that were largely unforeseen, and pressure is created for further changes to rectify anomalies and make the system manageable.

The constitutional reform may be taking place in the English manner – piecemeal, pragmatic, incremental without any overall design or plan – but a radical break with past practice is still taking place. The full implications of the changes may not be clear for ten or twenty years, but a watershed has already been passed and there is no going back (Barnett 1997).

- This is also the view of *constitutional traditionalists*, who are however utterly dismayed by the turn of events. They fear that the essence of the old constitution is being destroyed – devolution will lead inexorably sooner or later to the departure of Scotland from the Union, and the operation of the European Treaties is steadily depriving Britain of self-government by undermining parliamentary sovereignty. Many speak in apocalyptic terms of the *Abolition of Britain* (Hitchens 1999) and the *End of Britain?* (Redwood 1999), or lament the passing of England and its tradition of self-government (Scruton 2000). Others declare that England needs to prepare for the inevitable, by re-establishing itself as a self-governing, independent sovereign nation again. If other nations in the Union choose to leave, England should do nothing to detain them, but should calmly assert its own national interests, and resist incorporation into a European federal state (Heffer 1999).

The nature of the Constitution

The Constitution of the United Kingdom which traditionalists still so fiercely defend is in fact the *English* Constitution, the product of long-drawn out battles between Crown and Parliament in the seventeenth century, and the political settlement reached after the 'Glorious Revolution' of 1688 had deposed the legitimate King, James II, and his heirs, because they were Catholics, and placed a Dutch Protestant Prince, William of Orange and his consort, Mary Stuart, on the throne. The essentials of this Constitution were therefore established before the Union with Scotland in 1707, which did not interfere with its essential core, the sovereignty of the Crown-in-Parliament.

Apart from an incremental widening of representation during the nineteenth century most of the features of the Constitution present in 1688 are present still. This degree of formal institutional continuity, although disguising some major changes of substance, is still remarkable. The flexibility of the Constitution, the ease with which it has been adjusted to the vastly dissimilar circumstances of a largely agrarian country with representation and political voice limited to a political class of ten thousand families, to an urban and industrial society with universal suffrage, has often been regarded as its supreme virtue (Johnson 1999; Norton 1992), and superior to the written constitutions of other states. But in the last thirty years its virtues have been increasingly questioned.

Critics of the English constitution have pursued two main lines of attack. The first is that the United Kingdom is the last of the *anciens régimes* of Europe, possessing the only constitution to have been drawn up before the modern era. It badly needs a new constitutional settlement, based on citizenship and popular sovereignty, to reflect the reality of its politics. Anachronisms such as the unaccountable prerogative powers of the monarch, the status of British people as subjects rather than citizens, a voting system which often produces wildly disproportional relations between votes cast and MPs elected, and a second chamber which until 1999 still had a majority of its members selected on the basis of heredity should be swept away (Barnett 1997; Hutton 1995; Holme & Elliott 1988; Freedland 1999). Transparency and accountability have to be increased.

The second strand of criticism is not so concerned with whether the constitution is modern or not, but with the fact that it is no longer balanced (Mount 1992). It has lost the distribution of power between its various parts which in the eighteenth and nineteenth centuries was so much admired. The steady growth of the power of the elected house of Parliament, the Commons, and therefore of the executive and above all the Prime Minister, at the expense of the Crown and the Lords and to some extent the judiciary, has meant that the Constitution has been 'hollowed out'. The forms may have stayed the same, but at the heart of British Government is now an 'elective dictatorship'; the executive has come to wield a disproportionate amount of power. The Constitution must be 'rebalanced' by giving power back to Parliament (Lords and Commons), to the Monarch, and to the Courts, so making the executive accountable again.

These different strands of criticism have fed the constitutional debates and helped shape the demands for particular measures of reform. Elements of both types of thinking can be found in many of the proposals which have been put forward and implemented. But neither of them is fully reflected in the policy of the Government, which has sought to retain the supremacy of the executive and has avoided or modified any measures which seriously threaten to encroach upon it. Rebalancing the Constitution to improve the representativeness and accountability of British government have not been priorities; the government has been more concerned with improving the delivery of public services. This tension which is both institutional and ideological has been reflected in many of the conflicts and muddles that have characterized the constitutional reform programme.

The English Constitution has many peculiarities, which sets it apart from constitutions in other democracies. One of the most notorious is that this Constitution is not 'written' by which is meant that it is not *codified* in a single written foundation document like the American Constitution. The English Constitution is written in the form of Acts of Parliament and legal judgments. But the lack of a founding document or of the notion of a 'basic law', a set of legal precepts beyond the ability of Parliament to amend through simple majorities, make the English Constitution highly distinctive and idiosyncratic, as well as bestowing upon it its fabled flexibility and adaptability. Lacking the possibility of appeal to a founding document the Constitution can evolve according to the dominant fashions and opinions of the moment.

Nevertheless this flexibility has limits. The English Constitution is marked by two key doctrines – parliamentary sovereignty and the rule of law. The first reflects the fact that since 1688 the seat of sovereignty has been recognized as Parliament, more precisely the Crown-in-Parliament. This does not mean that sovereignty resides with backbench MPs but rather that the executive of the British state rules through Parliament and is dependent upon Parliament for its legitimacy (Judge 1993). The significance of the upheavals of the seventeenth century was that the Crown lost the ability to rule without the support of Parliament. The powers and prerogatives of the Crown have been transferred to the executive which in the democratic era owes its position to its ability to command a majority in the House of Commons rather than royal patronage. But although parliamentary government is different from the royalist absolutist government which it displaced, it is still a form of executive government, which gives prime importance to the formation and sustaining of a strong executive, and secondary importance to reflecting or representing the electorate.

The United Kingdom appears at first glance to be the model of a unitary state, with all powers vested in a central authority rather than dispersed or divided as in a federal system. But this centralism co-exists with different arrangements for governing England, Scotland, Wales and Northern Ireland. Having a single ultimate source of authority in the state does not rule out allowing considerable variation in regional arrangements, which is why the UK has sometimes been described as a 'union state' rather than as a 'unitary state' (Rose 1982). This state was formed through a series of unions of other nations within the British Isles with England, but each one was different, which is reflected in their governing arrangements. With the coming of formal devolution the oddities and anomalies of this 'union state' have been brought into full view.

The second principle of the English Constitution is the rule of law, which implied that government had to act within the law and respect individual rights which had grown up through custom and convention. The idea of a rule of law which placed restraints upon the actions of the executive has been one of the most important elements of the balanced constitution but, as with most features of the constitution, it has lacked codification and has depended upon the executive abiding by conventions which restrain its powers. The doctrine of parliamentary sovereignty and the unified executive take priority. No Parliament is able under this doctrine to bind its successor. Each new Parliament is formally sovereign and in principle there is nothing it cannot do. In practice its powers are hedged around by constitutional conventions and political realities. But because there is no conception of a basic law as in Germany, or even of a particular category of laws which are so fundamental that they need a different procedure before they can be amended, judges are unable indefinitely to overrule Parliament and the executive if the latter is determined on a particular course of action.

The constitutional reform movement in Britain in the last two decades has tackled head-on the traditional doctrines which have informed the constitution, and radicals such as Charter 88 have demanded a new constitutional settlement to put the UK constitution on a similar basis to the constitutions of other democratic states around the world (Evans 1995). They have argued for a codified constitution with the entrenchment of key provisions to safeguard the liberties of the citizen and the accountability of the executive, rather than relying on conventions and common law.

Developments in the constitution in relation to the devolution programme, the European Union, and the electoral system are discussed in other chapters. The remainder of this chapter focuses on constitutional developments in relation to Parliament, the Monarchy and the Judiciary.

Parliament: House of Commons

One of the areas where least progress was made in the first term was the reform of Parliament itself. The present day House of Commons has often been contrasted unfavourably with its mid-nineteenth century predecessor, when MPs were more independent of the executive. The rise of party and the whipping system enabled the executive to re-establish control over the Commons, to the point where governments seldom lose votes in Parliament, and the number of rebellions against the party whip, although higher in some Parliaments than others, rarely reaches levels which cause the executive difficulty, except where it commands only a narrow majority (Norton 1995; Cowley 2001).

The problem has been much discussed but few plausible suggestions for reform have come forward, because any reform that made a difference would have to tackle one of the central tenets of the doctrine of Crown-in-Parliament by separating the legislature from the executive. This was a central feature of the US Constitution, intended to limit the power of the executive to control the legislature. In the UK the position has been exacerbated by the size of modern government, which means that in any Parliament more than one hundred MPs out of 659 are part of the ministerial team, and therefore obliged to vote with the executive. Party divisions and the adversarial nature of the Commons means that on the majority of issues most backbench MPs will vote according to their party rather than according to their conscience. Opposition as a result has tended to become stylized in the modern House of Commons, epitomized by the ritual jousting matches of ministerial questions and set-piece debates. The main opposition party has little incentive to change these rules so long as it has a prospect of power (Riddell 1998).

Although MPs have the ultimate sanction over Governments and no Government can survive without maintaining support in the House of Commons, the initiative always remains very much with the executive, and instances of successful backbench rebellion are few. With such a large majority the Blair Government has been in little danger of being defeated outright in the Commons, but there have nevertheless been a number of significant rebellions, for example over single parents, disability benefits, reform of the House of Lords, and war with Iraq. The need for Government to placate its backbenchers is always there, and leads to deals and compromises on controversial legislation (Cowley 2001). The device of Early Day Motions and threats to vote against the Government or abstain are means of exerting pressure to achieve changes, and there are numerous occasions when Governments consider it prudent to make changes in legislation to accommodate the anxieties and concerns of their supporters (Stage 2 of House of Lords reform in 2002 is an example).

The other route by which MPs seek to influence Government and make it accountable is through the system of scrutiny, particularly the Select Committees, which have gradually been accorded more powers and more independence, and which offer an opportunity to interrogate ministers, civil servants and other witnesses about particular decisions and programmes. These Committees still have fewer powers than their equivalents in the United States, in particular their powers to compel witnesses to attend or to get access to the documents they want are limited. But a number of them, particularly when chaired by effective politicians, have achieved a high profile for their reports. The Public Accounts Committee, the Public Administration Committee, the Transport Committee and the Foreign Affairs Committee have all been successful in this respect in the recent past. But Government is still able to disregard them if it chooses.

There has been a long discussion as to how to make the Select Committees more effective and give them more powers. One of the difficulties is that, while the Commons is structured on adversarial party lines, and the majority party is expected to sustain the executive, party considerations will also often enter into the deliberations of the Select Committees. All MPs who belong to the party that forms the government become in effect part of the executive so long as they accept the party whip, which is why the withdrawal of the whip is treated as such a serious matter and occurs so rarely. But so long as MPs see their primary duty as either supporting or opposing the executive, it is very hard for a genuinely independent legislature to emerge – one capable of resisting the executive and forcing it to be accountable. Nevertheless some steps are being taken. There was controversy after the 2001 election when Government Whips tried to change the chairs of two key select committees, Donald Anderson and Gwyneth Dunwoody. They were regarded as insufficiently loyal to the executive. The change was successfully resisted by MPs and subsequently there was pressure for the decision on the appointment of Select Committee Chairs to be taken away from the Whips.

The changes to the Select Committee system were part of a more general package of reform put forward by Robin Cook as Leader of the House of Commons from the 2001 election until he resigned over war with Iraq in March 2003. Using the all-party Modernization Committee, established in 1997, as his vehicle, Cook built on the report of the Commons Liaison Committee, *Shifting the Balance* (House of Commons 2000), which had been dismissed by the Government before the election. Amongst the proposals were changing the hours of the House of Commons to get rid of late-night sittings, so making the Commons less of a gentlemen's club and more a working legislature. These reforms, long sought by many women MPs, were finally passed in October 2002. Cook also proposed a significant procedural change, by which bills which did not complete all their stages in one session could be carried forward to the next session, instead of having either to be axed or to start again at the beginning (Cook 2003).

All parties professed themselves in favour of strengthening the Commons. The Conservatives had produced a report chaired by a political scientist, Lord Norton, several of whose recommendations were similar to those subsequently proposed by Robin Cook (see Box 2.1). But Labour and the Conservatives as the two parties of government

---

Box 2.1   The Norton Commission to strengthen Parliament, 2000

Main Recommendations
- Carry-over for all public bills from one session to the next
- Strengthening Select Committees. Appointments no longer to be made by Whips
- Prime Minister to appear before Liaison Committee of Select Committee Chairs twice a year
- Reforming Question Time, for example use of 'unstarred questions', and return to two sessions a week
- Scrutiny of English bills by English MPs
- Size of the Cabinet restricted to 20 and junior ministers to 50

Source: Constitution Unit (2000)

---

were lukewarm about any measures which would seriously hamper the executive. So too were many backbench MPs. Robin Cook's proposal to allow MPs to determine the membership of Select Committees rather than the party Whips was defeated by MPs themselves.

Much of the talk of the *decline* of Parliament seemed misplaced. Parliament was pretty much what it had always been, the seat of sovereignty, but in practice dominated by the executive. Complaints that power was being increasingly concentrated in the hands of the Prime Minister and the executive at the expense of Parliament had some substance, but were also part of an established pattern which went back at least to Lloyd George. A small but significant step in the other direction was the announcement in May 2002 that Tony Blair would meet the Liaison Committee, composed of all the chairs of Select Committees twice a year to answer questions. But despite concessions like these the increasing pressures on the executive were bound to make Parliament seem more peripheral to the process of Government, unless it acquired much greater powers to act as an independent legislature. That would almost certainly require a change in the electoral system, which would break the stranglehold of the two major parties. Despite being part of the original reform package agreed with the Liberal Democrats, the prospect of electoral change receded during Labour's second term, although changes in voting systems were agreed and implemented for several other elections, including the Scottish Parliament, the Welsh Assembly and the European Parliament. Other more limited changes aimed at redressing some of the imbalance between Government and Parliament remain possible. One idea is that the patronage powers of the executive should be curbed by making all major public appointments subject to parliamentary approval.

Parliament: House of Lords

The second chamber in the Westminster Parliament was throughout the twentieth century its most obvious anachronism. By the end of the century it was the only second chamber in the world which still used heredity as the principal basis for determining membership. The power of the House of Lords to reject legislation passed by the Commons had been drastically restricted in 1911 and was further reduced in 1949. This hollowing out of the Lords alarmed those who favoured a more balanced constitution, since a weak second house posed little serious challenge to a determined executive with a majority in the House of Commons. Almost everyone came to agree that the Lords should be reformed, but there was no agreement on what should replace it, or what its powers should be. For many reformers the important thing was to get rid of the hereditary principle, but they were divided as to whether it would be better simply to abolish the Lords and have a single chamber legislature, on the grounds that this guaranteed the purest expression of the popular will, or whether the Lords should be elected, thus acquiring its own democratic legitimacy. An elected second chamber could be expected to be more robust in resisting the diktats of the House of Commons, but it opened up the prospect of legislative deadlock, with both Houses of Parliament claiming democratic legitimacy and neither being prepared to defer to the other.

One solution was to make the second chamber into a wholly appointed House – filling it with people who had acquired some expertise, many of whom would not be prepared to stand for election, but who might have something useful to contribute to the detailed scrutiny of government legislation. But this notion was attacked on the grounds that there was far too much patronage in the hands of the executive already, and that an appointed House would mean that it was no longer independent but would become dominated by the executive.

Reform of the Lords had always got bogged down in arguments of this kind. The Labour Government after 1997 decided to break the logjam by reforming the Lords in two stages. In stage 1 the right of hereditary peers to sit in the Lords would be removed. In stage 2 the new powers and membership of the upper chamber would be defined, including its size and its procedures. Cynics suggested that Labour would complete Stage 1 but not Stage 2. It would be quite happy with a reform which removed the automatic Conservative majority which the hereditary principle ensured, without creating a second chamber which could be a rival to the Commons. Stage 1 was duly piloted through the Commons and the Lords with the assistance of a deal with the Conservative and crossbench peers which preserved ninety-two hereditary peers in the reformed House. The Wakeham Commission set up to consider the form which Stage 2 should take was given the explicit brief that the new chamber should not challenge the supremacy of the Commons. It recommended a chamber that was largely appointed with a small elected element, ranging from 12 to 35 per cent. Critics of the Wakeham report fastened on the lack of democratic legitimacy and the enlargement of the scope for patronage, and refused to be mollified by the proposal that appointments to the second chamber should be made on the recommendation of an independent appointments commission.

Labour pledged in its manifesto in 2001 that if re-elected it would proceed to implement Stage 2 of Lords reform. But it became clear after the election that this would not be plain sailing, because there was no consensus in Parliament behind the Wakeham proposals. The Liberal Democrats favoured an 80 per cent elected second chamber elected by proportional representation. Not to be outdone, the Conservatives now reversed their earlier support for the status quo and also advocated an 80 per cent elected House of Lords, but elected by the simple plurality method, with constituencies based on the shires. A large number of Labour backbenchers also expressed their support for a largely elected second chamber. In the Lords however most opinion favoured a largely appointed second chamber. There was a particularly sharp split in the Conservative party between their representatives in the two Houses.

The Lord Chancellor, Derry Irvine, came forward with proposals which stayed quite close to Wakeham's blueprint, opting for a very large second chamber (600 members) with 120 elected peers (only 20 per cent of the total) and a statutory Appointments Commission. But the remit of this Commission was limited to appointing 120 crossbench peers. There would be 16 bishops and 12 law lords but crucially the political parties between them would still nominate 330 party representatives. Irvine also rejected Wakeham's proposals for long terms of office for elected and appointed peers, and the staggering of elections to the upper house, which Wakeham had wanted in order to ensure it was independent of the executive.

The reaction to Irvine's plan in the House of Commons and in sections of the media was derisive, and it quickly became obvious that his proposals had no chance of winning a majority in the House of Commons. No Labour MP could be found to support the White Paper; most of the party wanted a second chamber that was predominantly elected and with fewer members. The Public Administration Committee

---

Box 2.2   Stage 2 of House of Lords reform

Wakeham Commission proposals
- Mixture of elected and appointed Peers
- Elected Peers 12 – 35 per cent of total
- Independent Commission for all appointed peers
- Peers to serve for 15 years: staggered elections

Government proposals
- Mixture of 600 elected, appointed and nominated Peers
- 20 per cent elected out of 600 (120) (five-year terms)
- 20 per cent appointed by Independent Commission
- 55 per cent nominated by political parties
- 5 per cent Bishops and Law Lords

Liberal Democrats
- 80 per cent elected, single transferable vote

Conservatives
- 80 per cent elected, simple plurality

Joint Committee proposals/choices
- Fully appointed
- Fully elected
- 80 per cent appointed
- 20 per cent elected
- 80 per cent elected
- 20 per cent appointed
- 60 per cent appointed
- 40 per cent elected
- 60 per cent elected
- 40 per cent appointed
- 50 per cent elected
- 50 per cent appointed

---

proposed a second chamber of only 350 members with 60 per cent elected and 40 per cent appointed by an independent Appointments Commission, half of whom would be crossbenchers (Public Administration Committee 2002).

To take matters forward Robin Cook as Leader of the Commons proposed a joint all-party Committee of both Houses. The views represented on the Committee were extremely diverse, and a consensus looked unlikely, but the Committee was charged with bringing a set of options to be voted on by both Houses of Parliament, out of which it was hoped a way forward to a permanent reform would emerge (Cook 2003). A number of alternatives were proposed – ranging from 100 per cent elected to 100 per cent appointed, with various permutations in between. In the event, all such proposals were voted down by MPs in February 2003, the consequence being, no consensus having emerged, that stage 2 reform was to be further delayed.

Yet whether or not Stage 2 is completed in the lifetime of the current Parliament, it is already clear that the old House of Lords has gone. The new House, already enjoying a greater legitimacy than the old, showed itself ready to throw out government proposals with considerably less restraint than the previous House of Lords had exercised. The executive remained nervous of giving the House of Lords greater legitimacy and greater powers, but it seemed to have few ways of avoiding it.

The Monarchy

The Crown tended not to be a direct target of the constitutional reformers, partly because of nervousness about popular support for an institution which remained remarkably constant, even through the succession of *anni horribili* of the 1990s which saw the tabloids feasting on the marriage breakups and celebrity antics of the Queen's children. Yet the position of the Monarchy is at the heart of any serious constitutional reform, since Crown-in-Parliament is the centrepiece of the Constitution. Like the House of Lords, the Crown had in practice lost most of its powers, although not by statute. The conduct of the Monarch had been increasingly circumscribed by conventions, particularly over the royal assent to legislation (no Monarch has vetoed an Act of Parliament since 1707), over the choice of Prime Minister, and decisions to dissolve Parliament and call a general election.

There has been considerable comment about 'anachronistic' features of the monarchy, such as the Acts of Parliament which require the Head of State to be a Protestant, prevents him or her from marrying a Catholic or divorcee, and enforces male primogeniture. A modest reform agenda for the Monarchy has emerged, much of which appears to be embraced by the circles around Prince Charles, and some of these restrictions may therefore change in the years ahead, although the initiative for them is likely to come from the Palace rather than from Downing Street. The transition will be difficult however since the English Monarch is a constitutional Monarch like no other. The Monarchy is intimately bound up with both Church and Parliament, so that a change in even so apparently minor a matter as the personal religious faith of the Monarch will have many other constitutional consequences. The Monarch can hardly be Head of the Church of England if he or she is no longer a member of it. Once the character of the Monarchy comes under scrutiny there will be pressure to bring Britain into line with other states and lay down in precise, codified terms the role and duties which the British Head of State is required to perform (Fabian Society 2003).

If at some point in the future Britain were to have a new constitutional settlement, its starting point would inevitably be the Sovereignty of the People rather than the Sovereignty of the Crown-in-Parliament. The British constitution is unlike any other democratic constitution in the world because it is not the people but the Crown-in-Parliament that is legally sovereign. This is upheld by elaborate charades, such as the State Opening of Parliament, in which all the participants act as though all power still resides with the Monarch and the MPs are her lowly and dutiful servants, and the preamble of Acts of Parliament, which suggests that all legislation emanates from the will of the Sovereign. The primacy of the people and its representatives, something which has long been a political reality, continues to be denied by the traditional protocols of Her Majesty's Government, still devoted to the pretence of monarchical absolutism.

One of the arguments for leaving the Monarchy alone is that it has acted in the past as a support for reforming governments (Bogdanor 1995). The Blair Government, it is suggested, is able to carry through far-reaching constitutional changes precisely because it does not seek to touch the Monarchy. The stability and continuity associated with the Monarchy places it above party politics and provides a point of unity and cohesion which allows quite uncongenial changes to be accepted, because they are done with the authority of the Crown. By opening the new Scottish Parliament the Queen helped to legitimize it, and therefore made it acceptable even to those who had opposed it on principle. In the same way the Queen has signed the Act of Parliament which does away with the hereditary principle in the House of Lords, a principle to which she must be supposed to have more than a fleeting attachment. So long as the Monarch does not take sides in party politics, but always acts on the advice of ministers, and reads the speeches which ministers prepare, she becomes a Head of State beyond political competition, a focus for national unity, but also a cipher.

The performance of this role, however, requires extraordinary self-discipline on the part of the royal family. The present Queen has this in abundance, but the strain does sometimes show in other members of the royal family. A recent example was the leaking, in September 2002, of the contents of letters sent by the Prince of Wales to Government Ministers, which expressed very clear views about a range of subjects from hunting and the countryside to genetic foods and political correctness. The only way a constitutional monarchy of the British kind can survive is if the royals keep their private political opinions strictly to themselves. This is a difficult thing to do, since they are being asked to perform a highly visible public role, but expected not to express their views publicly.

The public role which the Monarchy has developed in place of a political role is one in which it devotes itself to public service. The Royals have come to identify themselves with every form of public and voluntary service in the community, from the Armed Forces to campaigns such as the World Wildlife Fund. Princess Diana extended this into new areas with her support for the victims of Aids and landmines. The Crown now sponsors a great variety of associations and events in civil society (Prochaska 1995). This role is not overtly political, although in its support for a public ethos and the value of public service it can at times clash with the attitudes of the Government, as was apparent in the Thatcher era.

One of the greatest problems for the future of the Monarchy is how to reconcile the hereditary principle with the celebrity principle. After Diana the hunger of the tabloids for celebrity royals is intense, but celebrity cannot easily be manufactured, and the genetic lottery which the hereditary principle enshrines, makes it unlikely that many royal heirs will instinctively possess it. But it is also hard for the royals to avoid media exposure and the pitfalls which come with it. Raising young royals to dedicate themselves to a lifetime of duty and discretion is not likely to grow any easier.

Abolition of the Monarchy is a distant project, but serious reform may not be far away. Although underlying support for the continuation of the Monarchy has remained fairly constant at around 70 per cent, and was so even through the worst of the troubles in the 1990s, almost two thirds of British citizens now do not expect there to be a Monarchy in fifty years time (Fabian Society 2003). The funeral of the Queen Mother and the Queen's Jubilee in 2002 consolidated support for the Monarchy in 2002, but it remains highly vulnerable to media squalls and scandals. The case for serious reform in the interests of the Monarchy itself will increase, and it will also be difficult for the Monarchy not to be affected by the other constitutional changes in progress, which are likely to lead to changes in the way it operates, especially after the present Queen dies.

One reason why the position of the Monarch remains secure is because it suits the other monarch in the British system, the Prime Minister. The trappings of royal absolutism, particularly the royal prerogatives and the powers of patronage, were long ago appropriated by the Prime Minister, and have never been subjected to parliamentary control. This gives the British Prime Minister more executive authority than any other democratically elected President or Prime Minister. There is much talk of the Prime Minister becoming more like a President, but there is no need for the Prime Minister to become a President, because he already enjoys the powers of a monarch, in the sense that he has usurped the executive authority in the shape of the prerogative powers and patronage powers which monarchs once used to exercise. If the role of the Monarchy was ever therefore to be constitutionally defined, the same would need to be done for the Prime Minister. The temporary residents of 10 Downing Street have never been keen. The prerogative powers free the Prime Minister from much scrutiny and accountability in Parliament, and help preserves the primacy of the executive.

The judiciary: accountability and transparency

The principle of undivided and unlimited sovereignty in the English Constitution required a unified system of law. Although judges are independent, the separation between politics and the law is less clearcut than in the United States. There is no equivalent of the Supreme Court which is able to strike down legislation as unconstitutional. In Britain the head of the legal system, the Lord Chancellor, not only appoints judges but is also a senior member of the Cabinet and presides over the House of Lords. The Law Lords who form the ultimate court of appeal also sit in the House of Lords, and can participate and vote in debates. Constitutional reformers have sought to change this system, and have demanded a separation between Parliament and the courts, specifically making the Lord Chief Justice the head of the legal system, and removing the power of the Lord Chancellor over judicial appointments. Some changes have been initiated. A Judicial Appointments Commission now scrutinizes candidates for the judiciary and makes recommendations to the Lord Chancellor, but the final decision still rests with him. The need for a more representative bench, with more women and ethnic minority candidates is acknowledged, but progress has been slow.

What is occurring, however, in the law as in other fields, is a trend towards more formal regulation and the adoption of more explicit standards and procedures to promote transparency and accountability. The obligation on MPs to register their interests and the appointment of an independent Parliamentary Commissioner to oversee it, the Nolan Committee on Standards in Public Life, the proposals for a civil service act to define the roles of civil servants and special advisers, the debate on how political parties should be funded, are all examples of this, and part of the wider political and cultural changes which are driving constitutional reform. Another instance is the 1999 Freedom of Information Act. Although much watered down from the original proposals, this legislation when it eventually comes into force will nevertheless create an important precedent, a serious dent in the culture of secrecy of British Government. Written rules are replacing conventions.

In the legal field another important example has been the 1998 Human Rights Act which incorporated the European Convention on

Human Rights into English Law, and came into force in October 2000. Traditionalists were strongly opposed, arguing that it would undermine parliamentary sovereignty, but the welter of trivial and vexatious cases they predicted would ensue has not in fact materialized. The Act imposes a legal framework which will be hard to change or remove. In doing so it creates a space beyond Westminster in which the judges can operate, giving them a set of criteria by which they can hold ministers and their departments to account. In the past the main weapon open to judges to criticize ministers was the common law. But judgments made in the light of common law could always be overturned by Parliament passing a new statute. The Human Rights Act cannot be overturned in this way, and this gives judges a new power they may well exploit in the future.

There are signs that judges are beginning to do just that, and to claim a new role for themselves. In 2001 the Senior Law Lord, Lord Bingham, expressed support for combining the Appellate Committee of the House of Lords and the Judicial Committee of the Privy Council into a new Supreme Court (Constitution Unit 2001). The Lord Chief Justice, Lord Woolf, argued in 2002 in the light of recent asylum cases that the judiciary had an important role in defending human rights if Government sought to infringe them (*Guardian*, 18 October 2002).

The reason why constitutional traditionalists dislike innovations like the Human Rights Act so much is because it represents a form of constitutional entrenchment. They see the distinctiveness and the flexibility of the old English constitution being destroyed by measures like devolution for Scotland and Wales, the incorporation of the European Convention on Human Rights, and the signing of EU Treaties which makes European Court rulings binding on English and Scottish courts. The principle that no Parliament is able to bind its successor is broken. No future Westminster Parliament, for example, will be able to abolish the Scottish Parliament in the way that the Thatcher Government abolished the Greater London Council. In that sense the Parliament has to accept restraints on its actions, which although not embodied formally in a written constitution amounts to much the same thing.

There are other important instances of this trend. One of the most intriguing is the decision by the Blair Government in 1997 to give operational independence to the Bank of England. Although criticized from right and left by those who favour discretion over general rules in the way the public realm is organized, many constitutional reformers welcomed the move precisely because it established a more accountable and transparent process for the determination of interest rates, reducing the monopoly of power held by the executive (Barnett 1997). Analysts of these moves towards a regulatory rather than a discretionary state argue that by reducing the power of 'Parliament' and politicians to take these decisions it 'depoliticizes' the process of government, handing it over to specialists and technicians (Burnham 2001).

Similar objections have been raised to the operation of the European Treaties and what constitutional traditionalists see as the granting of powers to the European Court to override the decisions of English and Scottish courts. This has given rise to the fear that by participating in the European Union, Britain will end up as part of a European federal state and lose its right to self-government. In the Factortame case in 1990 British judges decided that the application of an Act of Parliament could not overrule the exercise of rights under European Law. This was regarded by traditionalists as a major surrender of parliamentary sovereignty. Fears were also aroused by the implications of qualified majority voting in the Council of Ministers, agreed to by the Thatcher Government in the Single European Act, and extended by the Treaty of Nice. The British Government could be outvoted in the Council of Ministers, but forced to accept their decisions as binding.

These issues are being discussed at the European Convention set up in 2002 under the chairmanship of Giscard d'Estaing to consider the appropriate constitutional arrangements for a Union that already has fifteen members and is planning to admit ten more. Its agenda included ways of improving the democratic legitimacy of the EU: clarifying the competencies of the EU institutions, member states and the regions: the status of the EU's Charter of Fundamental Rights: and the role of national parliaments. Federalists such as Joschka Fischer, the German Foreign Minister, urged the Convention to propose a framework for a federal state, with a clear division of powers between different levels, and a written constitution that is legally binding and enforced by a Constitutional Court. The attraction of a federal solution is that it provides a set of rules for resolving issues without necessarily setting up a strong centralized government; the division of powers could be set with only minimal powers being granted to European institutions like the Commission, so giving states rights to resist creeping Europeanization if they did not want it (Siedentop 2000). The British favoured an intergovernmental solution, the drawing up of a Statement of Principles by the Council of Ministers, which would set out the powers of the EU and those of member states, but would be a political rather than a constitutional document. Eurosceptics argued for the retention of all powers in the Council of Ministers, ending qualified majority voting, and giving each country an absolute veto on every issue. With twenty-five members such a proposal would make common action at the European level virtually impossible.

Conclusion

The programme of constitutional reform which the Blair Government initiated is unlikely ever to be codified through a constitutional convention in a single written document. But cumulatively it represents an important stage of evolution away from the flexible monarchical constitution of the past, which had Parliamentary sovereignty and executive supremacy at its heart, towards a regulatory state, in which the power of the executive and the Westminster Parliament, while still significant, is restrained by the existence of subordinate, supranational and parallel powers which it has willed into existence but cannot will away. The Scottish Parliament is an example of the first, the EU Commission and the European Court examples of the second, and the new judicial activism an example of the third.

The decline of the central importance of Parliament in sustaining a strong, flexible centralized executive authority may also in time make further reforms more likely, most notably to the exercise of the royal prerogatives and powers by the Prime Minister, particularly the powers of patronage and appointment, and the power to sign treaties and declare war. In the more transparent and accountable polity that is emerging, these powers, although cherished by the executive, are harder to defend. The same may be true of the electoral system itself. The Labour party remains for the moment strongly attached to simple plurality voting, especially since the wildly disproportional results of 1997 and 2001. The plans to hold a referendum on changing the voting system have so far come to nothing. But versions of proportional representation are now being used for elections to the Northern Ireland Assembly, the Scottish Parliament, the Welsh Assembly, and the European Parliament. They are being actively discussed for local elections and the House of Lords. It is quite likely that at some stage in the development of the constitutional reforms pressure for electoral reform at Westminister will return. It is probably the only way to make the House of Commons an effective legislative chamber, with greater independence from the executive.

The heroic phase of constitutional change may be over, but the reforms still have a long way to run, and there are many uncertainties as to how they will turn out. In a recent democratic audit, Britain was shown to have some strengths but also many weaknesses (Weir and Beetham 1999). The constitutional reform programme has begun to address some of these. The kind of framework which is being established means that although there is unlikely to be any sudden rupture in continuity and a new beginning for the British state, the content of the British constitution and the way it operates are undergoing some major changes, which are unlikely to be reversed. Whether the result will be that Britain breaks up into its component nations, or whether it creates a new, more federal structure for the different elements of the United Kingdom remains to be seen. Similarly whether the system of representation is reformed and Parliament, including a reformed second chamber, is restored to a prominent position in the British state, or whether the executive contrives to hold on to a monopoly of power, is not yet decided. Whether Britain votes to join the Euro and becomes a full partner in European integration, or continues to stand aside, and by refusing to engage becomes a marginal player semi-detached from the eurozone also lies in the future. What is clear however is that the way in which these different constitutional issues are resolved will have the greatest possible consequences for the future conduct of British politics.

Chapter 3

The Europeanization of British Politics

BEN ROSAMOND

It is now commonplace to argue that a full understanding of contemporary British politics is impossible without a comprehension of the European Union (EU) and Britain's place therein. This chapter considers the importance of European integration for British politics via a discussion of the concept of 'Europeanization'. It suggests that much of the public debate in Britain about the EU is built around a rather simplistic dichotomy that fails to capture the sheer complexity of the Europeanization of British politics. The EU's importance is underscored dramatically by the fact that a decision about Britain's monetary sovereignty is imminent. While other member states have replaced their national currencies with the Euro, Britain remains outside of the Euro-zone. Adoption of the single currency would commit Britain to a particular form of economic governance by removing the national capacity to set interest and exchange rates. The argument is, at one level, technical, a calculation of costs and benefits, but it is also an intensely political issue embracing three key questions:

- normative and symbolic debates about the propriety of surrendering (or pooling) national sovereignty in a key area of 'high' politics;
- strategic debates about the international alignment of the British state; and
- issues of internal party management and inter-party politics.

Important though it is, the Euro is not the only pressing matter concerning the future of the EU. Indeed the future scope, character and even name of the EU are now matters for intense debate across the continent. This debate is driven by two impulses. The first is a widespread and developing concern among policy elites that the EU lacks legitimacy and is generally poorly understood by the citizens of its member states. This problem is particularly acute in Britain where opinion surveys routinely reveal low levels of knowledge about, and low levels of trust in, EU institutions. With such concerns in mind a European Convention was convened in 2001 under the directorship of former French President Valéry Giscard d'Estaing.

The Convention's mission was to think openly about the structures, functioning and transparency of the EU. With this in mind, the Convention produced a draft constitutional treaty in October 2002 (European Convention 2002). This was designed to rationalize the existing treaties while rendering them comprehensible to the ordinary citizen. The deliberations of the Convention raise all manner of questions about the character of the EU and the Convention's existence has stimulated widespread debate amongst politicians. For instance, the British Foreign Secretary Jack Straw (2002) agreed with the notion of a simplified constitutional document, but advanced a vision of the EU as an intergovernmental body rather than some sort of federal super-state.

The second impulse is enlargement. In October 2002 the European Commission recommended that ten countries, mostly from central and eastern Europe, would be ready to join the EU in 2004 with another two ready by 2007 (Commission of the European Communities 2002). While new member states are not admitted unless they have achieved certain levels of institutional, economic and legal convergence with the EU, enlargement nonetheless poses major challenges to the institutional fabric and decision-making capacity of the EU. The arrival of new member states raises deep political issues about redistributive policies of the EU such as the Common Agricultural Policy and regional development ('cohesion') funding. In short, an EU of 25 or 27 members will be a very different entity from that joined by Britain in 1973.

One way of exploring the national and international interactions involving Britain and the EU (and the EU and Britain) is to look at the ways in which the EU impacts upon the opportunity structures that frame politics within Britain. At the level of the party system, the 'EU issue' fits poorly with the established fault lines of British politics and has not simply been absorbed into intra-party politics. It raises questions of authority and identity and hits head-on certain peculiarly British (or, perhaps more accurately, *English*) conceptions such as 'parliamentary sovereignty'. Moreover, as European integration increases, it becomes harder for parties to manage the issue. This is especially true of the Conservative party, which has long been internally divided between pro and anti-Europeans (Baker, Gamble and Ludlam 1994; Cowley and Norton 1999), but also creates difficulties for Labour, as future debates on monetary union might well demonstrate.

Europeanization and British debates about the EU

Public debate has focused on two starkly opposed views of Britain's European future. On one side is a claim that Britain is being absorbed into a European system of government. On the other is the argument that national governments will continue to loom large as the bearer of national destinies, in spite of European integration. This debate is bound up with the idea that the assimilation of Britain into a 'Europolity' automatically entails the loss of national sovereignty and, more precisely, the transfer of policy competence to supranational European institutions. Thus, for Eurosceptics of various shades the assimilation scenario is an irretrievably bad thing. Eurosceptics on the right articulate concerns about the diminution of national autonomy and express fear about the emasculation of national identity. Some on the left fear that the EU is fatally inscribed with the logic of neoliberalism. If so, the pooling of economic policy competence implies nothing less than the surrender of progressive or social democratic possibilities in Britain.

Box 3.1 Britain and European integration: landmarks since 1997

1997	The newly elected Blair government signs the social protocol originally excluded from the Treaty on European Union. The Treasury stipulates its five economic tests for the suitability of the UK joining the single currency. The Treaty of Amsterdam refines aspects of the Maastricht Treaty, but is most notable for introducing the idea of 'flexible' integration and making the Schengen agreement on the removal of internal border controls part of the *acquis communautaire*. The UK (along with Ireland) remains outside of the Schengen area
1998–9	Negotiations commence with twelve countries (mostly from Central and Eastern Europe) seeking membership of the EU
1999	The UK (along with Denmark and Sweden) exercises its right (as negotiated at Maastricht) to remain outside of the single currency. Greece does not meet the convergence criteria until 2001
2000	The Draft Treaty of Nice lays out the institutional reforms needed to prepare the EU for its forthcoming enlargement
2002	Twelve of the fifteen member states adopt the euro as their currency. Denmark, Sweden and the UK remain outside of the euro-zone

Even defenders of the EU and closer British engagement with European integration find themselves using zero-sum vocabulary replicating this imagery (see also Rosamond 2002). One recent example is the New Labour government's presentation of the Draft Treaty of Nice at the end of 2000. The Nice European Council sought to streamline and reform the EU's institutions and policy-making processes in time for the entry of multiple new member states from Central and Eastern Europe. The negotiations leading up to Nice had focused on the number of Members of the European Parliament, the composition and size of the European Commission, the formula to be used for establishing voting weights in the Council and the identification of policy areas where qualified majority voting (QMV) – as opposed to unanimity – would be used in the Council. While this could be construed as a largely technocratic exercise designed to promote efficiency and to prevent institutional gridlock in an EU of 25-plus members, the last two of these issues were clearly regarded by the Blair government as potentially combustible. The Treaty extended QMV to some 30 new areas, but unanimity was retained in areas such as taxation and social security, and a decision to move to majority voting in areas such as asylum and cohesion (regional development) policy was deferred. The requirement for unanimity means that a single member state can – should it wish – effectively veto any legislative initiative in the areas in question. The government, like all of its predecessors in similar circumstances, presented the outcome of Nice as a substantial negotiating victory. Speaking to the House of Commons shortly after the summit, the then Foreign Secretary Robin Cook pointed out that

> [t]he Treaty of Nice provides for qualified majority voting in 31 articles . . . They are substantial changes that we wanted because we wanted to get rid of the veto of other countries on tougher management of the Community budget; because we wanted to ensure that we have tight rules on structural funds, so that they cannot be mismanaged; and because we wanted to ensure that we can change the rules and procedure of the European Court of Justice, so that Britain can get its cases heard faster and more fairly. Those are gains for Britain. (*Hansard*, Commons Debates, 12 December 2000, Column 468)

The point of this illustration is to show how the EU is conceptualized within the British political system. The defence deployed by Robin Cook was designed to show that the scenario of future assimilation is Eurosceptic scaremongering. At the same time it demonstrates how an oppositional, 'us versus them' version of British involvement with the EU remains embedded in the language of domestic political exchange, despite UK membership for thirty years. It also reinforces the idea that – in terms of its acceptance of integration and its dealings with other member states and supranational institutions such as the Commission – Britain is the 'awkward partner' in the EU (George 1998).

This prevailing British political discourse of European integration tends to rely on two premises that are challenged by most academic work on the EU:

- The first is the notion that the EU is a monolith, inspired by a single project. Few scholars take this as read.
- The second premise is that the EU and 'British politics' are separate spheres of action.

As noted below, there is some (modest and highly qualified) support for a version of this second proposition in the EU studies literature. However, the idea that the three choices faced by the British are (a) 'the EU does things to Britain', (b) 'Britain resists the encroachment of the EU', or (c) 'Britain seeks to acquire greater influence over EU developments' is somewhat simplistic. It fails to capture the complexities of the EU while, at the same time, underestimating the ways in which Britain participates in the shaping of this system. Moreover, it underplays the persistence of national diversity within the context of deeper integration and the development of a supranational governance regime in the EU.

To make these points is not to suggest that we are living through a period of politics 'as usual'. There is clearly something afoot in contemporary European politics and Britain is part and parcel of these transformations. As a result, it is necessry to explore the shape and scope of the Europeanization of British politics, shifting emphasis from thinking about the nature of the 'diplomatic' exchanges between Britain and the EU that have tended to characterize the 'awkward partner' debate (Buller 1995; George 1995, 1998; Wilks 1996). The academic literature on the EU and integration, dividing crudely into two camps, 'intergovernmentalist' and 'transformationalist', are bound up with alternative notions of 'Europeanization'. Using examples we can discuss the ways in which the EU 'inputs' into the British political system. Europeanization can be understood in four ways:

- enforced Europeanization or Europeanization by obligation;
- Europeanization through national adaptation;
- 'ideational Europeanization' – the Europeanization of beliefs and discourses; and
- Europeanization as feedback.

The notion of Europeanization as feedback takes us away from thinking about Europeanization as a top-down process by addressing the extent to which UK preferences are 'uploaded' to the EU level.

The Europeanization of governance

Much of the academic literature on the EU and the Europeanization presents a rather more nuanced picture than the cut and thrust of day-to-day public debate allows. That said, there is little consensus among the main schools of thought in EU studies. Intergovernmentalists see the EU as a forum through which governments strike mutually beneficial bargains and so they argue that the key transformations in the European political economy over the past fifty years have been engineered by states. National executives remain 'gatekeepers' between the European-level negotiating game and domestic politics. Thus, while European integration has a significant impact upon the domestic politics of the member states, this perspective sees the EU as very much a 'second order' political system in that the preferences taken by national governments to the European level emerge in the crucial arena of domestic exchange. Moreover, some intergovernmentalists offer the counter-intuitive observation that governments actually acquire autonomy as a consequence of integration and the growth of European-level institutions. Milward's discussion of the origins of the European Communities uses the phrase 'rescue of the nation-state' to describe the way in which the pooling of sovereign capacity in limited areas enabled European governments to deliver policy programmes capable of sustaining important domestic coalitions (Milward 1999). Moravcsik (1993, 1998) suggests that governments benefit from the information-rich setting of the EU's intergovernmental institutions. Moreover, bargains struck in the Council are conducted more or less free from domestic constraint and '[n]ational leaders undermine potential opposition by reaching bargains first and presenting domestic groups with an "up and down" choice' (Moravcsik 1993: 515).

In contrast, other scholars consider the EU to be part of a radical re-engineering of the fabric of European governance. States remain important sites of loyalty and policy output, but they co-exist with other nodes of authority in a system of multilevel governance (MLG). This account presents a stark challenge to the two-level game imagery of intergovernmentalism. Hooghe and Marks describe MLG as 'the dispersion of authoritative decision making across multiple territorial levels' (Hooghe and Marks 2001: xi). The scenario presented is one where, over the past half-century, authority has drifted away from central governments, both upwards to the European level and downwards to local and regional authorities. In short, both integration and devolution form two parts of a process through which European governance is being transformed. But this transformation does not stop with the simple redistribution of competencies between tiers of authority. The European multilevel system does not consist of discrete political regimes situated at different levels. Rather local, regional, national and supranational spaces overlap and political actors interact across the various levels. Thus the EU polity consists of 'a set of overarching multilevel policy networks' (Marks, Nielsen, Ray and Salk 1996: 41). Moreover, because European integration is uneven across sectors, it is risky to generalize about the direction and scope of contemporary European governance. But while the drift of integration does not necessarily present us with the prospect of a coherent 'superstate', this transformationalist position holds that significant alterations to European political space are underway (Kohler-Koch 1999; Rosamond 2001).

These intergovernmentalist and transformationalist positions represent alternative accounts of Europeanization. This much-used term is often used to describe the creation of European-level institutions and governance capacity. This suggests the birth of a supranational system that either replaces or sits alongside the domestic polities of member states. In some accounts Europeanization (in this sense) would be accompanied by two phenomena:

- The first is loyalty transference from national to European authority as interested actors come to discern that they are stakeholders in a new post-national political system. So, for example, trade unions – ever keen to pursue the interests of their members – may come to understand that employment rights legislation is now largely a matter of European Community law. This would require a strategy of adaptation to reorient action to the new, more meaningful European *loci* of authority.
- The second is the prominence of actors populating a genuinely transnational space, which, in turn, is actually brought about through the integration of the European economy. Such actors may include firms who begin to engage in cross-border production activity as a consequence of the creation of the European single market. At the same time these actors develop an interest in the creation of more harmonious supranational rules. For example, the continued existence of distinct national merger regulations is an obstacle to the effective exploitation of the possibilities of a single market. Firms in this position develop a stake in the creation of a uniform European competition policy regime.

However, Europeanization is more usually and precisely used to denote the *domestic* impact of the EU. As such, Knill and Lehmkuhl (1999) identify three mechanisms of Europeanization:

- The first is the non-negotiable effect of EU norms upon national politics. They have in mind cases where the EU engages in the positive prescription of an institutional model. This forces domestic arrangements to fall into line with tightly defined European requirements.
- The second consists of the alteration of what Knill and Lehmkuhl call 'domestic opportunity structures'. This describes situations where the EU contributes to the reconfiguration of the game of domestic politics by altering the balance of power among actors, thereby affecting the resource dependencies that exist between them. The point to note here is that the impact of 'Europe' will not be uniform from country to country. Pre-existing patterns of politics come under threat, but these extant institutions, policy communities and political cultures will also shape the way in which the EU transforms domestic politics. Europeanization in this sense can produce highly variable outcomes in distinct national settings as organizations and actors adapt in (nationally) particular ways to EU inputs (Ladrech 2001). Europeanization, as Radaelli (2000) notes, is not about convergence towards a single model. Indeed, it may describe the retention of national diversity, albeit under changed conditions and in a new form.
- The third is the transformation of beliefs and expectations among domestic groups and policy actors. Here we are alerted to how the EU contributes to shifting the 'ideational matter' of domestic politics (Knill and Lehmkuhl 1999).

Ladrech (2001) makes two further important observations:

- First, we should not expect to see uniform Europeanization, even within the same political system. Integration is uneven across sectors, so the nature of the incentives to adapt will vary accordingly. Also, while there may be discernible state traditions that will feed into perceptible national policy styles (Dyson 1980), institutional arrangements and policy communities are likely to differ from sector to sector within national political economies.
- Second, Europeanization should not be seen as a one-way process. The adaptive responses of actors in national settings will feed back to the European level, thereby influencing the nature of future EU inputs.

The quality of feedback between the national and the international, the means by which it is delivered to the European level, and indeed whether it can be delivered at all, are matters for debate. At its most conspicuous, this feedback can be described as the (attempted) projection of national policy preferences to the European level (Bomberg and Peterson 2000). In other words, then, the question of Europeanization cannot simply be discussed in terms of 'Europe in Britain'. It must also address the question of 'Britain in Europe'.

As suggested earlier, using the vocabulary of Europeanization in this dynamic fashion takes us away from thinking about the British polity as a simple recipient of EU inputs. Britain is (at least) a co-author of many of those inputs. In some cases, the nature of those inputs may reflect the success of an upward projection of British preferences. However, the extent to which this process resembles the two-level game metaphor favoured by intergovernmentalists is open to challenge.

Enforced Europeanization?

Membership of the EU brings with it many obligations for Britain. As a signatory to the Treaties, Britain is committed to the consolidated law of the European Communities, the *acquis communautaire*, as well as to various common policies. The principle of 'supremacy' means that European legislation takes precedence over any existing or future statutes in British law that might conflict with EU law (Wincott 2001). As the *acquis* grows, so the compromises to the autonomy of the British government become greater. Most EU law deals with rules governing market exchange and the free movement of goods, services and persons. The principle of the single market demands regulation at the European level and certain facets of the EU carry the inherent logic of supranational rather than European action. The best example of this is trade policy. The EU is a customs union, which means that it operates a common external tariff. The capacity for member states to vary levies on imports would allow for competition between national economies and this in turn would undermine the core principles of the EU Treaties. The practical consequences are the existence of a common commercial policy and the creation of a single voice for the EU in international trade negotiations. This means that British trade policy is now wholly Europeanized to the extent that it is not particularly meaningful to any longer talk about a British trade policy, at least in certain key areas such as trade in goods. As Figure 3.1 suggests, Europeanization is thus enforced (or is obligated) from Europe to the national level.

Figure 3.1   *Enforced Europeanization*

European Union

National Polity   National Polity   National Polity

Adoption of new obligations at the national level

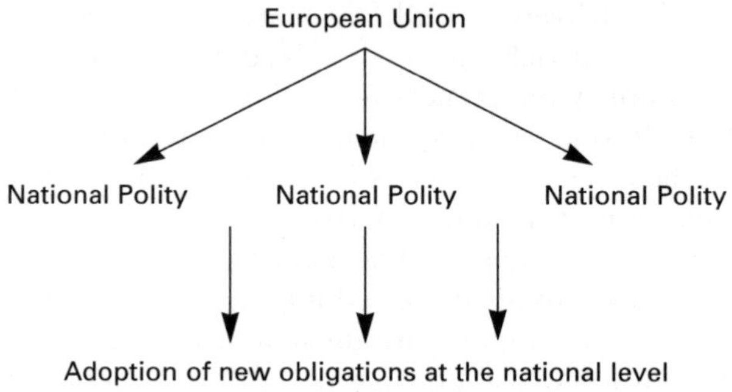

While it is important to recognize the significance of these obligations, it is also worth remembering that the extent to which Europeanization is forced upon Britain is at least open to question. For example, it is clear that the EU model of integration is constructed upon economic principles such as budgetary discipline, deregulation and privatization. These tenets of economic integration are embedded most explicitly in EU Treaties, but they have also been restated through the jurisprudence of the European Court of Justice, something that suggests member states are required to converge in terms of the norms and conduct of economic management. However, the extent to which convergence and structural adjustment is required is a function of the policy distance between member state and EU norms. In certain key areas this distance was comparatively small in the British case.

For instance, if convergence pressure is seen as coming on line with the Single European Act of 1987, then Britain can be seen as relatively unencumbered by new Europeanizing forces. As Schmidt notes, 'deregulation and privatization came before the European pressures; the Thatcher government was ideologically committed to dismantling state control of an economy that was in any event less state-dominated than either that of Germany or France' (Schmidt 1997: 172). A similar story holds for the model upon which economic and monetary union is founded: '[T]he commitment to sound money, an autonomous central bank, and freedom of capital movements were policies which Britain itself adopted independently in the 1990s' (Gamble and Kelly 2002: 98).

The limited extent of 'enforced Europeanization' is also clarified by the extent to which the idea of 'opting out' of certain policies has become a quasi-norm of a more flexible approach to integration in the EU (Warleigh 2002). The classic instance of such derogation is the 'opt

---

Box 3.2 The Maastricht convergence criteria

1. The avoidance of excessive government deficits, to be less than 3% of GDP for annual debt and 60% for the stock of government debt;
2. Inflation to be no more than 1.5% higher than the best 3 performing member states.
3. Currency to stay within the margins of the European Monetary System for at least 2 years;
4. Long-term interest rates to be no more than 2% higher than the 3 member states with the lowest rates.

---

out' of monetary union negotiated by the Major government at the Maastricht European Council in December 1991. This meant that Britain (along with Denmark and later Sweden) was able to choose whether to proceed to the irrevocable phase of monetary union. While the Maastricht stipulations, including the convergence criteria for admission to the single currency (see Box 3.2), were binding on the other member states, an enforced Europeanization did not apply formally to Britain. Yet following Maastricht, government budgets, not least those of the Major government towards the end of its tenure, were geared precisely to ensuring that the British economy met the strict criteria set for inflation, budget deficits, exchange rate stability and interest rates by the 1992 (Maastricht) Treaty on European Union (TEU). Moreover, the Major government and its New Labour successor both subscribed to the EU's Stability and Growth Pact, an agreement designed to underwrite and give substance to the economic orthodoxy at the heart of monetary union (see HM Treasury 1996; 2001b). Equivocation about the merits of entering the Euro aside, the Treasury has undertaken significant preparatory work for British entry (HM Treasury 2001a).

There can be little doubt that the Stability and Growth Pact (and monetary union more generally) impinge significantly upon the monetary and fiscal autonomy of EU member states. The interesting thing about Britain is that successive governments have seemed unwilling to commit to the level of enforced Europeanization consistent with monetary integration. At the same time, Conservative and Labour governments have chosen restrictive policy paths that represent *de facto* subscription to the underlying principles of the euro and its associated regime of economic governance. This observation is rather less paradoxical, however, if we consider the other senses in which the term Europeanization is used.

Europeanization and national adaptation

As suggested above, EU 'inputs' are moulded by the context into which they arrive. They may bring about transformations within domestic political economies, but these changes emerge from the complex interaction of national institutions, practices and ideas with 'Europeanizing' norms. The routine business of governments and administrations in member states is intimately bound up with things European. The volume of directives requiring transposition into national law is considerable. Once embedded, these have to be implemented and policed. Thus the impact of the EU in this sense goes well beyond the task of inserting directives into national law. Member states have considerable scope in deciding how these are implemented, so national traditions of policy making and administration are potentially significant shapers of Europeanization. The other main European legal instrument is regulation. To be in force regulations do not require national legislation to be enacted, but their successful application is again a matter largely dealt with by national administrative frameworks.

Thus, as Figure 3.2 indicates, there is considerable scope for variation in patterns of Europeanization across the member states. But national administrative and regulatory traditions are never static. Indeed, national administrative reforms can have an independent effect upon the capacity for effective transposition of directives into British law. Knill's (1998, 2001) comparative studies of the interplay between national administrative traditions and various European environmental

Figure 3.2   *Europeanization through national adaptation*

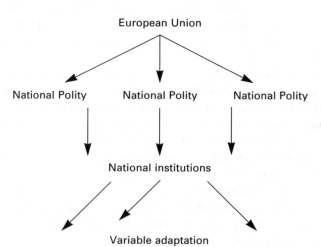

directives suggests that the Thatcher government's extensive package of administrative reforms created a national style of regulation that allowed for relatively straightforward adaptation to the new European norms. At the same time, Knill also notes that the constellation of domestic environmental and consumer pressure groups in favour of the input of European standards was strengthened (1998). Thatcherite reforms in the 1980s brought into being a network of relatively autonomous regulatory bodies and downgraded Britain's rather centralized and formalistic administrative traditions. The reformed system offered more points of access for organized interests, many of which were advocates of the implementation of European standards into British environmental regulation.

Despite the administrative changes of the past two decades, the relatively unitary character of the British state remains an important shaper of the character of Europeanization in Britain. Haverland's (2000) study of the implementation of the Packaging Waste Directive (1997) finds that the transposition of this measure in British law and the necessary administrative adaptations were accomplished with remarkable success compared to elsewhere in the EU. This observation runs counter to expectations because the detail of the directive posed fundamental challenges to the established regulatory style in this policy domain. Haverland's explanation is that the largely centralized character of the British state enables smooth transposition whereas federal systems with several layers of authority of administrative competence contain more veto points where the implementation of directives can be subverted or undermined.

But as Bulmer and Burch (2001) note, national legislative and administrative apparatuses can also be transformed through Europeanization just as they have an independent impact upon the nature of Europeanization in Britain. The need to deliver both consistent responses to European inputs and coherent positions within EU-level institutions has prompted heightened coordination efforts between departments and between key bureaucratic players such as the Cabinet Office, the Foreign Office and Britain's Permanent Representation in Brussels. Specialist subdivisions of departments have also emerged to deal with the intricacies of EU legislation. Bulmer and Burch, like others (Buller and Smith, 1998) find that much of the adaptation they describe has been fashioned in ways consistent with Whitehall traditions and the culture of the British policy process. Echoing Knill (see above), they note that a cultural predisposition to share information between departments has contributed to the relative success of policy coordination among ministries (Bulmer and Burch 2001: 86). Moreover, while the Europeanization of the British administrative apparatus has been more or less consistent with the culture of Whitehall, Bulmer and Burch also make the interesting observation that the pattern of adaptation since 1973 is itself a legacy of decisions made in the early 1960s. The model designed to co-ordinate business during the British applications to join 'the Six' has been remarkably resilient and, once again, demonstrates the inherent 'stickiness' of institutions as well as the long-term consequences of particular institutional choices.

Ideational Europeanization

Ideational Europeanization refers to alterations to attitudes, beliefs and understandings among political actors as well as to those processes of socialization and learning that promote such cognitive change. Under this heading, we are also concerned with the impact of European integration upon the underlying discourses and prevailing rhetorical patterns within British politics. Many of the adaptations described above can be thought of in these terms. Europeanization is intimately bound up with the ways in which politicians, officials and other political actors understand the imperatives set by the EU. This induces a re-calibration of what is deemed to be politically possible. For example, policy makers in Westminster and Whitehall come to understand that any policy innovation needs to be compatible with European norms (Bulmer and Burch 2001). This offers a partial explanation for why certain policy ideas – for example the re-imposition of exchange controls or the introduction of extensive state aids for ailing industries – remain off the political agenda in Britain.

British discourses of European integration have always intersected with pre-existing, embedded ideas about the conduct of politics and policy making. As is well understood, the powerful doctrine of 'parliamentary sovereignty' has been a historic obstacle to the reform of the British state generally and to the ceding of authority to the supranational level in particular (Marquand 1988; Hutton 1995). Britain's historical orientation to an open international economy has had complex effects upon attitudes to European integration among political elites. On the one hand it suggests that Britain is self-consciously located within a global rather than a regional (European) economic space. On the other, it has promoted neoliberal policy orientations that have been (as least for the past quarter of a century) largely compatible with the ethos of the Treaty of Rome and its successors (Schmidt 1997). This intersection of political identity and political economy questions (Gamble 1998) remains firmly at the heart of the debate about European integration within British politics. As Gamble and Kelly point out with regard to monetary union:

As far as the British political class was concerned . . . the direct policy implications of EMU [European Monetary Uninon] were not the problem; it was the way EMU challenged the British discourse about Europe and entrenched conceptions both of Britain's place in the world and the nature of the policy process. (Gamble and Kelly 2002: 99)

The point to make here is that 'ideational Europeanization' need not necessarily refer to the emergence of pro-European attitudes. Indeed, it may even induce the exact opposite. Perhaps more precisely, it may denote the 'infection' of a policy discourse with European concerns or it might alter the underlying parameters of what it means to be 'pro' or 'anti-European'. As Figure 3.3 suggests, ideational Europeanization involves European initiatives interacting with prevailing national norms, often prompting adaptation through policy learning.

Across the continent 'Europe' is often invoked as an imperative by governments seeking to pursue particular (and usually unpopular) legislative courses. Here Britain appears to be a strange case in that

Figure 3.3   *Ideational Europeanization*

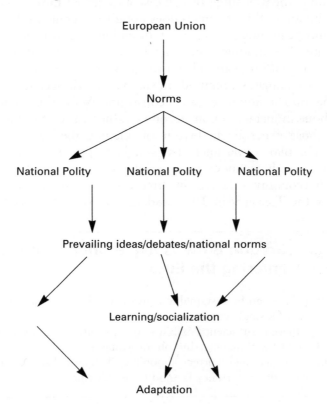

there is little evidence of governments citing the imperatives set by the EU as the immediate cause of policy choices. This stands in marked contrast to the example of France where the convergence criteria set by the Treaty on European Union were used throughout the 1990s as explanations for public expenditure cuts and other potentially unpopular measures (Hay and Rosamond 2002; Schmidt 2001). French political elites were perhaps better placed than their British counterparts to invoke the benefits of 'more Europe', which could be invoked as a bulwark against US-led globalization (Jospin 2002). British governments – including the Conservatives under John Major – have striven to ensure that economic performance was aligned with the strict criteria for progression to monetary union stipulated in the TEU. This exercise in keeping Britain's options open was rarely, if ever, discussed publicly and the French or Italian solution of invoking the virtues of deeper European integration as a long run good to emerge from short-term privation via neoliberal policies was not really available as a rhetorical resource. British governments – and this is especially true of those in office since 1997 – have persistently blamed globalization rather than European integration as the decisive constraint on policy choice (Hay and Rosamond 2002: 158–9).

If anything, the prevailing British discourse about Europe – described at the beginning of this chapter – does not give leverage to the notion of the EU/European integration as a disciplining constraint upon the British state. The abiding concern with sovereignty and the popular projection of the European policy process as hard-headed international diplomatic exchange is premised on the worst case scenario of the EU developing into a non-negotiable constraint. With this in mind, the debate about monetary union becomes rather easier for Eurosceptics than for those generally in favour of aligning the UK to the single currency. The Blair government has sought to present monetary union as a predominantly technocratic question concerned with the welfare of the British economy – hence the 'five economic tests' (see Box 3.3) devised by the Treasury in 1997 and reiterated by Chancellor of the

---

Box 3.3   Gordon Brown's five economic tests for entering the Euro

1. Whether there can be sustainable convergence between Britain and the economies of a single currency;
2. Whether there is sufficient flexibility to cope with economic change;
3. The effect of EMU membership on investment;
4. The impact of the single currency upon the UK financial services industry;
5. Whether the single currency is good for employment.

Exchequer Gordon Brown ever since (see HM Treasury, 2001c). Thus a thorough Europeanization of British political discourse might enable cases to be made for a positive pooling of sovereignty and for monetary union as a means to combat the uncertainties associated with financial globalization.

Attitudinal shifts towards Europe are evident elsewhere within the British polity. The cases of environmental pressure groups and local authorities have also been mentioned earlier in this chapter. In her study of gender equality legislation, Cram (2001b) argues that the Equal Opportunities Commission has been a major stimulus for pro-EU sentiments, particularly amongst the constituencies it serves. In the same context, Cram also alerts us to the unnoticed elements of ideational Europeanization. Her notion of 'banal Europeanism' (Cram 2001a; 2001b) suggests that shifts in belief and expectation do not need to be large scale. The development of meaningful 'loyalties' to Europe will not be bound up with the development of allegiance to 'heroic' notions of the European idea or to symbols such as the European flag or Beethoven's 'Ode to Joy', the chosen European anthem. Attitudinal shifts occur inconspicuously as those parts of life regulated by the EU become routinized and normalized.

Europeanization as feedback

The foregoing, despite cautions about inherent complexity and the persistence of national variation, has looked at the effects of EU inputs upon the British polity. However, writers on Europeanization have also become interested in the reciprocal relationship between national and European levels of governance (Bomberg and Peterson 2000). In their discussion of national adaptation, Bulmer and Burch note that member states often attempt to 'export domestic policy models, ideas and detail to the EU' (2001: 76), and Börzel offers an explanation for this type of behaviour:

> An effective strategy to maximize the benefits and minimize the costs of European policies is to upload national policy arrangements to the European level . . . [U]ploading reduces the need for legal and administrative adaptation in downloading, that is, incorporating European policies into national policy structures. (Börzel 2002: 196)

This reminds us that the process of Europeanization is not simply about EU outputs that impact upon national political systems. The nature of those outputs is reflective of a process of political contestation that will involve, amongst other things, rival national conceptions of the substance and style of policy. It is difficult to show the causal logic of these processes of diffusion. The prevailing EU model of neoliberal integration embraces regulatory governance within Europe and open regionalism without Europe. As suggested above, this is quite consistent, in abstract terms at least, with Britain's long term economic policy priorities. This may, as Moravcsik (1998) suggests, have something to do with the preferences and relative bargaining power of key member states such as Britain. Alternatively, we might hypothesize that the market-driven norms of the integration project reflect the extensive cross-border power of particular economic ideas.

The case of regulation is quite instructive, and its use as the primary mode of governance in the single market is one of the foremost features of the EU (Young and Wallace 2000). In terms of Europeanization, this can be read as setting imperatives for the evolution of regulatory-cum-competition states in the member states. However, the insight offered by Majone (1996) is that the EU's emergence as a regulatory state is bound up with broader processes in the transformation of governance across the world. Moreover, the model of regulation may be a case of a policy transfer from the United States. Others see the regulatory state, which by definition is significantly less bothered with matters of redistribution, as a consequence of globalization (Cerny 1997). Such developments are consistent with the preferences of the British state over the past 25 years, but whether these reflect the successful transplantation of British priorities to the rest of the EU is hard to show.

As Figure 3.4 demonstrates, what might appear to be enforced Europeanization, may in fact be the reappearance into a national polity of preferences that the national state has uploaded to the EU. For example, competition policy looks like a *prima facie* case of enforced Europeanization as described above. The logic of a single market dictates that economic activity should be conducted on a level playing field. Distortions to the operation of the market are wholly incompatible with the EU Treaties. It therefore makes inherent sense that the governance of the European economy in areas such as anti-trust, the regulation of state aids and merger regulation should be conducted at the European rather than the national level. This is the precise function of EU competition policy. Moreover, the European Commission has extensive powers in this area. Yet the growth of the European-level competition regime paralleled the emergence of similar policy-making competencies in the member states. The application of the subsidiarity principle (in effect the idea that authority should reside at the most appropriate level) means that the European Commission relies upon national competition authorities to do much of its work. Thus, there has been and continues to be a reciprocal

Figure 3.4   *Europeanization as feedback*

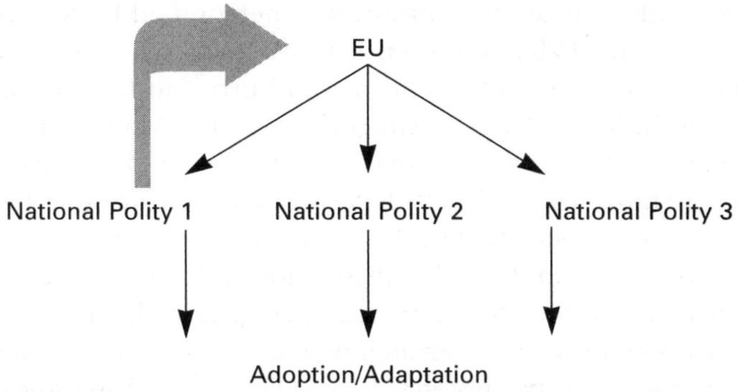

Note: In this diagram, a policy choice emanates from National Policy 1. It then feeds back into national political systems (including National Polity 1) from the EU level.

relationship between national and European developments, rather than a process where European initiatives have been developed in ways that 'trump' existing regimes in the member states (McGowan 2000: 118). Moreover, Britain enacted anti-trust legislation as early as 1965 and was among the first European countries to develop a competence in competition policy after the Second World War (Dumez and Jeunemaître 1996). European competition policy may have been 'imposed from without', but the nature of that regime – was at the very least – consistent with the evolving preferences of the British state in this area.

These issues of policy transfer are rarely unidirectional. It could be argued that the regulation of market activity in the UK after 1945 actually reflected the influence of an American model of competition policy. There is certainly much evidence of attempts to produce US-style anti-trust policies across Western Europe in the late-1940s and early 1950s. So one conclusion might be that European competition policy reflects the preferences of states such as Britain, which in turn reflect the preferences of the United States for a particular version of European economic order. Europeanization becomes, in effect, a version of Americanization. However, as studies of this period show, national variations remained a significant obstacle to the wholesale implantation of an American-style competition policy in Europe (Dumez and Jeunemaître 1996).

Social policy provides a similarly complex case. The path of policy in Britain, at least since 1979, has been towards welfare retrenchment and a definite retreat from the redistributive functions of the state with overwhelming faith placed in market solutions. This would seem to offer a stark contrast with the social policy impetus of the EU. The clash between Britain and the European Commission over the 'social dimension' to the single-market programme was personified by the confrontation during the late 1980s between Prime Minister Margaret Thatcher and Jacques Delors, then President of the European Commission. This culminated with the Major government's refusal at Maastricht to accede to the 'social chapter' of the Treaty on European Union, suggesting neoliberal resistance by the UK to forced Europeanization in the area of social policy. A protocol to the Treaty effectively permitted the other member states to 'borrow' the EU institutions to enact legislation under the terms laid out in the (excised) 'social chapter'. This derogation had the effect of dissuading the other member states from action in this area as this would open up the potential for distortions in market compatibility in favour of Britain (Liebfried and Pierson, 2000: 290). In a way British preferences prevailed, not only through the fact that the Conservative government was not locked into a new set of social policy norms, but also through the effect that Britain's stance had upon the behaviour of the other member states.

Even so, Britain did sign the resultant social protocol following the election of the New Labour government in 1997. However, the Blair government has followed a broadly neoliberal thrust in social policy (Hay 1999), indicating significant continuity with the previous Conservative governments and that in some areas (such as 'welfare to work') a form of Americanization has crept into British social policy (King and Wickham-Jones 1999). Labour's emphasis on flexible labour markets, a decline in welfare expenditure, the privatization of welfare provision and the consequent 'retreat' of the state from redistribution is a widespread trend across Western Europe. The two most obvious stimuli for this trend are globalization and the convergence criteria set by the Treaty on European Union for the achievement of monetary union (Annesley 2001: 12–13). But it is important to recognize that the Commission has rarely sought to impose a welfare model upon EU member states. The governance of socio-cultural issue areas remains relatively un-Europeanized and there is little EU-level encroachment into the traditional redistributive competencies of the welfare state. Rather, and in spite of the rhetoric associated with the social dimension, EU social policy has been about the ensuring of market compatibility and little else (Liebfried and Pierson 2000).

With this in mind, it is interesting to observe Britain's apparent influence on developments in EU social policy over the past few years. The relatively high levels of unemployment in Europe since the 1980s has seen the EU develop a concern with the promotion of employment, beginning with the 1993 *White Paper on Competitiveness, Growth and*

Employment (Commission of the European Communities 1993), continuing with the Essen European Council (1994), the Treaty of Amsterdam (1997) and the special European Council held in Lisbon in 2000. The means used to address these problems are largely consistent with British preferences and may reflect the successful 'uploading' of policy ideas to the European level. In particular, a concern to inject flexibility into labour markets has become a significant component of European-level employment initiatives (Liebfried and Pierson 2000: 275).

Conclusion

These examples show how Europeanization should not be construed as a one-way, top-down process. Indeed the imagery – still popular in British political discourse – of the EU as a separate political domain that fires regulatory 'shots' at Britain is shown to be problematic, not least because the ammunition for the EU's policy rifle is often exported from Britain. Even if the two-level game metaphor favoured by intergovernmentalists is retained, the interplay between the EU system and the British polity appears to be characterized by complex feedback loops. Moreover, ideas, policies and regulatory regimes that appear to emanate from the EU, may themselves represent successful exports to Europe from (for example) the United States.

European inputs rarely, if ever, enter Britain without modification. The formalities and practicalities of the EU policy process ensure this. But Europeanization – whether in terms of policy inputs or ideas – is shaped by established institutional, normative and ideational patterns. Thus to speak of the Europeanization of Britain is not the same as pointing to British politics and policy making converging towards a standard European model. National diversity is alive and well. However, this is not the same as saying that British politics is not changing in the context of European integration. It is. The evidence suggests that things are changing, particularly in terms of the opportunity structures encountered by groups within the British polity. That said, transformation is rarely predictable, and this is because the shapers of Europeanization are partially bound up with the complex and uneven character of the EU's policy process and undoubtedly embedded in the institutional matter of British politics.

Chapter 4

The Core Executive and the Modernization of Central Government

MARTIN J. SMITH

There is a growing consensus that power within British central government, specifically the core executive, is becoming concentrated in the office of the Prime Minister. Peter Riddell sees the office in Number 10 Downing Street as a Prime Minister's department in all but in name, Peter Hennessy talks of the 'Command Prime Ministership', and Michael Foley argues that the system has become Presidential with the Prime Minister now standing above Party, Parliament and even Whitehall. One Labour MP, Graham Allen (2001), has suggested that we forgo the pretence of Cabinet Government and accept the inevitable: that we now have a presidential system which if acknowledged, and with proper constitutional checks and balances, would provide a more effective method of governing Britain.

The culmination of a long-term process of centralization of power in the hands of the Prime Minister is seen in the declining role of Cabinet and the increased development of resources inside Number 10. The weekly Cabinet meetings rarely last an hour and usually do not involve substantive policy discussions (Holliday 2002). In addition, the period since the 2001 General Election has seen a reorganization of Number 10 Downing Street with the Prime Minister developing much greater policy capabilities and means for intervening in a wide range of policy areas. The Prime Minister's Office is increasingly perceived as the source of policy whilst it is argued that the role of Whitehall is to administer Number 10's agenda. As Tony Blair has admitted: 'I make no apology for having a strong centre. I think you need a strong centre' (Liaison Committee 2002: para 5). This could be seen as a definitive break with the traditional constitutional position that sees the Cabinet as the ultimate political authority and government departments as the sources of policy. Concurrently, another important change is said to have occurred. In developing policy and running the government, it is argued that the Prime Minister is relying much less on officials and increasingly using special advisers and outside sources for advice. According to *The Times* (10 January 2002),' Downing Street's battalions of political advisers and consultants have wrested power from the traditional civil service'. Again, this is changing the balance of power inside Number 10 and across government.

It is important to remember that the debate about the dominance of the Prime Minister is not new. Since the 1960s, academics, commentators and politicians have been suggesting that Prime Ministerial government has been replacing Cabinet government. Many within government insist there have not been major changes in the organization of government. Richard Wilson, the recently retired Cabinet Secretary, told the Public Administration Select Committee, in what can be seen as being nearest to a constitutional view:

> I do not think that it is a Prime Minister's Department in all but name
> . . . we do not have a Presidential role for the Prime Minister in this
> country. We have a system where legal powers and financial resources
> are vested in the Secretaries of State. The Prime Minister has few
> executive powers other than the administration of the Civil Service
> . . . His or her power varies from time to time according to the extent
> his Cabinet colleagues permit him to have that power, depending on
> whether the Cabinet is split, depending also on the strength of the
> Government majority particularly in the House of Commons and
> also popular opinion in the electorate and attitudes in the Party. The
> structure that we have is one that meets the needs of the Prime
> Minister but it does not imply that the role of the Prime Minister has
> fundamentally changed. I think the term 'Prime Minister's
> Department' implies a different role for the Prime Minister and a
> major constitutional change that I would tell you has not taken place
> (Public Administration Committee 2001).

Likewise, Blair has argued that a stronger centre does not weaken Cabinet government and he points to the increased number of Cabinet committees and bilateral meetings with ministers (Liaison Committee 2002).

In understanding the changing role of the Prime Minister it is important not to oversimplify the argument. To see the current core executive as dominated by an over-powerful Prime Minister is to misunderstand the complex network of relationships that are essential to the running of a modern state. The core executive model – which highlights the complexity and interdependency of central government – can be used to analyse the changes in Number 10 to assess the way the powers and relationships within government have changed. Whilst we can see that the resources and capabilities of the Prime Minister have increased quite significantly, this does not mean that he has complete autonomy. Indeed one of the paradoxes of the modern Prime Minister's office is that whilst institutional resources have increased, the power of the Prime Minister to achieve his or her goals has not.

Understanding the core executive

The work of a number of authors (see Bruce-Gardyne and Lawson 1976; Burch and Holliday 1996; Holliday 2002; Rhodes and Dunleavy 1995; Smith 1999) has suggested that the traditional understandings of the relationship between Cabinet and Prime Minister oversimplify the debate by analysing it in terms of whether we have Prime Ministerial/Presidential or Cabinet government. The core executive approach suggests the Prime Minister is one actor, albeit a significant actor, within the institutions and relationships that make up the core executive. In order to appreciate the complexities of policy making within the core executive it is necessary to recognize several key factors:

- All actors within the core executive have resources (see Table 4.1).
- In order to achieve goals, resources have to be exchanged.
- Notions of Prime Ministerial government, Cabinet government or 'Presidentialism' are irrelevant. Power within the core executive is based on dependency not on command.
- To understand the operation of the core executive, the structures of dependency have to be identified.
- These structures of dependency are often based on overlapping networks. Frequently these networks do not follow formal organizational structures and this can lead to fragmentation and conflict over responsibility and territory.
- Even resource-rich actors, such as the Prime Minister, are dependent on other actors to achieve their goals. Therefore, government works through building alliances rather than by Prime Ministerial command.
- Actors operate within a structured arena. Traditional approaches to central government have placed too much emphasis on personality. Prime Ministers, officials and ministers are bound by external organization, the rules of the game, the structures of institutions, other actors and the context within which they operate. Therefore, the nature and form of the core executive is not dependent on the personality of any one actor.

Table 4.1 *The resources of prime ministers, ministers and officials*

Prime Minister	Ministers	Officials
Patronage the Prime Minister appoints MPs to government jobs	*Political support* ministers can often have considerable support within the party	*Permanence* officials are permanent and ministers temporary. Consequently, much of the ministers' task is learning the job
Authority within the British system the post of PM is recognized as carrying tremendous authority. Ministers immediately react differently to a colleague who becomes PM	*Authority* the minister within a department has a high-level of authority. The British Constitution means the minister's word is law	*Knowledge* officials have detailed information to the minister
Political support/party the Prime usually has the support of the party	*Department* through the control of a department a minister has access to tremendous bureaucratic resources	*Time* as a body, officials have considerable time
Political support/electorate the Prime Minister's resources are greatly increased if he has popular support	*Knowledge* departments have considerable informational resources concerning particular policy areas which are often absent to the Prime Minister	*Whitehall network* officials have contacts throughout Whitehall which again provides a good source of information
Prime Minister's Office the Prime Minister has institutional support through the office	*Policy networks* ministers become enmeshed within policy networks that control the making and delivery of policy	*Keepers of the Constitution* senior officials see themselves as upholding the Constitution. Consequently they can define what behaviour is acceptable for ministers and officials
Bilateral policy making the PM can have a major impact through intervening in departmental policy through policy making with ministers	*Policy success* if a minister is seen to be successful, he/she is in a very strong position	

The degree of dependency that actors have on each other varies according to the context. As the political and economic situation changes, actors may become more or less dependent. Economic success may provide a Chancellor of the Exchequer with more freedom, and political success may provide the Prime Minister with greater room for manoeuvre. Economic failure means the Chancellor needs more support from the Prime Minister. Political failure means the Prime Minister needs more support from the Cabinet. In particular, because of the distribution of resources, the strength of government departments and the existence of overlapping networks, the core executive is fragmented making central coordination extremely difficult.

The relationships between ministers, between ministers and officials and between ministers and the Prime Minister do not primarily depend on personality. They are structured relationships that are shaped by the rules of the Whitehall game, the institutions of government, past policy choices and by the external political and economic context. Asking whether there is Prime Ministerial government does not take us far in understanding the operation of central government. Different actors and institutions need each other. Cabinet Ministers and Prime Ministers have resources, but to achieve goals they need to exchange resources. The process of exchange – the forging of alliances – depends on the particular context. If a Prime Minister has just won an election he or she is less dependent than a Prime Minister who is very unpopular in the polls. It also depends on the tactics and strategies that ministers and Prime Ministers use. The Prime Minister has no authority if it is not recognized by ministers. Continual overriding of the wishes of the Cabinet by the Prime Minister will undermine that authority. Even dominant Prime Ministers need to exchange resources.

Clearly the Prime Minister has resources that are unavailable to other ministers, among them the traditionally cited formal resources of patronage, control of the Cabinet agenda, appointment of Cabinet Committees and the use of the Prime Minister's Office. The Prime Minister also has the less tangible resources, including the ability to intervene in any policy area. Only the Prime Minister really has any collective oversight; most ministers lack the interest, time, ability or institutional support to be involved in other areas of policy. This oversight enables Prime Ministers to involve themselves in any area of policy making they choose.

Crucially the Prime Minister does have a degree of authority that is greater than any other minister. Authority is the acceptance of power without the need to exercise formal capabilities (Wrong 1988). A crucial rule of the Whitehall game is that ministers and civil servants accept the authority of the Prime Minister. Nevertheless, unlike other resources, which are fairly objective, Prime Ministerial authority is largely relational and is dependent on the standing of the Prime Minister. In particular, the Prime Minister has greatest authority after an electoral victory and particularly if it is an unexpected one such as that of Edward Heath in 1970 (Campbell 1993: 289). From this perspective the key point about the Labour administration is not that Tony Blair has become all-powerful, but that the resources of the Prime Minister have clearly increased and new patterns of dependency have developed.

From personalism to institutionalism in central government

The reconfiguration of the core executive has resolved around five elements: the institutionalization of policy-making capabilities within Number 10; the development of joined-up government; the modernization and changing role of the civil service; the increased policy activism of the Treasury; and the emergence of new external patterns of dependency as a consequence of EU integration, greater global pressures and devolution. Within this configuration, the role of the Prime Minister, as do the roles of all other core executive actors, necessarily changes. Recently, Tony Blair defined the Prime Minister's position:

> The Prime Minister's role as head of Her Majesty's Government, her principal adviser and as Chairman of the Cabinet are not defined in legislation. These roles, including the exercise of power under the Royal Prerogative, have evolved over many years, drawing on convention and usage, and *it is not possible to precisely to define them.* [emphasis added] (quoted in Allen 2001: vii)

As this quote suggests, for much of the twentieth century the role of the Prime Minister has been vaguely specified. Indeed, what the Prime Minister does has often depended on what the Prime Minister has wanted to do. In that sense, it has always been personalistic with the impact of Number 10 varying with the preferences of the particular Prime Minister and the role of the office changing with its particular holder or even within Prime Ministerships. The Prime Minister is able to change the structure of Whitehall almost at whim by abolishing or creating new departments. This is a trait common to most Prime Ministers. Margaret Thatcher merged the Departments of Trade and Industry and divided the Department of Health and Social Security. John Major abolished the Department of Energy and merged Employment and Education. Tony Blair has been particularly active, abolishing the Departments of Environment, Transport and Agriculture, creating (and then remaking) new conglomerates such as the Department of Local Government, Transport and the Regions (DLGTR) and The Department for the Environment, Food and Rural Affairs (DEFRA), and streamlining the Home Office. Likewise the structure of the Prime Minister's Office has changed with each incumbent. Harold Wilson only created the Policy Unit in 1974, and when Margaret Thatcher came to power in 1979 she initially paid little attention to it, preferring instead to rely on ad hoc advisers (Kavanagh and Seldon 1999).

Similarly, each Prime Minister has played very different roles in terms of policy making. Some have been relatively inactive whilst others have taken a much more interventionist role. Thatcher intervened directly in a range of policy areas such as the economy, education and health. She was always relatively well briefed about what was going on in all departments (Marsh, Richards and Smith 2001). On the other hand, John Major was, according to Anthony Seldon (1997: 38) 'a conciliator' who liked to encourage discussion and reach a consensus in Cabinet. Much of what a Prime Minister does depends on how he or she carved out their role and the particular interests they had. Thatcher made a big impact on her government not because of the institutions of her office, but because of her personal hyperactivity. She often intervened in areas where she was not properly informed. Most Prime Ministers pay considerable attention to economic and foreign policy (Rhodes and Dunleavy 1995) (and most recently Northern Ireland). This leaves less time for intervention in other areas, but because of their authority Prime Ministers are able to focus their attention in policy areas in which they are interested.

What seems to have occurred under Tony Blair is that this mechanism of personalized intervention has become institutionalized through the use of special advisers and by changes in the structure of Number 10. Figure 4.1 demonstrates the organizational structure within Downing Street established after the 2001 General Election. Significantly, a party special adviser, not a civil servant, heads each of the key divisions, Communications, Policy and Government Relations. The significance of these changes relates to how they affect the resources that are available to the Prime Minister and how they affect the structures of dependency within the core executive. Further changes followed in the summer of 2002 with the appointment of a new Cabinet Secretary, Sir Andrew Turnbull. Under Turnbull, there has been the creation of a separate office of the Deputy Prime Minster, and the creation of a new post of Security and Intelligence Coordinator and a Permanent Secretary in the Cabinet Office. In addition, a new team on reform strategy now reports directly to the Cabinet Secretary. These changes highlight how the

Figure 4.1 *No. 10 organization chart (after 2001 general election)*

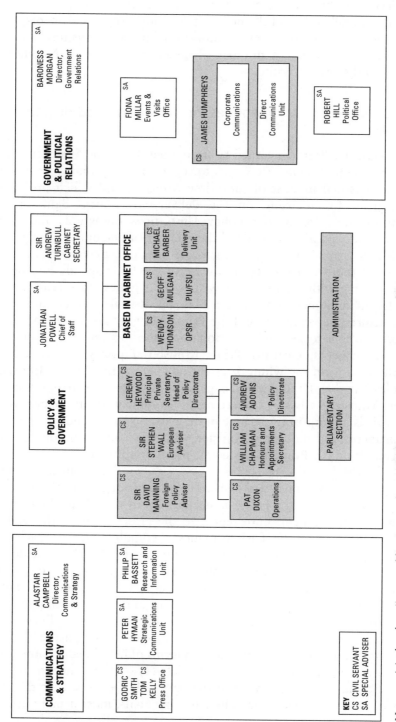

Note: original on http://www.publications.parliament.uk/pa/cm2001&2/cmselect/cmpubadm/262/1110101.pdf

emphasis of the Blair government is increasingly on public service reform and delivery, and the new organization contains elements of the old structure and some new organizations and relationships. Some of these changes suggest a number of changes in the way Number 10 relates to the rest of Whitehall.

The creation of new capabilities for the making and delivery of policy

Tony Blair has been concerned to strengthen the Prime Minister's influence over departments. He wants to do so in a way that does not rely on the personal interest of the Prime Minister, and which provides a mechanism for focusing on the delivery of policy. Blair initially expanded the size of the Policy Unit, now known as the Policy Directorate, and almost doubled the number of personnel compared to the Major years. The Policy Directorate does not 'make policy', rather it ensures that departments are aware of the Blair agenda and deliver policy in line with Number 10's wishes. This policy steer, reinforced in regular bilateral meetings between Blair, his officials and relevant ministers, ensures Departments and the Prime Minister are agreed on policy objectives. This forges an institutional relationship between Number 10 and departments, ensuring Prime Ministerial policy activism is not wholly reliant on the whim or attention span of the Prime Minister. It enables Number 10 to develop capabilities to direct departments by the Prime Minister's advisers overseeing and commenting on policy proposals. This is an important change in the patterns of dependency between departments and the Prime Minister, with departments becoming more dependent on the Prime Minister for policy initiatives.

While the Policy Directorate oversees policy development, strategic policy capability is provided by the Forward Strategy Unit (FSU) (based in Number 10) and the Performance and Innovation Unit (PIU) (based in the Cabinet Office). Both report to the Prime Minister through the Cabinet Secretary. The FSU 'provides a complimentary capacity for doing more private work, generally working bilaterally with departments rather than on cross-cutting issues, and reporting directly to the Prime Minister and Secretaries of State (Cabinet Office 2002). The institution with the greatest significance in terms of the relationship between the Prime Minister and departments is probably the Delivery Unit. Reporting to the Prime Minister, its objective is to ensure that the government delivers on its priorities in terms of health, education, crime and transport. Its rationale is that the delivery of policy, not the making of policy has been a problem in the past. The Delivery Unit therefore checks progress is being made in achieving goals, most usually through bi-monthly meetings between the Prime Minister and the relevant minister, and through meetings of the Public Expenditure Cabinet Committee (PSX). Through the establishment of Public Service Agreements (PSAs), departments are set specific targets for the delivery of policy. This is another major change in the relationship between the centre and departments. In the past, departments have always had sole responsibility for the delivery of services, but now the Delivery Unit institutionalizes Number 10's role in the oversight of what had traditionally been a relatively autonomous area of departmental activity. In addition, the Office of Public Service Reform is charged with improving the government's capacity to deliver services more effectively. It provides strategic oversight of the modernization of Whitehall (discussed below) and ensures departments implement reforms. It also ensures that the central elements of the Blair agenda are transmitted throughout government.

These changes at the centre have systematized what in the past was always an ad hoc process, increasing the resources of Number 10 and changing core executive patterns of dependency. The pattern of relationships between Number 10 and departments has therefore become more complex in both policy making and policy delivery. Nevertheless, the institutional support for the British Prime Minister remains less than his or her European counterparts. As Tony Blair pointed out to the Liaison Committee, the

> Number 10 Office has roughly the same or perhaps slightly fewer people working for it than the Irish Taoiseach's. To put this in context, the Prime Minister has fewer staff than either the French Prime Minister (never mind the combined staffs of the French President and Prime Minister combined), or the German Chancellor. (Liaison Committee 2002: para 6).

The modernization of Whitehall: changing relations between ministers and civil servants

Wider changes are occurring within the core executive, particularly in terms of changing relations between ministers and civil servants. Since 1979, there have been two key developments. First, there have been significant reforms of the Civil Service, culminating in New Labour's modernizing government agenda. Second, relations seem to be changing between officials and ministers, which again have consequences for the structures of dependency within the core executive. The Thatcher administration was distrustful of the Civil Service and undertook a radical, but slow burning programme of reform. This was aimed at making the Civil Service more efficient, particularly through the introduction of private sector management techniques such as the Financial Management Initiative, privatization, and the creation of Next Steps agencies. One consequence was a reduction in the number of civil servants, down from 748,000 in 1976 to 470,800 in 1997 (interestingly this had increased to 482,690 in 2001). The Major administration sought to make officials more responsive to the public, particularly through the Citizen's Charters and by market testing. It reformed the senior levels of the Civil Service through the Fundamental Expenditure Reviews (FER) and the Senior Management Review (SMR). The FER originated within the Treasury as attempts to ensure its functions were discharged effectively and that organizational reforms would be geared at improving performance. As a consequence, many of the Treasury's tasks were hived off with the subsequent loss of 25 per cent of senior posts. These reforms sought to strip out layers of management, pushing detailed policy work down the Whitehall hierarchy so that senior officials could concentrate on management (Marsh, Smith and Richards 2000). As a consequence, there were some significant reductions in the number of senior civil servants within departments.

The Blair government has continued the reform process initiated by the Conservatives. In 1999, it published a Modernizing Government White Paper, outlined plans for further reforms. These reforms are aimed at improving the delivery of public services by making them more available, responsible and flexible; by joining up the process of government; by improving the quality of services; and through using information age technology (HMSO 1999). Thus Labour has maintained the commitment of the Thatcher governments to improving management. Better management, however, is not the only concern. Attention has also been paid to the issue of improving the making of public policy. There has been a great deal of reflection over the nature of the policy process. Hitherto, there has been little critical thought about the policy process in Britain. The widely held assumption was that the Civil Service is good at policy advice and the cliché of the 'Rolls-Royce Machine' has become an unquestioned truth. This may seem a relatively mundane and unimportant issue, but its implications in terms of policy making and power within the core executive may be profound.

From the government's perspective reform needed to look in detail at the way in which policy was made and the importance of integrating policy making and delivery. Moreover, harking back to some of the reforms of the Heath government in 1970, there was a desire to improve strategic capability and to make policy making more evidence-based. The implications were that the 'making' and the 'delivery' of policy had to be seamless, and to this end, government needed to be more 'joined-up'.

Joined-up government

The persistent dilemma faced by the Labour government is the desire to multiply the sources of policy advice, pluralise service delivery and to decentralize power, whilst simultaneously ensuring that it achieves a coherent set of goals. At the same time, the constitutional mechanism for ensuring departmental cooperation, the Cabinet and its Committees, seems to have been undermined to the point that the full Cabinet is now a symbolic part of the Constitution. Consequently, one of the mantras of the government is the need for joined-up government at the policy making and the delivery level. From the government's perspective:

> The 'tubes' or 'silos' down which money flows from government to people and localities have come to be seen as part of the reason why government is bad at solving problems. Many issues have fitted imperfectly if at all into departmental slots. Vertical organization by its nature skews government efforts away from certain activities, such as prevention – since the benefits of preventive action often come to another department. It tends to make government less sensitive to particular client groups whose needs cut across departmental lines. It incentivises departments to dump problems on each other – like schools dumping unruly children onto the streets to become a headache for the police ... Over time it reinforces the tendency common to all bureaucracies of devoting more energy to the protection of turf rather than serving the public. (Mulgan 2001)

Consequently, the government has created bodies like the Social Exclusion Unit, the Delivery Unit, the Forward Strategy Unit and various task forces to overcome departmentalism. In some ways, under the guise of ensuring a co-ordinated approach, this has further extended the reach of Number 10 into departmental affairs. However, whilst there are some examples of the success of a joined-up approach, such as Welfare to Work, the approach has also created a number of confusions within the core executive. First, there has been a proliferation of bodies involved in policy making. The result is that the centre becomes more rather than less fragmented. Second, there is a considerable tension concerning where or with whom responsibility for these bodies lies. In Constitutional terms how are units and task forces accountable to Parliament, and in what practical sense are they responsible to Number 10 or the Cabinet Office? And third, what is the relationship between these bodies and departments? Whereas the rules governing the relationship between departments, the Cabinet, the Treasury and the Prime Minister have always been understood, those between departments and units and task forces is now less clear.

The impact on power within the core executive

The changes outlined above effectively change the relationship between ministers and civil servants and they have important implications for the core executive. Whereas the constitutional framework of the relationship between ministers and officials derives from the Haldane notion of symbiosis (see Foster 2001, Richards 1997), there is today a bifurcation of roles as ministers concern themselves with policy making and officials with 'management' of the policy process. As a result, there is a significant change in the role of officials as their traditional monopoly of policy advice is being eroded. Ministers are turning to a myriad of organizations and advisers for policy inputs, thus mirroring the changes that are occurring inside Downing Street. For Sir Andrew Turnbull, the Downing Street model, one of an increased number of Special Advisors working with Civil Servants, was the model for all departments (*The Times* 1 May 2002). The traditionalist interdependent pattern of policy making, one where policy originated from a department rather than a minister, is being replaced by a pattern which grants very discrete roles for ministers and their officials. As a consequence, ministers are much less reliant on the Civil Service than they once were. Previously, officials were influential because they had permanence and ministers relied on them for information and expertise (Foster 2001). However the resignation of Stephen Byers from the Department for Transport, Local Government and The Regions in 2002 demonstrates the types of problems that arise from conflicting interpretations of the roles of officials and special advisors. His inability to manage effectively the personnel in DLTR led to conflict and discord. In particular, Byers appears to have failed to resolve tensions between his own political advisers and the permanent officials within the department. As a consequence official loyalty broke down and the public conflict resulted in Byers resigning.

Traditionally, policy making within Whitehall was made largely within departments, with a senior civil servant placed in charge of gathering options and commissioning proposals that would be passed up the departmental hierarchy, reaching the permanent secretary then going to the minister. When an issue was highly political, or there was an urgent need to manage a crisis, a minister would summon his or her senior civil servants and work through various options. When policy crossed departmental boundaries, officials worked out policy in the first instance, usually through informal bilateral meetings, and this was followed by bilateral agreement by ministers or through formal Cabinet Committees, where the final decisions would be taken. In areas where there was long-term interdepartmental policy, formal Inter-Departmental Committees would be established both at official and ministerial levels. One such example was the Inter-Departmental Committee on the issuing of export licences for arms sales, which included the Ministry of Defence, the Department of Trade and Industry and the Foreign Office. Here, ministers were highly dependent on their officials for advice, and officials often pre-arranged decisions. While officials were careful to gauge the wishes of their minister, they were influential in terms of policy outcomes.

Today, however, the processes of policy making seems to have changed quite considerably, although some of the old patterns still remain in place. The increased emphasis on management (combined with the stripping out of middle layers of departments) has meant that senior officials (grades 1 and 2) now take on a managerial role, while less senior officials (lower grades 5, 7 and higher executive officers) now undertake much detailed policy work. To some extent, top officials are excluded almost completely from policy making, as seems to have happened with the last Cabinet Secretary Richard Wilson, whilst policy advice has started to come increasingly from lower level officials. Officials have therefore become less important as a source of advice, and some commentators suggest this has 'diluted the quality of advice available to ministers' (Foster 2001: 730).

More significantly, there has been a general increase in the number of special advisers in Whitehall and in a number of areas they have taken on an increased importance. As mentioned above, special advisers, most notably Jonathan Powell and Alastair Campbell, occupy key, influential positions within Number 10. Likewise in the Treasury, Gordon Brown's closest adviser is his Special Adviser, Ed Balls, who is now the government's Chief Economic Adviser. All advice from civil servants first goes through Brown's Special Advisers, who

> act as gatekeepers, letting civil servants know what the Chancellor is interested in and acting as a filter for policy ideas coming from below. An official knows that he or she is getting somewhere when they get a half-hour slot with Ed Balls. (*Guardian*, 15 April 2002)

In addition, Brown also has a collection of ad hoc advisers, charged with undertaking 'blue skies' thinking and with keeping the Chancellor in touch with new and innovative policy ideas. Like the Prime Minister, the Chancellor has also used people from business to undertake reviews of particular issue, the recent report on funding the NHS being a case in point. He clearly has a sense of an agenda that he is trying to develop which does not owe its existence to the traditional concerns and ways of seeing that exist within the Treasury. Hence the May 1997 decision, which shocked senior officials, to give independence to the Bank of

England without consulting Treasury Officials. In Brown's early period in office at least, there was considerable consternation within the Treasury that Brown was seen to be ignoring official advice.

The changes within Number 10 and the Treasury are indicative of change in the sources of policy. Increasingly, policy is coming from sources outside of departments and officials. These and other changes have a number of consequences:

- *Ministerial activism.* While it has always been the case that some ministers have been highly policy active (Headey 1974), ministers are increasingly proactive in policy making. During the Thatcher administrations, the extent and degree of that policy activism became much greater. For example, in the Department of Social Security, Peter Lilley carefully and systematically set about reforming the social security system and at the Home Office, Michael Howard forced through significant changes in penal policy, in a much more confrontational and less strategic manner (Marsh, Richards and Smith 2001). The Blair administration has continued this policy activism. When first elected in 1997, the new government was keen to 'hit the ground running' and had therefore worked out detailed policy options in opposition, which it used the Civil Service to implement. Ministers have distinct agendas. For instance, David Blunkett, very proactive at the Home Office, has in a short period made key changes in policy on cannabis, asylum seekers and crime.
- *Policy transfer.* Increasingly ministers and Number 10 are looking oversees for new policy ideas. There is a conscious effort to undertake comparative analysis of policy and to see what policy ideas can be used in Britain. One clear example is the development of the Welfare to Work policy in Wisconsin, which has been extremely influential in terms of Labour's view on welfare reform and tackling unemployment.
- *The use of task forces.* The government has created an array of ad hoc bodies with the intention of crossing departmental boundaries and providing a range of sources of advice. The exact role, or indeed names, of these bodies is not clear but according to a response to a Parliamentary Question between May 1997 and October 2000 there were over 200 'live' task forces drawing upon individuals from the private, public and voluntary sector, including academics and civil servants. Some task forces are chaired by ministers, but others are not, and the topics they cover is extremely diverse.
- *The use of specialist units focusing on particular issues.* Such units examine particular issues in-depth and to develop policy proposals. A number of these institutions such as the Social Exclusion Unit, the

Women's Unit and the Performance and Innovation Unit are attached to Number 10, but are specifically seen as cross-departmental rather than Prime Ministerial bodies. These units have been supplemented by the so-called 'Tsars', individuals appointed from outside the civil service to develop policy where specific problems have been identified. Examples include the former Drugs Tsar, Keith Halliwell, attached to the Home Office, and the Rough Sleepers Tsar, Louise Case. These bodies repeat the pattern of developing non-traditional sources of policy advice that do not rely on traditional officials. They use outsiders and cut across departmental boundaries.

In constitutional terms, post-1980 developments in the organization of central government have proved as significant for British politics as Scottish and Welsh devolution, the Humans Rights Act, and Freedom of Information. The roles played by various actors, be they the Prime Minister, ministers, officials or outsiders, have changed, and as a consequence new patterns of policy making have emerged and with them new forms of dependence. Ministers have become more policy active, and in particular the policy activism of the Prime Minister, having being institutionalized with the development of Number 10, depends less on personal whim and preference. All ministers rely less on officials for policy advice and now use a multiple of policy sources. There is an implicit recognition that officials are generalist administrators who are not experts on policy matters, whether it is teenage pregnancy, global warming or the management of the economy. Detailed investigations into such public scandals as Arms to Iraq, the BSE crisis, and more recently, the 2001 Foot and Mouth Epidemic, often demonstrated the poor quality of Civil Service policy advice. Indeed, much Civil Service advice was technically flawed, invariably being concerned with presenting the minister and the respective department in the best possible light. Andrew Rawnsley (2001) identified the failure of officials at the old Ministry of Agriculture Fisheries and Food to deal with Foot and Mouth as being behind Blair's determination to reform the civil service in his second term. Their failure to act caused untold damage to the British livestock industry. The 'Rolls Royce Machine' seemed not to be working. Increasingly, the civil servant's role is to organize the multiple sources of advice available to ministers.

As a consequence, the balance of dependence between officials and ministers has changed. Ministers are far less dependent on their officials than they used to be, and they now draw on sources of policy advice that are not controlled by the departmental machine. This would also seem to suggest that ministers are more dependent on the Prime Minister, particularly when policy development appears to be occurring hand in hand with Number 10, and the role of Cabinet in policy making seems to have completely disappeared. However, this is a charge the Blair administration strongly denies. Blair himself argues that policy continues to be made in departments and he does not accept that Cabinet government has been weakened:

> I think the fact that you have roughly doubled the number of Cabinet sub-committees is an indication that Cabinet Government is strong . . . I chair regular ministerial meetings . . . I do not accept that the checks and balances are not there. (Liaison Committee 2002, para 9)

The limits of Prime Ministerial power

However downgraded the role of the full Cabinet, it is important to realize that there are major constraints on the powers of the Prime Minster. This chapter has commented on the institutionalization of Prime Ministerial power, and suggested how this process has occurred within the context of more general reforms in the processes of policy making. However, this does not mean that we now have a 'Command Prime Minister' or some form of 'Presidentialism'. There are still tremendous constraints on the Prime Minister, which means he or she continues to be highly dependent on other actors and institutions within the core executive. Among such constraints are:

Time and events

The ability of the Prime Minister to intervene in a vast array of policy areas is limited by the time available and the pressure of particular events. Much of Tony Blair's time as Prime Minister has been taken up with dealing with particular issues or crisis management. This is demonstrated by the period following 11 September, a wholly unexpected event, after which the Prime Minister found much of his time was taken up with travelling the world to build support for the war in Afghanistan. Other crises such as the fuel protest, Foot and Mouth, Kosova, and now Iraq, dominated the Prime Ministerial agenda for long periods of time. Even Margaret Thatcher, often portrayed as intervening in all areas, could only intervene in key areas of particular interest to her. One official, formally in her Private Office, recounted:

> If I think back to my time in her office, in the first year, 1981, we mainly dealt with the rampant recession and the management of the

economy; managing the political debate on that. And, of course, the wet and dry problem [referring to left and right wing members of the Cabinet]. The second year was dominated by the Falklands war and during the several months in which the war was fought, she didn't do any domestic business at all. The third year was mainly about winning the election. (quoted in Marsh, Richards and Smith 2001: 119)

The increased institutionalization of Prime Ministerial resources does mean that Prime Ministerial intervention is more systematic, but Number 10 still lacks resources in relation to departments. Whilst the Department of Health may have hundreds of people working on health policy, the Downing Street Policy Directorate only employs two such people (Kavanagh and Seldon 1999). This means still that unless the Prime Minister is proactive, the role of the Prime Minister is still reactive. However effective the Prime Minister's Office is, there is still only one Prime Minister. Downing Street can inform the Prime Minister about what is going on in departments (and also inform departments about what the Prime Minister is thinking), but the Prime Minister cannot pay attention to everything at any one time. Prime Ministers tend to have a long-term impact only when they concentrate on an issue over a sustained period of time. For example, Prime Ministers from Jim Callaghan onwards have paid considerable emphasis on education, and John Major and Tony Blair have both pushed public sector reform. Indeed, the Prime Minister's effectiveness depends to some extent on the nature of the ministers. Some ministers are agents of the Prime Minister who carry out his bidding, others are political allies who achieve shared goals on a more equal basis. Other still are rivals who may eventually challenge the Prime Minister or seek his or her post. Ministerial and Prime Minister relationships are constantly in flux. Political realities make it impossible for Prime Ministers to control what goes on in all departments.

The changing role of the Treasury

There has always been a high level of interdependence between the Prime Minister and the Chancellor of the Exchequer. The existence of a good working relationship between them has often been crucial for the success of the government. The Thatcher government was at its most successful when Thatcher and her Chancellors, first Geoffrey Howe and then Nigel Lawson, shared goals and worked together. After 1985, disagreement between Thatcher and Lawson over the goals of economic policy, and the means of achieving them, proved to be a major factor in Thatcher's downfall in November 1990.

Likewise, when John Major and his Chancellor, Norman Lamont, disagreed on economic policy after Black Wednesday in 1992, the government was never able to recover the perception of economic competence. At present, the relationship between Tony Blair and his Chancellor, Gordon Brown, has been particularly important. Brown has a high degree of autonomy in terms of economic policy, principally because of the support he enjoys within the party as Blair's de facto second in command, the apparent success of his economic policy, and because of his private deal struck with Blair over the Labour leadership in 1994 (see Rawnsley 2001). Consequently, although Blair is kept closely informed about economic policy, he has generally left control of economic policy to the Chancellor. This suggests that the notion of a Bonapartist Prime Minister is wide of the mark.

More importantly, by controlling public expenditure, the Chancellor has always had an impact on the coordination of government policy and, because government policy involves 'getting and spending', this grants him or her considerable influence on a wide range of policies. This influence has usually been negative, however, and in the sense that the Treasury can stop departments attempting to develop certain policies. Under Brown this has changed. Through the Comprehensive Spending Review (CSR), set up to ensure that departments justified their policies and planned spending over a three-year cycle, this Chancellor has been able to shape the direction of policy in a strategic way. In areas as diverse as education, social security, health policy and transport, the Treasury under Gordon Brown has had a major influence on the direction of policy. Indeed, the strength of Brown's policy influence was seen in the 2002 budget when his decision to fund NHS expenditure through increasing National Insurance effectively sealed the direction of NHS reform and removed some radical 'Third Way' solutions from the agenda. Likewise, policy such as Welfare to Work and reform of Social Security reform have largely been initiated within the Treasury, not necessarily within the Departments responsible for such policy areas.

The irony is that Treasury capabilities for intervention are much more established than those of Number 10. The Treasury now has expenditure teams, each headed by a senior civil servant, which are responsible for expenditure in each policy area (Deakin and Parry 2000). Through control of public expenditure, the Treasury has a powerful lever for ensuring compliance, one that is absent in Number 10. Whilst this development is a clear constraint on departments, it is also a major constraint on the Prime Minster who has difficulty forcing through policy change without the Chancellor's support.

The continuing importance of departments

Despite the changing role of the Prime Minister and the Chancellor and their increased resources, it is still the case that the majority of policy is made and implemented within departments. Departments provide a unique concentration of financial, bureaucratic, knowledge and, in certain cases, political resources. Ministers still have a great deal of control over policy and a change of minister in a department often results in a change of policy. Policy in relation to Transport, Education, Immigration and Asylum, and Foreign Affairs has changed rapidly with the appointment of new ministers. Blair has regular meetings with his departmental ministers in order to discuss the priorities and success of departments. Many commentators see the growth of bilateral meetings between ministers and the Prime Minister as an indication of growing presidentialism. However, it is possible that these meetings are an indication of the Prime Minister's continued dependence. In a whole range of policy areas it is very difficult for the Prime Minister to achieve his goals without the support of the minister concerned. As the Prime Minister cannot continually sack or reshuffle ministers, he needs to build alliances that are mutually beneficial. Likewise, for ministers to achieve their goals, there is a great deal of benefit to be gained from winning the support of the Prime Minister, particularly if the policy entails a battle with the Treasury for extra resources. Clearly, with joined-up government and increased policy capability in the Treasury and the Prime Minister's Office, departments have lost their monopoly in policy making. However, they continue to control great swaths of the policy process and a successful minister with high public or party support can constrain the ambitions of the Prime Minister.

The shrinking world

Rose (2001) makes the point that the result of changes within the core executive is that the Prime Minister now has 'more control over less'. While a Prime Minister may be increasingly powerful in the Whitehall world, policy making in the real world has increasingly shifted from that arena. As Figure 4.2 suggests, many commentators argue that power has shifted upwards to the international arena, outwards to the private and voluntary sector, and downwards to agencies, quangos and devolved institutions.

Increasingly the Prime Minister has less control over key elements of public policy. For example, during her time in office, Margaret Thatcher was continually excised over the issue of interest rates, but now such decisions are taken by the Bank of England Monetary Policy Committee.

Figure 4.2   *The hollowed out state under Labour*

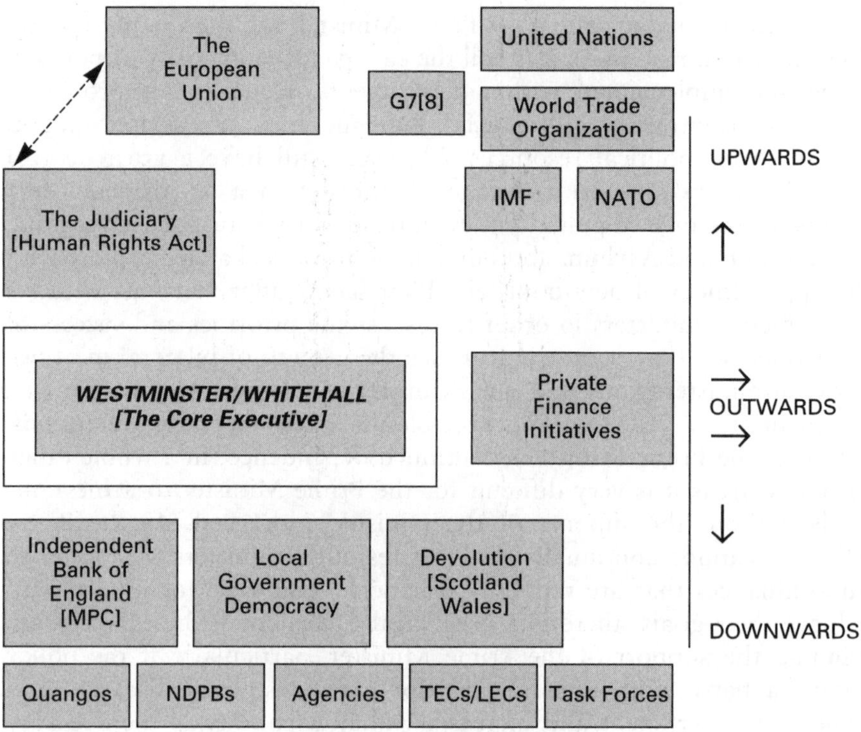

The European Union	United Nations	
	G7[8]	World Trade Organization
The Judiciary [Human Rights Act]	IMF	NATO

UPWARDS

↑

WESTMINSTER/WHITEHALL [The Core Executive]   Private Finance Initiatives

→
OUTWARDS
→

↓

Independent Bank of England [MPC]   Local Government Democracy   Devolution [Scotland Wales]

DOWNWARDS

Quangos   NDPBs   Agencies   TECs/LECs   Task Forces

The Scottish Parliament and the Welsh Assembly have made decisions that run counter to policy in Westminster. Achieving an integrated transport policy is extremely difficult when most transport is controlled by the private sector. As Rose reminds us, within the European Union (EU) the Prime Minister is just one leader among fifteen leaders, and therefore his influence in the EU is often quite slight. There can be little doubt that the majority of departments are now deeply involved with the EU on a day-to-day basis. Bulmer and Burch point out how the EU has become integrated into the system of British government and, in areas such as procurement, trade policy, agricultural policy and the environment, this has had a significant impact on the policy options available to the British government (see Richards and Smith 2002: chap. 7). Consequently, the Prime Minister's impact within the EU depends on making alliances with other countries. The Prime Minister may have a clear agenda, and may know what he or she wants to achieve, but achieving it may be difficult when he or she does not control those who deliver public goods. The paradox is therefore that the more power the Prime Minister appears to have, the less he is able to achieve.

Conclusion

In recent years major changes have occurred within the British core executive. The ability of the Prime Minister to intervene in policy areas has been increased, and the relationship between the political members of the core executive and the official members has been changed. The resources inside Number 10, the office of the Prime Minister, have been strengthened and through the use of joined-up government, public service agreements and the use of alternative and varied sources of advice, the role of the Prime Minister in policy making has become more proactive. As important a change has occurred as a result of the Civil Service becoming less involved in detailed policy making and being more likely to be gathering policy advice than directly giving it.

However, these reforms have been grafted on to existing patterns of policy making. They do not mean Britain now has presidential government. The Prime Minister has more resources, but is still dependent on other actors and institutions for the use of those resources. He or she needs the support of ministers. Within the Blair administration the Prime Minister is greatly constrained in economic and social policy by his relationship with the Chancellor. Moreover, the Prime Minister is also constrained by events and institutions outside the core executive, such as constitutional change, deeper European integration, and the prevalence of international crises. Consequently, the extra resources of the Prime Minister (and the systematization of his or her ability to intervene in policy) have to be understood within the context of the British political system. These, above all other things, constrain the actions of the Prime Minster, preventing him or her from ever having a unfettered hand in the formation of policy or the governance of the country. The argument of Rhodes (1995) and Rose (2001) is that British government has been hollowed out and thus the Prime Minister has more control over less. However, we have to be careful not to exaggerate the extent to which central government has changed. Whilst the organization of the central state, and the context within which it operates, has changed greatly, central government is still the key actor within the British political system. It has developed new relationships internally and externally but it continues to be in a powerful position. Government has the resources and the authority to intervene effectively within society (examine, for example, education) and even in relation to the EU it is clear that in many areas Brussels is more dependent on nation states than states are on the EU.

Chapter 5

Political Culture and Voting Participation

GEOFFREY EVANS

One of most immediate and substantial problems for the British political system has been the level of voting in recent elections. As expected the 2001 British general election yielded a comfortable Labour victory, with some consolidation of the Liberal Democrat seat gains from 1997 and little evidence of a resurgence by the Conservatives. But it was remarkable in one way: voter participation fell to 59 per cent, down by over 12 per cent on levels in 1997, and down over 18 per cent on the (admittedly quite high levels) in 1992. This change followed a significant decline in voting in the local and European elections in the 1997–2001 period. So the change has generated academic and media discussions pondering the general 'health' of British democracy. Does this dramatic fall in the level of voting signal a marked decline in commitment to the democratic process? And is there a growing level of disaffection from the British political system as a whole? Or are these recent developments instead just a temporary reflection of the current nature of party competition, with no long-term implications for citizens' involvement in democratic processes? We also need to consider whether the decline in voting is a uniquely British phenomenon, or whether it can better be understood from a wider perspective, in which case parochial remedies are unlikely to be sufficient to alleviate the problem.

A related concern in recent years focuses on the extent to which political participation is socially inclusive. Are particular types of groups, such as the working class, ethnic minorities, women, and the young, more politically disengaged than others? Differences in participation between social groups have long been in evidence, but the suggestion in media commentaries is that have they been exacerbating. Finally, though conventional political participation in the form of voting may have declined, other forms of political action might well be flourishing, or even undergoing a revival.

Participation and political culture

Involvement or participation in politics involve both behavioural and cognitive factors. The two are usually inter-connected:

* *Political behaviour*: behavioural political participation is usually divided into orthodox (or conventional) participation like voting, party membership and contacting MPs or councillors; and unorthodox (unconventional) participation, such as protests, demonstrations, marches and even 'terrorist' violence (Brady 1993 Parry, Moyser and Day 1992). A direct mode of influence from electorate to politicians is responding to public opinion polls, citizen juries and focus groups, but it involves very few people at a time. For the vast majority of the population voting remains the primary procedure through which they are involved in politics. So although protests against 'global capitalism' continue to disrupt G7 meetings and other international summits, unorthodox participation in Britain remains the preserve of a relatively small minority of people, although in the last few years undertaken as much by conservative groups (such as the Countryside Alliance) as radical ones (such as the anti-war protests in relation to Iraq). But even the Countryside Alliance elicits sporadic and relatively small-scale participation when compared with the size of the electorate.
* *Political culture*: cognitive aspects of participation are less easily specified and measured, but reflect an important element of 'political culture', a notoriously contentious concept usually taken to refer to sets of subjective beliefs, values, and identities, and even knowledge, pertaining to politics (Almond and Verba 1963, Eckstein 1988). Studies that adopt a political culture approach tend to explain political actions by assuming that they derive from normative orientations learned mainly, but not exclusively, from the family and other institutions of socialization, and which are subject to substantial continuity over time. In this sense, explaining short-term change in cultural terms is rather problematic. Nevertheless, if we accept that political culture concerns aspects of beliefs about politics that relate to the duty to vote, trust in politicians, and perceptions of the effectiveness of the political system, then we can examine evidence about the nature of these beliefs, whilst remaining agnostic about the possible role of the family and other sources of political socialization, such as education and the media, in forming them. Changes in political culture are of particular interest because they can provide explanations of changes in patterns of behavioural political participation.

Explaining participation

Attempts to explain levels of political participation have traditionally emphasized socio-economic factors and resources. Class, level of education, gender, age and social networks all have substantial effects on people's propensity to vote or to participate in politics through unorthodox means (Parry *et al.* 1992, Verba *et al.* 1995). In Britain, social class, housing tenure, age, gender and education have been strongly associated with higher turnout (Pattie and Johnston 1998). In general, people in more advantaged circumstances and with more resources to draw on, tend to have a greater propensity to act politically than do the disadvantaged.

A limitation here is that these background influences normally change rather gradually, and so such shifts cannot explain large-scale, short-term shifts of the type seen in levels of voting between 1997 and 2001 (and between 1992 and 1997). Moreover the direction of social change even suggests that we might expect to see the opposite trend. Over time the electorate has gradually become more educated and more middle class, both background factors associated with a greater likelihood to vote and to participate more generally. So other things being equal, there should have been increasing political participation over time. Thus, socio-demographic factors, or 'resources', do not offer a plausible explanation of falling political involvement over time.

In contrast to the emphasis on social structure, the 'institutional perspective' identifies the key factors explaining variations in turnout across countries and over time as being the administrative or organizational arrangements directly relevant to voting – such as the adoption of plurality rule voting or some more proportional system; the procedures for voter registration; the use or not of compulsory voting; the age of voting, and so on. Certainly, such institutional change historically has affected voting levels in Britain: the lowering of the voting age to 18 partly accounted for the low levels of turnout at the 1970 general election, for instance (Heath and Taylor 1999). Likewise the Thatcher government's introduction of the 'poll tax' based on the electoral register caused a substantial number of people not to register on the electoral roll in the period 1988–92, thereby decreasing turnout (McLean and Smith 1994). However, there were no important institutional changes between 1997 and 2001 that could be expected to impact on turnout, and yet the decline in the proportion of people voting was far larger than at any previous election. So again, this traditional approach is of limited usefulness.

A declining culture of participation?

Focusing on the prevailing subjective political culture is a potentially more fruitful approach for understanding participation in Britain. People might fail to participate in politics because:

- they lack a sense of civic obligation;
- they have little belief in their ability to influence politics (their sense of political efficacy) or in the effectiveness of the political system (Reef and Knoke 1999);
- they do not trust their political representatives, or do not identify closely with any of the parties; or
- they lack a general sense of interest and involvement in politics (Teixeira 1992).

In practice it is not always possible to disentangle the causal impact of these cultural or social psychological characteristics of voters from that of the conduct of politics itself. If politics becomes sleazy or boring, then voters become more disillusioned or less interested in it. So voters' beliefs are likely to be conditioned by changes in the political context, at least in part. Nevertheless, such responsiveness to the immediate context can provide at least part of an explanation of the sudden short-term changes in turnout. The question, therefore, is whether Britain has seen a growing alienation from politics, as reflected in declining levels of civic obligation, political efficacy, trust in politicians, and interest in politics?

In the 1990s there was certainly much debate about declining levels of trust in MPs and in the political system, seen in large part as a response to the long period of Conservative rule and to the government's reputation for 'sleaze' (Curtice and Jowell 1997). Similar analysis has been given by many commentators of the period leading up to and following the 2001 election, though this time not directed against the Conservatives. A conventional wisdom has it that: 'There is a growing feeling of alienation which is coupled with the view that the politicians are not listening to the people. This is bringing all forms of democracy into a considerable measure of disrepute' (Michael Brown, the *Independent*, 6 June 2002).

Academic research *partly* confirms this opinion. The 2001 British Social Attitudes survey shows that a growing number of people have little faith in how they are ruled. No less than 66 per cent agreed with the statement that 'people like me have no say in what government does', up from 57 per cent immediately after Labour's 1997 victory, and up from 48 per cent in 1987. Similarly, 70 per cent agreed that they do

Figure 5.1   *Voters' perceptions of political efficacy and trust in government*

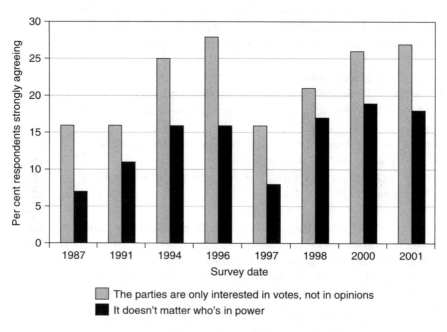

not trust governments of whatever party to put the interests of the nation ahead of those of their party, again up from 65 per cent in 1997 and 60 per cent in 1987. Most strikingly, 76 per cent agreed that parties were 'only interested in people's votes, not their opinions', compared with 62 per cent in 1997 and 55 per cent in 1987. Figure 5.1 shows that the proportion *strongly* agreeing with these statements has also increased over time, after initially falling back in the Blair 'honeymoon' period after the 1997 election. So both indices measuring trust in the motives of politicians and what is usually termed 'political efficacy' have been in decline, consistent with an increase in what is usually (though rather fancifully) termed 'alienation' from parliamentary politics. Yet in the same period, levels of reported political interest did not follow this pattern: three in every ten people expressed either 'a great deal' or 'quite a lot of interest' in politics in 1997, the same proportion as in 2001, and indeed previous elections.

Similarly, Figure 5.2 shows that there is no clear evidence of a decline in recent years in survey respondents answering that it was a duty to vote. So scepticism about politicians and parties does not seem to have been accompanied by a similar decline in political interest or in commitment to the act of democratic participation itself.

Figure 5.2   *Voters' interest in politics and perceptions of a civic duty to vote*

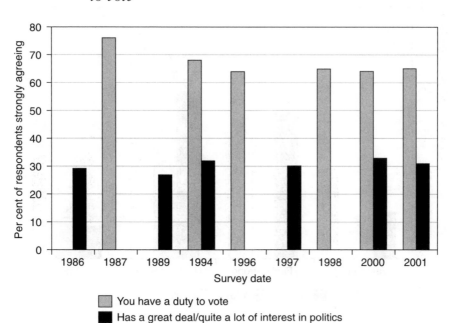

However, one element of voters' social psychology that *has* clearly changed substantially over recent decades is their degree of partisan attachment to the main political parties (Crewe and Thomson 1999). People who are 'party identifiers' are far more likely to vote than are the non-aligned (Butler and Stokes 1974). Although not usually considered as part of a growing malaise in political culture, levels of 'party identification' have dropped continuously over many years, after starting to do so in the 1970s (Saarlvik and Crewe 1983). This change gives at least some basis for expecting lower turnout in 2001 than in 1997, but again Figure 5.3 shows that excepting very strong identifiers, most change in the levels of party identification occurred before 1997, so that only a small amount of recent changes in participation can be attributed to this form of voter disengagement.

Participatory culture and (non)-voting

Looking in more detail at the evidence of increasing disillusionment with politicians among the British electorate, Bromley and Curtice (2002) argue that this trend had at most a minor role in accounting for

Figure 5.3   *The decline of party identification*

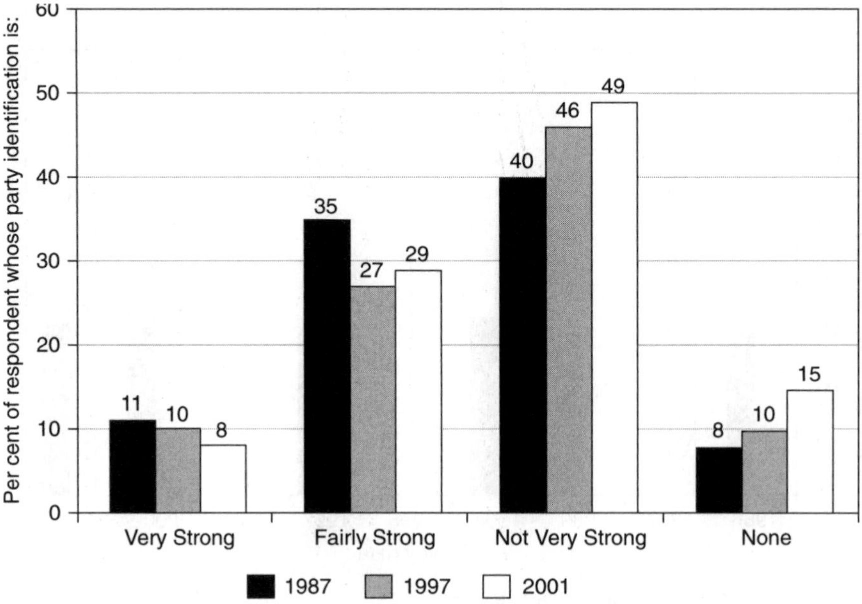

the declining voting levels between 1997 and 2001. People who distrust politicians are somewhat less likely to vote than those who trust them. In 1997, 84 per cent of people who said that they trusted governments to 'put the nation's interests first' voted, but so did 76 per cent of those who did not. Similar figures (87 and 78 per cent) are found for respondents who believed that parties are interested in people's opinions and those who do not. So the growth in distrust cannot possibly account for more than a small part of the fall in turnout in recent years.

In contrast, Bromley and Curtice argue that three characteristics clearly do mark out voters from non-voters: (i) whether voters feel they have a duty to vote; (ii) whether they have an interest in politics, and (iii) whether they have an emotional attachment to a political party. Thus while 87 per cent of those who expressed 'a great deal' or 'quite a lot' of interest in politics voted in 1997, only 66 per cent of those with 'not very much' or 'no interest at all' did so. Similarly, 86 per cent of those who agreed that it was 'everyone's duty to vote' participated, but only 51 per cent of those who did not. The 2001 British Election Study found similar results for the impact of a sense of civic duty and a sense of efficacy on turnout (Clarke *et al.* 2002). So perhaps the decline in turnout occurred because more and more voters are disengaging from politics? This would not appear to be the case: as Figure 5.2 above shows, there is no evidence that reported interest in politics has declined. Similarly, there is also no clear evidence of a decline in survey respondents agreeing that there is a duty to vote in recent years.

However, Bromley and Curtice (2002) do plausibly argue that the gradual increase in the proportion of non-partisan voters creates a larger constituency of de-aligned citizens whose responses are more calculating than they might have been in earlier years of higher turnout levels. At one time most people might well have voted without thinking too much about the costs and benefits of doing so. But nowadays more people deciding to vote or not are influenced by what the parties have to offer and the nature of the electoral competition itself.

Why bother? Voting and the character of party competition

The idea that a greater proportion of the electorate are 'up for grabs' places more weight on 'rational choice' approaches to voting, which focus attention on the nature of party competition and the resulting political options confronting voters, rather than on voters' individual characteristics. On rational choice principles there is less incentive to turn out and vote if: (i) the main parties offer similar policy packages; or (ii) the result is a foregone conclusion (Aldrich 1993). On the first issue here, the convergence of party positions, between 1992 and 1997 the Labour policy agenda shifted to the right in a pronounced fashion. For the first time in post-war history, Labour's manifesto showed a preponderance of right-wing positions over left-wing ones, and was even to the right of the Liberal Democrats' position (Budge 1999). The Conservatives meanwhile remained more or less as they had been in 1992. These shifts did not go unnoticed by the electorate who also perceived a pronounced decline in the ideological gap between the parties. Since that time the main party policy positions have not diverged (Bara and Budge 2001). So by the time of the 2001 general election there were few differences in policy between the main parties compared to previous elections and the narrowest perceived gap between the two main parties in modern times. The only major issue on which the parties took clearly different positions was European integration (specifically, the adoption of the Euro), an issue which allowed the Conservatives to acquire a small amount of votes from Labour between 1997 and 2001 (Evans 2002). Research on previous elections suggests that the smaller the perceived differences between the two major parties, the more likely voters are to abstain (Heath and Taylor, 1999; Pattie and Johnston, 2001) – and the same pattern can be seen in 2001. Low turnout in recent elections may not therefore represent a 'crisis for democracy' but rather a realistic response to the belief that there was not much to choose between the main parties on the main issues.

Second, on the closeness of the parties, at no point in the run up to the 2001 general election did Labour's lead in the polls falter. The government was clearly expected by voters to retain its large overall majority, and the election was seen as a foregone conclusion, reducing people's incentives to vote. It is worth noting that the exact way in which such considerations are weighed by voters has been the subject of debate. One approach emphasizes the closeness of the constituency competition – the more marginal the seat, the greater the chance that an individual's vote might be decisive, and hence the greater the incentive to vote. Consistent with this view, *aggregate* research on recent general elections has demonstrated a positive association between constituency marginality and turnout (Denver and Hands 1997, Pattie and Johnston 1998). In 2001 turnout was 10 per cent higher in marginal constituencies than in 'safe' seats (Whiteley *et al*. 2001; Curtice and Steed 2001). In contrast, studies that have examined *individual level* or survey data have found little link between marginality and turnout (Pattie and Johnston 2001). Hence it has been argued that the overall closeness of the *national* election is the factor most likely to affect turn out across elections.

Indeed, on rational choice grounds, it could be argued that even in a marginal seat there is little incentive to turn out and vote if the overall election result is a foregone conclusion. Thus low turnout in 1997 and 1983 occurred when there were substantial differences in the party vote shares, while high turnout in 1964 and February 1974 occurred when the electoral competition was close run (Heath and Taylor 1999), a pattern also found in earlier elections. There are exceptions to this pattern, particularly the 1992 election when the pre-elections polls were wildly inaccurate, misleadingly indicating a very close race when in fact the Tories were well ahead. But this mis-signal could well have accounted for the unusually high turnout that year. In 2001, voters' perceptions of the closeness of the national competition predicted some individual differences in turnout: those who saw the race as closer were a little less likely to stay at home (Whiteley *et al*. 2001).

If the main parties offer similar programmes and at the same time the election outcome seems certain, then there should be a particularly marked drop in levels of voting. Some of the highest turnouts in British elections have occurred – in 1950, 1951 and 1992 – when there were both large differences between the parties and (perceived) close races. The wide gap between the Conservative and Labour parties in 1983 and 1987 was not associated with high turnout, but this can be explained by the Tories' clear opinion poll leads. Without a close electoral race, large ideological differences between the parties count for little in the voter's decision-making. Conversely, the apparently anomalous pattern observed in the 1970 election, when the pre-election polls indicated a fairly close race yet the turnout was rather low, can be accounted for by the very low proportion of the electorate (32 per cent) who perceived much of a difference between the parties. This hypothesis of dual influences still awaits more detailed individual-level analysis but it seems to fit the 2001 election result well.

Overall, the perceived closeness of the election, in conjunction with the perceived ideological difference between the parties, seems to offer the most convincing explanation of over-time differences in turnout, not just for the decline in turnout from 1997 to 2001, but throughout the series of post-war British elections. However, in its most convincing form, this argument also includes the notion that closeness and difference have their effects *when voters are not closely attached to parties.* Partisan identification is far less widespread than it used to be – nearly two out of three voters now say they either do not feel any kind of bond to a party at all or at most not a very strong one. So the proportion of voters who can be influenced by the closeness of the competition between the parties and the differences between them is correspondingly greater. Bromley and Curtice (2002) show that amongst those who said that they felt a duty to vote, had an interest in politics or had a sense of attachment to a political party, the turnout levels hardly fell at all between 1997 and 2001. By contrast, voting plummeted amongst people who did not have such involvements.

Social inclusion

A further concern for political leaders and political scientists alike has been in what sorts of people are involved in politics. The involvement of women, ethnic minorities, the working class and 'young people' have all occasioned particular concern. At the level of the political elite the picture is mixed. Recent initiatives have increased the number of women in positions of political power such as the Cabinet, though the proportion of female MPs has remained more or less constant since the celebrated arrival of 'Blair's babes' in 1997 (Lovenduski 2001). Ethnic minorities likewise now have their first 'black cabinet minister' in Paul Boateng, though only 12 MPs (Saggar 2001). Many of the Prime Minister's closest political advisers have even been characterized as extremely youthful (sometimes perhaps resentfully so by older colleagues). In contrast, the representation of people from working class occupations, or even working class backgrounds, is hard to monitor and no official body has been charged with

promoting it. It seems likely that working class representation in top positions is in decline, partly because the working class as it is usually defined
has shrunk to just over half the size it was only 40 years ago.

At the level of mass political participation, however, differential political involvement is less easily changed by the appointment of a few new
faces. Aggregate analyses show that in 2001 constituencies containing a
large ethnic minority or many welfare dependent people had lower
turnout rates (Whiteley *et al.* 2001). However, in constituencies where
the main competition was between the Conservatives and the Liberal
Democrats, there was no significant effect here (Curtice and Steed 2001,
McAllister 2001). This pattern is possibly because of the high levels of
support for Labour amongst most ethnic minorities and people dependent on welfare. Turnout tended to be higher in Conservative-held seats
because of their affluent, middle class composition, while Labour voters
in the party's safe seats may have felt that their party was going to win
easily. Older voters and women were less likely to abstain than were
younger voters and men (Whiteley *et al.* 2001).

Disaffected youth?

Turnout by young people in 2001 was at an all time low (Whiteley *et al*,
2001). A study of over 10,000 young people indicated that voting by
18–24-year olds was down to only 39 per cent, reflecting a trend
commented on at several points in the 1990s (Mulgan and Wilkinson
1997, Jowell and Park 1998). Journalistic commentators have thus been
quick to conclude that young people: 'were alienated from the political
process by cynical MPs, spin and a relentless focus on the negative
aspects of their lives'(Womack 2002). Academic analysts have also
pointed to the crucial significance of learning to vote routinely during
one's formative years and how failing to get 'the voting habit' has long-
term consequences (Plutzer, 2002). Figure 5.4 shows that the fall in
participation between 1997 and 2001 is noticeably greater among the
young than among other age groups, which *prima facie* seems to
confirm these concerns.

However, we should be careful to remember that low turnout does
not necessarily indicate disinterest in politics *per se*. Bromley and
Curtice (2002) show that along with other indicators of disengagement,
interest in politics amongst the young did not decline between 1997 and
2001, although it was never particularly high. Qualitative research
suggests that young people care more about non mainstream political
issues such as environmentalism or animal rights (White, Bruce and
Ritchie 2000), both issues that were of little salience in the campaigns
of the main political parties (Henn, Weinstein and Wring 2002). If the

Figure 5.4 *Turnout levels in 1997 and 2001 by age group*

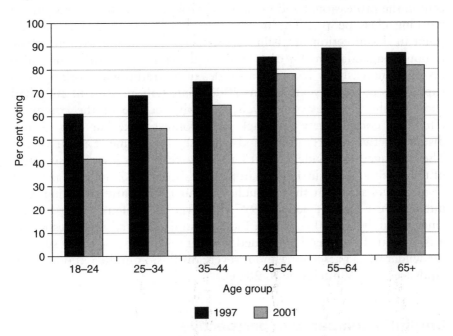

parties gave more emphasis to such matters then the growing disparity in participation between younger and older members of the electorate might perhaps be open to correction.

Working-class abstention?

In the 1997 general election Labour 'reached across the class divide' and obtained more support from the middle classes than at any point previously (Evans, Heath and Payne 1999). But what happened to Labour's traditional heartland of support amongst working class voters? Were they likely to abstain as the party moved firmly onto middle-class ideological terrain? The theme of manual workers feeling cut off from politics is a frequent one in media commentary. 'Alienation from the political process is running deep, but nowhere deeper than among the working class' (Crow and Rix 2002). There is some evidence from America that as the Democrats moved towards the centre of the political spectrum class differences in turnout increased (Weakliem and Heath 1999). Heath and Taylor (1999) suggest that this might have been the case in Britain: between 1992 and 1997 non-voting grew by 4 per cent among the professional and managerial class, whereas in the working class it increased 7 percentage points. Among previous Labour voters (its 'heartland' voters), for whom a change in Labour's policy distinctiveness might have had most impact, non-voting grew by 1 per cent in the professional and managerial group, but by 6 per cent among working class people. The numbers involved are small, but they do point in the direction of disillusion with Labour in the working class. Labour's agenda on Europe, gays and ethnic minorities has also diverged increasingly from the attitudes of its traditional working-class supporters in recent years (Evans 2000). Safe Labour seats in 2001 had some of the lowest voting levels, possibly because of the combined effects of complacency and lack of a contest risk, but also greater distance between party policy and working-class former Labour voters. There is suggestive evidence that Labour were seen as less representative of the working class in 1997 than previously. In 1987 some 47 per cent of all voters said that they thought Labour looked after working-class interests very closely, but by 1997 this level had fallen to 34 per cent. Unfortunately, the 2001 British Election study omitted this question so it is unclear if this trend continued. So there is little evidence to support the wilder media assertions about severe disillusion in the Labour heart-lands (see also Whiteley *et al.* 2001).

Britain in comparative perspective

It is important to recognize that the minutiae of British political life could fade into the background if the changes in turnout are not unique to the UK. Any trend that is generic to established democracies cannot be seen as a specifically British problem. There is academic consensus that turnout has declined steadily throughout all established liberal democracies since the 1950s (Dalton and Wattenberg 2000; Grey and Caul 2000, Franklin 2001). Yet there is little agreement on what has caused this change. Of course, considerable *cross-national* variations remain in turnout rates – mainly caused by voluntary voter registration, the size of voting districts, using proportional representation or plural-ity rule electoral systems and compulsory versus voluntary voting laws (Blais and Dobrznska 1990, Jackman and Miller 1995). But most advanced industrial democracies have still experienced the same general trend of declining turnout over a 40-year period. This might suggest that we should let Britain's political culture off the hook. To explain this outcome a more general level of explanation is needed – one that is present across a wide range of democratic societies.

A popular view is that a 'crisis of democracy' looms as the public become increasingly alienated from the democratic system by its failure to deliver what citizens want (Fuchs and Klingemann 1995). Greater centralization and lowered opportunity for participation is another candidate for alienation. But is this the case? Are people really more dissatisfied with democracy and its institutions nowadays? In Britain we have found little evidence of marked change in this respect. And recent extensive analysis of perceptions and attitudes across a wide range of advanced industrial democracies reaches similar conclusions, suggesting that accounts of a global democratic `crisis' are greatly exaggerated (Dalton 1999, Klingemann 1999).

One possibility is that declining turnout simply reflects increasing rationality among the electorate (Whiteley 2002). This follows the analysis of Downs (1957) who argued that the chances of an individual vote affecting an election outcome are negligibly small so a rational voter should ask: Why bother to vote? Let someone else make the effort. If your party wins you get the benefit, but avoid the (admittedly small) costs of voting. Equally if a disliked party wins, at least you have not had to bear the costs of voting, and the outcome would have happened anyway even if you tried to prevent it. So an increasingly calculating citizenry could reason in this way, rather than following norms and traditions (Rose and McAllister 1986). Whiteley (2002) notes an exception to the general turnout trend in Scandinavia, hypothesizing that voters are insulated from the effects of individual calculation because: 'These are countries with high levels of "social capital" in which individuals trust each other and where individuals are linked together in networks of civic engagement'. However, arguing that greater interpersonal trust and social capital promote and maintain political involvement has been criticized as really more a hopeful aspiration than a proven case at present (Seligson 2002, Evans and Letki 2003).

An alternative view, however, which would require no assumptions of such a marked change in the electorate's character is that it is not *voters* who are becoming more rational but *parties*. If all major parties place an increased emphasis on finding centrist policies designed to appeal to the median voter and using sophisticated methods like focus groups and opinion polls, then, inevitably, the views of more 'extreme' or specific issue groups are given less prominence in the pursuit of general popularity. This change could then boost unorthodox political activity among people who increasingly find that their personal concerns are not addressed in an increasingly catch-all, centrist politics – presumably groups whose identities or values lie a long way from the centrist concerns of the main political competitors. The Countryside Alliance could be seen as just such a group. Urban voters dominate in the main parties' electoral calculations. Rural concerns are always likely to be at a disadvantage in the calculus of overall electoral costs and benefits.

A supportive finding here from comparative evidence is that citizen involvement in politics is perhaps not so imperilled. Indeed some studies

Table 5.1   *Reported political action, 1986–2000*

% saying they had	1986	1989	1991	1994	2000
Signed a petition	34	41	53	39	42
Contacted their MP	11	15	17	14	16
Contacted radio, TV or newspaper	3	4	4	5	6
Gone on a protest or demonstration	6	8	9	9	10
Raised the issue in an organization they already belong to	5	4	5	4	5
Spoken to an influential person	1	3	5	3	4
Contacted a government department	3	3	4	3	4
Formed a group of like-minded people	2	3	2	3	2
Done none of these	*56*	*48*	*37*	*53*	*47*

Source: Bromley, Curtice and Seyd, 2001.

provide cross-national evidence of substantial increases in political activity over a 25-year period (Norris 2002). And in Britain, Table 5.1 shows that between 1986 and 2000 there were small increases in the proportions of respondents who said they had actually engaged in a variety of non-electoral forms of political participation. These included signing a petition (up from 34 to 42 per cent), going on a protest or demonstration (up from 6 to 10 per cent), and contacting their MP (11 to 16 per cent) (Bromley, Curtice and Seyd 2001). Similar increases occurred in those who expressed a potential to engage in various forms of political activity, such as signing a petition, going on a protest or demonstration and contacting their MP. But these politically active people tend to be the same ones who vote, so their extra-curricular political actions serve to add to current patterns of representation rather than to spread the range of options to habitual non-voters.

Admittedly, these interpretations of trends in involvement rely on answers to questions in social surveys, which is only one type of evidence. A systematic analysis of people's actual involvement in non-voting forms of participation would be useful. For the present, however, the survey evidence provides a useful counterweight to the fashionable tendency to see civic involvement in politics in 'disaffected democracies' as being in a parlous state (Pharr and Putnam 2000). Moreover, there is clear evidence that demonstrations and other forms of political action, such as national strikes, are a continuing part of the British political scene. In September 2002, 400,000 or so people marched for 'liberty and the countryside', with a set of right-wing causes being represented as a protest for liberal values. The Conservative leader, Iain Duncan Smith proclaimed 'I am marching today in defence of our freedom' (*Sunday Telegraph*, 22 September 2002) and the *Daily Telegraph* linked the campaign to equality of treatment: 'Prince Charles tells Blair: "Farmers are being treated worse than blacks or gays"' (ibid). The protest was then followed in February 2003 by a 1.5 million strong march in London proclaiming opposition to war on Iraq, a rather different expression of liberal values.

Conclusion

In June 2002 the Electoral Commission organized a conference on turnout asking 'what can be done to reverse the decline and by whom?' In searching for explanations of and solutions for the current turnout malaise, the British political elite are probably right to believe that, over the long term, voters' trust in politicians has declined. But is restoring trust the main route to getting voters back to the polls? Political trust and cynicism have not changed that greatly and cannot explain over-time trends in turnout. Analyses of the 2001 election suggest that low turnout reflects election-specific factors, primarily the lack of close party competition at a national and constituency level and voters' feeling that the overall outcome was a foregone conclusion and that their vote would have little weight in shaping it. These attitudes were most pronounced among the increasing proportion of the electorate who lack a strong attachment to one or other of the main political parties. Evidence for any 'crisis' due to increased working-class abstention is slim; it could not explain much of the 2001 fall in turnout and on the evidence available it cannot be said whether any change here is caused by disillusionment with Labour politics or complacency about a Labour win. Until another general election result is in real doubt, and at the same time the parties divide over an important issue so as to galvanize British politics, there is no reason to expect noticeably higher levels of participation. Meanwhile British political culture has become *more* supportive of formal civic engagements and informal protests, and demonstrations and unconventional political participation still provide an important outlet for those who feel their views are not adequately represented by mainstream politics. So it would to appear to be only *electoral* participation that is in decline (Margetts 2000).

Various modes of voting have been encouraged as a way of boosting turnout. Gordon Brown has allocated £10 million per annum for new initiatives to combat the prevalent sense of alienation or mood of non-participation. The government also published a report that sets out 'the principles that underpin further policy development and proposes what could be done to make e-democracy a reality' (see www.edemocracy.gov.uk). However, although surveys suggest 57 per cent would be willing to vote online if they had the chance, less than half of households are online, and they are disproportionately those where people are already more likely to vote (Walker, 2002). Other changes are likely to be more significant. Consistent with recent comparative evidence, postal voting in Britain had moderately positive results when tried in the 2002 local elections and holds the prospect of a slight increase, though not one that will be of great impact. Franklin's (2001) estimate is that using compulsory voting can increase turnout by 6–7 per cent; postal voting by 5–6 per cent; and Sunday voting by 6–7 per cent. However, comparing systems with and without such features is inevitably problematic given the many other ways in which they also differ, so these estimates are only tentative. More extensive institutional intervention such as adopting proportional representation might be thought to hold more extensive prospects for increased legitimacy and hence popular participation in elections. However, changing to PR carries no immediate guarantee of more involvement. In 1993 New Zealand changed its electoral system from plurality rule to an additional member system (called the 'mixed member proportional system' there). In the first election under the new system turnout rose by 1.7 per cent. However, in the second election three years later turnout fell to an alltime low of 74 per cent (Vowles, 2001). Moreover, since the pre-election days of the mid-1990s the Labour Party's commitment to proportional representation withered on the vine. With no government enthusiasm for PR, there is little likelihood of it being adopted for Westminster elections.

The combination of little difference between the parties, plus a result that is a foregone conclusion, plus an electorate where many voters are no longer pre-committed to any given party would appear to provide the most convincing answer to the puzzle of (non)turnout in Britain today. We have become an increasingly 'de-aligned' or 'disengaged', or 'choosy', or 'rational' electorate, depending on the spin of different authors. Although there is a somewhat more generalized political cynicism now than in earlier more innocent times, it would be wrong to claim that large sections of the electorate are 'alienated' from democratic politics, or from our particular party system. Instead voters are more *demanding* than they used to be, and it is not at all clear what initiatives will change this stance. Changes in political culture work hand-in-hand with the current state of a de-polarized, one-party dominant political context to de-politicize an electorate who might well have more personally important things on their mind than national politics. If this situation changes, however, as with the re-appearance of new issues dividing the main parties or closer party competition, then we should expect to see a resurgence of behavioural participation. Whether scepticism will in turn be replaced by open-hearted endorsement of politics or politicians is more doubtful. In the meantime, however, there is no evidence that other forms of political participation have declined.

This analysis implies that if Labour continues to command substantial leads in the opinion polls, we might well find that turnout in the next general election remains relatively low or declines further. On the other hand if the Conservatives gradually recover support, as we might expect, or the Liberal Democrats increase their vote, then subsequent general elections could be regarded as closer contests, and turnout can be expected to increase. However, there is also the possibility that the ideological difference between the parties plays a role in voters' decisions to turn out and vote: if Labour remains close to the centre of the political spectrum, and the Conservatives also move back towards the centre ground, the lack of difference between the parties might imply continuing low turnout. Electoral politics in 2001 simply became an unexciting one horse race. Restoring faith in politics will not in itself get voters back to the polls. But the re-emergence of an effective opposition just might.

Chapter 6

Changing Voting Systems

JOHN CURTICE

Not so long ago, the debate about alternative electoral systems in Britain appeared to be entirely academic. In practice, all elections were held using one method, called plurality rule. Candidates secured election simply by winning more votes than their competitors, a plurality but very frequently not a majority (less than 50 per cent) of all votes, in a single member district. Parliament or any other elected body was then composed simply by the amalgam of results all these local contests. Only the use of the Single Transferable Vote (STV) for many elections in Northern Ireland since 1973 breached what appeared to be the standard and centuries-old British way of doing things.

But since Labour came to power in 1997 that tradition has been challenged and uprooted. Instead of being a country where things are always done the same way, Britain has become a laboratory of electoral experimentation and change, often as part of Labour's wider programme of devolution and constitutional reform. But pre-existing election systems for the European Parliament have also been changed and new systems of election have been seriously proposed but not yet implemented for Westminster elections (Jenkins, 1998), for a reformed House of Lords and for Scottish local government. The Labour government has so far not implemented the pledge it made in its 1997 manifesto to put a recommendation on reforming House of Commons elections to the public in a referendum, and did not repeat it in 2001. But it is committed to initiating in 2003 a review of the experience of proportional representation in Britain so far, to inform a further consideration whether a change to the Commons electoral system should take place. To assess the questions that will need to be answered by such a review, this chapter reviews the new voting systems now in place. It also focuses on three issues at the heart of academic and policy debates about the relative merits of plurality rule and alternative more proportional electoral systems:

- which kind of electoral system is more conducive to high levels of electoral participation;

- what impacts do electoral systems have on elections' role in liberal democracy; and
- what difference electoral systems make to the kind of representation that voters enjoy.

Varieties of electoral systems

The principle behind the plurality rule is a simple one. Those candidates who get most votes in a local area get elected, whether they have a majority of the votes cast or not. In elections to the House of Commons every constituency elects just one MP under the classic Single Member Plurality System (SMPS). This system was also used for electing the British MEPs in the European Parliament during 1979–94, and is employed for choosing all Scottish local councillors. Plurality rule can also be used in multi-member electoral districts, as it often is in English and Welsh local government. To elect three councillors in one ward, for instance, voters can cast one vote each for three different candidates, and then the top three candidates with most votes win.

The Additional Member System (AMS, also known outside the UK as the Mixed Member Proportional system) was first implemented in Germany after 1945. It became one of the leading alternatives for use in Britain in the mid 1970s (Blake 1976) and was adopted in New Zealand in 1996. AMS is part of a larger 'family' of mixed or parallel electoral systems, where representatives are chosen in two different ways, an approach also used in Italy, Japan and other countries (Shugart and Wattenberg 2001). AMS retains the use of SMPS in local districts but adds an additional election of some representatives using a more proportional system. These 'additional members' (also often called the 'top up' representatives) are elected from lists of candidates nominated by each party in such a way that the total representatives for each party is made (quite) proportional to the share of the total vote cast for those parties.

Some features of AMS are standard. All three existing implementations of AMS in Britain, for the Greater London Assembly, the Welsh National Assembly and the Scottish Parliament, give voters two votes, one cast in the local SMPS election and one in the party list stage. Other details of AMS systems can vary significantly. A key variation is the proportion of seats that are elected by SMPS and the proportion that come from party lists. In Germany, these proportions are 50:50. By contrast, in all the British AMS systems more than half of the seats are elected by SMPS. In the Greater London Assembly the local members comprise 56 per cent of all seats, in the Scottish Parliament 57 per cent and in the Welsh Assembly no less than 66 per cent. A second potentially important variation is in how the party list seats are allocated across one big or several less big 'top up' constituencies. The Greater London Assembly uses a single London-wide constituency but Wales is divided into four separate regions for the party list election, and Scotland into eight regions.

The Alternative Vote Plus system was proposed by the Independent Commission on the Electoral System (Jenkins, 1988) and is based on yet a further possible variation of AMS. Its first key idea was that the proportion of locally elected MPs should be as high as 80 to 85 per cent of all seats, keeping party list MPs to a minimum needed for 'broad proportionality'. A second innovation was not to elect MPs in the local contests by SMPS, but instead to use the Alternative Vote (AV) method there. Under AV, voters no longer place an 'X' against the name of one individual candidate, but instead they are invited to rank the candidates in an order of preference, numbering them 1, 2, 3, etc. If no single candidate secures more than half of all first preference votes (those people have numbered 1), then the bottom candidate is eliminated and the second votes of people who supported him or her are redistributed amongst the remaining candidates, in accordance with the number 2 preferences marked. This process of eliminating the bottom candidate and redistributing these voters' later preferences continues until one candidate has secured over half of the eligible votes, and so can be said to have majority support.

The Supplementary Vote (SV) is a simplified version of AV. It is used for electing the London Mayor, and for the directly elected mayors in other localities in England. Here voters are simply asked to express a first preference and a second preference, not by marking a '1' and a '2' on their ballot paper but instead by putting an 'X' in one column to mark their first preference and then another 'X' in a second column to indicate their second preference. This procedure avoids mixing up X voting and voting by numbering preferences which might otherwise have been confusing, for instance when voters are choosing the London Mayor and the Assembly on the same day.

Proportional Representation Party list systems also come in many varieties across the world. One version was introduced in Britain for the first time in the European elections in 1999. That was a 'closed' list system. Voters cast one vote for different lists of candidates put up by the parties. Which candidates are elected is determined by how many people support each party, and then by the order in which they are ranked on their party's list. So, for example, if a party is entitled to three seats, the top three persons on its list will be elected. Voters cannot pick or choose within each party's slate of candidates. By contrast, in an 'open' list system voters can express a preference for an individual candidate chosen from inside each party list. So if a party's overall vote share meant it had won three seats, then its most voted-for three candidates would be elected, not the top three on a list drawn up by the party leadership. 'Flexible' lists are a compromise between these approaches. Voters can choose to support either a whole party's slate, or a particular individual candidate within it, and in some circumstances those individual preference votes may overturn the rank order proposed by the party.

Any party list system requires larger constituencies, so that several representatives can be elected for each area. In the European elections, rather than Britain forming one large constituency electing 84 members, it is divided into Scotland, Wales and nine English official government regions, whose population size varies a lot. So the number of MEPs elected in each region also varies, from four in the North East region of England to eleven in the South East. Within each region seats are allocated by a formula designed to ensure that seats are proportional to votes. (There is no direct mechanism for ensuring that seats won across the country as a whole are proportional to votes, but the result was quite close.)

The Single Transferable Vote (STV) gives voters the same task as with the Alternative Vote, namely to rank candidates in order of preference. But whereas under AV just one candidate is elected in a local constituency, under STV multiple candidates are elected to represent a wider area. This means that each party may nominate more than one candidate, for instance five people if there are five seats to be won. And whereas under AV the threshold for election is half the vote, under STV there is a 'quota' that depends on the number of candidates to be elected. This quota level is the smallest number of votes that only the number of candidates to be elected can possibly achieve. It is set as [the number of votes cast] divided by [one more than the number of seats to be elected], plus one extra vote. Thus if there are three candidates to be elected and 100 votes have been cast, the quota would be (100/4) + 1, that is 26 votes. Anyone meeting this quota is elected immediately, and any 'surplus' votes they have (above the quota level) are redistributed to those voters' second preference candidates. If this leaves some seats still unallocated (as it normally does), then STV shifts over to eliminating the bottom candidate like AV above, and then redistributing these voters' second preferences. The process continues in this way until all the seats have been won by a candidate reaching the quota level of votes.

The level and quality of electoral participation

Do some kinds of system make it more likely that people will vote and that their votes will express their true preferences? Advocates of proportional systems point out that under SMPS many constituencies are 'safe' constituencies where one party is so strong locally that the outcome is a foregone conclusion. There is much less incentive for voters in safe constituencies to vote. It is only in more 'marginal' constituencies (which may well be relatively rare) that the outcome locally is closely fought and open to change, and in practice only voters in these constituencies have an effective say in which party will form the next government. So we should expect turnout to be lower in elections held using SMPS than it is under elections using some system of proportional representation where 'every vote counts' (Farrell 2001, Franklin 1996, Katz 1997).

But advocates of SMPS have a rejoinder. They point to the alleged complexity of many proportional representation (PR) systems. Under SMPS voters can easily understand that whoever gets most votes gets elected, whereas under any PR systems who wins is determined by counting more complex counting procedures (even involving mathematical formulae) that leave most voters unsure just how their vote contributes to the election of an MP. And ballot papers under SMPS are relatively simple affairs on which voters place a single cross. Under alternative systems voters are often presented with longer and more complex ballot papers, and sometimes may have to vote twice or more. (For instance, voters in London elections could cast four votes, first and second preference for Mayor, and local and London-wide votes for the Assembly). This greater complexity is supposed to act as a disincentive for voters to go to the polling station and to be a factor which makes mistaken or invalid votes more likely amongst those who do go.

Recent British experience of alternative electoral systems certainly suggests that introducing proportional systems is certainly no immediate panacea for enhancing turnout. Turnout was lower at each of the major elections that were held between 1997 and 2001 using an alternative electoral system than it was in either the 1997 or 2001 general election held under SMPS. Furthermore, turnout in the 1999 European Elections was as much as nine points lower than at any previous European election held under SMPS. However, turnout in 2001 using SMPS was lower than at any previous election since 1918, and even in 1997 voting levels were low compared with other post-war elections. So sticking with SMPS can apparently no longer be relied upon to bring voters to the polls either.

In fact Table 6.1 can tell us relatively little about the impact of electoral systems on turnout. It compares the voting turnout for different institutions that have very different powers, and as a result different levels of importance in voters' minds. Turnout for the House of Commons may well be higher than it is for any other British political

Table 6.1   *Turnout at elections in Britain 1997–2001*

Year	Institution	Electoral System	% voting
1997	House of Commons	SMPS	71.4
1999	Scottish Parliament	AMS	58.2
1999	Welsh Assembly	AMS	46.4
1999	European Parliament	Party List	23.1
2000	London Mayor	SV	33.5
2001	House of Commons	SMPS	59.1

institution irrespective of the voting system being used, simply because more people think it matters. After all turnout in Westminster elections has always been much higher than in European or local elections, even though the former once were and the latter still are conducted under the plurality rule. Comparing the 1999 European election turnout with those from 1979 to 1994 does not suffer from this flaw. But even here the lower turnout in 1999 could just as well be the result of the apparent decline in turnout at *all kinds* of election (general election, local and European) after 1997, rather than indicating any impact from using the party list system.

To be able to make a judgement about the claims made by advocates on each side of the argument, we need more direct evidence of about whether different kinds of system do in fact matter. We need to examine two key questions. Is it true that turnout is markedly higher in marginal constituencies than in safe seats? And is there any evidence that voters were confused by any of the alternative electoral systems? Table 6.2 addresses the first question by comparing the turnout in marginal and not so marginal seats in the 2001 general election, and at first sight it shows a clear effect for turnout to be less in safe seats. However, a closer look reveals there is only a clear difference between the turnout in marginal and not so marginal constituencies in seats that were being defended by Labour. In places with a sitting Conservative or other party MP, turnout was almost the same across marginal and safe seats. In part this reflects the fact that more Labour constituencies in 2001 were *very* safe and so might be expected to have particularly low turnouts. But it is also the case that turnout is lower the stronger the Labour vote is in a constituency, irrespective of how marginal it is, so this pattern has the effect of exaggerating the difference in turnout between marginal and not so marginal seats.

Using a more complex statistical approach (a regression analysis) takes this complicating factor into account, and does suggest that

Table 6.2   *How turnour in 2001 varied by the marginality of seats and by the party holding the seat*

	Average % turnout in	
	Marginal seats	Not so marginal seats
Labour MP in 1997	62.3	55.8
Conservative MP in 1997	63.4	63.1
Other MP in 1997	63.7	62.7
All seats	**63.0**	**57.7**

Note: A 'marginal' seat is defined as one where the winning party had a majority over the second party in 1997 of less than 10 per cent of all votes. A 'not so marginal' seat is one where the leading party's majority was greater than this level.

turnout is in fact lower in safe seats than in marginal ones. On average it can be shown that turnout is a little over three percentage points lower in a seat where the defending party starts off with a 20 per cent majority than it is in one where the two parties start off neck and neck. (The regression equation here explains over half the variance in turnout in 1997). Marginality does then have some influence on turnout, but its impact should not be exaggerated. At the same time one likely reason why turnout was so low in both marginal and safe constituencies in 2001was because voters anticipated that Britain's SMPS electoral system was going to give Labour a second large parliamentary majority (Bromley and Curtice 2002). Voters would not have anticipated such a 'clear win' outcome under a more proportional system.

Turning to our second question, is there evidence that more proportional electoral systems are more complex in ways that make it less likely for people to vote or to cast a valid vote if they do go to the polls? In surveys of voters conducted immediately after the devolved elections in Scotland, Wales and London respondents were asked first whether they found the ballot papers difficult to complete, and then whether they found it difficult to understand the relationship between votes and seats (Curtice *et al.* 2001 and 2002). In each case relatively few voters said they thought it was 'very' or 'fairly' difficult to complete the ballot papers. In Scotland and Wales they amounted to no more than one person in ten, although in London this figure was double at one in five. However, two in five people said that they found understanding how votes were converted into seats difficult. Even so, it does not appear that this problem, understanding how seats were allocated, had much impact on turnout for all three elections. Those who found it difficult to understand how votes were converted into seats reported the same level of turnout as people who did not report such a difficulty (Curtice *et al.* 2002).

Meanwhile at the 1999 European election, Home Office research concluded that difficulties in understanding the new party list system, or indeed dislike of the system, were not in any way responsible for the low turnout (Home Office 1999). And evidence from the 1999 British Social Attitudes survey indicates that people who were opposed to electoral reform were almost just as likely to say they had voted in the European election as were those who favoured new voting methods. Only in one instance, when 2 per cent of people voted invalidly in the 2000 London mayoral race, was there clear evidence of people being confused by newer ballot papers. So overall, the arguments from advocates of SMPS that newer systems discourage turnout or less reliable voting do not receive much support.

Some critics of the Additional Member System have suggested that people view their local vote as a first preference vote, and the party list or 'top-up' vote as a second preference vote – consequently voting for the wrong party. However, when voters in Scotland and Wales were asked both for whom they had voted in the 1999 devolution elections and which was their first preference party, most people gave both their votes to their first preference party. In Scotland 83 per cent gave their party list vote to their first preference party while 88 per cent did so in the local SMPS contest. In Wales the equivalent figures were 81 per cent and 88 per cent respectively.

One reason why voters might fail to vote for their first preference party in an election is because they decide to vote tactically. Electoral reformers often argue that under SMPS rather than 'waste' their vote on their first preference party which has no chance of winning, people opt to support their second preference in order to ensure the defeat of another party or candidate which they positively dislike. In this way, they say, SMPS undermines the quality of electoral participation. In contrast, because 'every vote counts' in systems of proportional representation they are better able to ensure that the votes people cast are a true reflection of their real preferences.

Contrary to this argument, however, some critics of the Additional Member System point out that in Scotland, Wales and London it uses SMPS in the local contests, and so cannot reduce tactical voting effects here. Meanwhile a party list vote can be a 'wasted' vote too if a party wins so many of the local SMPS contests that it cannot win any further party list seats, a situation that Labour faced in much of Scotland and

Wales in 1999. However, in practice somewhat fewer voters reported voting tactically in the AMS elections than in recent general elections. In Scotland, 6 per cent of voters reported voting tactically in their SMPS contest and just 4 per cent on the party list vote. In London the figure was somewhat higher at 7 per cent apiece. But these levels were still below the 10 per cent of people who reported voting tactically at the 1997 general election. The impacts of PR systems here should not be exaggerated. The Liberal Democrats have always in the past been pictured as the party most disadvantaged by SMPS, because they accumulate many votes running second or third without getting a realistic chance of winning. If people were put off voting Liberal Democrat for fear of wasting their votes then the advent of PR systems should have given the party a significant dividend of new votes. Yet in the Scottish, Welsh and London elections the Liberal Democrat share of the party list vote was almost exactly the same as in the 1997 general election. In the 1999 European election Liberal Democrat support was nearly 5 per cent less than their 1997 general election vote. So any feeling that, 'A Liberal vote is a wasted vote', evidently has not had much impact on the party's overall performance in SMPS elections.

Despite the passion with which both sides in the SMPS versus PR controversy argue their case, the impact of electoral systems on the level and quality of electoral participation is not sufficiently strong or certain for it to be decisive in determining which system should be used in any particular election. There is little evidence that new electoral systems create confusion amongst voters. But equally it appears that people are not much influenced to turn out by whether or not their vote appears likely to have an influence on the outcome of an election.

The role of elections

The second set of claims about SMPS versus more proportional systems are about two different conceptions of the proper role of parliamentary elections in a modern liberal democracy. Advocates of SMPS argue that elections are primarily about choosing a government. What matters is whether an electoral system makes it possible to hold the current government to account and replace it with an alternative if voters are disappointed with its performance. A key strength of SMPS is that the party that wins most votes usually wins a clear majority of seats, even though it may well have won less than half the vote – because third parties usually receive little reward. This feature means that who becomes Prime Minister is determined directly by who can win the most votes, and not by post-election coalition bargaining between multiple parties. The winning party also commonly has a sufficient legislative majority to deliver 'strong', effective and stable government. However, at the same time governments often make decisions in the knowledge that it will take only a relatively small proportion of the electorate to switch sides for the principal opposition party to replace them in office at the next election.

Advocates of more proportional systems, in contrast, regard elections as primarily about the election of a representative assembly. They suggest that the legislature should be a microcosm of the political opinions of the country as a whole, so that the House of Commons can adequately represent and reflect public opinion in its deliberations. They see no problem in who forms the next government being determined by a process of post-election coalition bargaining – because if each party is represented in the legislature in proportion to its share of the vote then any majority government formed will have the backing of a majority of voters. It is undesirable, they argue, to give an artificial majority to a government in fact based on only a minority of voters' support.

This dispute is a choice about competing values, so empirical evidence cannot help us judge whether elections should be about choosing a government or electing a representative legislature. But we can establish the degree to which recent experience of British elections upholds the claims that are made by both sides about the ability of their preferred electoral system to facilitate the ends that they advocate. Is it the case that SMPS gives voters a choice between alternative governments? And are the alternatives that have been used in recent British elections sufficiently proportional to ensure that a majority government can only be formed by parties which have won a majority of the vote between them?

At first glance, the experience of recent British general elections has more than amply confirmed the claims that are made on behalf of SMPS. In 1992 the Conservatives won a narrow victory with just under 43 per cent support. Five years later in 1997 the Labour opposition defeated the incumbent Conservative government, winning an overwhelming overall majority of 166 on just over 44 per cent of the vote in Great Britain. Labour repeated this feat in 2001 with a majority of 167 on just 42 per cent of the vote. So an alternation of government and clear overall majorities have seemingly been delivered in abundance.

Yet all is not as it seems. There is no simple relationship of votes to seats won that voters can know in advance. First, comparing the winning vote shares in 2001 with those in 1992 and 1997, Labour in 2001 got less support than the Conservatives' in 1992 – yet won huge majorities. The Tories in 1992 on the same vote share secured a majority of just 21 – which proved insufficient to withstand the by-election losses and defections that the government endured over the next five years. Second, the Liberal Democrats in 2001 won just under 19 per cent of the vote, well below the 26 per cent high tide support of the Liberal/SDP Alliance in 1983. Yet whereas the Alliance secured just 23 seats in 1983, the Liberal Democrat vote in 2001 earned the party 52 seats, its highest tally since 1929.

These apparent inconsistencies in the operation of SMPS raise important doubts about the claims made on its behalf. While it might be considered defensible for the electoral system to give the winning party a bonus so that it has on overall majority, it would not seem reasonable for different parties to receive a different sized bonus when they win an election with a similar share of the vote. And if it is considered reasonable for the electoral system to discriminate against small parties, should citizens not be able to anticipate that this discrimination will be consistent from election to election, and indeed from party to party? But recent experience in Britain indicates that SMPS cannot be relied upon to display these two qualities at all.

Just how far SMPS currently treats Labour more favourably than the Conservatives is shown hypothetically in Table 6.3. This analysis starts from the outcome of the 2001 general election and looks at what would happen to the parties' seats if there different swings of the size indicated in each and every parliamentary constituency. (We assume that in all other respects conditions remain exactly as they were in 2001, including the share of the vote won by other parties, the electorate and the turnout in each constituency.) On a 2 per cent swing from Labour to the Conservatives, Labour retains a big majority, but it still has a lead in votes to justify that. On a 4.7 per cent swing Labour and the Conservatives would be level-pegging in terms of votes, but Labour has 140 more seats, giving it an overall Commons majority of 69. The Conservatives would have to win 3.7 per cent *more* of the overall vote than Labour before the current government would no longer have the 330 seats required for an overall majority. The Tories would have to be no less than 8.3 points *ahead* of Labour in votes terms before they had the same number of seats as Labour. Finally, to get an overall Commons majority of 1, the Tories would need to be 11.5 points ahead of Labour.

So SMPS is currently biased towards Labour, such that there appears to be a danger that a future Conservative victory in votes may not be reflected in a victory in terms of seats. Moreover there is a minor precedent for this happening. In February 1974 the Conservatives won 0.8 per cent more support than Labour, but ended up with four seats fewer than Labour. Such a bias can occur because the SMPS does not follow any consistent law on the reward that parties gets in seats for any given victory in terms of votes shares. The outcome all depends on geographical

Table 6.3 How changes from the 2001 pattern of votes under SMPS would affect Labour and Conservative seats

% swing to Con:	% Votes			Number of seats			Outcome
	Con	Lab	Lab lead over Con	Con	Lab	Lab lead over Con	
No change	32.7	42.0	9.3	166	413	247	Lab overall majority
2	34.7	40.0	5.3	184	401	217	Lab overall majority
4.7	37.4	37.4	0	224	364	140	Lab overall majority
6.5	39.2	35.5	-3.7	263	329	66	Lab just loses majority
8.8	41.5	33.2	-8.3	297	297	0	Hung Parliament
9.3	42.0	32.7	-9.3	305	290	-15	Hung Parliament
10.4	43.1	31.6	-11.5	330	269	-61	Tory majority of 1
12	44.7	30.0	-14.7	351	249	-102	Tory overall majority

Notes: There are 659 seats in the Commons, so a government needs to have 330 seats for a majority over all other parties.
Source: Curtice and Steed (2001)

patterns, on how the main parties' votes are distributed across the local constituencies. At all the general elections since 1987 Labour's vote has been more efficiently distributed than that of the Conservatives. Labour does better in smaller constituencies, both those with smaller electorates and those with lower turnout levels. Labour has increased its vote most in seats that were previously marginal between itself and the Conservatives, and its vote has grown least in its safe seats (Curtice 2001). Between them these two patterns were responsible for John Major's lack of a safe majority in 1992 and Tony Blair's unusually large majorities in both 1997 and 2001.

Of course, it is not inevitable that the current bias in Labour's favour will persist. Some of Labour's advantage from winning more seats in smaller constituencies will be pruned back by a review of parliamentary boundaries currently under way, which perhaps might ensure that any future Conservative lead in votes will also be reflected in a lead in seats. Yet a clear danger that it will not be so remains. SMPS simply cannot be relied upon to fulfil consistently the claims that are made on its behalf by its advocates.

Turning to the second inconsistency identified above, there has been an apparent decline in plurality voting system's discrimination against smaller parties. Again this effect (which is proclaimed as a certain virtue by SMPS advocates) actually depends on how a party votes are distributed across constituencies. A medium or small party that wins most of its vote in a small number of constituencies can do relatively well at winning seats. Only a smaller party whose vote is scattered evenly across the country suffers. In 1983 the Liberal/SDP Alliance vote was very evenly spread, but this was less true of the Liberal Democrat vote in 2001 – hence the party's better reward in terms of winning seats. (Of course, the Liberal Democrats in 2001 also benefited from the slump in Tory support, since they compete differentially with Conservatives at constituency level. Even so, if the relative Tory and Liberal Democrat votes were restored to 1983 levels, but with the 1997 pattern of voting across areas, the Liberal Democrats would win more seats than they did in 1983). At the other extreme amongst smaller parties, Plaid Cymru's vote in Westminster election is so highly concentrated in a small number of constituencies that its 0.8 per cent of support in Great Britain was almost proportionately rewarded in 2001 with 0.6 per cent of the seats. So once again what is thought to be a key characteristic of SMPS in fact depends on electoral geography. So it becomes more understandable that despite the continued use of SMPS in Commons elections, nearly one in eight of the MPs elected in 2001 now sit for parties other than Labour or the Conservatives.

If there is reason to doubt whether SMPS is a reliable mechanism for meeting the aims of its advocates, what can be said of the claims put forward by advocates of more proportional systems? Have the new systems shown so far that they reliably deliver a sufficiently proportional outcome, such that only a party or coalition of parties with a majority support commands a majority of the seats? Table 6.4 shows immediately that some of the alternative electoral systems strictly fail this test. After the 1999 election, Scotland has been governed by a Labour–Liberal Democrat coalition with 46 per cent of the votes but 56 per cent of the Scottish Parliament's 129 seats. In Wales a Labour–Liberal Democrat coalition was formed in October 2000 with 57 per cent of the Assembly's 60 seats, supported by 48 per cent of the electorate – although this is admittedly quite close to majority support, since any election system must have some small distortions. In the Greater London Assembly there is no formal executive, but the Assembly is run by a less formal Labour–Liberal Democrat–Green coalition, supported by 56 per cent of voters and with nearly 66 per cent of the assembly seats. In the European Parliament there is also no executive formed, but the outcome was far from being exactly proportional.

Disproportionalities occur for several reasons (see Curtice and Steed 2000). In Scotland and Wales there were insufficient party list seats to overcome the over-representation of Labour in the outcome of the SMPS contests, and the top-up seats were allocated on a regional and not a national basis. In all four elections in Table 6.4, a particular counting method was used to allocate seats (called the D'Hondt formula), which is somewhat favourable to larger parties (Lijphart 1994). And in all four elections very small parties did not get the minimum votes needed to win a list seat, which effectively varied from around 5 to 7 per cent in Scotland and Wales, to 7 to 8 per cent in the European Parliament elections (Dunleavy and Margetts: 302). In London a party must by law win 5 per cent of the list vote before it can win a list seat. These thresholds severely limit the ability of other smaller parties to win seats, and mean that larger parties are still somewhat over-represented. The bigger the vote going to the smaller parties, the stronger this effect is. So proportional electoral systems are never perfectly proportional and hence the executives formed from them may well be supported by less than 50 per cent of voters.

The Supplementary Vote as used in London and other recent mayoral elections might be expected to rectify this problem, for in the event that no candidate wins a majority outright, under this system voters' second preferences are taken into account. Yet in the London Mayoral election, the victor Ken Livingstone's share of the first and second preference votes counted by SV was still only 49 per cent of the valid first preference vote. Equally in twelve subsequent uses of the system to elect

Table 6.4 Seats and votes in recent PR elections

Party	Scotland 1999		Wales 1999		London 2000		European Parliament 1999	
	% vote	% seats	% vote	% seats	% vote	% seats	% vote	% seats
Labour	34	43	35	47	30	36	28	33
Conservative	15	14	17	15	29	36	36	41
Lib Dem	12	13	13	10	15	16	13	12
Nationalist	27	27	31	28	–	–	5	5
Green	4	1	3	0	11	12	6	2
Others	8	2	2	0	15	0	12	7

Notes: The vote percentage shown is the party list (or top up) vote in the three AMS elections, and the single party list vote for the European Parliament. 'Others' includes Northern Ireland parties for the European elections.
Source: Dunleavy and Margetts (2001: 308).

Mayors in various parts of England in 2002, only on five occasions did the victor have a majority of the initially expressed vote. This occurs because some voters do not give a second preference, or allocate it to a candidate who gets eliminated from the second round by not being in the top two. In the London Mayoral election 17 per cent of those who voted gave no second preference; and amongst voters for London candidates outside the top two, almost two thirds did not give their second preference to Livingstone or Norris, who were in the run-off second stage (Cracknell and Hicks 2000).

It should also be noted that the Alternative Vote Plus system recommended by the Jenkins Commission would also fail to ensure that national governments have the support of a majority of the electorate – because no more than 20 per cent of Commons seats would be allocated on a proportionate basis, not enough to offset the SMPS biases in the local constituencies. Also the top-up seats would be allocated in only ones and twos, county by county. The commission itself accepted that its system would still have given the largest party an overall majority at three of the four elections held between 1983 and 1997, as would also apply for the 2001 election.

So whatever the merits of the different roles of elections put forward by the advocates of SMPS and more proportional systems, in truth there are important weaknesses in the arguments of both camps. In neither case can it be said that the instrument chosen to fulfil the role they have in mind is a reliable and consistent means of ensuring that that role is fulfilled. SMPS does not always ensure that the (correct) winner has a safe overall majority; neither does it consistently discriminate against third parties. Meanwhile more proportional systems are not necessarily sufficiently proportional to ensure majority governments have the expressed will of a majority of the electorate. The reality of electoral systems evidently does not always match their rhetoric.

Representation

What kind of representation is delivered by different electoral systems? Advocates for SMPS argue it ensures that all MPs are accountable to a clearly defined body of voters and encourages them to represent the interests of all their constituents (Bogdanor 1985, Carey and Shugart 1992). To be elected individual candidates need more votes than anyone else locally. They cannot get elected simply by being at the top of their party's list, nor in marginal seats can they rely only on being popular amongst the voters who support their party anyway. Incumbent MPs are encouraged to develop a reputation as an effective individual local representative, in the hope of winning over marginal votes from other parties' supporters locally. They can do this by taking up the grievances of individual constituents in their dealings with government and other organizations and by advocating the interests of their constituency as a whole in Parliament. And voters have a valuable reassurance that there is always someone specific to whom they can turn if they feel unfairly treated by the state.

Those who back more proportional systems are in contrast not as concerned about MPs' ability to advocate their constituents' interests as they are to ensure that the legislature as a whole reflects the social diversity of society as a whole (Plant 1991). As well as accurately mirroring the balance of political opinion in the country, a legislature should also more broadly reflect the distribution of different genders, ethnic backgrounds and other social characteristics in the whole population. Multi-member constituencies are an essential feature of more proportional systems, and they make it easier for parties to put forward a much more socially balanced ticket than SMPS with its single member constituencies whose MPs are drawn mainly from the predominant social groups. Any party putting forward a list for election will want to include someone from each of the key social groups in an area, or run the risk of losing votes as a result.

How valid are these theoretical claims in practice? For SMPS advocates to have an effective point then some voters at least must be willing to vote on the basis of how good the incumbent MP is (or another party's candidates would be) as their local representative, rather than just because they represent the particular party they support. There is some evidence of such an effect. The MPs with most incentive and opportunity to develop a personal vote are those who have captured a marginal seat from an MP of a different party at the previous election, who might fear that their seat could easily return to the opposition if the tide of political fortune reverses at the next election. For these MPs any extra votes that could be gathered by developing a personal vote could make the difference between future victory or defeat. And indeed MPs in such circumstances have tended at recent elections to perform more strongly than the party they are representing, suggesting that they have been able to develop a favourable personal reputation over the previous four or five years (Norton and Wood 1994).

Even so, the scale of such personal voting should not be exaggerated. It appears that an energetic local MP in a marginal seat can typically win an extra 1,500 votes at most. Such a total could be crucial in a tight contest and probably helped some new Labour MPs in 1997 to defend highly marginal seats successfully in 2001. But notice that a personal vote could do nothing to save those Conservative MPs who saw their party swept away by an electoral avalanche in 1997. Equally, the degree to which MPs are in any form of contact with individual constituents should not be exaggerated either. The 1997 British Election Study found that just one in eight voters reported having had any kind of contact with their local MP over the previous year, with the vast majority of people not even receiving a direct mail shot from their representative.

Moreover it is far from clear that modest but potentially significant personal voting only occurs under SMPS. Proponents of AMS argue that it encourages voters to vote for whoever they think is the best individual candidate in the local SMPS contests that are the first stage of AMS, secure in the knowledge that they can still vote for their preferred party at the party list stage. So voters might be expected to be *more* likely to cast a personal vote under AMS than under SMPS. And certainly in the 1999 Scottish and Welsh elections those who had already made a name for themselves in their constituency as a Westminster MP consistently outperformed their less well-known colleagues. The Labour rebel Dennis Canavan was able to secure election to the Scottish Parliament in 1999 within his local area, standing as an Independent MP against the official Labour candidate endorsed by the Labour leadership. And of course, in the 2000 London mayoral election under SV, Ken Livingstone won even more dramatically as an independent, after the national Labour leadership put in place a more acceptable official Labour candidate via an electoral college process. So while some personal voting may occur under SMPS, it clearly can occur in other proportional systems as well.

What of the claim that voting systems using multi-member constituencies will create legislatures more representative of the social composition of society as a whole? On one aspect of this proposition, the representation of women, alternative systems appear to do better than SMPS. Less than one in five MPs elected to the Commons in 2001 under SMPS were women, compared with two in five of those elected to the Greater London Assembly in 2000 and the Welsh Assembly in 1999. Over a third of Scottish MSPs in 1999 were also women. But multi-member constituencies do not necessarily ensure that more women are elected, for in the 1999 European election only a quarter of MEPs elected were women.

Nor is there any simple relationship between the use of party lists and the level of female representation (Curtice and Steed 2000). In the Scottish and Welsh elections, women were in fact relatively more successful in the local SMPS contests than they were on the party lists. The main factor enhancing women's representation here was a change in Labour rules requiring constituencies to be paired in twos, with each pair selecting two candidates, one a man and the other a woman.

Similarly in the European elections for 1999 the only major party to achieve gender balance was the Liberal Democrats party, who required that all of their regional party lists should intersperse male and female candidates equally. So it is party selection rules rather than electoral systems per se that determine whether gender balance is achieved.

Overall it appears that claims about the nature of representation provide little reason to prefer one kind of electoral system over another. Personal voting, and the local constituency work by MPs that supposedly goes with it, is not all that important, nor is it found only under SMPS. And multi-member party lists will not necessarily result in elected winners being more socially representative.

Conclusion

The available evidence casts considerable doubt on the validity of many of the claims often made on behalf of SMPS or more proportional systems. It appears that using SMPS or one of its alternatives does not have a sufficiently strong impact on the level or quality of electoral participation for this to be a sufficient reason for preferring one rather than the other. Equally neither side appears to have a decisive case when it comes to the kind of representation that the various systems encourage. So the choice of electoral system seems to depends on our view about what we want elections to do – directly elect our governments, or produce a representative assembly. But neither SMPS nor many of its proportional alternatives can necessarily be relied upon to deliver the values with which it is associated. Given such intellectual uncertainty, it is odds on that the electoral system for the House of Commons will be determined by politicians' calculations of political advantage, and not the lessons of dispassionate analysis of how Britain's alternative proportional electoral systems have worked in practice.

Chapter 7

Political Parties and the Party System

RICHARD HEFFERNAN

In Britain, as elsewhere, political parties find themselves challenged by electoral volatility, falling turnout, declining membership and disappearing activists. Interest groups and new social movements seem increasingly the primary articulaters of public opinions and concerns, as do the journalists and commentators of the news media. One single-issue pressure group, the Royal Society for the Protection of Birds, claims more members than all the parties put together, and a staggering 98.5 per cent of British citizens do not even belong to a political party. For some commentators, parties, previously 'engines of civic activism have become the symptoms of civic malaise' (Gamble and Wright 2002: 123).

Although they face testing times, parties retain a number of important roles in liberal democracies, among them socializing citizens as voters and mobilizing voters as citizens. Most importantly, parties continue to link citizens to political institutions, and parties alone still facilitate the key process of representative government, determining which actors hold what legislative and executive posts at national, regional and local levels. Having created 'political identities, framed electoral choices, recruited candidates, organized elections, defined the structure of legislative politics, and determined the outputs of government' (Dalton and Wattenberg 2002: 262), British parties provide key linkage between citizens and the state, and as a result, 'democracy without political parties is unthinkable' (ibid).

As *political organizations*, parties recruit and train political elites, propel them into public office, and articulate and aggregate a range of political interests. They then express those interests within government on a local and a national level. As *electoral actors*, parties provide choices for voters and help attach voters to the political process by creating ties of affinity. They instil a sense of identification and partisan loyalty, and also facilitate citizen participation. As *governing institutions*, parties form governments, organize majorities within the government,

119

and provide the elected personnel of government. They develop and enact public policies, help translate public preferences into government action, and make government accountable to citizens at large by providing electoral choices at subsequent elections.

The three major British parties, Labour, the Conservatives and the Liberal Democrats, find themselves in government or opposition at a variety of levels: the national, in Westminster and Whitehall; the regional, including the Scottish Parliament and the Welsh Assembly; the local; and, much less significantly, within the European Parliament. Recent developments in British politics have impacted on parties in new and significant ways and this chapter considers changes that have taken place between parties and the electorate and within parties themselves. Parties have reformed themselves: 'First, parties have tended to become more centralised and professionalised; second, they have become more cognizant of citizens opinions and demands; and third, party and (especially) leader image has come to assume a prominent thematic role in campaigning' (Farrell and Webb 2002: 123). As a result, British parties have changed significantly in the past thirty or so years, particularly in regard to the electoral linkages they possess, the organizational structures they develop and the policies they present. Such party change has inevitably sponsored change within the party system, the overarching framework within which British parties operate.

Electoral change and its impacts: the fragmentation of the British party system

In May 1997, having been effectively dead in the water in 1983, 1987 and 1992, the Labour Party secured its largest parliamentary majority ever, a thumping 179, the largest enjoyed by any single party since 1906. In June 2001, Labour was re-elected in another landslide, this time with a majority of 166, securing a second term with a more than solid majority for the first time in the party's history. In terms of the party system, the changing nature of British party politics is well attested. Labour and the Conservatives won 90.3 per cent of the vote between them in 1945–70, but only 74.8 per cent in 1974–97. The vote of the principal third party, the Liberal Democrats (and before them the Liberals and the SDP/ Liberal Alliance), averaged 7.1 per cent in 1945–70, but 19.1 per cent in 1974–97. Whereas 92 per cent of seats in 1970 were direct contests between Labour and the Conservatives, this fell to 65 per cent in 1992. In 1951, 96.8 per cent of voters supported either Labour or the Conservatives on a turnout of 82.5 per cent. In 2001, only 74.8 per cent of voters did so, and turnout had fallen to 59.4 per cent. The 'golden

---

Box 7.1 Party system development since 1945

- the 1945–70 period was the classic era of two-party majoritarianism;
- the 1970–97 period might be best described as two-party-plus majoritarianism, as other parties, most notably the Liberals and nationalist parties in Scotland and Wales grew in strength; and
- the post-1997 period has seen the further fragmentation of this two-party plus system, although the emergence of a multi-party system at Westminster (and in government in Whitehall) remains stymied by Britain's plurality electoral system

---

era' of two-party politics, something based upon strong and stable levels of loyal party support, is no more.

The British party system has changed, but in many ways remains the same. More parties compete for votes, while only two parties, Labour and the Conservatives, are still best placed to form a single party government by winning an overall majority of seats in the House of Commons. The established party system has changed, but it has been fragmented, not overturned. The two-party system dominated by Labour and the Conservatives has been eroded, particularly in light of the post-1974 resurgence of the 'third party', the Liberal Democrats, and the growth in support for nationalist parties in Scotland and Wales.

Yet, while the two-party system has clearly expanded to embrace additional parties, only the two major parties, Labour and the Conservatives, can form a single party government under Britain's electoral system. This is why, at the same time as it can no longer be described as a classical two-party system, Britain cannot be described as a genuine multi-party system. As its party system fragments, Britain may be described as a 'two-party-plus' system, particularly as multi-party systems can be discerned as coming into being in the devolved assemblies in Scotland and Wales.

Party change, and therefore party system change, while prompted by a number of social, political and economic variables, owes much to changes enacted in two key party environments. Firstly, changes in established electorates of belonging from which parties draw support, something which is reflected in declining levels of party identification. Secondly, an alteration in the electoral system. Of these, the first environment has seen significant change in the past twenty-five years, but the second, at least in regard to Westminster elections, remains the same.

Changes in established electorates of belonging and declining levels of party identification

Over time, the hitherto reliable electoral bases on which the two major parties depended, their *electorates of belonging*, have dwindled in both size and significance. Electorates of belonging, first identified by pioneering studies of voting behaviour in the 1940s, helped explain electoral stability, because electors were identified as supporters of one party or another and voted for their chosen party. The classic model of voter behaviour argued that electors were essentially partisans in their voting behaviour, voting according to their party identification, often in a manner reflecting their occupation and how their parents voted (Butler and Stokes, 1974). Social class mattered enormously, and, so called 'deviant voters' aside (and, to the detriment of the model, there were a great many of these), it was expected working-class voters should vote Labour and middle-class voters vote Conservative. Had class determined all electoral outcomes, the Conservative Party would never have won an election, but it was in government for sixty-seven years of the twentieth century. Truth was, working class electors did more likely vote Labour, but many voted Conservative, particularly if they were deferential or patriotic, and certainly if they were politically chauvinistic in their outlook.

Persuasive theories of voting previously owed much to the concept of *party identification*, which was seen as the key to an elector's stable and enduring partisanship. Here, electors 'associate themselves psychologically with one or other of the parties, and this identification has predictable relationships with their perceptions, evaluations and actions' (Campbell *et al.*, 1960: 90, Butler and Stokes 1974). As a form of partisanship, party identification provides a 'perceptual screen' (ibid.) that gave the dominant cue to voting behaviour, just as someone's support for a football team determines his or her attitude to a football match. When combined with related social-group cues, most notably class background, partisan attachment was seen as the major determinant of how electors voted. However, in contrast to past high and stable levels, the past twenty-five years have seen a significant decrease in levels of party identification. Between the 1960s and the 1990s the percentage of strong party identifiers in Britain decreased by 26 per cent (Dalton 2002). Now less than half the electorate have any form of stable identification with either of the major parties, including the Liberal Democrats and the Scottish and Welsh Nationalists (Sanders 2002: 79). Most significantly, by the late 1990s, the percentage of strong identifiers, those sticking with a party through thick and thin, has fallen significantly to 16 per cent (Webb 2000).

British political parties therefore find themselves within an unstable – and, when compared to the past, an increasingly unreliable – electoral marketplace. They compete with one another for votes – and office – by convincing an ever more sceptical electorate that they have a more attractive set of leading politicians and policies than their opponents. Votes, the hard currency in which parties trade, are now more fluid and less reliable, voters being more capricious now than ever before. In large part, this reflects the erosion of group-based politics, a phenomenon encouraged by the decline of collectivism amid the rise of individualism. This has been further exacerbated by rising social mobility, specifically geographical, educational and occupational mobility, the erosion of class as a measure of identity, and the emergence of new political issues that cut across traditional partisan boundaries (Inglehart, 1990; Dalton 2002a). As traditional ties of attachment binding electors to parties have weakened, citizens make their electoral choices with less partisan predisposition. As electoral volatility has risen, party fortunes have been much less predictable and, as a result, the fragmentation of the two-party system has become a reality.

Parties and the electoral system

The demise of the two-party system has been disguised by the lack of proportionality between seats and votes prompted by Britain's Single Member Plurality System (SMPS). Electoral systems have as dramatic an effect on electoral outcomes as do electoral preferences, and SMPS has bolstered Labour and the Conservatives by disproportionably allocating them more seats in the House of Commons. Tony Blair, as did Margaret Thatcher and John Major before him, led his party to victory under an electoral system where a party with the largest minority of the votes cast, some 42–44 per cent, invariably secures a reliable parliamentary majority, some 54–64 per cent of the seats in the House of Commons.

Were British elections decided by a strictly proportional allocation of Commons seats according to votes won, Blair-led Labour would not have formed a single party government in 1997 or in 2001. Most likely, a Labour–Liberal Democrat coalition government would have been formed. As Table 7.1 suggests, SMPS still advantages both Labour and the Conservatives. Although other parties are better represented in Parliament they are still grossly under-represented. The system underpins the relative dominance of Labour and the Conservatives in Westminster. This is because, as Duverger's law long ago suggested, SMPS fashions a 'two-party' system in terms of competition for seats, although electors in Britain have long ago set about creating a 'two-party-plus' system in terms of competition for votes.

Table 7.1   *Vote and seat share, 1979 and 2001 general elections compared*

	1979		2001	
	Vote (%)	Seats (%)	Vote (%)	Seats (%)
Conservatives	43.9	53.6	32.7	25.2
Labour	36.9	42.4	42.0	62.5
Liberal/ Liberal Democrats	13.8	1.7	18.8	7.9
Others	5.4	2.3	6.5	4.4

This situation at Westminster can be contrasted to Scotland and Wales where there are emergent multi-party systems, encouraged by the Scottish Parliament and the Welsh Assembly being elected under a broadly proportional electoral system, the Additional Member System (AMS). At present, under AMS, although Scotland and Wales have been long dominated by the Labour Party in Westminster elections, Labour governs the devolved assemblies only in alliance with the third party, the Liberal Democrats. The Scottish and Welsh party systems are in the process of diverging from the English party system, and under devolution it remains to be seen if this will have an impact on the British party system as a whole. In addition, the British delegation to the European Parliament is now drawn from seven parties, with the Green Party and the UK Independence Party winning seats in 1999 along with the Scottish Nationalists and Plaid Cymru. In 1994, only four parties were elected. This is because the 1999 election was held under a Proportional Representation List system, and the 1994 election under SMPS. Of course, irrespective of whichever electoral system applies, European elections remain second-order elections of little importance or policy significance. Obviously, PR list systems proportionally convert votes cast into seats won, but this does not happen in Westminster elections under SMPS.

The reform of SMPS in elections to devolved assemblies has considerably altered the dynamic of party competition in Scotland and Wales. This has more in common with consensus democracies rather than majoritarian democracies (Lijphart 1999). Party interactions are being changed as a result, and this has encouraged the emergence of multi-party systems and coalition governments in Scotland and in Wales. Not so at Westminster. Although we can clearly see an erosion of the classic two-party system *within the electorate*, the continuation of that system *at Westminster* owes much to the electoral system in spite of increasing electoral volatility born of partisan dealignment.

Organizational change: the emergence of the modern British political party

SMPS and its effects notwithstanding, as Britain's established electorates of belonging have shrunk, the 'two-party-plus' system has emerged. Established parties still guide citizens' political behaviour and encourage some degree of political loyalty, but such loyalty is undoubtedly weaker in the modern political world. The ties of attachment binding electors to parties have become looser and looser, electoral behaviour is much more volatile, issue voting more prevalent, and parties have had to change organizationally in order to successfully compete in the electoral marketplace.

Organizational change in line with electoral demands is not new. The post-1867 extension of the franchise, finally embracing all men over the age of 21 in 1918 and all women in 1928, had a dramatic effect on parties and the role they saw themselves playing. Having to tout for votes in a much larger electoral marketplace, parties had to reinvent themselves. The traditional form of organization, the elite based cadre party, was unable to effectively mobilize citizens as voters or socialize them into party supporters. The era of the mass party therefore came into being. Although a social democratic party such as Labour, established by the trade unions to provide for the independent representation of labour within parliament, naturally possessed a mass base, one drawing on both an individual and affiliated membership, the Conservatives had to acquire one, and did so quickly and successfully.

As 'mass parties', both parties organized a large membership base, pursued firm ties to their key electorates, and continually emphasized their central ideological traditions. Now, at a time when electors are far less likely to possess a party identity or vote according to that party identification, parties have to respond to 'issue voters' (Sanders 2002). While still seeking a broad electoral appeal, one beyond their traditional electorate, parties have divested themselves of the 'bureaucratic form' of the mass party. Cast adrift within the de-aligned electorate, Britain's 'catch-all' parties have had to become 'electoral professional' parties, altering their organizational form as a result of broadening their electoral base (Panebianco 1988, Webb 2000). They have put in place campaigning structures that empower the party's office holders, principally the parliamentary leadership, and de-emphasize the role of members and party bureaucrats.

Box 7.2   The modern electoral professional party

- is dominated by a powerful and predominant leadership,
- has a smaller membership;
- has a very low voter/ member ratio;
- is orientated toward 'opinion electorates' rather than 'electorates of belonging';
- emphasizes issues or personalities rather than ideology;
- its campaign professionals supersede members and representative bureaucrats; and
- it is increasingly reliant on corporations, wealthy individuals or government for financial support (Panebianco 1988, Wolinetz 2002, Koole 1996)

The historical transformation of parties embraces a transition from old style pre-democratic 'cadre parties' through large membership based 'mass bureaucratic parties' to 'catch all parties' to 'electoral professional parties' (Wolinetz 2002, Katz and Mair 2002, Webb 2000). In turn, electoral professional parties are in turn giving way to 'modern cadre parties', such parties being elite driven, top down organizations, and lacking a genuine mass membership base. Such parties seek to satisfy their desire for office by maximizing their potential vote. Less reliant on voter loyalty than before, they hustle for votes, finding ways of selling their policy preferences by opinion polling and focus groups, projecting themselves in ways suggested by campaign professionals (O'Shaughnessy 1990, Scammell 1995, Wring 1996). Here, party office holders, the senior leaders, seek votes by eschewing a purely sectional interest or appeal. Whilst having to deploy a programme for government, parties no longer tailor their programme to its 'electorate of belonging', but to a broader 'national interest'.

As such, the rise of the electoral professional party has been accompanied by a decline in party membership. Labour membership, having risen under Tony Blair from 280,000 in 1992 to 420,000 in 1997, fell to some 280,000 in January 2002. The Conservatives currently claim a membership of some 318,000, although 256,797 members voted in the September 2001 leadership ballot between Iain Duncan Smith and Kenneth Clarke. Trailing the field, as one might imagine, are the Liberal Democrats with 100,000 members, although only 51,000 members cast votes in the 1999 leadership contest. Labour's brief resurgence in the mid 1990s is seemingly a blip in a spiralling downward trend. The calamitous collapse in party membership is best evidenced by that of the

Table 7.2 *Contrasting party membership, 1953 to 2002*

	Conservatives	Labour
1953	2,805,000	1,005,000
1975	1,120,000	675,000
1982	1,200,000	420,000
2002	318,000	280,000

Notes: Conservative Party membership figures for 1953, 1975 and 1982 are estimates, the party not establishing a national membership roll until 1999.

Young Conservatives, which had 160,000 members in 1949, a time when it was a finishing school for thousands of aspirant Tory MPs, but mustered only 5,000 members in 1994. Such is the parlous state of party membership, only 12,000 London Labour Party members – in a city with a population of over 7 million – cast a vote in the November 2002 ballot to select Labour's 2004 candidate for Mayor. While all parties would prefer to have a larger membership base, the truth is that they now have to function without one. In changing from 'exercises in mass mobilization toward professionally managed enterprises that sought to project the best possible image' (Wolinetz 2002: 160), party campaigns now appeal beyond committed party supporters to all voters. In this respect, party members have perhaps become a luxury party leaders conclude they do not need.

In becoming detached from traditional electorates of belonging and the members and monies these provided, parties find themselves in need of alternative resourcing. Corporate funding helps plug the gap, but modern parties often exploit their relationship with the state, given the fact that neither executive nor legislative government is possible without their participation. With dwindling membership inevitably come cash flow problems. All parties now raise revenue in fundamentally different ways to how they used to, and are now predominantly funded by donations, either from wealthy individuals or from big business.

In Labour's case 8 per cent of its income currently comes from members' subscriptions, 27 per cent from trade union affiliation fees, and 35 per cent from donations. In the Conservatives' case around 90 per cent of their funding comes from political donations, and donations account for 66 per cent of the Liberal Democrats' funding. In recent years corporate funding has flooded to Labour. This perhaps testifies to Tony Blair's business friendly image and the party changes he has introduced. Having provided no less than 75 per cent of Labour's funding in the early 1980s, trade unions now only provide some 27 per cent. Indeed, such is the degree of trade union opposition to much of Labour's policy, particularly its commitment to a Thatcherite flexible labour market and the privatization of the public sector, some unions, particularly the GMB, UNISON and the RMT, have significantly reduced the monies they provide. There can perhaps be no greater proof of the organizational transformation of the Labour Party than its vastly changed financial base. Donations from corporations and wealthy individuals such as Paul Hamlyn, Michael Ondaatje, and Lord Sainsbury, Bernie Ecclestone, Lakshmi Mittal, and Richard Desmond, owner of Express Newspapers and any number of Razzle Magazines, largesse invariably solicited by Blair's personal fundraiser, Lord Levy, now help pay the party's bills.

The Conservatives have been recently bankrolled by a mere handful of donors. Under William Hague, party leader 1997–2001, Michael Ashcroft, the controversial businessman and party treasurer, was its most high-profile donor. At the 2001 general election, the Tory campaign was funded by two big donations, from John Paul Getty Jnr and the bookmaker Stuart Wheeler, who each gave £5m. Such is the financial pressures currently afflicting all parties, Labour found itself some £9 million in debt in mid 2002. For some commentators, the crisis of party funding is such, state funding of political parties may well find itself slowly creeping up the political agenda as a result. This is particularly so, when parties can spend between £12 and £15 million at a general election, and when membership subscriptions are likely to continue to fall.

Intra-party politics: privileging the party in public office

Political parties contain a number of strata, most particularly leaders, sub-leaders and non-leaders (May, 1973). Located in the extra-parliamentary party, party members are non-leaders, and they may be further subdivided into active and non-active members. The formal distribution of power within parties is skewed toward leaders rather than members, although sub-leaders, MPs not within the leadership, possess some influence over the party as members of the parliamentary party. The division between the parliamentary and the extra-parliamentary party is now more acute then ever, and the 'party in public office', the leadership of the parliamentary party, had become more powerful over time. Labour Party campaigning has been almost wholly focused on Blair as Labour leader, and both Iain Duncan Smith and Charles

Kennedy (for good or ill) dominate as the public face of their parties. There is nothing intrinsically new in this, but the political centrality of the party leader is a key feature of the growing personalization of politics. While political leaders have always been central to the British political process, this owes much to the centrality of the news media in modern party electioneering. As a result, party leaderships run their political parties from the centre, and parties are geared to serve first, the needs of the leader, second, the parliamentary leadership, and only third, local affiliates.

As the power of the parliamentary party has increased, the degree of autonomy possessed by its leadership has also increased. Because active non-leaders are more radical than leaders, leaders therefore prefer non-leaders not to restrict their autonomy in competing in the electoral marketplace. Parties therefore institutionally deny non-leaders with the opportunities and resources that enable them to influence party policy, so allowing leaders to lead from the front.

Today is certainly the age of the non-mass membership. Yet, however few in number they are, members provide much needed income and support. They cheerlead their leaders, certainly, but active members also run the party at a local level, particularly in local government. They also provide key personnel from which the national party will draw, specifically by selecting parliamentary candidates. This is why, while denying members real power, parties have periodically to consult them and, in some cases, provide them with certain powers. For example, whereas MPs used to elect the party leader, members now elect them, the power of nomination being retained by MPs. The Liberal Democrats have a members' ballot, the Labour Party an electoral college comprising MPs, members and affiliated trade unionists, and the Conservatives Party allow members to choose between two candidates presented to them by the parliamentary party.

Recent party reforms, introduced across all parties, have established mechanisms enabling party members to individually – but not necessarily collectively – express views on matters leaders present to them. For example, Labour balloted its members in 1995 on reform of its aims and objectives, Clause Four of its constitution, and in 1997 on its draft election manifesto, and the Conservatives balloted its members on organizational reform in 1997 and on its policy on European Monetary Union in 1998. In each of these cases members were invited to support or reject proposals presented to them, but not to amend them, or to substitute proposals of their own. This apparent extension of a limited democracy allows members to be reactive, not proactive. It is directed at individual members, not organized active members. This is because

the often disorganized and atomised mass membership of the party
. . . is likely to prove more deferential to the party leadership and
more willing to endorse its proposals. It is in this sense that the
empowerment of the party on the ground remains compatible with,
and may actually serve as a strategy for, the privileging of the party
in public office. (Katz and Mair 2002: 129)

Plebiscitory democracy has been encouraged because it empowers
leaders. As a result, older style forms of party democracy that could challenge them, based around the Annual Conference and the Party
Executive, have been significantly downgraded. For instance, while the
Conservative Party Conference has long been only advisory, its decisions
influential, but never binding, the once powerful Labour Party
Conference has had its role in policy making stripped away. It no longer
can instruct the parliamentary party, and has become to all intents and
purposes a 'main showcase for the Prime Minister, other members of the
government and for a review of progress and achievements' (The Labour
Party 1999: 13). When the 2002 Party Conference called for a review of
the government's Private Finance Initiative by 67.2 per cent to 32.8 per
cent (*The Times*, 1 October 2002), ministers made it immediately clear
they would ignore the vote. Labour *policy deliberation* is delegated to a
National Policy Forum, representing ministers, MPs, party members and
trade unionists, but *policy formation* remains under the direction of the
party leadership and its staffs (see Seyd, 2002). The same may be said, in
different forms, of the Conservatives and the Liberal Democrats.

Party leaders, both Conservative and Labour, have long dominated
their parties. As McKenzie famously noted in the 1950s, party leaders
might take note of party opinion, but they have the ultimate power of
decision:

Effective decision-making authority will reside with the leadership
groups thrown up by the parliamentary parties (of whom much the
most important individual is the party leader), and they will exercise
this authority so long as they retain the confidence of their parliamentary parties. (McKenzie 1964: 635)

Never was a truer opinion expressed, and it is one applicable today, and
perhaps now more than ever. Within the modern Labour, Conservative
and Liberal Democrat parties, party elites are increasingly able to set
out their policy stall as the party's policy stall. Leaders addresses the
electorate – and the party itself – from a distance, making full use of the
news media to frame and disseminate their message, packaging their
appeal, and always seeking favourable media coverage.

Leadership predominance, political collegiality and the party in public office

Political differences are often found within the leadership or between the leadership and elements of its parliamentary party. Since the late 1980s the Conservative Party has been bedevilled by party infighting among the upper reaches of its parliamentary party, most notably regarding Europeans and Eurosceptics, and most recently between traditionalists and modernizers under William Hague and now Iain Duncan Smith. In contrast, Labour, which attempted to kick itself to death in the early 1950s and early 1980s, has chosen not to rock the New Labour boat through infighting. While internal dissension can still be a feature of party life, party loyalty runs deep among MPs, for instinctive tribal and partisan reasons as well as for baser careerist ones.

A party may speak with many voices, but it remains the case that fewer voices than ever seemingly determine its political direction. Leadership predominance, considerably reinforced by modern 'catch-all' electioneering, encourages the marketing and packaging of the party leadership, not the wider political party (Swanson and Mancini, 1996, Scammell 1995, Jones 1993, 1999). Such predominance inevitably grants power, but only provided the leadership is able to deliver the public goods the party wants, principally electoral popularity and policy success. Leaders invariably lead (and may squabble in so doing), and members usual follow or complain (or else exit the party).

Sub-leaders and non-leaders can criticize, however, and disputes over policy can and do arise. Attitudes towards European Monetary Union are one such example. Numerous others may be cited. For example, at the time of writing, Labour MPs are sharply divided over British support for a US-led invasion of Iraq, as was demonstrated by the unprecedented parliamentary revolt in which 139 Labour MPs voted against their government as the Commons voted for war. Such disputes are invariably amplified by a news media always keen to report party divisions. Intra-party disputes have also been evidenced in the wake of recent moves to decentralize power. Devolution deepens regional identities among voters, and may in time encourage party reform, with more power taken from the national parties and given to their Scottish and Welsh counterparts. There has been Labour infighting in London, where Ken Livingstone, denied the Labour nomination for Mayor by a Tony Blair-led fix, romped home as an independent, and in Wales, where Alun Michael, Blair's candidate for leader of the Welsh Assembly, was forced out by his Labour colleagues. Still, parties are dominated, for good or ill, by their elites.

Of course, when speaking of the party leadership, it should be empha-sized that a party leadership is to some degree collegial, not individual.

Tensions and differences are an every day reality within a party's high command. Winston Churchill once rightly advised an MP that 'he would face his opponents in the House of Commons chamber, but sit surrounded by his enemies'. Long established, overlapping, multi-focal enmities within the present Labour elite demonstrate this simple fact. Tony Blair, Gordon Brown, David Blunkett, John Prescott, Robin Cook, and Peter Mandelson have all had their differences, many of them being key players in a number of 'bad blood' networks (Rawnsley 2001, Macintyre 2000).

Although differences can cause significant problems, leaders have to hang together with their fellow leaders, for fear, as they say, of hanging separately. This ultimately prevents political disagreements destabilising a party, but not always. Leaders who do not provide the goods the party needs inevitably see themselves as surplus to the party's requirements, as Michael Foot, Margaret Thatcher and John Major can recently testify. Current debates about the Conservative Party leadership illustrate the point. After the Conservative's 2001 defeat, William Hague, who, despite impressive parliamentary skills, was a weak leader of a hapless party, fell on his sword. The election to succeed him, conducted under new rules whereby MPs select two candidates from which the party membership in the country choose a winner, attracted five candidates, the initial frontrunner, Michael Portillo, joined by Kenneth Clarke from the left, Iain Duncan Smith from the right, and two others, Michael Ancram and David Davis. In the final parliamentary ballot, the result was desperately close, with Portillo, long a fixture on the party's Thatcherite right, but now a declared 'moderniser', being dumped by MPs by a single vote.

As a result, Clarke and Duncan Smith, candidates perhaps symbolizing the European divide that had rent the post-Thatcher Conservative Party, went forward to the membership ballot, won by Duncan Smith, 155,933 votes to 100,864. One year on, however, Duncan Smith has yet

Table 7.3   *MPs' voting in the Conservative leadership race 2001*

	First Ballot	Second Ballot	Third Ballot
Michael Ancram	23	17 (eliminated)	–
Ken Clarke	36	39	59
David Davis	23	18 (withdrew)	–
Iain Duncan Smith	39	42	54
Michael Portillo	50	51	53 (eliminated)

to stamp his authority on a fractious party, and one worried about its electoral prospects. His personal poll ratings are poor, and even normally loyal MPs and members of the front bench express deep alarm at his lack of impact, particularly on the opinion polls, where the Tories were still marooned at around 30 per cent at the beginning of 2003. With the present leader unable to dent Labour's poll lead or mount any sustained opposition, the Conservative leadership looks anything but settled. Indeed, such is the crisis of confidence, whispers of plots to unseat Duncan Smith abound. A Portillo–Clarke axis is said to be eager to oust him in favour of Clarke, Portillo having claimed he no longer wishes to be leader. David Davis, sacked by Duncan Smith as Party Chairman in the summer of 2002, also waits in the wings. Portillo and Clarke represent the 'modernising' wing of the Conservatives, Davis, the 'traditionalists'. Both are ready to pounce, should the underperforming leader fall. With the support of only 15 per cent of Conservative MPs needed to launch a challenge, Duncan Smith's leadership, already decidedly shaky, will most probably be sunk, if he is not able to improve the Conservatives' electoral prospects as the 2001 Parliament unfolds.

Even if the leader enjoys considerable personal power by being 'first amongst equals', party leaderships are composed of multiple actors. Power within the party is not his or her sole prerogative but is shared among party leaders (and other such power brokers within the party). No one is indispensable, or ultimately bigger than the party itself. The post-1994 relationship between Tony Blair and his Chancellor of the Exchequer, Gordon Brown, clearly demonstrates that a degree of collegiality is still to be found within the upper reaches of the party elite (Rawnsley 2001). Similar obligations to work together bound together John Major, Michael Heseltine and Ken Clarke in the latter years of the Major government (Major 1999, Heseltine 2000).

While fewer party members now exercise less and less influence, extra-parliamentary avenues of resistance to leadership direction have been steadily closed down. A 'law of anticipated reactions' does however encourage an underperforming leader to ultimately act only with the support of her or her party. Some leaders, Neville Chamberlain or Edward Heath, perhaps even Margaret Thatcher at the end of her leadership, forget this. Of course, successful leaders enjoy the confidence of their parties, and at worst earn their grudging respect. Tony Blair has commanded substantial support among his Labour MPs, even when pushing reducing social security payments to single parents or cutting disability benefits in 1998 and 1999. While careful to manage the Chancellor, Gordon Brown, Blair enjoys the support of his senior colleagues. This is not unusual. Only seriously underperforming party leaders forfeit party support, such as Margaret Thatcher in 1988–90

Box 7.3   The parliamentary party as key leadership resource

Party leaderships are still collegial to some degree. However, in both government and opposition, a key resource available to the party leadership is a unitary, centralized, and disciplined parliamentary party; and this resource enables a party leadership, able to lead its parliamentary party, to dominate a weak, uninfluential extra-parliamentary party.

---

and John Major for most of the 1992 Parliament. Leading members of the Cabinet or the Shadow Cabinet – but by no means not all of them – can and do check the power of the party leader. He or she can check theirs. Senior party colleagues offer advice to the leader, object to or amend their proposals, and in extreme cases, can veto such proposals.

If never entirely masters in their own house, successive party leaders have drastically reduced the checks and balance their party can bring to bear against them, therefore making the parliamentary party much more powerful than the extra-parliamentary party. This is a key feature of the electoral professional party: '[A]s party organizations adapt to the demands of contemporary democracies, they tend increasingly to revolve around the needs and incentives of the party in public office' (Katz and Mair 2002: 130). For good or ill, policy is decided more and more by the parliamentary leadership and is less and less influenced by the wider membership (Panebianco 1998, Webb 2000). The leadership's policy preferences, not those of the wider membership, invariably are the party's preferences, provided the leadership can carry its parliamentary party.

Political realignment within the reworked British party system

In the golden era of alignment in the 1940s and 1950s, Labour argued for 'collectivism' and 'socialism', the Conservatives 'individualism' and 'freedom'. Labour, eager to change the world for the better, was pitted against the Conservatives, the party ready to prevent the world being changed for the worst. Labour, the party of the left closely allied to the trade unions, set about representing working-class interests by advocating social-democratic politics. The Conservative Party, the party of the centre right, emphasized patriotism, tradition and stability, appealing to the middle classes, property owners and the non-radical working classes. Today this distinction between the parties no longer applies, as a simple comparison between 'New' and 'Old' Labour attests.

Historically, the British party system was characterized by two broad families of ideas. One family might be described as

> left – a belief in the social, reduction in inequality, the provision of public services, regulation of enterprise, rehabilitation of criminals, tolerance and respect for minorities – and another broad family of ideas that might be called right – an honouring of our institutional fabric, a respect for order, a belief that private property rights and profit are essential to the operation of the market economy, a suspicion of workers' rights, faith in the remedial value of punitive justice and distrust of the new. (Hutton 2002: 12–14)

Yet, as Hutton rightly suggests, in Britain 'these distinctions no longer operate. The senior party of the left does not champion the family of liberal left values . . . New Labour cherry picks from both traditions. . . Thus it is the party of both enterprise and regulation, of flexible labour markets and of trade unions, of repression and rehabilitation, of change and no-change' (ibid). Unlike Old Labour, New Labour professes a belief in 'a Third Way because it moves decisively beyond an Old Left preoccupied by state control, high taxes and producer interests' (Blair 1998: 1).

In programmatic terms this is a classic example of far-reaching party change within a reformed party system. Labour's transformation was a response to a series of interrelated electoral, ideological and organizational crises (Shaw 1994). Here, electoral objectives – the need to attract sufficient votes to successfully seek office – dovetailed with dominant ideological preconceptions – the idea that Old Labour had been wedded to wrong policies, 'excessive government spending, high direct taxation, egalitarianism, excessive nationalization, a politicized trade union movement associated with Luddism, and an anti-enterprise culture', a charge first made by the arch-Thatcherite Keith Joseph in 1979 (Heffernan 2001: 23).

The transition from Old to New Labour was a slow, incremental process, enacted over time, for a variety of purposes, but primarily for electoral and ideological reasons. In July 1995, Tony Blair had set out the principal motivation behind the creation of New Labour. 'To become a serious party of government Labour required a quantum leap . . . [we] had to reconstruct our ideology and organization. . .[marking] the long march back from the dark days of the early 1980s when, frankly, we were unelectable' (Blair 1995). Old style redistributive, tax and spend statist politics were out. In their place, market enhancing, supply-side policies which would bring benefits to 'haves' as well as 'have nots', appealing to voters who had hitherto provided the core of the Conservative electoral coalition which propelled Labour into the wilderness after 1979. Old Labour politics were seen to be part and parcel of these economic problems, 'no longer an adequate solution to the problems of an underperforming market economy which was over-regulated, over-governed, over-taxed and over-managed' (Heffernan 2002: 756).

Labour's 1997 policy prescriptions were therefore markedly different from those of the past. In the 1980s, opposing the Thatcher government tooth and nail, the party stood to the left. It now stands to the right, having embraced many of the policies associated with the Thatcher governments. Some commentators describe this as the wholesale abandonment of Labour's social democratic traditions (Leys 1996; Panitch and Leys, 1997). Others suggest Labour has simply modernized its organization and programme (Blair 1998b, Kenny and Smith 2001; Driver and Martell 2002). Others still argue Labour has accommodated its policy and practice to a Britain fundamentally altered by eighteen years of radical Conservative governments of the New Right (Hay 1999, Heffernan 2001).

Whatever the explanation for the transformation of the Labour Party, policy changes brought about under Tony Blair (and his predecessors Neil Kinnock and John Smith), have helped reform the party system, in light of the major party of the left having moved to the right. As Labour has risen and the Conservatives have fallen, the third party, the Liberal Democrats, have successfully built on a firm electoral base, winning 52 seats in 2001 and consolidating their position as the largest third party in the House of Commons since 1929. Undoubtedly, Labour's current policy stance – and the policy record of the Blair government – reflects the fact that ideological differences between the parties has narrowed significantly. All parties are now avowedly post-socialist and pro-market.

With New Labour straddling the centre ground of politics, the British party system has been changed radically. While still flanked by the Conservatives to its right (and so remains the left-placed major party), Labour now finds the Liberal Democrats, the Scottish Nationalists and Plaid Cymru placed firmly to its left, together with the much smaller Greens and such miniscule leftist groupings such as the Socialist Alliance. In moving to its right, Labour has become a reformed centre party, pitching its policy to its left and right alike.

Now firmly established as the third party, the Liberal Democrats continue to present challenges to both Labour and the Conservatives. During the 1997 Parliament, policy differences between Labour and the

Liberal Democrats centred on tax and spend. Led by Paddy Ashdown and then Charles Kennedy, the Liberal Democrats excoriated Labour for its stewardship of the public services, savaging the government in language often reminiscent of Labour's charges against Thatcherite Conservatives in the 1980s. They claimed ministers had done too little, too late, and had squandered the opportunity to make lasting reforms. Proposing a penny increase on income tax to pay for increased spending in education and social services, the Liberal Democrats firmly placed themselves to Labour's left at the 2001 election. Yet, while occupying this space, they still aspire to displacing the Conservatives as Labour's main opponents. This suggests the party should tack to the right, particularly as its target seats are invariably Conservative held marginals, yet it is not clear that Charles Kennedy will totally abandon Paddy Ashdown's efforts to negotiate some settlement with Labour (Ashdown 2000, Denver 2002).

Such is the weakness of the Conservatives, the Liberal Democrats hope to replace them as the main opposition party in British politics, but a recent study shows what is needed is 'a swing from Tory to Lib Dem comparable to that from Tory to Labour in 1997 (about 10%), and a further swing of similar proportions from Conservative to Labour' (Whiteley 2002). Currently in second place in 58 Conservative-held seats (and second to Labour in 51 seats), seats which invariably have large majorities, it is unlikely the Liberal Democrats can overtake the Conservatives without Labour making further inroads into the Conservative vote (ibid). Placed to Labour's left, yet faced with challenging the Conservatives, not Labour, it would seem the Liberal Democrats are not best placed to win over Conservative voters. Such is the political disarray of the Conservatives, however, that Labour and the Liberal Democrats marching separately could erode further their remaining support, something that would prompt a significant reworking of the party system, pushing the Conservatives into third place, in seats gained, if not votes won. We shall have to see if such a scenario transpires. In the meantime, having eventually to choose whether they are more anti-Labour than anti-Conservative, the Liberal Democrats seem happy to fight on two electoral fronts (particularly in the north of England where Labour-Liberal Democrat relations remain hostile). Yet, the party is instinctively closer to Labour than the Conservatives, however, and both parties are in coalition administrations in the devolved Scottish and Welsh assemblies. Should parliamentary arithmetic ever require it, a Labour-Liberal Democrat coalition at Westminster can be quite easily imagined. Facing the proverbial mountain to climb to claw their way back into contention at the next election, the Conservatives are still down, but who can yet say if they are definitely out. Whatever happens, Labour's reinvention has itself reformed the party system, indicating the extent of the seismic shift witnessed in the left–right location of political parties in the past twenty or so years.

The end of traditional party politics?

For good or ill, in spite of the rise of new social movements or the emergence of newer forms of direct democracy, representative government in a liberal democracy can only be facilitated by political parties. The form of party politics, both the party system and the parties that comprise it, is therefore changing, not ending. Changes in political parties, expressed in organizational, institutional and programmatic terms, are far-reaching and permanent. Although the major parties retain many of the trappings

---

Box 7.4   Key features of the modern British political party

- the party leadership, the party in 'public office', is the heart of everything the electoral professional party does, and this has become the key feature of contemporary party politics;
- having transformed themselves into less ideologically pure parties, parties see competence, not ideology, as the key to electoral success, office seeking being increasingly prized over policy seeking.
- while still possessing certain ideological proclivities, parties are no longer tied to certain points in the political spectrum thanks to the preferences of their electorates of belonging. They are freer to roam across that spectrum in their catch-all quest for votes;
- parties compete for votes 'by marshalling more resources in the national party office, by hiring more professionalized and technically skilled staffers, and by maintaining the national party office as the locus for political control' (Dalton and Wattenberg 2002: 269);
- party memberships continue to decrease;
- other than choosing between leadership nominees presented by the parliamentary party, members have nominal consultative, not decisional rights over policy formation;
- election campaigns are now expensively fought out at the centre, not at the locality, local campaigns being mere adjuncts of the national campaign;
- parties now communicate with all of the electorate by means of the news media, and not directly through the party or its members; and
- party resources at the local level have declined, and those at the centre have increased, and money is spent at the centre, not at the locality.

of their pasts, not least their names and some of their historical traditions, they have, in common with parties elsewhere, changed significantly over time. Changes in the party system are as far-reaching as changes in the parties themselves, but it remains to be seen if they are to be as permanent. The deadening effect of SMPS notwithstanding, the British party system remains today a work-in-progress. The post-1992 haemorrhaging of electoral support from the Conservatives aside, British politics has seen party realignment within the existing party system, not electoral dealignment. Although the electoral fortunes of Labour and the Conservatives have been reversed since the 1980s, the ideological conflicts between them now differ fundamentally. In the 1980s the policy programmes of Labour and the Conservatives were almost diametrically opposed as left and right faced off against one another, none more so than in the general election of 1983. This is no longer the case, although each party continues to compete fiercely with the other for votes.

In light of the calamitous defeats of 1997 and 2001 (and having trailed in the polls since 1992) it may be expected the Conservatives will attempt to reform themselves to restore their electoral fortunes. It remains to be seen whether they will be able to do so in as spectacular and successful a manner as did Labour. Any Conservative comeback may not so easily be assumed, particularly in light of the party's performance in 2001. Caution is needed, however. Following successive election defeats the political science literature of the 1980s was littered with books and articles heralding the imminent electoral demise of the Labour Party. Yet, the party not merely survived, but thrived. Before second-guessing the future, we should perhaps analyse the present by looking at the past. Yet, having become catch-all, electoral professional organizations, British parties are no longer what they used to be. As a result, the party system, while outwardly looking the same, is not what it used to be either. Both the system and the parties that comprise it have changed significantly in the past twenty-five years. It remains to be seen if they will change further in the future.

Chapter 8

The Media and Politics

RAYMOND KUHN

The persistent charge of an obsession with spin levelled against the Labour government by its critics illustrates the extent to which the media have become fully implicated in the conduct of contemporary British politics. Such is the everyday interaction of the media and politics that the professionalization of communications behaviour by political actors has become a fact of life. As a result, politicians place great emphasis on mediated leadership, image projection and marketing strategies in the making of their political messages. For example, because policy decisions have to be framed for the media to be sold to the public, the Labour government's news management activities are central to the government's day-to-day modus operandi. This reflects the interdependent nature of the relationship between government and media – and between politicians and political journalists – in the production of political news. The ensuing contests over the news agenda illustrates the limits on the power of political actors to structure news stories and control the framing of issues in the face of a sceptical and sometimes hostile news media.

The political communications media

Given the pervasive mediatization of politics, it is necessary to establish a broad overview of the political communications media, the terrain within which political news is produced, published and broadcast. On this supply side, the main political communications media in Britain remain those which have dominated since the late 1950s: television, national newspapers and, some way behind, radio. Television as a source of political information has continued to expand in the multi-channel digital age, with rolling news channels such as BBC News 24 and specialist outlets such as BBC Parliament complementing traditional news programming on generalist free-to-air channels. The number of radio stations with a news focus has also grown since the start of the 1990s, while the total of national newspaper titles – ten dailies and eleven Sunday papers – has gone up as a result of two new entrants to the Sunday market since the 1997 election, *The Business* and the *Daily Star Sunday*.

In addition, new information and communication technologies such as the Internet increasingly provide alternative means of information distribution. Internet websites differ from traditional media in that they allow a variety of political actors – from mainstream parties to anti-globalization protestors – the possibility of direct access to the public, bypassing the gatekeeping and filtering functions traditionally performed by journalists. At the same time many established media organizations, such as the BBC and the *Guardian*, have established a strong web presence to complement and reinforce news and comment supplied by their traditional offline outlets (Coleman 2001: 683–4).

The Labour government too has made a huge commitment to use of the Internet. Under its project UK Online it has a stated objective of making Britain a fully networked society by 2005 (http://www. ukonline.gov.uk). This involves widening public access to the Internet and ensuring that as many government services as possible are available via web-based technologies. For instance, the Number 10 website, run by a team of three civil servants, was re-launched in February 2000 to promote the UK overseas, communicate government news and infor-mation, explain the role and history of Number 10 as a building and an institution, and demonstrate the Government's commitment to new technology (http://www.number-10.gov.uk). In 2001 the Number 10 website had over 3.2 million visitor sessions and its discussion forums proved so popular that they outgrew the site and had to be moved to the Citizens' Portal. The government's e-Democracy website provides information on how citizens may increase their participation in politics through use of the net, including electronic submission of petitions to Number 10 and the introduction of electronic voting experiments across the country (http://www.e-envoy.gov.uk).

It may be that some of this activity smacks of public relations initia-tives designed to demonstrate Labour's modernizing credentials through a high-profile symbolic presence in the use of new technology. It is certainly too early to make the wide-sweeping claim that 'one-stop, non-stop e-Government portals will revolutionize not just the way public services are delivered but government itself' (Silcock 2001: 91). Yet it is also likely that at a more modest level the Internet is changing how citi-zens interact with government departments and that the public will expect more services to be delivered online where practicable.

Faced with this overall increase in the supply of news and political information, one commentator has recently argued that the 'political public sphere . . . is larger, denser, and accessible to more people than at any previous point in Britain's cultural history, and it continues to expand' (McNair 2000: 39). Moreover, it is not just in terms of the number of media outlets or the amount of content that the provision of political information has grown in recent years. It has also expanded in time, with a 24-hours news culture now firmly part of the mediatized political environment. This poses organizational and resource problems for political communication actors in their attempts to keep on top of – or better still anticipate – fast moving stories. In addition, the supply of information has extended in space, with the instantaneous availability of news delivered from anywhere around the globe. The events of 11 September in the United States were a perfect example of this time-space compression. Within minutes of the terrorist attacks taking place, news media organizations in Britain were taking 'live' feeds from across the Atlantic and clearing their schedules to keep audiences up to date on developments as they happened.

On the demand side, it is difficult to make sweeping generalizations about audience usage of this enlarged political public sphere. Nonetheless, some broad trends can be identified.

First, television has long been the most important source of political information for the majority of the population. This seems set to continue in the near future with the projected growth in the number of households, already around 50 per cent, receiving multi-channel digital broadcasting services.

Second, just as there are more opportunities within the expanded media market for the politically interested citizen to obtain information, there is also greater freedom for audiences to escape from politics by focusing on entertainment content. In a zapping culture, both sets of political communication professionals – sources and journalists – have to compete more than ever before to gain and retain the audience's attention.

Third, while total circulation figures for national newspapers have been on the decline for some time, sales of the elite broadsheet newspapers (such as *The Times*, the *Guardian* and the *Financial Times*) and of the middle-market *Daily Mail* have held up reasonably well in comparison to the popular tabloid press (the *Sun*, *Daily Mirror*, *Daily Star*) and the ailing middle-market *Daily Express*. A similar trend can also be seen in the national Sunday market. This suggests that while there is still a strong demand for print-mediated political journalism, this is largely confined to readers from the upper social categories A, B and C1.

Finally, the number of people regularly using the Internet for political communication remains relatively small. This is in part because the technology has not yet reached the saturation level of television in British households (in 2001 only 33 per cent of voters had home Internet access), in part because the web is a 'pull' technology where consumers actively have to search out information (in contrast to television which is a 'push' technology) and in part because the Internet has come into a news and information market which is already highly saturated (Ballinger 2002: 232). Nonetheless, in time the Internet may come to rival television for some sections of the electorate. For instance, Coleman argues that for 'the younger generation, who are the most turned off by politics, the Internet is already becoming *the* trusted source for political information' (2001: 686, emphasis in the original).

If one aggregates these four demand trends, it is possible to talk, albeit rather schematically, of an information gap in British society. On the one side are those – more affluent, more educated, more interested in politics – who have access to and make selective use of a wide range of political communications media. On the other are those – less affluent, less educated, less interested in politics – who tend to rely overwhelmingly on television, supplemented by the uneven coverage of a tabloid newspaper. Inequalities of access to the Internet have further increased this imbalance between information-rich and information-poor, creating a digital divide which risks further marginalizing already disadvantaged social groups (Silcock 2001: 94–5).

Public relations politics

The professionalization of political advocacy was highlighted by Blumler and Gurevitch in the middle of the 1990s as 'arguably the most formative development in the political communication process of present-day democracies' (Blumler and Gurevitch 1995: 207). The authors supported this thesis largely with reference to the publicity activities of political parties during the short period of election campaigns. There is now a rich academic literature in this field, both cross-national comparative (LeDuc *et al.* 1996, Swanson and Mancini 1996) and with particular reference to the British case (Kavanagh 1995, Norris, 1997b, Crewe *et al.* 1998, Norris *et al.* 1999, Butler and Kavanagh 2002, Geddes and Tonge 2002).

In this context the 2001 election campaign represented more of a consolidation accompanied by some incremental adjustment in parties' campaign methods and media coverage rather than a radical or revolutionary shift. There was certainly nothing comparable to the impact of the arrival of television as an election communications medium in the 1959 contest. It is true that some features of what Norris (1997b) has called post-modern campaigning have entered British electoral practices in recent years: the use of focus groups, the targeting of selected tranches of the electorate and the spread of party websites on the net.

However, the long-awaited 'Internet revolution' has still failed to materialize, with only 18 per cent of voters with Internet access (6 per cent of the total electorate) using this technology for political communication purposes during the campaign (Ballinger 2002: 226).

Essentially the 2001 election was dominated by the traditional mass media rather than specialist 'narrowcast' channels of communication. Moreover, campaigning innovations – John Prescott's fight with an elector aside – had limited impact on what was generally considered by politicians, media and the public alike to have been a lacklustre contest. Finally, there was little worthy of note in the coverage of the campaign by the 'old' media: no dramatic swing-back to the Conservatives in national newspaper partisanship, no face-to-face leadership debate on television and no really new issues to grab voters' attention.

Over and above the behaviour of parties in formal election campaigns, the professionalization of political advocacy has expanded, first, to incorporate other political actors such as corporate organizations, pressure groups and new social movements and, second, to cover the long periods of political communication between elections. As a result, contemporary British politics is now influenced to a significant extent by the promotional culture of a 'public relations democracy' (Davis 2000 and 2002).

The government and major parties are undoubtedly the most visible political actors involved in this self-promotional culture. For example, after its 1997 election victory Labour placed communication at the heart of its approach to government, with ministers and their special advisers constantly engaged in harnessing the news media in the task of promoting Labour's achievements to the electorate. The political communications approach of Labour in its first parliamentary term consisted of the following mutually supportive elements (Kuhn 2002):

- first, clear *goals* – to drive and shape the news agenda so that this focused on the 'big picture' of policy proposals and achievements rather than being dominated by events and personalities;
- second, a coherent media management *strategy*, comprising well-planned proactive and reactive components (Heffernan and Stanyer 1998);
- third, good *organization* and resource management, including the establishment of a Strategic Communications Unit in Downing Street to plan and coordinate ministerial announcements and the restructuring of the Government Information Service – renamed the Government Information and Communication Service – to improve the provision of official information to the media;

• finally, the use of highly professional *personnel*, at the heart of the government's news media management, symbolized by the contribution of Alastair Campbell (Oborne,1999), first as the Prime Minister's Official Spokesman and later as Number 10's Director of Communications and Strategy.

In terms of resource allocation, for example, Labour's commitment to the communication aspects of contemporary government can be judged by the significant increase in the number of civil service information officers employed in ministerial departments. This amplifies a trend stretching back to the beginning of the Thatcher premiership in 1979. For instance, there were 11 information officers employed at the Cabinet Office in 1987, 14 in 1997 and no fewer than 23 in 1999 (Davis 2002: 21). In addition, according to some critics the Central Office of Information, set up to disseminate public information of a non-party political nature, has increasingly become a tool of the government. More controversially, under Labour there has been a huge rise in the total of politically appointed special advisers, several of whom exercise a communications rather than a policy function (Scammell 2001: 520–6). For instance, in 2002 there were 81 special advisers working across goverment, of whom about half worked on media-related activities. The BBC political correspondent Nicholas Jones estimated that 'the duties of almost half of the twenty-six political appointees assisting Blair in Downing Street involved briefing the news media, and that for most of this group it was their primary occupation' (Jones 2002: 30–1). Finally, the amount of taxpayers' money spent on government publicity and advertising more than doubled between 1997 and 2001–2, rising from just over £110 million when Labour came to power to over £270 million five years later. In short, just as in opposition the party under Blair's leadership had placed a strong emphasis on the importance of presentation and promotion, so once in power Labour, 'more than any of its predecessors, tried to conduct itself as a campaigning government' (Butler and Kavanagh 2002: 22).

The mediated leadership role of Tony Blair has been vitally important in this context. For some politicians and commentators, Blair has been instrumental in providing a presidential dimension to Labour in power (Foley 2000). Whatever the substantive validity of this claim, there is no doubt that in media terms Blair strongly personifies the Labour government. In part this merely serves to confirm the conventional view that television tends to personalize political debate and so inevitably reinforces the status of the leader at the expense of their immediate colleagues (Deacon, Golding and Billig 2001: 670). In the 2001 campaign, for example, Blair was quoted in free-to-air national television and Radio 4 news programmes almost five times more frequently than the next Labour politician, Gordon Brown. Indeed, Blair was quoted more often than *all* other Labour politicians put together (Harrison 2002: 140). In similar fashion William Hague for the Conservatives and, even more so, Charles Kennedy for the Liberal Democrats dominated their party's campaign news coverage. These examples illustrate the phenomenon which Foley calls 'leadership stretch', that is the way that 'party leaders have increasingly stretched away from their senior colleagues in terms of media attention and popular awareness' (2000: 205).

Yet Blair's highly personalized leadership style is not confined to election campaigns. Nor is the apparent presidentialization of his public role attributable merely to the automatic impact of television on political presentation. Rather Blair has actively and consciously sought to focus media attention on his own function as leader by deliberately associating himself with high-profile policy proposals. For example, in a memo leaked to the media in the spring of 2000, during a period when the government was going through a bad news trough, 'he asked his aides to provide him with "headline grabbing inititiatives" on touchstone issues that would change public perceptions of the government' (Butler and Kavanagh 2002: 27). In the memo Blair tellingly added that he should be personally associated with as much of this as possible.

Government and political parties are now involved in what has become a permanent campaign to dominate headlines and drive the news agenda. Leaders are now selected, in part at least, on the basis of their capacity to perform well on television. If judged by the public to be successful in this respect, as shown by Charles Kennedy in the 2001 election, then this can be an electoral asset for the party as a whole. More important than a leader's personal telegenic skills, however, is the ability to convey through the media an image of leadership which is consonant with public expectations about how a leader should perform. Party leaders now spend a considerable amount of time appearing in the media – communicating their policies to the electorate and trying to win over public support. Since symbolically they embody the values of their party, leaders need to pay close attention to their media image.

Blair, for example, has tried with considerable success to portray himself as a combination of strong leader and everyday family man. His highly proactive stance during the war in Kosovo in 1999 and his unflinching 'shoulder to shoulder' support for President Bush's 'war on terror' in the aftermath of 11 September were eloquent media manifestations of Blair playing the role of international statesman. Television news footage of the Prime Minister talking to British troops on active duty in the Balkans or visiting 'ground zero' in New York can be seen as created media events where good pictures are the principal object of the exercise. In addition, Blair has not been averse to displaying a tough side to his mediated persona in statements on domestic policy issues such as crime and anti-social behaviour.

Yet he has also cultivated a concerned, emotional side to his image, evident when he talks about the 'caring' issues of education and health. A complex mix of values, including competence, pragmatism and personal integrity, has been fused in a coherent media image where the notion that Blair is a politician the voter can trust is central. If that image is tarnished in Labour's second term by the failure of the government to deliver on its promises on public services, or by association with scandal, or by public perceptions of a Prime Minister who is out of touch with voters' concerns, then this will have a negative impact on the electoral popularity of the Labour party as a whole.

While there is no single template for a successful mediated image, one which is weak or incoherent, such as that of William Hague as Conservative party leader, is potentially highly damaging. Between the 1997 and 2001 elections Hague projected a confused image: for example, attending the Notting Hill carnival at the start of his leadership conveyed a message of multicultural social inclusiveness which was at odds with the controversial speech in the spring of 2001 where he claimed that a second term of Labour government would turn Britain 'into a foreign land'. While the Conservative leadership claimed that this speech was about Britain's relations with Europe, rather than race, this was not how it was spun by party advisers and subsequently covered in the media (Butler and Kavanagh 2002: 62). By the end of his four years as party leader, Hague had failed to project a positive, coherent media image. His successor, Iain Duncan Smith, has so far been no more successful. In his case the problem after over a year as party leader was not so much a contradictory media image as a non-existent one – characterizing himself as 'the quiet man' was one attempt to turn a negative into a positive.

To further a party's chances in conditions of the permanent election campaign, leadership image projection may be combined with the successful political marketing of issues and policies. Lees-Marshment argues that Labour under Blair became 'a classic Market-Oriented Party' (Lees-Marshment 2001: 181) and that this market-orientation has continued with Labour in government. From this marketing perspective, media management activities go beyond trying to obtain favourable coverage on isolated issues or even dominating the news agenda. More fundamentally, the Labour government has sought to use the media to promote the 'New Labour' brand in the electoral marketplace, just as private companies, such as Nike and Benetton, do in the commercial sphere (Klein 2000).

A key aspect of this has been to associate Labour with certain values which, although undoubtedly personified by Blair, at the same time go beyond simple image projection. Here the use of the media – along with the employment of other techniques such as opinion polls and focus groups – can be seen as part of a much broader marketing process. The brand image is designed to create positive feelings in the target market – the electorate. The leader's image, the government's policies and the party's values, all contribute to maintaining the integrity of the 'New Labour' brand. In this political market, the great fear is that the brand may take on negative associations and so become 'contaminated', as the party's marketing guru, Philip Gould, contended 'New Labour's' had become in the summer of 2000.

While the government and the main political parties enjoy privileged status as sources in securing media coverage and access, other political actors engaged in public relations politics have to strive harder to gain media recognition. To some extent this is a problem of organization and financial resources. Resource-poor groups may find it difficult to make sufficient investment on a routinized basis to maintain an active presence in a communications environment of many competing sources. This is a particular problem for minor parties and some small pressure groups. Conversely, other groups, such as Greenpeace, are well resourced and can afford to provide the media with well-packaged material, such as video news releases, and maintain a high quality website.

Yet under certain circumstances even politically marginal groups can hope to influence the news agenda and issue framing. This is because the capacity for political actors to gain access to the media is not determined by economic resources alone. Even resource-poor groups can foster 'exchange relationships' with journalists (Manning 2001: 178) and can accumulate what Davis calls 'media cultural capital' (2002: 173–7). This involves an understanding of news values as part of an 'accommodative' strategy by the group to meet the demands of media organizations.

Nonetheless, while the media may be more open to alternative sources than some deterministic analyses allowed for in the past, this does not mean that there is a level playing-field. Because of their status, expertize and central position in the political process, some political actors are more likely than others to enjoy routinized media access as a matter of course. One of these is clearly the core executive. With a Prime Minister who constantly tends to his mediated leadership image, a government which concentrates so much attention on presentation and self-promotion, and a Conservative opposition still rebuilding itself after two consecutive landslide defeats, Labour in power might reasonably have expected to dominate the news agenda and secure favourable coverage. Focusing on the two years either side of the 2001 election, the following section demonstrates that this has not been such a straightforward task.

Labour and news management

Almost exactly a year before the 2001 general election Tony Blair was slow hand-clapped by sections of the audience as he was giving a speech at the annual conference of the Women's Institute. Television news coverage that evening showed an obviously embarrassed Prime Minister failing miserably to get his message across to the representatives in the conference centre. The story in the next day's newspapers concentrated not on the government's proposed policy initiatives – the formal substance of the speech, but rather on this very public failure of prime ministerial communication, the resonance of which was hugely amplified by being shown on television.

Soon after its election victory the Labour government became embroiled in a much more serious negative communications story. When Jo Moore, the special adviser to the Transport Secretary Stephen Byers, encouraged staff to take advantage of the 11 September events as a 'very good day to get out anything we want to bury', her advice was made public via an unauthorized leak to the media. This gave rise to a controversy which ranged from the inappropriateness of her comment in this particular instance to the ethics of spin-doctoring in general. While Moore survived the first onslaught of media-led public disapproval, her image was irreversibly tarnished and she later resigned from her position following a highly mediatized dispute with the civil servant in charge of the department's communications section (Jones 2002: 271–343). For some critics Moore personified everything that was wrong with Labour's approach to communication in government: too much emphasis on presentation and spin; the short circuiting of official channels of communication by non-accountable special advisers, always seeking to secure maximum partisan advantage from every ministerial announcement; and the amorality of the belief that all is fair in news management, with the only criterion of success being the quality of the subsequent media coverage.

In their different ways, these two examples illustrate the downside of Labour's constant concern with the communication aspects of contemporary governance. A government which devotes so much attention to news management has made the painful discovery that its spinning activities may rebound to its disadvantage in the face of dissident sources, critical journalists and a sceptical audience. In the months either side of the 2001 election, Labour's reputation as a media-savvy political outfit, if not exactly past its sell-by date, certainly required some serious qualification.

The apparent turnaround in Labour's record of news management was all the more striking in the light of what appeared to be a largely successful approach in this area of operations after Blair became leader of the party in 1994. The professionalism of Labour's news management activities in opposition was much commented on, not least by political journalists who contrasted it with the failed efforts of the Conservatives during the Major premiership (Jones 1995, 1999 and 2002, Oborne 1999, Johnson, J. 1999).

Once in government Labour continued to cultivate its relations with leading journalists in the press and broadcasting media, while also engaging in the use of various techniques to seek to ensure favourable news coverage (Barnett and Gaber 2001: 106–13). These included:

- firebreaking, whereby a diversion is deliberately constructed to take journalists off the scent of an embarrassing story. For example, in the case of the revelation of Robin Cook's extra-marital relationship with his secretary in 1997, Labour spin doctors put out two other stories to divert media attention away from the Cook affair, one regarding a possible breach of the Official Secrets Act by Chris Patten in his book about his period as governor of Hong Kong and the other about a possible reprieve for the royal yacht *Britannia*;
- pre-empting, as in the case of the government minister Nick Brown, who in late 1998 admitted that he was gay to minimize the impact of revelations to this effect which were about to appear in the *News of the World*;
- milking a story, whereby advance notice of a governmental initiative is trailed in various media in a drip-by-drip fashion in advance of the official announcement so as to obtain the maximum amount of favourable coverage;
- kite-flying, where controversial proposals are floated via the media to test public reaction;
- managing expectations, which is particularly evident around the time of the Budget, when public expectations may be reduced via media briefings in advance of the Chancellor's speech, thus giving the Chancellor more favourable publicity if the formal announcement contains an unanticipated tax or spend bonus.

In the aftermath of the 1997 victory Labour enjoyed an extended honeymoon period with much of the news media: the 'media coverage that the Labour government has received, sleaze and scandals aside, was for its first three years in power mostly positive' (Barnett and Gaber 2001: 122). Yet while this assessment is largely true, the situation which it described was not to last. Why then did Labour increasingly encounter problems with the news media in the months running up to the 2001 election and after? To answer this question requires a critical examination of the dynamic, interdependent relationship between these two sets of political communication actors, going beyond an approach which is solely source – or media-centred (Schlesinger 1990).

Government and the news media: differences and disagreements

The government's inability to determine the news agenda owes much to the operationalization of news values by professional media personnel. In a highly competitive commercial environment, characterized by the relentless pursuit of audiences and advertisers for market survival, decision-making in newsrooms focuses attention on those stories which satisfy criteria of newsworthiness (Tumber 1999). In the period immediately following the 1997 election, the changeover to a Labour government after eighteen years of Conservative rule was in itself eminently newsworthy. The news media wanted to cover the arrival of a fresh cohort of MPs at Westminster, the appointment of new ministers and their advisers in Whitehall and, not least, the installation of a charismatic incumbent at Number 10. In short, New Labour in government was the story.

Once the novelty of a Labour administration had worn off, however, there slowly emerged a tendency towards the re-application of 'normal' news values by journalists and editors, with sections of the media adopting a more critical or even adversarial stance towards the government. Stories increasingly tended to emphasize conflict and disunity, negative events and Labour personalities in trouble. Examples included:

- the possible link between large financial donations to the Labour party by several private individuals and the favours from government that may have resulted;
- allegations of impropriety and incompetence against a succession of government ministers, including Geoffrey Robinson, Peter Mandelson, Keith Vaz and Stephen Byers;
- the London mayoral contest in 2000, where the official Labour candidate, Frank Dobson, given the personal endorsement of the Prime

Minister, suffered a heavy defeat at the hands of the Labour rebel, Ken Livingstone, standing as an Independent;
- the almost universally critical coverage by newspapers of the Millennium Dome as a visitor attraction during its financially disastrous year of operation in 2000;
- the fuel blockade in the autumn of the same year, where several tabloid newspapers did not just report and comment on the events, but gave editorial backing to the demands of the protestors for a cut in fuel duty;
- the foot and mouth crisis in 2001, where criticism of government policy from a variety of sources, combined with lurid pictures of slaughtered animals, secured extensive media coverage. In addition, the story fitted a pre-established news framework of public concern about food safety constructed during the previous BSE crisis.

Eminently newsworthy, all of the above were 'good stories' in media terms. However, they often provided negative headlines for the government. The relationship between Alastair Campbell and news journalists in the lobby became increasingly soured. Campbell initially enjoyed three hugely positive features in carrying out his function as the Prime Minister's Official Spokesman. First, the role itself had been clarified at the very start of the first Labour term to give it a more robustly defined status. Lobby briefings were put on the record and Campbell was the first Number 10 press secretary to attend Cabinet meetings on a regular basis. Second, Campbell was highly valued by journalists as a source because of his well-known proximity to Blair in the inner circle of key ministers and top advisers (Hennessy, 2000). In ways comparable to the role of Bernard Ingham as Number 10 press secretary during the Thatcher premiership, Campbell was regarded by journalists as speaking with the authority of the Prime Minister in providing the government's line on an issue. The well-publicized closeness of the relationship between the two was even the subject of frequent satirical sketches on the *Rory Bremner* comedy show on television. Third, as a former journalist and political editor at the two *Mirror* titles and *Today*, Campbell knew the world of the news media, and particularly tabloid journalism, from the inside. He did not have to second guess what journalists might do with a lead; he knew from his own experience how a story would play in different media outlets.

Yet Campbell also had a highly adversarial style in lobby briefings. At times the very force of his personality and the colourful language he chose to employ to express his thoughts on a matter exacerbated what of necessity is frequently a tense and conflictual relationship between two sets of political communication actors. Campbell had opened up the process of lobby briefings to the public by putting a summary on the Internet from the beginning of 2000 (http://www.number-10.gov.uk). He had also allowed a BBC camera team to film the insider relationship between Number 10 and lobby journalists in the hope that the programme would belie the Labour government's reputation for 'control freakery' (Cockerell 2000). Yet there were signs that, as with the Chancellor of the Exchequer's former press adviser, Charlie Whelan, in the first eighteen months of the Labour government, Campbell was in danger of becoming the story rather than just its source. The centrality of his role, in a government now subject to increasing criticism for its attempts to spin its way out of trouble, began to devalue his day-to-day credibility in lobby briefings. As a result, in June 2000, Campbell was moved to a more strategic role in overseeing government communication, rather than being actively engaged in the daily struggle to set the next day's headlines.

Even this move away from the front line did not end the running battle between Campbell and some news media. In June 2002 stories in the *Spectator* magazine, the *Evening Standard* and the *Mail on Sunday* that Number 10 had intervened to try to enhance the Prime Minister's role at the funeral ceremony for the Queen Mother led to furious denials from Downing Street, with Campbell writing formally to the Press Complaints Commission (PCC). Although in substantive terms the initial story may not have seemed particularly significant, it played into a news framework in some papers of an increasingly arrogant Prime Minister. Downing Street was thrown on to the defensive. Even several media not involved in the original revelations framed subsequent developments – Downing Street versus the press – in terms of a government climbdown, presenting Campbell as one of the 'losers' in the affair and questioning whether he had lost his touch.

Another factor for the media's increasingly critical coverage of the Labour government in the two years before and after the 2001 election is linked to the changed nature of newspaper partisanship over the past decade (Deacon, Golding and Billig 2001: 673–6). Since the early 1990s a process of partisan dealignment on the part of several newspapers has taken place, with newspaper support now frequently more issue-oriented than party-based (Seymour-Ure 1998). It is true that several national newspaper titles supported Labour in the 2001 campaign – even more than in 1997 – giving the impression that press support leant heavily towards Labour to the detriment of the Conservatives. However, despite the massive *quantitative* advantage Labour enjoyed in terms of both the number of individual titles and the size of their circulation figures, in *qualitative* terms newspaper support for Labour during the 2001 campaign 'was generally subdued, often qualified and sometimes critical' (Scammell and Harrop 2002: 156).

Not even under Blair has Labour been able to turn round the pro-Conservative editorial views of the *Mail* and *Telegraph* titles. Yet even among those papers which backed the party in 2001, support for Labour in government has generally been highly conditional. This is a far cry from the 'hallelujah chorus' of pro-Conservative newspapers which idolized Mrs Thatcher in the 1980s. Whereas Mrs Thatcher could largely command allegiance from a phalanx of sympathetic press owners and their editors, the Blair government has had to bargain to obtain newspaper support.

The Murdoch-owned newspapers, especially the mass-selling tabloid the *Sun*, are a good example of this exchange relationship. In opposition, Labour under Blair courted Rupert Murdoch with considerable success, evidenced by the *Sun* supporting a Labour victory in the 1997 election and afterwards in opening up its columns to numerous articles published under Tony Blair's byline. In return for its support, the Labour government offered the paper's political editor, Trevor Kavanagh, insider titbits of information – such as the date of the 2001 election – ahead of its being made available to other parliamentary lobby journalists. Along with the continued repudiation of 'Old Labour' style policies, the deal helped ensure that between 1997 and 2001 the tabloid did not switch sides in the party battle.

Nonetheless, the *Sun*, never renowned for its positive attitude towards continental Europe or Brussels, remained a fierce critic of Labour's stance on Britain's relationship with the European Union. In particular, it has steadfastly criticized the government's stated policy of support in principle for British adoption of the single European currency. In so doing, it is only one of several newspapers which have participated actively as advocates – for and against – on this issue in their editorial columns, commentary and news coverage. In recent years, coverage of Europe by several national newsapers, including the *Mail* and *Telegraph* titles, has been framed from a strongly-held Eurosceptic position (Wilkes and Wring 1998, Anderson and Weymouth 1999). Murdoch announced in the summer of 2002 that his four titles (the *Sun*, *The Times*, *News of the World* and the *Sunday Times*) would support a 'No' vote – a clear example of the proprietor laying down the line to be adopted by his papers. In circulation terms the Europhile newspapers are far outsold by the Eurosceptic press. This raises two issues for the government. First, will Labour be able to shift some national newspapers round to a more balanced or even supportive position in the run-up to the referendum campaign? Second, if not, can Labour and the pro-Euro camp win a referendum in the face of intense opposition from large sections of the press?

Process journalism

A further explanatory variable is tied to the importance of *process journalism* in contemporary political coverage. Process journalism refers to stories which comment on and evaluate the behaviour of political actors (party strategies, leadership tactics, personality rivalries) in contrast to policy journalism which explains issues and assesses policy proposals (McNair 2000: 42–60). Process journalism is frequently characterized by a highly adversarial stance on the part of the news media. In this context journalists ascribe to themselves the role not of mere reporters of – or commentators on – the political process, but rather of critics willing to condemn aspects of its functioning and prepared to engage in highly personalized attacks against politicians, both individually and as a group. Scandals are an obvious case in point, with financial wrongdoings and sexual infidelities given high profile coverage, as in the final years of the Major government when 'sleaze' provided the frame for many news stories about the Conservatives. In these circumstances the media, especially national newspapers, can easily fulfil an oppositional role in news coverage and commentary.

In the case of the Labour government 'spin' rather than 'sleaze' provided the narrative link for much process-oriented news coverage either side of the 2001 election, as journalists 'unpacked' the government's news management activities. With media attention on the attempted official spin taking centre stage, government presentation of an issue rather than the substance of policy became the news frame. For example, while stories about government spending plans in the early years of the Labour government tended to be covered as policy stories, journalists later became wise to the misrepresentation of figures by spin doctors. As a result, subsequent news stories focused increasingly on the government's attempts to manipulate presentation, for instance on NHS waiting list figures or the number of schoolteacher vacancies. In addition, the increased prominence of columnist journalism in national papers provided commentators, such as Richard Littlejohn in the *Sun*, a regular platform from which to criticize leading politicians.

There are several reasons for the place accorded process journalism in the media's coverage of politics. First, since political actors pay considerably more attention to public relations and promotional strategies than ever before, this development is a legitimate matter of public interest for journalistic commentary. Second, journalists enjoy an 'insider' position in the political communications environment. They can write about a political game in which they are perfectly familiar with the players, rules, strategies and tactics and can communicate that 'insider information' to their audiences. Third, writing about process is often easier than writing about policy. Process journalism can focus on human interest stories – who's in and who's out of favour in the govern-mental entourage. When combined with other media coverage such as the newspaper serialization of a politician's memoirs and, perhaps, a television documentary – as in the case of Mo Mowlam's Cabinet demo-tion and subsequent resignation from politics (Mowlam 2002) – then the news story has all the ingredients of a political soap opera, with its heroes and villains, intrigue and plotting, treachery and deceit. In contrast, a focus on policy may require knowledge and skills which many lobby journalists quite simply lack. Finally, process journalism covers information which audiences can easily understand and situa-tions with which they can empathize. Conversely, in an age of increas-ingly technical debates – for example, on the issues of climate change, genetically modifed food and currency convergence – and a more complex decision-making process involving largely remote and unfamil-iar supranational and global actors such as the European Union and the World Trade Organization, it is more difficult and time consuming for audiences to grasp the essential features, far less the details, of many policy issues.

The final factor in this interdependent relationship between govern-ment and news media relates to an aspect of the way in which journal-ists behave collectively as 'competitor–colleagues' (Tunstall 1971). Although journalists constantly want to scoop their rivals working for other media, at the same time they are prone to behaving as a 'pack', often agreeing on the main lines of a story before it goes to their respec-tive news editors. The ultimate manifestation of this journalistic 'pack' behaviour is the ritualistic feeding frenzy which surrounds a metaphor-ical political 'kill'. This is the phenomenon known as *attack journalism* (Sabato 1991).

Attack journalism

Two notable examples of attack journalism were evident either side of the 2001 election. The first involved Blair's confidant, Peter Mandelson, in a case of alleged involvement in the granting of UK passports to three wealthy Indian brothers who had given money to the Millennium Dome project in which the minister had previously been closely involved. Media coverage of the Hinduja affair focused on both Mandelson's actions (what happened?) and his subsequent account of his behaviour to the media and the Prime Minister (had he told the truth?). Confusion on both counts led to Mandelson being forced to resign from govern-ment for a second time at the start of 2001 to jubilant howls from the baying news hounds (Rawnsley 2000: 210–34; Jones 2002: 237–70).

The *Sun's* leader column was particularly blunt: 'He is out on his ear again because he is a lying, manipulative, oily, two-faced, nasty piece of work who should never have been allowed near the Government in the first place' (the *Sun*, 25 January 2001).

The second example of attack journalism concerned Stephen Byers. His failure to dismiss Jo Moore over her 'bury bad news' e-mail, his controversial decision to put Railtrack into administration, but most of all his apparent propensity for prevarication, evasion and economy with the truth made him into an iconic hate figure for several newspapers. The news framing of Byers after September 2001 firmly concentrated on his honesty in his dealings with Parliament and the media more than his ministerial competence – though that too was called into question by some journalists. Hunted without mercy, Byers resigned from his ministerial position in May 2002. The newspaper headlines (29 May 2002) which greeted his resignation tell their own story: 'BYE BYE LIAR' (*Daily Express*); 'Special Notice: We apologise for the late departure of Stephen Byers from Platform No10. This was due to a signal failure to realise he was a useless little fibber who should have buried himself months ago.' (*Daily Mirror*); 'HE'S QUIT (. . .and it's about time, Byers) (the *Sun*); 'BYE BYE BYERS Disgraced Minister who lied and lied again finally bows out (still insisting that he doesn't tell lies)' (*Daily Mail*); 'A good day to bury Byers' (*Daily Telegraph*).

Spin as problem, not solution? How can government manage news management?

By the end of the first year of its second term Labour had become acutely aware that its reputation for spin had turned against it and was being used by sections of the news media as a weapon to attack the government. Yet Labour seemed confused as to who was primarily responsible for this degradation in the relationship between government and media. In an article in *The Times* the then Labour chairman, Charles Clarke, accused the media of being 'pious and hypocritical' and of doing their best 'to bring democratic politics into disrepute' (12 June 2002), while in contrast the Leader of the House of Commons, Robin Cook, called on Labour to put its own house in order and end its obsession with spin.

Dissatisfied with much news coverage, Labour introduced a reform of the lobby briefings, opening up the morning sessions to a wider cross-section of journalists, including specialist and foreign correspondents, allowing a journalist to chair the session and permitting ministers who brief in person to be filmed for television (*Guardian*, 3 May 2002). The government argued that these American-style reforms were a genuine attempt to be more open with the media and less 'buttoned up' about the next day's headlines. However, according to leading lobby journalists such as Trevor Kavanagh, political editor of the *Sun*, and Adam Boulton, political editor of Sky News, the government's aim was to minimize the disruptive potential of the traditional lobby correspondents who were accustomed to 'grilling' a government spokesperson on a particular issue in comparative secrecy. Some lobby correspondents feared that the new media briefings would become more orchestrated by government, for example through the choice of journalists invited to ask questions and in the lack of opportunity to engage in sustained interrogation, and so give ministers more power to shape the news agenda.

The Prime Minister's first monthly televised press conference under these new arrangements took place on 20 June 2002, with Blair confidently fielding questions on a variety of subjects 'live' in front of the cameras. The press conference in early September was broadcast from the Prime Minister's Sedgefield constituency and concentrated on the issue of a possible military strike against Iraq. These highly mediatized events, reminiscent of President de Gaulle's press conferences in France in the 1960s (Chalaby 2002), may allow the Prime Minister to control the agenda in a more direct fashion than normally allowed by traditional lobby briefings. They are also part of a broader strategy to bypass lobby correspondents, which in the past has included Number 10 targeting regional newspapers, women's magazines and ethnic minority publications to get its message across to the electorate. Televised press conferences may also give the Prime Minister the opportunity to exploit his presentational skills and have the best soundbites replayed in the evening television news programmes. However, there is a potential downside to such an approach. If the government is on the defensive on an issue, then the Prime Minister is potentially exposed to attack from journalists without the intervening shield of a government spokesperson. Televised prime ministerial press conferences are not a risk-free option for the Labour leader.

Despite these innovations, there must remain doubts that in the immediate future at least Labour will be successful in radically changing its news management relationship with the media. In part this is because the image of 'spin' and 'control freakery' has now become so associated with New Labour that journalists will find it difficult to believe that the government is committed to changing its ways. Indeed, perhaps the public call for a cutback on spin by leading Labour sources, including ironically Campbell and Mandelson, is itself a spin on spinning – the kind of double bluff worthy of inclusion in a Le Carré spy novel.

Moreover, even if Labour were committed to radical reform of its approach to news management, is such a policy feasible? News management and self-promotion are an integral part of the way in which Labour has functioned under Blair's leadership. Since communication has been deliberately made integral to its mode of governance, by definition this cannot be easily excised. While Labour officials may argue that they are abandoning 'spin', not communication, the distinction may not be so easy to apply in practice. If so, it may well be that Labour is locked into a spiral of spin.

In any event there are good reasons for Labour to continue to pursue an active communications strategy. With a 24-hours news culture and a huge variety of media outlets, there is now a voracious appetite on the part of journalists for fresh primary material. In these circumstances, government has to work hard to try to drive and dominate the news agenda. The alternative would be to risk abandoning this terrain to other sources, including opposition parties, and to allow journalists themselves to fill the vacuum with their own speculative commentary. This is neither a desirable, nor a feasible option for government. News management is an essential part of contemporary politics. What is at issue therefore is not *whether* the Labour government should seek to influence the news agenda (it has no option), but rather *how* it should do so to best effect.

Conclusion

The media play a central role in the process of political communication. Political actors, therefore, want to use the media for their own purposes: to recruit members, mobilize supporters, persuade voters, communicate with citizens, raise issues and influence policy making. Labour under Blair's leadership has done more than any other political actor in Britain in recent years to embrace the concept of public relations politics by professionalizing its relationship with the news media. Yet as this chapter has shown, it is misleading to present the media in a subordinate passive role in their relationship with powerful political actors, including the government. Instead, the news media are active participants in the process of political communication. It is true that sometimes they may seem to act as transmission belts for the dissemination of a message from politicians to the electorate. Yet it is also the case that the news media frequently fulfil a watchdog role, serving the interests of the citizenry by making politicians accountable. At other times sections of the media appear to be following their own agendas, guided by interventionist proprietors and editors. In short, the power relationship between politicians and the media is not reducible to a simple model in which politicians lead and the media follow.

Where does this leave audiences, who themselves are increasingly presented in academic literature as empowered actors rather than passive receivers in the process of decoding media texts? It is clear that the media exercise an important influence on audience attitudes, knowledge and behaviour. Indeed, the alleged power of the media to exert an influence on the behaviour of audiences in the short term – for instance, the impact of national newspapers on voting patterns in British general elections – continues to be an active field of academic research (Newton and Brynin, 2001). In the longer term, by giving issues more or less salience in news coverage, the media help to set the political agenda for audiences, influencing not so much what people think as what they think about.

In this media age of politics, some commentators see in the expansion of the public sphere and the semiological sophistication of audiences as grounds for relative optimism. McNair (2000) and Norris (2000), for example, are comparatively upbeat in attributing to the media a positive influence on informing and educating citizens. McNair argues that there is little evidence of a dumbing-down of political journalism in contemporary Britain, while Norris maintains that because of a 'virtuous circle', attention to the news media gradually reinforces civic engagement, just as civic engagement prompts attention to the news. Others are less convinced. Blumler and Gurevitch (1995: 203) talk about a crisis of public communication, whereby 'the political communication process now tends to strain against rather than with the grain of citizenship', while Franklin (1997) refers to the triumph of entertainment values in news production, resulting in a product which he calls 'newszak'. For proponents of the 'media malaise' theory, the media have made audiences more cynical about politicians and the political process and turned them away from political participation.

The debate between these cultural optimists and pessimists is set to run and run. This is not just because of the conceptual and methodological difficulties involved in this area of research – for instance, how does one define and then measure 'dumbing-down' in news coverage over time? More fundamentally it is because the impact of the media on politics is a matter of huge public interest. At the heart of the 'media malaise' controversy lies a disagreement about norms and values in determining what properly constitutes political communication in an information-rich society and mass democratic polity.

Chapter 9

Politics in Scotland

JAMES MITCHELL

A new orthodoxy has emerged in British politics. Scotland is different and the United Kingdom is no longer a uniform, unitary state. Media attention now focuses on the differences that exist within the United Kingdom and in particular how the Scottish Parliament, elected for the first time in 1999, has given rise to these differences. It is now generally accepted that Scottish politics is distinct in a number of ways:

- political institutions;
- public policy;
- party system; and
- public opinion.

The old orthodoxy was that Britain, if not the United Kingdom, was fairly homogeneous. Central political institutions – the Monarchy, Parliament at Westminster, Cabinet government – united the country. So too did the party system especially the dominant two parties within it. The Labour and Conservative parties carved up Britain between them leaving the odd scrap to the Liberals. Class determined how people voted. Policies determined at the centre were, more or less, uniformly applied throughout Britain, for example, the 'national' in the National Health Service referred to British National. Devolution has been viewed as a transformative experience for the United Kingdom, undermining old certainties and creating new territorial divisions.

Devolution has indeed been symbolically significant as much as for any change in the substance of politics. Devolution signifies the end of an old orthodoxy that was never very accurate but was widely believed and in being believed was itself important. Even if factually inaccurate, when something is believed to be true it can affect political behaviour. The myth of the 'one and indivisible' British nation said much about Britain's understanding of itself. Equally, the new myth of Scottish distinctiveness is just as inaccurate but, again, is important and has consequences simply because it is believed. To understand contemporary Scottish politics, it is necessary to separate out myth from reality

161

and to take account of the many continuities as well as the differences that devolution has brought about.

A Scottish political system?

The unions that created Britain did not result in one uniform nation. The Union of Crowns in 1603 and the Union of Parliaments of 1707 created one Monarchy for Scotland and England and then one Parliament in place of two. Much else remained as before, and union did not entail uniformity and assimilation. The treaty establishing the common Parliament at Westminster also protected important Scottish institutions including Scots law and the established Church of Scotland. Aspects of law rooted in pre-union times, notably criminal law and legal institutions such as the courts, retain a greater degree of distinctiveness in Scotland, while newer bodies of law, related to the welfare state or company law, are more uniform across Britain. Hence, not all aspects of law are different in Scotland from England. It is commonly, but mistakenly, assumed that Scottish educational distinctiveness was protected in the Treaty of Union, but education was largely under the control of the churches, not the state. This ensured a diverse pattern of educational provision both within Scotland and England and between Scotland and England. Educational provision was based on the organization and ethos of the Church of Scotland, and this prompted the form of state education that emerged in Scotland during the nineteenth and twentieth centuries. Two myths regarding Scottish education have had some basis in hard evidence, each existing as much in the minds of policy makers and the public as in reality. The first was the national myth: Scotland was quite different from England in education. The second was the egalitarian myth: Scottish education was democratic offering opportunities to a wider group of people than existed in England and Wales. A similar pattern of development emerged in education as in law. In some respects Scottish education with its separate roots was different from that in England, but many post-union developments ensured that the pattern on either side of the border was broadly the same.

Notably, no effort was ever made by the Westminster Parliament to impose uniformity across the state. At times, diversity was celebrated, but more often simply unquestioned, and territorial pluralism was practised across a wide range of institutions and policies. There was a common army but Scottish regiments existed within it. Unlike other European states in the nineteenth and early twentieth-centuries that attempted to impose uniformity top-down, Westminster's attitude towards Scotland was largely one of pluralistic indifference. This pluralism became so ingrained that it was rarely questioned, and having to take account of some 'Scottish dimension' within government caused occasional irritation but little hostility. This accepted pluralism could be used by Scots seeking special treatment. It led to calls for the appointment of a Cabinet Minister to look after Scottish affairs from the middle of the nineteenth century, culminating in the establishment of the Scottish Office in 1885. Similarly, almost a century later it led to calls for a Scottish Parliament. Notably, the nature of the Union agreed between Scotland and England and its development thereafter ensured the survival of pre-union Scottish distinctiveness. It provided a base for a home rule movement that would be almost inconceivable in, for example the north of England which suffered similar, indeed worse, economic problems than Scotland.

It would be mistaken, however, to focus exclusively on what made Scotland different politically from England. There was much in common between constituent parts of the Union, not least a common Monarchy, a single Parliament and a vast range of institutions and policies developed in the twentieth-century, most notably associated with the welfare state. One of the most intriguing aspects of twentieth-century Scotland was observed by Paul Scott, an octogenarian former diplomat and leading figure in the home rule movement: 'Scotland of the [19]80s had become more conscious of distinctiveness and more anxious to preserve it against the pressure for global conformity; but, paradoxically, it had become markedly less distinctively Scottish in practice.' (Scott 2002: 239–40). As a result, over time Scotland has become less Scottish, at the same time Scots became more Scottish.

A consequence of this Scottish British diversity has been that there is no agreement on the extent of Scottish distinctiveness. One of the oldest debates amongst students of Scottish politics has been whether or not a Scottish political system exists or existed. The debate was first provoked in 1973 by the publication of James Kellas's book *The Scottish Political System* (Kellas, 1973). While Kellas conceded that the boundary between a British political system and the Scottish system was not always clear, he argued that a Scottish political system existed and that Scotland had many coherent and distinct institutions and organizations (Kellas 1984: 18). An alternative view, focusing largely on political institutions, argued Scotland was governed through distinct British based 'policy networks' and that the main political institutions operating in Scotland were British institutions because power was 'retained and concentrated at Westminster and Whitehall' (Keating and Midwinter 1981: 1–2). Others contended that if the term system 'is to have any meaning in political science it must relate to a distinctive sovereign and autonomous set of political institutions governing within defined territorial boundaries, which clearly Scotland does not have' (Booth and Moore 1989: 15). Although they disagreed on the form it took, all writers did acknowledge that a distinct Scottish dimension to politics existed pre-devolution.

Because the Anglo-Scottish Union involved compromise it preserved a degree of Scottish distinctiveness. What emerged was a union, rather than a unitary state, and this had significant implications for the development of the United Kingdom. Jim Bulpitt maintained that a dual polity operated for much of the twentieth century, between 1926 and 1961, and that the centre allowed Scotland, Wales and Northern Ireland, along with English local authorities, a fair degree of autonomy enabling the centre to concentrate on 'high politics'. The de facto devolution of 'low politics' gave rise to limited interaction between the centre and the periphery (Bulpitt 1983: 134–63) creating what Bulpitt called territorial politics, 'that arena of political activity concerned with the relations between the central political institutions in the capital city and those interests, communities, political organizations and governmental bodies outside the central institutional complex, but within the accepted boundaries of the state, which possess, or are commonly perceived to possess, a significant geographical or local/regional character.' (Bulpitt 1983: 1) In truth, territorial politics were seen by many political scientists as being a peripheral interest in all senses, and most students of politics and most of the public, focusing on 'high' and 'national' politics, had little interest in them. Beyond those studying Scottish or territorial politics, the orthodox view was that Britain was a relatively homogeneous political community. Political science textbooks asserted the United Kingdom was a unitary state, not often considering what that meant, far less considering whether it was accurate. For the most part, writing on British politics, journalistic as well as academic, would concentrate on metropolitan politics. At most, they might give passing acknowledgement to the United Kingdom's diversity.

Scottish institutions and policies pre-devolution

Distinct Scottish institutions existed before devolution, although many of these were British institutions. However, the Scottish Office, set up in 1885, had an unusual niche within Whitehall, and over time it began to accumulate a number of responsibilities. Scottish Office ministers, appointed by the British Prime Minister, were answerable to the Westminster Parliament as were all other ministers. Unlike ministers appointed to the Northern Ireland Office (set up in 1972) or the Welsh

Office (set up in 1964), Scottish Office ministers traditionally represented Scottish constituencies in the House of Commons (or had a Scottish connection when members of the House of Lords). They had some degree of autonomy in determining public policy, but found themselves constrained in a number of ways. First, Scottish policy rarely diverged dramatically from English policy, not least because political parties contested elections on a fairly common manifesto across Britain. Although the main parties in Scotland produced Scottish manifestos, these were little different in content from the 'national' manifesto. Unsurprisingly, the Secretary of State for Scotland broadly followed the same policy agenda as his Cabinet colleagues. Second, the Scottish Office was another spending department (and a fairly weak one, at that) and it had to negotiate its annual budget with the Treasury or derive that budget from expenditure formulae based on decisions affecting other spending departments. In other words, the Scottish Office was not in any position to develop new expensive policies, but had to work within tight spending controls determined by the government as a whole. Again and again, when an imaginative Scottish Secretary, of whom there were very few, came up with an innovative policy, he would be told by the Treasury it was unacceptable on the grounds that it would create a precedent and a similar, much more expensive demand, because of relative size, from other ministers. For the most part, then, the Scottish Office followed the lead of English spending departments. Policy divergence tended to be at the margins. Often it merely involved differences in emphasis. In addition, the Scottish Office did not spend its budget allocation directly, but instead allocated it to local government and numerous other government agencies. It was, to a large extent, simply Scotland's Ministry for Local Government.

Despite these constraints, the Scottish Office was able to carve out a distinct role for itself in policy terms. First, because it allocated budgets to local authorities it could take important decisions on priorities and the distribution of resources. Second, although it could not act as the catalyst for new, innovative policies in Cabinet, the Scottish Office was able to press for additional sums of money from the Treasury on the basis of some Scottish claim. Whenever evidence pointed to Scotland having a pressing case for more resources because, for example, it had more severe problems, it was possible to win more monies in the Whitehall spending round. Over time, such small victories accumulated and the Scottish Office would jealously guard its gains. In housing, for example, Scotland's historically poor conditions meant that from the First World War onward grants to build housing tended to be more generous in Scotland. Such historic, cumulative decisions account for Scotland's generous share of British public spending today. Naturally,

Scottish ministers came to see their job, in common with other spending ministers, as defending and increasing their department's share of public spending. Third, not all public policies are costly, and it was possible for the Scottish Office to develop distinctive Scottish policies where cost was not significant. This was most likely where distinct Scottish practices already existed, for instance, in education and social policy. Here Scotland had a long history of distinctiveness that allowed a degree of separate (or at least parallel) development of policy. In the 1960s, for example, policy on juvenile crime in Scotland was imaginatively reformed with the introduction of children's panels. At the same time, however, the Scottish Office under a Labour Secretary of State, Willie Ross, blocked the Home Office's liberal policies legalizing homosexuality which were introduced in England and Wales. Homosexuality was only formally decriminalized in Scotland when the Thatcher Government enacted the Criminal Justice (Scotland) Act in 1980.

In essence, Scottish public policy largely followed that in England and Wales, but there were differences of emphasis and occasionally of substance. These have tended to emerge incrementally or because there already existed separate treatment. The overall trend was towards greater homogeneity because much policy affecting the lives of people living in Scotland was not the responsibility of the Scottish Office. For instance, a pensioner in Glasgow received the same pension as one in Glossop; social security and unemployment benefits were the same in Aberdeen as in Aberystwyth; business people operated within the same framework of company law in Bathgate as in Bath, although different courts and criminal proceedings would operate in Scotland and England and Wales should they fail to operate within these same laws.

Other institutions should also be noted. For instance, a distinct Scottish media has long existed, and the expectations of many social scientists that the emergence of modern communications would lead to homogeneity were dashed. Television and radio contributed to a sense of Britishness but from relatively early on broadcasting acknowledged the regional dimension and allowed for local outputs. BBC television first broadcast Scottish programmes in Scotland in 1952 and Scottish Television was launched in 1955. Other forces accentuated Scottish distinctiveness and provided a Scottish voice, operating alongside forces for homogeneity. Scottish newspapers easily outsold London-based papers and while institutions that in earlier times had helped maintain a sense of Scottishness – notably the Church of Scotland in the nineteenth century – were declining in significance, other institutions were taking their place maintaining a sense of Scottish distinctiveness. State intervention, as we have seen, did not involve homogeneity across Britain. Not only did the Scottish Office exist, but also state intervention spawned or augmented the activities of distinct Scottish pressure groups. The educational lobby in Scotland was emphatically Scottish. The National Union of Teachers did (and does) not operate north of the border. Instead the Educational Institute of Scotland (EIS) was the largest teachers union and would emphasize its Scottishness in its dealings with the Scottish Office. British-wide pressure groups would generally have Scottish branches that had a variety of degrees of autonomy from the London headquarters.

Public opinion and parties pre-devolution

At first glance, public opinion and party politics appear to have been fairly homogeneous across Britain. Differences existed but, according to the old orthodoxy, these could be explained not by national differences but in terms of people's class location. The same parties dominated Scottish politics for most of the twentieth century as dominated English politics, with Labour and the Conservatives taking more than the lion's share of votes and seats. In fact, this appearance of homogeneity masked considerable differences. In much the same way that Christian missionaries adopted the forms of local customs, folklore and religions in their proselytizing abroad, British parties adopted local styles in appealing for the vote in Scotland. The Conservative Party was not, in fact, known by that name in Scotland for about half of the twentieth century. Between 1912 and 1965, it was styled the Scottish Unionist Party. Notably, the Union in the title referred not to the Anglo-Scottish Union but the British Union with Ireland.

This title gave the Scottish Tories a number of advantages. First, it allowed it to appear distinctly Scottish and it was not seen simply as a branch of a London-based party. Second, it allowed it to appeal to working-class Protestants, a significant part of the electorate that might otherwise have been unlikely to support it, but who provided much of its electoral strength. It would be wrong to suggest that this was an appeal to Orange votes, as its appeal appears to have gone well beyond sectarian loyalties. It does, however, highlight a significant aspect of political behaviour that distinguished Scotland from much of England and Wales. Religion was more important in Scotland and continues to have a lingering significance in voting behaviour than old British orthodoxies about class voting admitted. The decision to change the party's name and incorporate 'Conservative' into its title has been seen in some quarters as having contributed to its decline (Seawright 1999: 127–45). From its highpoint in 1955, when 36 Scottish Tory MPs were elected compared to 35 Scottish Labour MPs, support for the party fell almost continuously thereafter. No Scottish Tory was returned in 1997, an election that saw 56 Scottish Labour MPs elected. Being in power in Westminster with large majorities, while not being the majority party in Scotland fed perceptions that 'English Conservatives' were imposing their will against Scottish opinion.

Labour in Scotland was the most centrally controlled party during most of the twentieth century, something reflecting the dominant ideology of the party as support for central planning and central governmental decision-making were reflected in the party's own organization. A 'Scottish Council of the Labour Party' existed and Scottish Party Conferences were held, although these were only marginally more powerful than their English regional equivalents. However, Labour was adept in appealing to voters in Scotland as a party that had Scotland's interests at heart. The party's ability to appeal on the basis of its working-class credentials combined with a strong Scottish identity proved electorally successful (Brand *et al.* 1994: 219–20).

The Scottish National Party (SNP) was the most obvious manifestation of Scottish distinctiveness, but found itself on the fringes of politics for most of the twentieth century. Home rule was a fairly marginal issue in Scottish politics until the latter part of the century. Issues that dominated Scottish politics tended to be the same as in England and Wales, although there were differences of emphasis and a few distinct issues would emerge. Bubbling away under the surface of Scottish politics, home rule only became a pressing issue in the late 1960s. The Liberals, having dominated nineteenth-century Scotland, found themselves marginalized in the twentieth century, able to maintain some support in geographically peripheral regions. In their own different ways, each party highlighted its Scottish credentials when most electorally successful in Scotland.

Why devolution?

Support for some measure of Scottish self-government existed throughout most of the twentieth century, but this support, though widespread, was shallow. Home rule was not a high priority and Scots continued to vote for parties that opposed home rule. This began to change in the 1960s as Westminster and Whitehall struggled to deal with a variety of economic and social problems and British nationalism – a political identification with Britain – became less attractive. The alternative of Scottish nationalism – a political identification with Scotland – became more attractive as the former lost much of its appeal. But support for Scottish devolution, specifically a Scottish Parliament, remained fairly shallow and reactive and amounted to little more than protest support.

However, the SNP picked up support in local elections, won famous by-elections in 1967 and 1973, and did reasonably well in general elections, especially in October 1974 when it took 11 of Scotland's 71 seats, winning 30 per cent of the vote.

The reactions of the other parties to these developments were inconsistent, confused and half-hearted in support for devolution. In 1968, Ted Heath, the then Conservative leader, shocked his party when he announced the Conservatives would support a limited measure of Scottish devolution. The following year, Labour, in government at the time, announced a Royal Commission on the Constitution to investigate the issue. On coming to power in 1970, Heath failed to deliver on the promise made in opposition. The SNP's performance in that year's general election, although much better than anything it had previously achieved, was less than had been anticipated, seemingly signalling that pressure for change had gone. Conservative support for devolution was quietly forgotten and once Margaret Thatcher replaced Heath in 1975 the party became hostile.

After 1974, however, Labour moved in the other direction to the Conservatives. The revival in SNP fortunes prompted Labour to deliver a measure of devolution. The problem was that the party was deeply divided on the issue and there were few members who were committed in principle to the policy. In order for the leadership to win the necessary support for a measure of Scottish (and Welsh) devolution, it had to promise a referendum on the matter. The referendum was duly held in March 1979 against a backdrop of falling support for the Labour Government. Although 52 per cent of Scots voted for devolution, a requirement had been included in the legislation stipulating that 40 per cent of the eligible electorate (not just those who voted) had to vote in favour. Because only 33 per cent of the total electorate supported devolution, the measure was rejected. This created a strong sense of grievance amongst supporters of devolution who felt they had been robbed of a prize they had actually won majority support for. Conversely, while such events created considerable disillusionment at the time, over the longer term they provided Scottish home rulers with some hope. Margaret Thatcher became Prime Minister in May 1979 and made it clear that she would not contemplate any measure of devolution. Her mistake, like that of Ted Heath a decade before, was to misinterpret Scottish public opinion. She assumed the referendum result showed little enthusiasm for devolution and, believed that the collapse in support for the SNP in the 1979 general election amounted to the end of the matter. It did not, and before too long, through the agency of the SNP, but also the Labour Party, the issue of Scottish devolution pushed itself to the forefront of the Scottish political agenda.

As noted, throughout most of the twentieth century, central government in London at Westminster, regardless of which party was in power, had been sensitive to the Scottish dimension of politics. It may have been fairly insignificant amongst its concerns, but Westminster was generally willing to accommodate Scottish distinctiveness. Although Britain was highly centralized, Westminster had made concessions to Scottish sensibilities, as indicated by the establishment of the Scottish Office. Each major party was sensitive to Scottish distinctiveness when in office, but when in opposition each in turn accused the governing party of failing Scotland in some way. This may not have been the main argument deployed by opposition parties against parties in government but was a recurring theme of Scottish politics. It ensured a continuing focus, however limited, on the Scottish dimension. One of the most under-examined aspects of post-war politics was the acceptance of a measure of territorial pluralism. Most significantly, Scottish public opinion believed that this had changed in 1979 (or was believed to have changed) with the arrival in Downing Street of Margaret Thatcher.

Thatcher's political agenda did not include much room for accommodating Scottish sensitivities. From her perspective, the Scots might occasionally vote SNP but in the final analysis they would always be British. Yet the Scottish public increasingly viewed Thatcher and her government as not only hostile to devolution but unsympathetic to Scotland. Labour in opposition, as had opposition parties in the past, were quick to play the Scottish card. It emphasized its Scottishness and attacked the Conservatives for being anti-Scottish. For its own reasons, the SNP, naturally, concurred with the latter part of Labour's strategy in Scotland. There were, however, some significant differences from the past. First, between 1979 and 1997 the Conservatives were in office for a long period of time. With their support declining during this period it became relatively easy and increasingly attractive for Labour to attack the Conservatives as anti-Scottish. Second, Margaret Thatcher seemed unwilling to make any effort to appease the Scots, appearing to be oblivious to the damage done to her party north of the border. From her perspective the Conservative position in Scotland mattered little so long as the party won majorities in England that would secure its position across Britain. The idea that a governing party should seek to command support from across Britain as a whole had been seemingly abandoned; although the Conservatives pursued the deliberate strategy of building support in their heartlands, the Scots damned them for neglecting Scotland. This had the effect of undermining Conservative support in Scotland but also fuelling support for Scottish devolution. Third, whereas support for Scottish devolution had in the past been widespread and shallow, it now became more deep-rooted and became associated with a broader progressive political coalition. This was most evident amongst Labour supporters and members, and Scottish Labour's grudging support for devolution in the 1970s was transformed into a genuine commitment by the late 1980s (Mitchell 1998).

The change of Prime Minister in 1990 made little difference to the Conservatives' standing in Scotland. Being softer on the Scottish question, willing to concede and conciliate when necessary, John Major's approach was quite different from Margaret Thatcher's, but he remained resolutely opposed to devolution, declaring it a 'threat to the Union'. A similar approach may have worked in an earlier period, but by the time Major became Prime Minister the devolution die had been cast. Although Labour's political transformation under Tony Blair involved the party jettisoning many past policy commitments, the policy of devolution in both Scotland and Wales remained sacrosanct. Blair might have been 'least happy about' the policy (Anderson and Mann 1997: 283), but it was here to stay. Any attempt to undermine the policy would have provoked divisions that would have seriously damaged the party and its prospects in Scotland.

By the 1997 general election, Labour was fully committed to both Scottish and Welsh devolution, so much so the half-hearted commitment evidenced by some Labour MPs in 1979 was a thing of the past. After 1989, Labour had discussed devolution with Scottish Liberal Democrats and other interested parties in a 'Constitutional Convention', but its policy remained much the same. That said, Labour had amended its policy, and it now referred to a Scottish Parliament where it had previously spoken of a Scottish Assembly, something symbolising a deepening of support for devolution. Labour had declared it would grant the parliament tax-raising powers and additional responsibilities long before the Convention, but within the Convention these commitments were firmed up in terms of level of commitment and watered down in terms of their content.

However, within the Convention, Labour did evidence a degree of radicalism in respect to how the Scottish Parliament should be elected. Labour reached an agreement with Liberal Democrats in favour of a hybrid electoral system, the Additional Member System (AMS). This mixed system combined the traditional Single Member Plurality System (SMPS or First-Past-The-Post) with a more proportional regional list system. In the 129 Member Parliament, some 73 MSPs were to be elected directly, and a further 56 'top-up' MSPs would be returned according to each party's share of the vote. This electoral system ensured there would be a more proportional relationship between votes cast and seats won and it restricted the ability of the party with the largest minority of the vote from receiving a large majority of seats in the Scottish Parliament. In practice this meant that Labour, which dominated Scottish politics under SMPS, winning 56 of the 72 Scottish Westminster seats in 1997, would be less likely to govern by itself and would probably have to govern in coalition with others, most likely the Liberal Democrats. The logic behind Labour's support for an electoral system which would prevent Labour dominating Scottish politics, as SMPS would have ensured, was not altruism on the part of the Labour Party, nor was it support for greater pluralism and consensus (Brown 2000: 47). It owed everything to rational calculation: discarding the prospect of governing Scotland on its own was the price Labour was prepared to pay for preventing the SNP from ever governing on its own. Jack McConnell, then Labour's Scottish general secretary, now First Minister in the Scottish Executive, confirmed in April 1997 that the electoral system had been devised to prevent the SNP winning an outright majority. Indeed, after the first elections to the Scottish Parliament in 1999, Labour formed a coalition with the Liberal Democrats, as had been widely predicted.

One of the enduring myths of Scottish politics has been the exaggerated significance attached to the role of the Constitutional Convention in the emergence of the Scottish Parliament. This myth, propagated in part by many of those intimately associated with it, has had the intention of understating the role played by the SNP in devolution, which had refused to participate in the Convention. In reality, however, Scottish devolution owed much more to the work of the Labour government elected in 1997 than to the Convention. Ministers sorted out the fine detail of actually establishing the Scottish Parliament, addressing trickier matters left un-addressed by the Convention. In addition, devolution owed a great deal to public pressures which culminated in the overwhelming support recorded in the second referendum held in September 1997.

The idea of a referendum had not originally featured in Labour's plans in the 1980s, nor was it discussed in the Constitutional Convention, but it was proposed unilaterally by Tony Blair in the summer of 1996. The referendum took two parts. The first question asked Scots if they wanted a Parliament and the second asked Scots is they wanted the Parliament to have tax-varying powers. Though the dual referendum infuriated the Liberal Democrats, it was to prove a sensible rational decision. Michael Forsyth, the Conservative Secretary of State for Scotland in the closing years of the Major government, frequently argued that only two new additions to Scottish politics would follow devolution: More politicians and more taxes, the 'tartan tax', as Forsyth persistently referred to the Parliament's tax-raising power, charges which helped provoke Labour's leadership at

Table 9.1 *Results of Scottish devolution referendum, 1997*

	% of votes cast	% of electorate
Q1. Support a Scottish parliament?		
Yes	74.3	44.7
No	25.7	15.5
Q2. Support tax-raising powers?		
Yes	63.5	38.1
No	36.5	21.9
Turnout		60.4

Source: Adapted from Mitchell (2001).

Westminster into proposing the pre-devolution referendums. The small cost in terms of Labour's credibility as a consensual partner in the Convention was compensated for by undermining Conservative attacks on devolution that focused on the spectre of a tax-raising assembly. The dual referendum also provided legitimacy to devolution from the outset. The establishment of the Scottish Parliament was the creation of political calculation and political interests. It had little to do with some vague notion of 'new politics', nor did its creation usher in a totally new type of politics. Finally, the referendums also allowed Labour to detach the issue of devolution from its 1997 general election campaign. Labour could argue in favour of devolution, but demonstrate that the decision would ultimately be made by the voters in a referendum, not by the government of the day.

Scottish institutions and policies after devolution

The creation of the Scottish Parliament, not least the establishment of a Scottish Executive exercising powers once held by the Scottish Office, marked a major change in Scottish politics. With the Parliament having been first elected in May 1999, the various institutions that have been established in the wake of devolution will take some time to bed in. An important development prompted by women's groups most notably in the trade unions, was a focus on the representation of women. At the 1999 elections for the Scottish Parliament, the Labour Party adopted selection procedures resulting in 50 per cent of its MSPs being women, 46 per cent of SNP MSPs were women, but the Liberal Democrats,

Labour's partners in the Convention, returned only three women out of its seventeen MSPs. The Convention had also sought to encourage more ethnic-minority representation, but in this it failed completely. Within the Parliament itself, its committee system has had to evolve, and, most significantly, its procedures have had to be adapted to take into account a legislature elected under an electoral system that contains an element of proportionality. In this regard, particularly within a political system where SMPS usually ensures single-party government, the current composition of the Scottish Parliament (and the Labour-Liberal Democrat coalition Executive) perhaps reflects a significant shift away from Westminster-style majoritarian politics toward a form of coalition politics.

Supporters of the Scottish Parliament have emphasized the differences between it and its Westminster counterpart. David Steel, its Presiding Officer (the equivalent of the Commons Speaker), for example, set out twelve differences between the Scottish Parliament and the Westminster Parliament in a speech in 2001: the Parliament has a fixed term of four years; there are no annual sessions and legislation can continue through all four years of the Parliament; the Parliament is elected by a system with a proportional element making it very unlikely that any one party would be able to form an Executive on its own; the Parliamentary chamber is a different shape to the House of Commons, it has a U-shaped chamber and government and opposition benches adjoin rather than face one another; more 'civilised' hours are kept by the Parliament with sittings rarely after 6.00 pm; the Parliament has a high percentage of women members; Bills are scrutinized by relevant committees and evidence taken from interested bodies before they are debated in the Parliament; a Petitions Committee receives public petitions; a weekly public 'time for reflection' led by different faiths reflecting their size instead of Anglican prayers before opening of Parliamentary business at Westminster; proceedings are webcast; the Parliament attempts to be more accessible to the public; a new modern Parliament, the Holyrood Parliament building in Edinburgh is being built (Steel, 2001). Whether these amount to a radically different form of politics is open to debate, but a significant number of commentators appear to believe that together these constitute a new form of politics.

While exclusively Scottish interest groups existed before devolution, there has been a growth in their number and activities since 1999 and they now increasingly focus their attention on the Scottish Parliament. The type of interest group that now has access to the Scottish Executive may owe much to the fact that Labour and the Liberal Democrats are in office, than to the creation of the Scottish Parliament itself. Members of the Scottish Parliament (MSPs) encourage interest groups to petition the Parliament, but the evidence that this has altered the content of policy is uncertain. Nonetheless, the refocusing of interest group activity in the wake of devolution has been reflected in news media attention. Scottish MPs at Westminster complain that they are increasingly ignored by a Scottish media that focuses on the Scottish Parliament, rather than Scottish politics generally. News media coverage of local government and of extra-parliamentary politics in Scotland can be said to have suffered as much as the Westminster-based House of Commons in recent years.

The Conservative charge that the Scottish Parliament would not be able to do anything that the Scottish Office could already do, except, should it wish, to raise taxes, proved not entirely correct. The most significant post-devolution change is that the Scottish Parliament reflects the wishes of the Scottish electorate, rather than a British electorate. With a Labour government at Westminster and a Labour–Liberal Democrat Executive in Edinburgh, this change may not be obvious, but it is likely to become much more evident when different parties are in office in Westminster and Edinburgh. Even in the context of the first Scottish Parliament a number of developments have taken place that would not have been possible had the Scottish Parliament not existed. First, the quantity of Scottish legislation that has been enacted has been much greater than in the past. Second, legislation has been passed that would not have been passed, even if time had been available, at Westminster.

The pre-devolution Westminster Parliament did make some time available for some exclusively Scottish pieces of legislation, but a lack of parliamentary time did prevent many measures, including many non-controversial measures, from being passed. In its first three years, the Scottish Parliament enacted over forty pieces of legislation. Most of this would have been supported by Labour in Westminster had devolution not existed, but some exclusively Scottish legislation would not have been passed for lack of parliamentary time. A few measures passed by the Scottish Parliament would not have been passed by Westminster, and these proposals did meet opposition from Westminster. Two pieces of legislation can be highlighted. First, the Liberal Democrats had campaigned to abolish tuition fees for Scottish university students, a policy first introduced by the Labour government in 1998. Although a watered-down policy was eventually passed, it was not one Labour at Westminster wanted, and it has created pressure in England and Wales for a similar measure to be introduced there. Second, in the case of free care for the elderly, Scottish policy had initially been the same as in England and Wales, but after the death of Donald Dewar, Scotland's First Minister (as Scotland's Prime Minister is called), and the election of his successor, Henry McLeish, the policy of the Scottish Executive changed and a different policy for Scotland emerged. This was opposed by Westminster, and once again has subsequently led to pressure in England and Wales to follow Scotland. Most significantly, thanks to devolution, these examples amount to a reversal of past practice when Scotland had generally followed England and Wales.

As in the past, however, very real political and constitutional constraints continue to limit the autonomy of Scottish policy making. Finance remains the major issue and the Scottish Parliament has only very limited power to raise its own money. It can only vote to vary, to raise or reduce, the rate of general taxation by some 3 per cent. However this is a power, one that is not available to the Welsh Assembly, which the Scottish Parliament has not used since Labour and the Liberal Democrats came to form the majority. Labour specifically gave a campaign pledge that it would not use the parliament's tax raising powers. As a result of this self-denying ordinance, the most significant power of the Scottish Parliament – as it is guided by the Scottish Executive – is to decide how to distribute monies voted to Scotland by the Westminster Parliament. Expensive new policies can only be introduced at the expense of existing policies. The formula used in determining Scotland's share of national monies provided by Westminster is largely based on decisions made affecting English spending priorities. If more money, say, goes into education in England and Wales, the Scottish total will increase even though the Scottish Parliament is not obliged to spend that increase on education.

Many commentaries list the 'powers' of the Scottish Parliament as the functions which have been devolved – including health, education, training and lifelong learning, local government, social work, housing, area regeneration, economic development, inward investment, tourism, transport, prisons, police, agriculture, sport, fisheries. Yet, this gives a false impression of what the Scottish Parliament can do and of the nature of post-devolution Scottish politics. There is far more overlap of responsibilities between Westminster and Edinburgh than this list implies. Devolution has not resulted in separate institutions determining policies separately for Scotland, but it has meant that new Scottish institutions do share some responsibility and power with Westminster-based institutions for policy-making.

Public opinion and parties after devolution

As noted above, Scottish party politics moved away from being dominated by the two main British parties some time ago. In terms of party representation, for some time now Scotland has had one dominant party, Labour, and three smaller parties, the Conservatives, the SNP and the Liberal Democrats, who compete for second, third and fourth place. In the 2001 UK general election, Labour's share of the Scottish vote was 43.2 per cent, something which under SMPS gave the party 55 MPs, some 76.4 per cent of Westminster seats. The SNP, by contrast, won 20.1 per cent of the vote but returned only 5 MPs, 6.9 per cent of Westminster seats. The Conservatives won 15.6 per cent of the vote and one MP, 1.4 per cent of the seats, and the Liberal Democrats, 16.4 per cent of the vote and 10 MPs, 13.9 per cent of the seats. As such, the adoption of AMS for elections to the Scottish Parliament has had a major impact on political representation in Scotland. That said, SMPS remains in place in local elections, allowing continued Labour dominance of local government, and in Scottish elections to the Westminster Parliament. Labour dominance in Scotland has long been evidenced in the number of MPs and Councillors elected, but this has not accurately reflected real levels of party support. The composition of the Scottish Parliament more accurately reflects public support for the parties and this has significant real (and potential) implications.

The main beneficiary of AMS in elections to the Scottish Parliament has been the SNP, traditionally the party most disadvantaged by SMPS. However, AMS also makes it difficult for the SNP to repeat Labour's pre-devolution dominance, making it difficult for the party to command an outright majority at Holyrood. The SNP, for some time Scotland's second party in terms of share of the vote, struggled to win seats in the Commons, but in the Scottish Parliament is now clearly Scotland's second party. As a result, the Conservatives and Liberal Democrats now compete for third place. AMS also enables other parties to emerge, principally the Scottish Socialist Party, a radical nationalist party, which has a Scottish Parliament seat held by its charismatic leader Tommy Sheridan. The Green Party also has one MSP and Dennis Canavan, a former Labour MP, was elected as an Independent MSP. Within the Labour-led Executive the Liberal Democrats have called for AMS to be extended to Scottish local government, but unremarkably, Labour has opposed this. Such a reform would undermine Labour's traditional hold on much of Scotland, and prompt dramatic changes in party politics. Hence Labour's opposition.

Despite these major institutional changes, specifically the Scottish Parliament and its new electoral system, public opinion in Scotland has remained fairly constant. According to opinion polls, support for the different parties fluctuates, but does so within the established usual parameters. Devolution has not killed off the SNP, as some Labour MPs claimed it would, but neither has it seen the SNP surge ahead. Public opinion on further constitutional change remains fairly constant too. Support for independence has rarely climbed above 30 per cent, but polls consistently record strong support for increased powers for the Parliament (Curtice, 2001) and support for undoing devolution is negligible. So far, then, devolution has not encouraged further changes in public attitudes north (or south) of the border.

Conclusion

In political terms, pre-devolution Scotland still differed in significant respects from the rest of Britain, and this was a result of institutional differences, which had a number of repercussions for public policy. While Scottish party politics and public opinion echoed those of the wider Britain, deeper analysis identified many differences, yet such differences were subsumed beneath the myth of the uniform, unitary state, a myth which held sway in people's minds. When compared with other European countries, territorial political differences within Britain were fairly unexceptional, but while other countries had long witnessed internal diversity, what made Scotland's position within Britain unusual was the nation's institutional form. No other region within a liberal democracy had anything like a Scottish Office, a territorial Department of State discharging a range of responsibilities headed by ministers, appointed by the Prime Minister, and accountable to a central Parliament. In two senses, therefore, devolution has normalized Scottish politics. First, there is now a widespread understanding of Britain as a multi-national political community, a union state, not a unitary state, although it can be argued that the territorial political diversity within that state might now be overstated where it was previously understated. Second, post-devolution, this territorially based political diversity within this union state, in Scotland, in Wales, and in (the particular case of) Northern Ireland, is reflected in the emergence of elected assemblies and political institutions below the level of the British central government.

As certain powers to influence particular public policies have passed from Westminster at the centre to new political institutions at the locality, the new orthodoxy is that devolution has radically changed Scotland. In some cases, this new orthodoxy reflects for the first time the awareness of Scottish distinctiveness. Yet, as discussed above, pre-devolution Scotland was already distinct in a number of respects. The issue is not whether Scotland is different as a consequence of devolution, but whether it is more different as a result. The Scottish Parliament and the Scottish Executive have proved to be major institutional innovations, yet the extent to which Scotland's relations with Westminster, both governmental and non-governmental bodies has changed is perhaps less clear. If public policy differences between Scotland and England and Wales are to be judged in terms of legislative output, the Scottish Parliament has made a significant difference. The party system has also altered as a consequence of changes in the electoral system, specifically the shift away from SMPS and the adoption of AMS. There have also been some changes in public opinion. However, as the one time Conservative Secretary of State for Scotland, Michael Forsyth, often stated, a new Scottish Parliament, like the proverbial young puppy, is 'not just for Christmas'.

It is difficult to assess the extent to which already existing devolution will create a dynamic of its own, a 'widening' and 'deepening' of the responsibilities granted the new political institutions. The Labour MP Tam Dalyell, a long established and vehement opponent of devolution, argued that the whole exercise would put Scotland on a 'motorway without an exit'. Devolution would therefore make Scottish independence inevitable. This is the principal objective of the SNP, but Labour expects (perhaps hopes) that devolution will copperfasten Scotland within the United Kingdom, while granting certain powers and responsibilities that confer a degree of 'authoritative autonomy'. Time alone will tell which perspective will prove correct. At present, poll evidence suggests that Scottish independence is not likely in the near (or distant) future. Moreover, while polls remain only temporal snapshots of public opinion (and, as such, they are open to change), they further suggest that electoral support for Scottish independence has stalled. However, the SNP has had a devolution dividend with its vote jumping in polls for the Scottish Parliament though it appears to have been a one-off benefit rather than a springboard to further advances.

So far, the pressure to create a Scottish Parliament consisted of two elements. First, it drew on a powerful sense of a Scottish identity. Second, it was encouraged by the dynamic of Scottish opposition to Scotland being governed by a party, the Thatcher and Major-led Conservatives, which Scotland did not elect and did not want. Devolution has considerably strengthened this Scottish distinctiveness. The degree of political interest in the Scottish Parliament and the Scottish Executive, fuelled by a news media focus on Scotland and its politics, has certainly helped promote an increased sense of Scottishness. While it may be expected that this will continue, there is no obvious modern equivalent of the Thatcher government around which a pro-Scottish oppositionalism can be mobilized. That said, it is not inconceivable that some such dynamic will emerge. When allied with the stronger Scottish base born of a heightened sense of Scottishness owing much to Scottish devolution, this might one day prompt new demands for Scottish independence from Britain. That, at any rate, is the hope of the SNP.

As the 2003 election looms, the prospect of major change in party support in the Scottish Parliament seems remote. The most likely outcome is that Labour will remain the largest party in coalition with the Liberal Democrats, with the SNP as the main opposition party. However, the Liberal Democrats appear set to replace the Conservatives as Scotland's third party and the Scottish Socialists are likely to pick up a few seats. Marginal change apart, the 2003 election looks likely to be similar to that of 1999.

Chapter 10

Politics in Northern Ireland

JONATHAN TONGE

The 1998 Good Friday Agreement offered the prospect of closure to a conflict lasting three decades in Northern Ireland. The Agreement attempted a permanent solution to Britain's Irish problem, or Ireland's British problem, which has endured for several centuries. Although sceptics continued to view the Agreement as merely a hope against history, a transition to a relatively peaceful Northern Ireland was achieved. The Agreement was an attempt to manage, if not resolve, Northern Ireland's political faultline, that between British unionists and Irish nationalists, through an interlocking set of political institutions. Political aspirations remain unaltered: (protestant) unionists remain committed to the maintenance of Northern Ireland's place within the United Kingdom, whilst (catholic) nationalists, although less unanimous in their constitutional preferences, broadly aspire to a united Ireland, or greater expressions of their Irish identity. By harnessing competing aspirations within a three-stranded framework, based upon power sharing in Northern Ireland, an all-Ireland dimension and a confederation of the British Isles, the Good Friday Agreement was an attempt to embed rivalries within permanently peaceful, constitutional politics.

The peace process attempted to end the violent pursuit of a united Ireland by republicans, mainly in the IRA, and to remove loyalist violence, which had been designed partly to emphasize the human cost of any British withdrawal from Northern Ireland. Since its creation in 1920, Northern Ireland has been an insecure state. For fifty years, sectarian discrimination by unionist governments and nationalist abstention had exacerbated the abnormality of the state, which was devoid of a proper system of government and opposition. Nationalist politics moved from abstention to civil rights protests in the 1960s and finally to armed insurrection in the 1970s. The seeming inability of Unionists to alter their political agenda led to the suspension of the devolved unionist government in 1972 and the introduction of direct rule from Westminster by the British Government. After 1968, 3,600 deaths occurred as a result of political conflict in Northern Ireland. If placed on a population pro rata basis throughout Britain, this would have meant a staggering 111,000 deaths, with some 500,000 people being charged with a terrorist offence (Hayes and McAllister 2000). Protagonists on all sides suffered losses, although civilians represented the largest category of deaths.

Political developments in the 1990s were predicated upon the need to include rather than marginalize the political representatives of paramilitary groups. These political and paramilitary organizations are outlined in Box 10.1. Several events were crucial in developing the peace process but the largest single factor in furthering the development of a peace process was the dilution of the agenda of republicans (see below). However, all sides involved in Northern Ireland also shifted their positions. In fostering a peace process, the British Government acknowledged that an outright military defeat of the IRA was impossible. The 1993 Downing Street Declaration made clear that Britain had 'no selfish, strategic or economic interest' in Northern Ireland and the British Government stressed to republicans that they were not fighting an anti-colonial war in Northern Ireland, but were merely upholding the present wishes of the majority of its population. This assertion of a non-colonial, non-territorial claim to Northern Ireland sufficiently interested republicans for the IRA to call a ceasefire in August 1994, reciprocated by loyalist paramilitary groups six weeks later. After the Conservative Government under John Major, dependent upon unionist votes in the House of Commons, failed to include Sinn Fein in multi-party talks in the mid-1990s, the IRA ceasefire fractured, only to be reinstated upon the election of a Labour Government in 1997. For its part, the Irish Government used the Downing Street Declaration to declare its willingness to discard Articles 2 and 3 of its Constitution, which lay claim to Northern Ireland, something that was crucial in securing unionist acceptance of the Good Friday Agreement.

The Good Friday Agreement: a new consociational democracy?

The 1998 Good Friday Agreement established a 108-member Northern Ireland Assembly and a power-sharing executive, the first elected by proportional representation under the Single Transferable Vote (STV) system. Although overly large for a population of 1.6 million, the vastness of the Assembly was justified on the grounds that it ensured the inclusion of a wide variety of opinion and it was awarded a large range of competences, including education, health, social services, agriculture and economic development. At its head lies the Executive, led by the First and Deputy First Minister, jointly elected to office with the consent of a majority of unionist and nationalist Members of the Legislative Assembly (MLAs), and ten departmental heads reflecting both unionists and nationalists. This consociational basis was the most important feature of the Good Friday Agreement (O'Leary 1999), which required representatives of competitive ethnic blocs to share power. This 'big tent' power sharing was reinforced by the need for parallel consent for approval of certain legislative measures in the Assembly. Protection for the nationalist minority was offered through such voting requirements. The Agreement contained a series of measures designed to achieve equality and parity of esteem for the two communities.

Within the Assembly, all shades of opinion – loyalist, unionist, nationalist, republican, are represented. According to the First Minister and UUP leader, David Trimble, at the first meeting of the Assembly in 1999, this was a 'pluralist parliament for a pluralist people', a repudiation of unionism's pre-1972 protestant parliament for a protestant people. Each MLA is obliged to designate as unionist, nationalist, or 'other'. Designations, party strengths and attitudes to the Good Friday Agreement are indicated in Table 10.1.

One central theme of the Good Friday Agreement, the need for the consent of Northern Ireland's peoples for constitutional change, contains little that is novel. The declaration of the British Government, that there can be no change in the status of Northern Ireland without the consent of a majority of its citizens, has been central to all political experiments since 1973. The 'green language', the embracing of nationalist aspirations, that was contained in parts of the Good Friday Agreement was countered by the realpolitik of the maintenance of the consent principle. Other aspects of the Good Friday Agreement did contain more novel thinking. The constitutional claim of the Irish Government to Northern Ireland was withdrawn, a move supported by the voters of the Irish Republic in a referendum in 1998. Combined with the referendum in Northern Ireland, a (limited) exercise in co-determination of the future of the island was initiated.

Previous attempts at power sharing, such as the 1974 Sunningdale Agreement, offered a coalition of the moderate centre, whereas the Good Friday Agreement pulled together a wider array of political forces, including the polar extremes. It brought together political leaders in an accommodation within political institutions, whilst acknowledging their competing identities. The desire of nationalists to be Irish and be awarded political expression of that Irishness was respected; a similar position was taken on the Britishness of unionists. Although a basic loyalty to Northern Ireland was encouraged through power sharing and a stake in the state, the Agreement also emphasized the need for a binational political approach. Strand Two of the Agreement established a

North–South ministerial council, comprising representatives from the Irish Dail and the Northern Ireland Executive. The initial role of the Council was to identify and oversee twelve areas of cross border cooperation, six of which were to be new implementation bodies.

Ulster Unionist members of the North-South Council believed the modest all-island dimension was ringfenced. The North-South Council did not constitute a dynamic, freestanding body. Further cross-border implementation bodies could only be introduced with the consent of the Irish parliament and, more significantly, the Northern Ireland Assembly.

Box 10.1   Main political and paramilitary organizations in Northern Ireland

Unionist/Loyalist: Common aim: retention of Northern Ireland's place within the United Kingdom

Constitutional organizations

UUP   Ulster Unionist Party: largest unionist party, pro-Good Friday Agreement, but divided on power sharing with Sinn Fein.

DUP   Democratic Unionist Party: main unionist rival to UUP, anti-Agreement.

PUP   Progressive Unionist Party: small working-class, socialist, pro-Agreement party.

UKUP   United Kingdom Unionist Party: small anti-Agreement party, supports full integration of Northern Ireland into the United Kingdom.

NIUP   Northern Ireland Unionist Party: small anti-Agreement party, broke from the UKUP in 1999.

UUAP   United Unionist Assembly Party: small anti-Agreement party.

Paramilitary organizations

UVF   Ulster Volunteer Force: pro-Agreement and on ceasefire, represented politically by the PUP.

UDA   Ulster Defence Association.: initially pro-Agreement, but now anti-Agreement and no longer on ceasefire, represented politically by the New Ulster Political Research Group.

UFF   Ulster Freedom Fighters: essentially the 'killing wing' of the UDA.

RHD   Red Hand Defenders: anti-Agreement maverick group, allegedly linked to the LVF and lacking a political agenda.

LVF   Loyalist Volunteer Force. Breakaway from the UVF, anti-Agreement.

→

Given a unionist majority in any Assembly, a proliferation of cross border bodies was unlikely. Nonetheless, the Democratic Unionist Party saw the North-South Council as a Trojan horse for Irish unity and declined participation. The limited cross-border bodies fell short of the joint sovereignty desired by some nationalists.

A further strand of the Agreement was the British–Irish Council, comprising representatives of the British and Irish Governments and devolved institutions throughout the United Kingdom. This offers a mildly confederal element, desired by unionists as a means of shoring

---

Centre parties

APNI   Alliance Party of Northern Ireland: pro-Agreement, rejects unionism and nationalism, mainly middle-class, based in east of Northern Ireland.

NIWC Northern Ireland Women's Coalition: offers input from women to politics, strongly pro-Agreement, neutral on Northern Ireland's constitutional future.

Nationalist/Republican: **Common aim: establishment of a united Ireland**

Constitutional parties

SF   Sinn Fein: pro-Agreement, became the largest nationalist party in 2001, still linked to the Provisional IRA, but now the dominant arm of the republican movement.

SDLP   Social Democratic and Labour Party: pro-Agreement main nationalist party from formation (1970) until 2001, much of its political thinking evident in the Good Friday Agreement, but now under electoral pressure from Sinn Fein.

Paramilitary organizations

PIRA   Provisional IRA: on ceasefire since 1994, apart from 1996–97, represented politically by Sinn Fein, began decommissioning weapons in 2001.

RIRA   Real IRA: tiny hardline breakaway from the Provisional IRA, in protest at Republican 'peace strategy', killed 29 civilians at Omagh in 1998, 32 County Sovereignty Committee is RIRA's political outlet.

CIRA   Continuity IRA: tiny hardline breakaway from the Provisional IRA, represented politically by Republican Sinn Fein, which broke in 1986 from Provisional Sinn Fein, over the latter's recognition of the 'partitionist' Irish Republic. Demands British withdrawal.

INLA   Irish National Liberation Army: very small anti-Agreement group, represented politically by far-left Irish Republican Socialist Party.

Table 10.1   *Northern Ireland Assembly prior to suspension, 2002*

Pro-Agreement unionist parties	Seats
Ulster Unionist Party+	26
Progressive Unionist Party	2
Anti-Agreement unionist parties	
Democratic Unionist Party	20
Northern Ireland Unionist Party#	3
United Unionist Assembly Party##	3
Independent Unionist++	3
UK Unionist	1
Nationalist parties (both pro-Agreement)	
SDLP	24
Sinn Fein	18
Other parties (both pro-Agreement)	
Alliance	6
Women's Coalition	2

Notes:
+ Peter Weir was expelled and joined the Democratic Unionist Party: see below
++ Total includes Roger Hutchinson, expelled from the Northern Ireland Unionist Party in December 1999.
# Elected as UK Unionist Party; resigned and formed Northern Ireland Unionist Party with effect from 15 January 1999
Elected as Independent candidates; formed United Unionist Assembly Party with effect from 21 September 1998

Northern Ireland's place within a restructured United Kingdom. Devoid of formal legislative powers, the British-Irish Council was an agenda-setting body, offering scope for bilateral or multilateral agreements. The importance of the second aspect of Strand Three was understated. In subsuming the Anglo-Irish secretariat loathed by unionists since set up under the 1985 Anglo–Irish Agreement, the British-Irish Intergovernmental Conference established under the Good Friday Agreement nonetheless continued to exercise some similar functions. In the absence of devolved institutions, the Intergovernmental Conference offered continuing Anglo-Irish intergovernmentalism.

The true novelty of the Agreement lay in its inclusivity. There was a deliberate enticement of republican and loyalist paramilitaries. Sunningdale offered nothing to republicans, beyond a review of

Table 10.2   *The Good Friday Agreement referendums 1998*

	Yes	%	No	%	Turnout (%)
Northern Ireland	676,966	71.1	274,879	28.9	81.0
Republic of Ireland	1,442,583	94.4	85,748	5.6	55.6

internment. The 1998 Agreement, in contrast, covered a broad range of human rights and equality issues, with the release of prisoners attractive to republicans and loyalists. By including parity, prisoners and policing issues within the Agreement, the widest possible constituency would enjoy a stake. The use of referendums, north and south, gave the deal broader legitimacy. Unlike other attempts at settlement, the Good Friday Agreement enjoyed a popular mandate. The May 1998 referendum on the Agreement produced a narrow majority in favour of the deal within the unionist community; a substantial majority overall in Northern Ireland and overwhelming majority support, albeit on a low turnout, in the Irish Republic.

The most optimistic scenario in respect of the new institutions was that they would unfreeze Northern Ireland's sectarian divide. On issues such as the eleven-plus examination, university tuition fees and healthcare, intra-party division may be more important than ethnic bloc politics. Cross-community or class-based alliances could be formed. For example, Sinn Fein and the PUP both oppose the eleven-plus examination and university tuition fees. The Agreement offered a potential withering of ethno-national politics as constitutional issues diminished in salience. Pessimists believed that the abnormality of Northern Ireland politics, in which national identity and religious affiliation determine party allegiance, would continue unabated. The electoral evidence thus far is examined below.

Practical and theoretical problems with the Good Friday Agreement

Despite its apparent popularity, the Good Friday Agreement was criticized on practical and theoretical grounds. Much early criticism centred less upon the constitutional architecture than the perceived moral ambivalence of aspects of the Agreement. Aside from ambiguity over weapons decommissioning, the micro-agenda of the Agreement included the release of paramilitary prisoners within two years and the establishment of commissions dealing with policing, human rights and equality.

Does consociationalism actually work?

However laudable the attempt to include most shades of opinion in power-sharing structures, the Good Friday Agreement was clearly a risky political project. Few divided societies have successfully employed a similar grand coalition of political rivals to resolve such divisions (Horowitz, 2001). Never a formal coalition, the Power-Sharing Executive proved an uneasy collective. It was hampered by the suspension of devolution on a total of three occasions in 2000 and 2001 over the lack of paramilitary decommissioning of weapons, before the IRA finally moved on the issue.

A more serious suspension and return to direct rule from Westminster occurred in October 2002. The UUP had already announced that its ministers were withdrawing from the North-South ministerial council, effectively rendering the body impotent, and said they would withdraw from the Executive if IRA disbandment was not achieved by January 2003. Following a highly visible police raid upon Sinn Fein's offices at Stormont amid allegations of IRA spying, the UUP and DUP served notice that their ministers would quit the Executive, leaving the British Government with little option but to suspend the political institutions. This fourth suspension appeared likely to bring about a longer return to direct rule from Westminster, pending a review of the Good Friday Agreement. Meanwhile, pressure increased upon the IRA to disband, in order that the institutions could be revived. Given the extent of change within republicanism, disbandment appeared a distinct possibility.

Aside from practical concerns of workability, the main intellectual criticism of the Good Friday Agreement has been that the designations of MLAs as unionist, nationalist or other, and the associated parallel consent rules, legitimize the existing sectarian division in Northern Ireland and deny a common humanity. Critics claim that a sense of Northern Irishness will not be developed whilst British unionist and Irish nationalist identities are encouraged. The need for parallel consent for measures among unionists and nationalist MLAs diminishes the importance of 'other' parties within the Assembly. According to the 1999 Northern Ireland Life and Times Survey, 30 per cent of Northern Ireland's voters do not see themselves as unionist or nationalist, yet this outlook was given little recognition. Elite accommodation, or consociation, within the Executive is fragile, whilst electoral polarity is heightened. With few incentives for moderation, the parties that do best are the stoutest defenders of their bloc. An examination of elections results confirms growing support for the 'stronger' green and orange parties, as Sinn Fein and the DUP have strengthened their positions within their ethnic bloc (Table 10.3).

Table 10.3 *Election results in Northern Ireland 1992–2001*

Election	UUP (%)	DUP (%)	SDLP (%)	SF (%)	Other
1992 General	34.5	13.1	23.5	10.0	19.9
1993 Local	29.4	17.3	22.0	12.4	18.9
1994 European	23.8	29.2	28.9	9.0	19.1
1996 Forum	24.2	18.8	21.4	15.5	20.1
1997 Local	27.8	15.6	20.7	16.9	19.0
1998 Assembly	21.3	18.1	22.0	17.6	21.0
1999 European	17.7	28.5	28.2	17.4	8.2
2001 General	26.8	22.5	21.0	21.7	8.0
2001 Local	23.0	21.5	19.4	20.7	15.4

Sinn Fein has also developed its electoral strength in the Irish Republic. The party had five candidates elected to Dail Eireann (the Irish Parliament) in the 2002 Irish elections. Its vote share of 6.5 per cent amounted to a trebling of the party's 1997 showing. Sinn Fein is the only significant all-Ireland party and further increases in the party's showing could see its elected representatives in government, as a coalition partner, north and south of the border.

With Assembly elections looming in May 2003, there is the prospect of the DUP and Sinn Fein becoming the largest Assembly parties. Even in a changed Northern Ireland, many doubted the viability of a DUP First Minister working with a Sinn Fein Deputy First Minister (or vice versa). For the DUP, such arrangements could be seen as a betrayal by its anti-Agreement electorate.

Policing

The Patten Commission on policing led to the change of name from Royal Ulster Constabulary to Police Service of Northern Ireland. Patten also demanded changes in recruitment, henceforth to be on a 50–50 Protestant–Catholic basis, to rectify the 88–12 per cent imbalance in respect of serving officers. Many unionists opposed these changes, and only 19 per cent of the Ulster Unionist Council, the ruling body of the UUP, supported the Patten changes. For Sinn Fein, the failure to implement Patten reforms in their entirety ('Patten lite') ensured that the party declined to support the Policing Board responsible for overseeing the work of the Police Service of Northern Ireland (PSNI). As a result, government ministers refused to back the state's police force, indicating the abnormality of politics in Northern Ireland. Given the rapidity of change within Sinn Fein, however, it would be little surprise to see this position reversed. In 2002, the new Chief Constable of the PSNI, Hugh Orde complained that his force was understaffed and suffering low morale. Rioting and the need to police parades (see below) had prevented the move towards a normalized society envisaged by the Patten Commission, when it proposed reductions in the size of the police service.

Decommissioning

Perhaps even more controversial was the issue of weapons decommissioning by paramilitary organizations. The Agreement insisted merely that participants to the Agreement must 'use any influence they may have, to achieve the decommissioning of paramilitary weapons within two years'. Accompanying letters from the British Prime Minister to the UUP leader, David Trimble, insisting that decommissioning was a necessary part of the process, were the closest that unionists came to establishing an actual, rather than moral case, in their insistence upon IRA disarmament. Under the terms of the Agreement, Sinn Fein's presence in the Executive was not conditional upon IRA decommissioning, although unionists argued that the links between party and paramilitary group were such that Sinn Fein would have huge influence upon the IRA and could persuade the organization to put weapons beyond use.

In 1998, the IRA indicated that 'voluntary decommissioning' would be a natural development of the peace process. The issue was one of sequencing rather than substance, given that the republican position had switched from past slogans of 'Not an ounce [of explosive]; not a bullet'. The IRA was willing to disarm, but according to its own timetable. In November 1999, the UUP Council indicated its willingness, narrowly, via a 58 to 42 per cent vote, to allow the UUP into government with Sinn Fein in advance of IRA decommissioning. The proviso was that IRA decommissioning had to begin by February 2000. With no IRA decommissioning having occurred by this stage the first of three Assembly suspensions occurred before the IRA began to get rid of its weapons in 2001. This prevented the collapse of the political process for a time, until allegations of IRA activity resurfaced in 2002. The role of the IRA appeared increasingly redundant, given the dependence of Sinn Fein's electoral support upon a non-violent republican outlook.

Continuing paramilitary activity

Despite the beginning of decommissioning by the IRA, paramilitary activity was still evident among loyalists and republicans. In 2001 and 2002, parts of Belfast witnessed the worst rioting in years. Republican and loyalist paramilitaries were involved on occasions, with the UDA particularly active in attacking nationalist homes in North Belfast. A dispute over the route of schoolchildren to the Holy Cross Catholic School, located in a Protestant area, descended into violence in 2001, illuminating the ability of sectarian territorial disputes to stir animosity, even after a political settlement. As sectarian violence and paramilitary punishment beatings continued, support for the Agreement declined in the Unionist community. This erosion of support was heightened by the discovery of three IRA personnel in Colombia, allegedly assisting the revolutionary FARC movement. The British Government announced that it would increase the monitoring of paramilitary ceasefires. Dissident republicans not on ceasefire also claimed a number of mainly low level attacks.

Parades

Sectarian tensions were also evident in controversies over the routes of unionist Orange Order parades skirting nationalist areas. The number of parades has increased in recent years, from 3,000 in the mid-1990s to approximately 3,500 annually by 2002. The number of contested parades has also increased, marches where nationalists have appealed to the Parades Commission for a rerouting of the march away from nationalist areas. The Parades Commission was established in 1997 to adjudicate on controversial parades, after the Orange Order's Drumcree parade led to violent protests from hostile nationalists and, subsequently, violence from loyalists angered at the rerouting of the parade. The increased controversy over parades reflects the downside of the stress upon expressions of identity favoured under the Good Friday Agreement. Natural expressions of identity for Orangemen are viewed as hostile actions by nationalists.

Ethnic bloc politics: the party system in Northern Ireland

Northern Ireland's party system remains confessional. The link between religion and voting (and party membership) remains the strongest in Western Europe. The UUP and DUP draw almost exclusively upon

Protestant support, as do fringe loyalist parties. The nationalist SDLP and Sinn Fein draw support from catholics. Cross-community vote transfers remain rare, but are nonetheless significant. The 1998 Assembly STV elections saw 34 per cent of final UUP vote transfers going to the SDLP (Mitchell 2001b: p. 44). More generally, final vote transfers across the divide amounted to 25 per cent from nationalists to Pro-Agreement unionists and 17 per cent of pro-Agreement unionists to nationalists (ibid.).

Most lower-preference vote transfers nonetheless take place within an ethnic bloc. The new moderation of Sinn Fein means that SDLP voters are increasingly disposed towards lower-preference vote transfers to their nationalist rival. Two-thirds of SDLP members did so in the 1998 assembly contest, a figure likely to rise. The willingness of voters to transfer within their ethnic bloc means that even those candidates attracting low support on a first count can still be elected. Forty-two per cent of DUP voters transferred to the UUP in 1998 (Mitchell, 2001b: 43).

There appeared to be electoral gain for the DUP in opposing the Good Friday Agreement, evidenced by the party's improved performance in the 2001 general and local elections. Optimists point to the fact that much of the DUP's campaign of opposition was based upon short-term 'side effects' of the Agreement, notably prisoner releases and policing reforms and the disinclination of the IRA, at the time, to decommission weapons. Increasingly, the DUP may have difficulty in sustaining the argument that the Provisional IRA's war is merely on hold, rather than abandoned in favour of politics.

Party memberships are drawn from a similarly exclusive religious base. Catholic membership of the UUP is less than 1 per cent. Fifty per cent of the party are members of the Orange Order, an organization that forbids its members to marry Catholics or attend Catholic Church services. The DUP has a high number of activists within the fundamentalist Free Presbyterian Church (Bruce 1986). Only two per cent of the SDLP's members are protestant (Murray and Tonge forthcoming). The tiny Northern Ireland Women's Coalition draws support from both sides of the religious divide. The Alliance Party, seemingly in terminal decline, also draws support from both communities, although only 20 per cent of party members are Catholic (Evans and Tonge 2001: 111).

Nonetheless, the Agreement offers fewer incentives to moderation for unionists than nationalists. For Sinn Fein, a return to violence by the Provisional IRA, a most unlikely prospect, would surely be disastrous for the party's electoral support. Admittedly, Sinn Fein's vote rose in the 1996 Forum elections, a period during which the IRA fractured its ceasefire. However, during that period, the exclusion of Sinn Fein from multi-party talks was seen as unjust by many nationalist voters. IRA violence was seen as a necessary means of forcing the entry of Sinn Fein into negotiations. There is little evidence indicating tolerance of any renewed campaign. According to a *Belfast Telegraph/Ulster Marketing Surveys* poll conducted in May 2001, 44 per cent of Sinn Fein support-ers believe that the IRA should decommission all its weapons, with a further 28 per cent supporting some decommissioning. In 2001, Sinn Fein became the larger nationalist party, in terms of first preference votes in the local elections and single preference votes in the general election.

For unionist parties, however, the rewards of participation in the Agreement were less clear. The deal was, in the word of David Trimble, the UUP leader, 'as good as it gets', an appraisal which, whatever its realism, was hardly a great electoral rallying cry. Within unionism, there has been an anti-Agreement electoral constituency to be farmed. Many 'no' unionists adopted such a position not merely on the basis that hundreds of paramilitary prisoners were released and the police force revamped, but also because they feared that the Agreement represented a transition to a united Ireland, a view also offered by Sinn Fein to republican doubters.

Inter-bloc rivalries persisted within the new institutions, although many of the decisions confronting the Executive and Assembly did not lend themselves to a unionist or nationalist standpoint. With most voters being allied to an ethnic segment and few located in the centre ground, intra-bloc contests to mobilize a particular ethnic pillar have become even more acute. Even as violence has ceased, rivalries within nationalist and unionist blocs have increased.

Nationalist and republican politics

Competition between the SDLP and Sinn Fein for the nationalist vote has intensified, although both parties are staunchly pro-Agreement. Although much of the Agreement reflected SDLP thinking, Sinn Fein captured the electoral spoils. The subsequent peace process was constructed upon many pillars, but the largest single influence was the softening of Sinn Fein and the IRA's political agenda. In 1988, the SDLP formally put the argument for an agreed Ireland to Sinn Fein, via the Hume–Adams talks. Hume wished to persuade Adams that the IRA's campaign of violence was futile, as a united Ireland could not be achieved by force. The SDLP leader argued that the British Government was now neutral on the future of Northern Ireland. As such, it was the one million protestant unionists who would need to be persuaded of the merits of Irish unity, not the British Government. Hume also argued that violence was morally wrong, a position supported by the Catholic Church, which dismissed the idea that the IRA was fighting a 'just war'. Furthermore, the SDLP leader insisted that violence was counter-productive for Sinn Fein, with many nationalist voters inhibited from voting for the party because of its support for the IRA's campaign.

The Hume–Adams talks paid dividends in helping move Sinn Fein from its unreconstructed 'Brits out' position. The path from republican fundamentalism had already begun in 1986, when abstention from the Irish Parliament, claiming jurisdiction over the 26 County Irish Republic, was dropped as party policy. From here on, the party would be prepared to enter partitionist parliaments. Diehard republicans opposed the change, arguing (correctly) that the change might be later extended to allow entry to a parliament in Northern Ireland. These fundamentalists left to form Republican Sinn Fein, giving Adams a freer hand in the modernization of Sinn Fein. Although still dismissive of the SDLP's view that the British Government was neutral on the future of Ireland, Sinn Fein acknowledged the need to persuade unionists, who republicans now accepted as British, of the merits of a united Ireland. Sinn Fein leaders now spoke less of a united Ireland and more of the need for self determination for all the people of the island, echoing SDLP ideas. Such language appeared in the Downing Street Declaration, issued by the British and Irish Governments in 1993 and designed to interest republicans. Although Irish self-determination was to be highly qualified, being based upon the North and South of Ireland co-determining their own futures, the Downing Street Declaration created space for the IRA ceasefire of 1994. This ceasefire was broken in 1996 but resumed in 1997, which led to Sinn Fein entering into talks leading up to the Good Friday Agreement.

Whatever the claims of the Sinn Fein leadership that it was entering the talks to negotiate for a united Ireland, there was no prospect of this outcome. According to the British Prime Minister, Tony Blair, speaking in 1997:

> My agenda is not a united Ireland and I wonder just how many see it as a realistic possibility for the foreseeable future. Northern Ireland will remain part of the United Kingdom as long as a majority here wish ... Unionists have nothing to fear from a new Labour Government. A political settlement is not a slippery slope to a united Ireland. The Government will not be persuaders for unity. (quoted in Tonge 2002: 179)

Enmeshed in the political process and anxious not to collapse the peace process, the Sinn Fein leadership nonetheless found itself signing up to an Agreement in April 1998, even though it reconstituted a power-sharing Executive and Assembly, something it had previously opposed, with Sinn Fein enjoying representation within both. At the Sinn Fein Ard Fheis in 1998, there was overwhelming (97 per cent) support for the Good Friday Agreement as skilful party management marginalized republican dissidents. Nonetheless, a split in the IRA did occur in 1997, over whether the organization's ceasefire should be renewed. A small number of volunteers left to form the Real IRA, whose bombing of Omagh in August 1998 caused the worst atrocity in Northern Ireland of the entire troubles, leaving 29 dead. The bombing appeared to stem the trickle towards republican ultras, represented politically by the 32 County Sovereignty Committee.

Sinn Fein now offers a revisionist republicanism, which, whilst still striving for Irish unity, has abandoned the old abstentionist approach in favour of a participatory form of politics. A party that sought to destroy the state of Northern Ireland possessed ministers managing its health and education services. Sinn Fein hopes that a logic for Irish unity will be created through the peace process and by the development of cross-border bodies. Against this, however, lies the stark reality that an increase in the number of such bodies is conditional upon (unlikely) unionist acquiescence in any Northern Ireland Assembly. Furthermore, the principle of consent for constitutional change within the Agreement means that nationalists are reliant upon substantial demographic change (i.e. a large rise in the number of catholics) to achieve a united Ireland. There is no demographic 'timebomb' confronting unionists. Differences between catholic and protestant birthrates are marginal and a significant minority of catholics are indifferent to the possibility of a united Ireland.

The severity of the electoral rivalry between Sinn Fein and the SDLP has undermined the concept of pan-nationalism developed during the early stages of the peace process. During that phase, the two parties cooperated in framing agreement over the need for Irish self-determination. With that phase over, following the referendum on the Good Friday Agreement, intra-bloc competition for nationalist votes was heightened. For the SDLP, often seen as an ageing, middle-class party, the repositioning of Sinn Fein has proved problematic. The party relied heavily upon the charisma of its former leader, John Hume, whilst party organization was sometimes neglected (Murray 1998). A majority of the party's members describe themselves as 'inactive'. The party's previous reliance upon the moral virtue of constitutional politics was rethought, as Sinn Fein distanced itself from violence. The SDLP nonetheless believes it is better placed to offer a form of civic nationalism acceptable to the unionist community, contrasting with the ethnic form maintained by Sinn Fein. Furthermore, the SDLP believes it is better placed to campaign on ordinary issues, due to its longstanding concern with 'normal' politics. However, the evidence suggests that the nationalist electorate view Sinn Fein as the stouter defender of their electoral bloc. Actual policy differences are nonetheless scarce, although Sinn Fein's refusal to join the board of the Policing Service of Northern Ireland remains one marker. The SDLP sees itself as a 'post-nationalist' party, while Sinn Fein continues to hold out the possibility of the construction of a distinctive Irish nation state.

Accounts of the rationale behind the changed politics of Sinn Fein vary. External factors are offered by Cox (2000), who suggests that the end of the Cold War meant that republicans shifted from their leftist, revolutionary rhetoric. Furthermore, the British and American Governments softened their approach, no longer fearing the establishment of a Cuban style regime on Britain's doorstep. This view finds some echo in the writings of Ryan (1994). These external referents may exaggerate the strength and the left-wing dimension to the Provisional IRA, an organization mixing leftist rhetoric with catholic piety according to its audience.

For some, the Provisional IRA was always a movement rooted in the defence of northern nationalists, rather than the promotion of purist republican ideals of a united Ireland. The politics of 1969 rather than the 1916 Easter Rising dominated the republican movement (McIntyre 2001). Internal explanations point to the changes within republicanism prior to the collapse of the Berlin Wall. The movement was already moving towards a more pragmatic republicanism. Sinn Fein was already engaged in electoral politics; abstention in the Irish Republic had been ended and the party had switched from an 'ourselves alone' approach towards a search for dialogues with other nationalists. As the republican movement sought an exit strategy from a war it could not win, it required confirmation from the British Government that Northern Ireland's place in the United Kingdom was not based upon colonial factors. The 1990 assertion by the Secretary of State for Northern Ireland that Britain had 'no selfish, strategic or economic interest' in Northern Ireland allowed republicans to hasten the pace of change and participate in a political process. Maloney (2002) suggests that Sinn Fein President Gerry Adams realized the IRA's war was unwinnable at a very early stage. An alternative explanation is offered by loyalists, who claim that the targeting of Sinn Fein and the IRA in the early 1990s by revived loyalist paramilitary groups impacted upon the republican movement.

Unionist and loyalist politics

Divisions within unionism have been greatly exacerbated by the Good Friday Agreement. The narrow (53–47 per cent) margin of support for the Agreement displayed within the unionist community in the 1998 referendum on the Agreement was followed by heightened competition between the pro-Agreement UUP and anti-Agreement DUP. This intra-bloc division was complicated by the opposition to the Agreement found within sections of the UUP. Whilst the UUP maintained its share of the vote, the DUP substantially improved its performance, gaining an extra 9 per cent of the vote in the 2001 general election, compared to its 1997 performance.

For a majority within the UUP, the Good Friday Agreement met the basic objective of the party by securing Northern Ireland's place within the United Kingdom. The constitutional claim of the Irish Republic to Northern Ireland has been withdrawn and the 1998 Northern Ireland Act in effect updates the 1920 Government of Ireland Act, ensuring that Northern Ireland remains part of the United Kingdom for so long as this is the will of the majority. Devolved government is desired by most unionists, notwithstanding the strong integrationist tendency within the UUP. Whilst acknowledging the imperfections of the deal, the pro-Agreement section of the UUP supported the assertion of successive Secretaries of State that the Good Friday Agreement is the 'only show in town'.

The pro-Agreement section of the UUP was engaged in a process of modernization, moving towards a civic unionism (Porter 1996). This form still has as its core the maintenance of the union, but is also one in which the Irishness of the minority nationalist community is recognized, legitimized and even encouraged. Politically, this is reflected in the acceptance of a limited all-Ireland dimension to political and economic arrangements. The crucial aspect for the UUP is to ensure control over cross-border bodies and the North–South Council, by locating the power of expansion within a northern Assembly in which unionists still enjoy a majority. With Strand One of the Agreement the dominant element, movement towards bi-national governance of Northern Ireland is only slight. Liberal and cultural unionists offer a less sanguine view of the impact of the Agreement. Liberal unionists believe in the superiority of the political system of the United Kingdom over that offered by the Irish Republic. As such, major concessions of sovereignty to the Irish Government are unacceptable. Although the project of the UUP leader, David Trimble, has been to modernize unionism and recognize the legitimate interests of the Irish Republic in the affairs of Northern Ireland, a belief in the innate superiority of the political order in the United Kingdom may still be apparent. This was illuminated by the UUP leader's speech to the Ulster Unionist Council General Meeting in March 2002, in which he urged delegates to 'contrast the United Kingdom state – a vibrant, multi-ethnic, multi-national liberal democracy . . . with the pathetic, sectarian, mono-ethnic, mono-cultural state to our South'.

In that same speech, however, Trimble also acknowledged, however, 'that a retreat into a sectarian laager would be a disaster'. Particular forms of cultural unionism, based upon an exaggerated sense of Orangeism, Protestantism and Britishness, are regarded with hostility by some nationalists. Cultural unionism remains strong, however, in both the UUP and DUP. Within the UUP, the Orange Order retains voting rights on the Ulster Unionist Council (the UUC), the ruling body of a party which has historically been more of a movement than a tightly bound organization. Membership of the Order, committed to the maintenance of the protestant ascendancy, remains important to many UUP members. More significantly, in terms of the modern debate within unionism, Orange Order membership has been an important variable in determining support for the Good Friday Agreement and for the UUP leader. Divisions within the UUP between pro- and anti- Agreement factions have been played out regularly in meetings of the UUC. Anti-agreement Unionists mobilized on a 'no guns, no government' platform, opposing Sinn Fein's presence in the Executive in advance of the IRA decommissioning some of its weapons.

For some members, divisions within the UUP are more tactical than substantial, mere devices to ensure movement from Sinn Fein and the IRA. However, the party also contains a sizeable minority who oppose the Agreement. The lack of unity was highlighted by the leadership contest within the UUP in 2000, when David Trimble was challenged by the Reverend Martin Smyth, an opponent of the Good Friday Agreement, who described himself as 'an Orangeman first and a politician second'. The contest displayed the faultline between ethnic unionism, centred upon Protestant-Britishness and concern over the ultimate destination of the Good Friday Agreement and a civic, more pluralist version of unionism, supportive of the Good Friday Agreement and devolved power sharing as the best means of avoiding the imposition of British-Irish joint authority over Northern Ireland. Slightly more than half of the UUC are also members of the Orange Order. Among such members, Smyth enjoyed the upper hand (51–48 per cent) of the votes in the leadership contest (Tonge and Evans 2001). Among non-Orange Order members, Trimble gathered two-thirds of the votes. The UUP leader has pledged to examine whether the Order should continue to enjoy voting rights within the ruling body of unionism's largest party.

Unsurprisingly, support for the retention of such rights is stronger among members of the Order than non-members.

Perhaps a more worrying variable for pro-Agreement unionists, however, is that of age. Extensive hostility to the Good Friday Agreement and the Trimble leadership is found among younger UUC delegates, notably those under 35 years of age. Older delegates are much more pro-Agreement. Occupation and income are also important. With the exception of a cluster of professionals, those in better paid, middle-class jobs tend to favour the Agreement.

The divisions within unionism have prompted discussions of a crisis of unionist identity. However, in terms of identity, unionists are relatively homogeneous, certainly more so than the nationalist or 'other' bloc. Unionists appear to know what they are; it is where they are going that divides them. Different interpretations of the political direction of the Good Friday Agreement, allied to distaste for some of its micro-agenda, created division within the UUP. Within the DUP, there was unremitting criticism of the Agreement, but the party does support devolution and power-sharing, albeit not with Sinn Fein. The DUP enjoys support from the loyalist urban working class and rural, church-going protestants. A fusion of secular populism and religious values has sustained the party, although its working-class base has been challenged in parts of Belfast by the pro-Agreement Progressive Unionist Party (the PUP), instrumental in developing a peace process within the loyalist community.

Other sections of working-class unionism were rapidly disillusioned by the Good Friday Agreement. The Ulster Democratic Party, linked to the paramilitary Ulster Defence Association (UDA) and Ulster Freedom Fighters (UFF) folded three years after the party failed to gain seats in the Northern Ireland Assembly. By 2002, the UDA and UFF were viewed as no longer being on ceasefire by the Secretary of State for Northern Ireland, John Reid, having been involved in a series of sectarian confrontations. For such working-class loyalists, the Good Friday Agreement is viewed as part of a continual process of gains for nationalists. For such loyalists, politics are still seen as part of a zero-sum game, in which progress for the 'other' community is viewed with suspicion. Continuing sectarian disturbances in parts of Belfast have emphasized the limits of the Agreement as a means of societal reconciliation. As the Agreement attempts to manage, rather than necessarily heal division within an institutional framework, those outside political institutions could maintain traditional hostilities. Physical separation of the communities in Belfast remains stark. Within the city, 35 of the 52 census wards are drawn almost entirely from a single religious denomination (Coulter 1999: 39).

Defending a consociational deal

The attempt at a consociational political deal in Northern Ireland can be defended. The Good Friday Agreement remains the political framework within which political divisions may be accommodated. It harnesses pre-existing political rivalries within a peaceful framework. Increased electoral support for Sinn Fein was a product of the party's new moderation rather than a mandate for militant republicanism. The DUP offered a voice for critics of aspects of the Agreement particularly painful to unionists. Its politics changed far less than those offered by Sinn Fein. Nonetheless, the DUP no longer viewed power sharing as essentially undemocratic, Furthermore, the party seeks a reworking of the Good Friday Agreement, rather than its entire destruction. The party participated in the Assembly and Executive, drawing salaries and expenses. Those seeing consociationalism as a causal factor in fostering sectarianism deny the prior state of Northern Ireland politics, in which ethnic bloc divisions persisted under a variety of regime types. What remains to be seen is whether the Agreement, renegotiated or otherwise, can turn a chilly peace into a process of political reconciliation. In this respect, the ambitions of the Agreement are modest. It seeks the management of difference rather than its eradication. Constitutional preferences remain divergent according to religious affiliation, as Table 10.4 indicates.

Northern Ireland has moved slowly into a post-conflict era. Despite various initial crises and the scepticism, the post-Agreement polity was characterized by relative tranquillity and, within the new political institutions, dull civility. The political institutions were dogged by instability, enduring four suspensions in their first four years. The inclusivity of the power-sharing deal, embracing historic enemies within the same government, was risky. This fragility was exacerbated by reluctance

Table 10.4 *Preferred long-term policy for Northern Ireland, 2001*

	Protestant (%)	RC (%)	No religion (%)
To remain part of the UK	79	15	46
Reunify with rest of the island	5	59	16
Become independent	5	6	10
Other/Don't know	10	17	23

Source: Adapted from Northern Ireland Life and Times Survey (2001)

among unionists to accept that 'armed struggle' had run its course for the IRA and Sinn Fein.

The transformation of Sinn Fein from supporters of armed struggle to constitutional politicians created space for the embedding of a set of institutions in which ethno-national division could be managed. Sinn Fein took most of its constituency on this journey, although the presence in prison of several dozen dissident republicans, members of the Continuity or Real IRA, illustrates that, for a small minority, an 'anti-colonial' struggle remains their preferred route. The least likely of possible scenarios, however, is a return to violence on the scale witnessed before the paramilitary ceasefires.

Devolved power sharing, linked to a modest all-Ireland ministerial council and cross-border bodies, has been accepted by most of the major political parties in Northern Ireland and the Agreement retains the support of a majority of the electorate, albeit not among unionists. Cooperative political relationships were beginning to emerge within the Assembly and its committees usually enjoyed unanimity, prior to the collapse (yet again) of the institutions in Autumn 2002. Devolved power sharing remains the goal of all parties and if such cooperative arrangements have a spillover effect upon the electorate, it is just possible to envisage an optimistic post-nationalist and post-unionist scenario developing, with a new focus upon social and economic agendas.

Perhaps the most realistic scenario in the short-term is that of continuing inter-ethnic rivalry alongside increased party competition within blocs. The bi-communality of the Agreement rendered it fragile, as both communities needed to feel they were gaining from its workings. Only the nationalist community gained in confidence, even though the constitutional provisions of the Agreement ought to have reassured unionists. A loss of confidence among the unionist community since the Agreement increased support for the anti-Agreement position of the DUP. The shift in the electorate raised the possibility of DUP-Sinn Fein First and Deputy First Ministers, a scenario to test the permanency of any power-sharing agreement.

Overall, the restructured Northern Ireland emerging from a protracted peace process is prospering. Economic regeneration is evident and political divisions are played out in a largely peaceful framework. An unthreatening role for the Irish Republic is accepted by many unionists and the Northern Ireland state is accepted, for the foreseeable future, by a nationalist population which has long abandoned the moribund abstentionism or paramilitary cheerleading which characterized part of its politics in earlier decades. Some nationalists hope that changing demographics, with the percentage of catholics among Northern

Ireland's population growing rapidly, will create pressure for union with the Irish Republic. This, however, may remain a distant prospect, given the diversity of constitutional preferences among Catholics. The real test for the Good Friday Agreement, renegotiated or otherwise, is whether it will ever create a sufficient sense of Northern Irishness, beyond the Irish nationalist versus British unionist political faultline, a division still played out in the continuing forms of societal sectarianism still evident in Northern Ireland.

Chapter 11

Politics in England and Wales

GILLIAN PEELE

The United Kingdom has traditionally been a heavily centralized state in which local government has enjoyed no constitutional independence and concern for efficient service delivery has outweighed interest in fostering a genuine arena of local democracy. Labour's post-1997 constitutional reforms radically changed the distribution of powers and the process of policy making within the United Kingdom. In addition to creating a separate Parliament for Scotland and an Assembly for Wales, the government established a new authority for London and promoted initiatives in regional government. These measures generated new patterns of intergovernmental relations and changed the context in which local government has to operate. English local government itself was profoundly affected by a series of modernizing reforms promulgated by Labour (especially by John Prescott from the office of the Deputy Prime Minister). These reforms were accompanied by rhetoric which promised a renewal of local democracy, partnership and greater freedoms for local authorities. The important analytic question, however, is the character of this 'new localism'. How far does Labour's apparent commitment to decentralization go? And how far does it conflict with Labour's other public policy objectives? Can we yet see the framework of a new structure of decentralized politics emerging across the United Kingdom?

Devolution and decentralization

Labour's devolution legislation is marked by two features that makes it inherently unstable. First it is asymmetrical in that, although wide-ranging powers over primary legislation were given to the Scottish Parliament, Wales was given an Assembly with much more limited power and no authority to make its own laws or to vary taxes. (Northern Ireland's distinctive problems mean that it was treated as a special case.) Second, there was little agreement about how to decentralize power in

England. Changes to the territorial management of the United Kingdom were thus made as much in terms of a pragmatic political adjustment as of a logical constitutional settlement. This approach may have its merits; but it means that there is likely to be continuing debate about the scope of the devolution arrangements and about their implications for the rest of the United Kingdom.

Developments in Wales underlined the extent to which the asymmetrical nature of the devolution settlement would keep the debate about powers and structures open. Wales also underlines the difficulty of developing a new style of politics to match new institutional arrangements. The first watershed in the Welsh system of devolution was the point at which Rhodri Morgan replaced Alun Michael as First Minister, following a no-confidence vote in Michael in January 2000. Morgan was seen as very much more independent of Whitehall and more responsive to Welsh sentiment than Michael had been. Michael's administration had been a minority Labour one; but Morgan entered a Partnership Agreement with the Liberal Democrats, an arrangement which had the advantage of providing greater security in relation to the Assembly Coalition but created its own tensions as a result of inter-party differences on policy. It also meant that the administration in Wales was more likely to develop a more distinctive policy agenda, which risked conflict with Whitehall. Indeed, one example of a major policy clash between Cardiff and Whitehall came in mid-2002 when the Welsh Assembly unanimously voted to follow the Scottish example and fund free personal care for the elderly out of taxation. Wales has also taken a very different line from England on such issues as student grants, tests for seven-year olds and league tables.

The coalition agreement between Labour and the Liberal Democrats in Wales had been obtained by a commitment to an independent review of the Assembly's powers and by an examination of the local government electoral system in Wales. (This Commission – the Sunderland Commission – reported in July 2002.) Both inquiries were potentially explosive. The independent review of powers, established under the Chairmanship of Lord Richard of Ammanford, although not due to report until 2003, has clearly placed the whole operation of the Welsh system of devolution on the political agenda. Specifically, it is expected that the Welsh Assembly's lack of primary law-making powers and tax-varying authority will be re-examined in a way which exposes the fragility of the argument for denying Cardiff what has been given to Edinburgh. The problems with the Sunderland Commission relate more directly to party interest and the eroding position of Labour in Wales. The Commission took a broad view of its mandate to examine the working of local democracy and was especially concerned about the high number of uncontested local elections in Wales, arguing that uncontested seats meant that, in 1999, 13 per cent of the Welsh population had no opportunity to vote. The Commission also found low levels of interest in, and information about, local government in Wales. To cure this situation, a majority of the Commission recommendations included lowering the voting age to sixteen and a switch from an electoral system based on Single Member Plurality System to one based on proportional representation, the Single Transferable Vote, in time for the local elections of 2008 (Commission on Local Government Arrangements in Wales 2002). This recommendation of a switch to proportional representation at the local level was bound to be highly controversial because it further threatened Labour's crumbling hegemony in Wales. The electoral system used for the Assembly (the Additional Member System) was blamed for weakening Labour's position in Wales, although Labour had undoubtedly also been damaged by the perceptions of a leadership 'stitch-up' to impose Alun Michael as leader (Flynn 1999). Labour's 2002 Spring Conference unanimously adopted a report rejecting any change to the local government electoral system. Morgan himself incurred hostility from his Labour supporters in the Assembly by proceeding with consultations on the Report.

Westminster's caution in relation to Welsh devolution had been partly caused by uncertainty about the depth of support for devolution there. That uncertainty reflected the potentially divisive character of Welsh nationalism, a potential highlighted by a series of inflammatory debates about the Welsh language and immigration into Welsh-speaking areas. In an attempt to circumvent the issues of cultural nationalism and Welsh identity, the Assembly has committed itself to a bilingual Wales. Nevertheless for Plaid Cymru's leader Iuean Wyn Jones the whole devolution scheme was inadequate. He branded the Assembly a failure and attacked Labour for trying to run Wales like a County Council (*Guardian*, 20 September 2002). Jones demanded enhanced powers for the Assembly by the time of the 2007 election. Indeed Rhodri Morgan in October 2002 himself admitted that many voters were still cynical about the Assembly and that it was hard to sell its achievements to the public. (*Guardian*, 14 October 2002).

Regionalism

It was noted at the beginning of this chapter that one of the destabilizing elements of Labour's approach to decentralization was the absence of any consensus about how to deal with the question of England. The

Conservatives had set up a system of government offices for the regions in the 1990s, but this was very much a question of decentralizing administration rather than in any way introducing a regional level of representation to government. Labour's manifesto in 1997 committed the Party to a modest expansion of regional government and in 1998 a bill to create Regional Development Agencies (RDAs) in each of eight English regions reached the statute book. These RDAs were to be 'economic powerhouses' in each region, and were generally promoted as instruments for improving the coordination of government policy, especially planning. Although the RDAs were initially to be scrutinized by non-elected bodies consisting of chambers of local representatives and there was a proclaimed intention to strengthen the regional input into policy-making, the legislation looked weak by comparison with the government's strategies for Scotland, Wales and indeed London. London had had its regional tier (in the form of a directly elected mayor and Greater London Authority) added in Labour's first term (see below). Three factors, however, ensured that regional issue did not disappear from view as many commentators had anticipated: first, the issue of English regionalism now had added salience. Second, John Prescott's own role as an advocate for regionalism. Third, the mobilization of support for regionalism in the regions themselves. The English issue had acquired a higher profile in response to devolution and Labour gave a much stronger commitment to regional government, enunciated with the publication of the White Paper, *Your Region-Your Choice: Revitalizing the English Regions* in May 2002. William Hague, leader of the Conservative Party until 2001, took up the idea (developed by the Conservative Peer and academic Lord Norton) of having special procedures within Parliament to confine voting on English issues to English MPs. Others argued for an independent English Parliament. For Labour, this appeal to *English* national identity was worrying intellectually and dangerous politically. One obvious way to deflect it was through a determined strategy to recast the devolution debate, at least as it applied to England, in terms which emphasized the decentralization of power, rather than any system of quasi-federalism for the component parts of the United Kingdom.

John Prescott himself has a long history of support for regionalism. Early in the 2001 Parliament it became apparent that Prescott supported by the then Secretary of State for Transport, Local Government and the Regions, Stephen Byers, was involved in a major Whitehall battle to promote regionalism. But Prescott and his allies had to overcome scepticism, not least from the Department of Trade and Industry, which wished to control RDAs, the Confederation of British Industry, which opposed elective regional authorities, and some chairmen of the RDAs themselves (Constitution Unit 2001). Prescott's personal enthusiasm for regional devolution was made clear in a speech announcing the new initiative, which would be 'the conclusion of a political dream I have held for decades. Giving the regions their own democratic voice and the chance to improve their economic performance, delivering jobs, prosperity and better public services' (Prescott, 2002).

The movement towards a bolder regional initiative was bolstered by emergent campaigns for democratically elected regional government in several parts of England. One of the earliest areas to mobilize support for regional reform was the North East, which organized a Campaign for a Northern Assembly as early as 1992. In 1998, in an imitation of the Scottish Constitutional Convention, a North East Constitutional Convention had been launched. Early in the 2001 Parliament it was noted that backbenchers, especially from the North East were raising the issue of regional devolution (Constitution Unit Bulletin, December 2001). The Campaign for Yorkshire also imitated the Scottish campaign by issuing a 'Claim of Right' in 1999, following this in 2000 with its own Constitutional Convention, and similar campaigns were launched in the West Midlands, the South West and the North West. All these campaigns claimed to have broad-based support in their areas. In order to coordinate these regional campaigns an umbrella group 'Campaign for the English Regions' (CFER) was founded in 2000 with financial support from the Joseph Rowntree Trust and from the trade union UNISON.

The 2002 White Paper itself acknowledged that support for developing the regional tier was not uniform across England. It argued that elective regional government would be introduced only where there was sufficient interest in the idea and when that interest had been tested in a referendum. Areas which did not want elective regional government (presumably areas such as the South East) would be free *not* to have it. Where an area did want an elective assembly, however, the government would be supportive because such a regional assembly could improve accountability, bring decision making closer to the people, revitalizing democracy by giving a new voice to the regions both within the United Kingdom and within Europe. Precisely what these regional assemblies would do was defined somewhat vaguely in terms of developing a strategic vision, setting regional priorities and integrating policy. Regions were promised more specific responsibilities, such as economic development, skills, housing, sport, culture and tourism, transport, land use and regional planning, environmental protection, bio-diversity and waste and public health. Democracy would be enhanced by giving these regional bodies powers to allocate funding and extensive scrutiny powers over quangos. The regional assemblies envisaged would be relatively small (between 25 and 35 members) and would have a leader and cabinet chosen by and fully accountable to the assembly. And they would be based on existing administrative boundaries used by the Government Offices and RDAs.

Although the government stated that most of the powers would come down from central government, rather than being removed from local authorities, the regional initiative is inevitably destabilizing for local government. Because it would be wasteful and confusing to combine regional government with the two-tier system of local government, in an area opting for an elective regional tier local authorities would have to move towards single tier unitary authorities. Thus the government proposes that in any region where there is sufficient interest to have a referendum on the issue, the Boundary Committee for England will first recommend a form of unitary local government for the region. If the referendum results in a yes vote the new structure of local authorities will come into being; if not, the status quo will be maintained. Consequently, the issue of structure in English local government is once more back on the agenda. This is not because of a direct determination to confront the issue, but as a by-product of regional policy. (Wales, like Scotland, had already been restructured on a single tier basis with 22 unitary authorities for Wales and 32 for Scotland.)

London

One regional government – that of London – was already up and working by 2002. The establishment of a directly elected Mayor for London and a new Greater London Authority (GLA) was a high profile part of Labour's first term programme and was presented as an important part of the general effort to modernize and decentralize British government. Unfortunately the wrangling over *who* would be the Labour candidate and the ultimate triumph of Labour MP Ken Livingstone, the former GLC leader, as an Independent, soured the initiative for many observers. Once Livingstone was elected, London's new political structure continued to backfire on the government. The electoral fiasco of 2000 was succeeded by a series of quarrels between Livingstone and the government, most notably over the best way of financing the modernization of London's Underground, where Livingstone, supported by the rail unions, opposed the government's preferred scheme of a Public Private Partnership (PPP). Ultimately, the case was taken to court and the government's position was upheld. PPP was to be revised to meet safety concerns. But the conflict underlined the difficult position of the mayor who, although ostensibly responsible for transport strategy, was subject to severe constraints on his policies from the centre. As two authorities put it, *The Mayor's Transport Strategy*, published immediately before the court case, was effectively nullified (Pimlott and Rao 2002).

Experience of London's government since 2000 raises more general doubts about the structure of the reform. The Mayor and GLA were superimposed upon a structure of local government in which the 32 boroughs (and the Corporation of London) continue to exercise most local government powers. The new directly elected Mayor's primary role is to devise strategies for cross-cutting policy areas such as transport, culture and the environment, as well as for the police and fire services. He is not responsible for service delivery. The 32 boroughs (whose number Livingstone would like to reduce) had become increasingly self-sufficient since the mid-1980s and following the abolition of the old Greater London Council (the GLC) they had developed new habits of working through administering the bodies which replaced GLC structures. For many boroughs the new Mayor and GLA were an expensive irrelevance, especially given the length of time it took to put comprehensive strategies in place. (In addition to delivering most of the key services of local government in London, the boroughs also exercised important responsibilities such as housing, which impinged on the Mayor's strategic portfolio.) Equally, there appeared to be a flaw at the centre of the reform in that the relationship between the Mayor and the GLA was blurred from the beginning. The directly elected Mayor was clearly intended to have his own legitimacy and provide high-profile leadership. He was to be able to appoint his own advisers from beyond the Assembly, although his so-called Cabinet is advisory and does not operate collective responsibility. The Assembly was intended to exercise broad scrutiny over the mayor, to which end it had been given some powers – notably the power to block the budget which it could do by a two-thirds majority, and the GLA members were also expected to act as representatives. It had been hoped that the GLA would be able to avoid the traditional style of party confrontation found at Westminster and would work more on a cross-party and functional basis. However, the fact that the highly controversial Livingstone was elected as an independent candidate against the manifest wishes of his former party and the Labour government put him in an extremely awkward situation. It was inevitable that in these circumstances he should attempt to build personal rather than policy or party coalitions. As Pimlott and Rao suggest, Livingstone tried to counter his isolation by using his patronage powers to draw in Labour members of the GLA, by giving them jobs running the many functional bodies or bringing them into his cabinet. Not only does this mean that the Conservative members are effectively frozen out (Pimlott and Rao, 2002), but it also dilutes the scrutiny role of the GLA. Instead of a new style of inclusive politics, Livingstone appears to have adopted a highly personalized style, one that is based to a large extent on patronage.

General dissatisfaction with the way in which the scrutiny process was operating and indeed more broadly with the relationship between the Mayor and the GLA was expressed in a document published by the Reaching Out Investigative Committee, chaired by Sally Hamwee, a Liberal Democrat. This Committee criticized the way in which Livingstone had failed to take notice of the consultation processes initiated by GLA officers and argued that this was making it difficult for the GLA to hold the mayor to account for his policies. It may be that some of these problems reflect the personality of Livingstone himself and that, if he were to be replaced by a more orthodox party politician, the structures (which depend so much on cooperation) would operate differently. It might be that London presents peculiar problems of governance. But at present, the London model underlines the difficulty of grafting new constitutional models onto an existing system and places a question mark over whether there is really scope for genuine regional government in England. It also undermines such support as there was for the introduction of directly elected mayors into local government (see below).

Local government

When it came to power in 1997 Labour expressed a highly positive view of local government, emphasizing its desire to modernize local government by giving local authorities greater freedom and removing some of the controls put in place by the Conservatives between 1979 and 1997. By contrast with the Conservatives' evident political suspicion of local government, Labour apparently saw it as an essential element in the polity. It committed itself to strengthening local democracy and reforming the internal structures and management processes of local government. But Labour's emphasis on public service delivery and performance, and its own distinctive approach to public sector management, has placed other constraints on local government. Thus Labour, while encouraging a greater role for local authorities as partners of central government, made it very clear that the framework of that partnership would reflect *central* values and that greater local authority autonomy would depend on achieving nationally set performance targets. Labour, although it made much of the fact that it had abandoned the pressure to test local provision against the market through compulsory competitive tendering (CCT) regime introduced by the Conservatives and rejected universal capping, nevertheless introduced its own more rigorous techniques for improving efficiency in local government. The Best Value (BV) framework (introduced in 1999), the Comprehensive Performance Assessment (CPA), Local Partnership Agreements and Beacon Councils all underlined Labour's desire to use new management techniques to drive up the quality of service delivery and council performance. And it was enthusiastic about raising new money for capital spending through Public Private Partnerships (PPP) and the Private Finance Initiative (PFI).

Of course, Labour had inherited a system of local government that had been extensively altered by Conservative policies. The strategic or enabling authority that increasingly replaced the traditional local authority could be seen as a way of shrinking the role of local government's presence in the community. Labour, by contrast, wanted to heighten the local authority role as the focus of the neighbourhood or community, giving local government a new leadership mission and requiring extensive interaction with a range of local stakeholders. Labour's White Paper, *Modern Local Government: In Touch with the People*, published in 1998, set out a radical vision of local government, one which attempted to create a new role for local government by making them 'outward looking and responsive' to their local communities. In addition, the White Paper undertook to make a comprehensive change in the internal structures of local government, to improve the decision-making process at the local level, and to enhance democracy.

The role of local government

Labour's stated vision of local government involved a cultural change. Instead of maintaining local authorities in their traditional form as rather cautious, legally-constrained organizations whose primary responsibility was to provide services for their residents, the government wanted councils to develop a much more entrepreneurial and proactive role as community leaders. The government wanted councils to become 'community leaders' and 'advocates of their constituents', being responsible for and able to respond to the needs of their communities. Part of the reason for local government's restricted role within the British system had been the constraints placed on local government by legal rules which confined almost all local government action to the provision of services for which there was statutory authority. Local authority action for which there was no legal authority could be challenged as being *ultra vires*; spending for which there no legal justification could also be challenged and councillors could be surcharged for any misuse of funds. Local authorities were used to seeing their role in terms of duties laid on them by central government. The Local Government Act of 2000 attempted to change this reactive conception of local government's role by placing an obligation on local authorities to develop a strategy to promote the well-being of their area, largely through reaching out to various local pressure groups and voluntary associations, as well as to other public bodies and to the business community. The legislation also introduced a new general power to do anything a local authority considered likely to promote the economic, social or environmental well-being of the area. The intention appears to be to promote the use of strategic partnerships and to provide new opportunities for people to become involved in decision making at the local level. The use of this power is itself subject to constraints, and some councils have pointed out the self-evident conflict between the creation of a broad power and the detailed regulations and prescriptions for local management issuing from London. Yet, although this new general power does not compare with the general legal competence enjoyed by local government in many other democratic systems, it does seem to indicate a desire to make councils more imaginative and creative. The 2000 Local Government Act also abolished the surcharge mechanism.

The representativeness of local councillors

Renewing local democracy was also a major theme of Labour's approach to local government, especially as Labour was forced to address a series of interlocking questions about the vitality of the local system and the people who ran it. Who were the councillors who ran the various local authorities? How far were their ways of working and their perceptions of their role appropriate to the needs of the twenty-first century? Were the structures of local authorities sufficiently geared to providing leadership and effective decision making? And could any structural changes be made to enhance the working of local democracy and enhance interest in local elections?

Recruitment of candidates to stand for local authorities has long been a problem for local government. Not surprisingly, local councillors differ in many ways from the population at large. One of the most comprehensive surveys of the 21,000 or so councillors taken in 2001 gives a good picture of local councillors. (Improvement and Development Agency 2001) It showed that councillors in office in May 2001 were predominantly male – 71 per cent – a figure that was very similar to that in 1997 when 72.6 per cent of councillors were men. Representation of female councillors was highest in the Liberal Democrat Party – 34.4 per cent – with Plaid Cymru scoring the lowest percentage of female representation. Female councillors were more evident in shire districts, London boroughs and unitary authorities.

Representation of female councillors was highest in the South East, South West and North West, and extremely low in Wales, a point also underlined by the Sunderland Commission. The vast majority of councillors in 1997 were aged over 45 – 86 per cent – with an average age of 57 years, an increase from the 1997 average of 55.6. Councillors from the shire counties and Wales tended to be slightly older than average; those from London boroughs and the metropolitan districts were slightly younger than average. A mere 2.5 per cent of councillors were of ethnic minority background, a decline from 1997. Labour had the highest proportion of ethnic minority councillors – 5.6 per cent – and representation of ethnic minority councillors was highest in London and the South East – 4.2 per cent. The employment status of councillors was also atypical of the population as a whole. Only 36.2 per cent of councillors were employees either full time – 26.8 per cent – or part time – 9.4 per cent – and self-employed councillors constituted 15.9 per cent of the total. A greater percentage of councillors were retired – 37.5 per cent – than were in full time employment. And there were significant differences between types of authority with only 17.4 per cent of councillors in the shire counties being in full time employment compared to 40.2 per cent of councillors in the London boroughs. Among the 52 per cent of all councillors in employment the majority – 61 per cent – were in the private sector and over half – 65 per cent – were in managerial, professional technical or executive jobs.

Thus the picture of the typical councillor suggests that council service is still as something for those who in the upper age groups and who are not in full time employment. Put slightly differently, those heavily affected by council policies, ethnic minorities, parents of young children and employees who have to travel to work, are not well-represented in the ranks of existing councillors.

Internal structures

One of Labour's major themes in its approach to local government after 1997 was that local government required strong leadership, which could only be achieved if there was a fundamental reform of the traditional internal structures of local government. Specifically, the Labour government wanted a clearer separation of the roles of executive and legislature within local government and the end of the blurring of decision making and representation processes entailed by the committee system. The traditional committee system was seen as slow and lacking in transparency. In order to effect a reform of local government structures Labour prescribed a massive reorganization of council constitutions and decision-making processes. The Local Government Act 2000 required that each local council undertake a consultation exercise to ascertain which of three acceptable models the local public wanted: a leader and cabinet; an elected mayor and cabinet; or an elected mayor and council manager, although some small district councils were allowed to retain a modified form of the old committee system. The overwhelming majority of the local authorities who undertook consultations opted for the form of governance which was most like the status quo, a council leader and cabinet. The new structures, although viewed sceptically by many observers, have sharpened the leadership provided by councils. There is a danger of allowing 'backbench' councillors to feel shut out of the policy process, a danger which can be partially overcome by sensitive use of group meetings.

Directly elected mayors had been urged by reformers of local government before Labour returned to office, specifically by Michael Heseltine when he was Secretary of State for the Environment in the Major government, and also by the 1995 Commission on Local Democracy. After 1997, the idea was taken up by Tony Blair and promoted by a number of modernizers within Labour ranks (Blair, 1998). Pressure groups such the New Local Government Network were also supportive of the idea. However, the idea of directly elected mayors also had formidable opponents, including John Prescott and most existing councillors. By the end of 2002 there had been at least 18 referendums on the introduction of a directly elected mayor, some of them forced by local petition against the wishes of the council; but only eleven local authorities had voted in favour. Thus, as of October 2002, the Local Government Association, the reorganized pressure group representing local government, calculated that the distribution of council constitutions (Table 11.1) contained only 11 directly elected mayors.

Moreover, when the votes to elect those mayors took place, many of the worst fears of traditionalists were realized. Five of the eleven directly-elected mayors currently in post have no conventional party

Table 11.1   *The constitutions of local authorities in England*

Constitution	Councils
Leader and cabinet	316
Mayor and cabinet	10
Mayor and council manager	1
Alternative arrangements	59

Source: Local Government Association (2002).

affiliation. In May 2002, independents were elected as mayor in North Tyneside, in Hartlepool and in Middlesbrough, despite these areas usually being Labour strongholds. The platforms of these directly-elected mayors differed, but all had an anti-establishment tinge. In North Tyneside a Conservative, Chris Morgan, was elected, and in Middlesbrough, Raymond Mallon, a former police chief known as 'Robocop' was elected on an anti-crime ticket. In Hartlepool, Stuart Drummond was elected after campaigning as 'Angus the Monkey', the mascot of the local football team, on a platform offering free bananas. In Watford, where Labour's Vincent Muspratt had been a strong advocate of directly elected mayors, the Liberal Democrat took the seat. The areas which voted for directly-elected mayors in October 2002 delivered similarly unpalatable verdicts to the major parties. In Bedford, independent Frank Branston defeated his more orthodox party rivals, while in Mansfield and Stoke, also Labour strongholds, two independents, Tony Egginton and Mike Wolfe, won. However, Labour did retain control of the London Borough of Hackney, one of the poorest local authorities in the country, when Jules Pipe succeeded in his bid to become mayor in a high-profile contest against the liberal Conservative Andrew Boff and hard left icon, Paul Foot.

How these independents will work out their own modus vivendi with their councils remains to be seen. What is clear is that the experiment has thus far not delivered the benefits which its advocates hoped for and that those who saw the opportunity to move to directly elected mayors as an encouragement for personality politics and populism have been proved to have a case. Certainly the Select Committee examining the workings of the 2000 local government legislation found that the concentration on the issue of internal structure had been a distraction for councils struggling to develop a new management agenda. And it commented acidly that the evidence suggested that electors had relatively little interest in the structures of local authorities as opposed to the services that they might obtain. Not surprisingly, the government distanced itself from the mayoral initiative, although in some ways moving towards the new form of government was made easier when in June 2002 it announced that local authorities would be able to choose whether to hold a referendum or not.

Local democracy

Arguments for local democracy have frequently been undermined by low turnouts at local elections and by public detachment from local government. Indeed, the Audit Commission makes explicit the link between low turnout and national intervention, and central government argues that its national mandate gives it a duty to address failures in priority services. Commercial and academic opinion research frequently reveals high proportions of citizens being unable to name a local councillor and large numbers, usually a majority, claiming to have had no contact with local representatives.

Low participation in local elections has recently generated concern in a number of quarters, including the Electoral Commission. Over the past twenty years, turnout at local level averaged around 40 per cent, but the last few years have seen turnout fall even lower. (Curtice 1999) In May 2002, turnout at the English local elections was 32.8 per cent. The introduction of directly elected mayors was intended to stimulate public interest, but many of these elections also recorded very low turnouts. Indeed, low turnouts in some areas were seen by many observers as contributing to victories by maverick candidates and independents. For example, the mayoral poll in which an independent won Mansfield in 2002 recorded a turnout of 17.9 per cent.

Young people and black and minority ethnic groups are particularly likely to be non-voters at local elections. Opinion poll material conducted by NOP for the Electoral Commission probed the reasons for public apathy in local elections and found a majority of the public expressed little belief that local elections would make much of a difference (Electoral Commission 2002). The majority thought local elections were not interesting and believed it was less important to vote at a local than at a general election. The same research also found 60 per cent of the public would be encouraged to vote at local elections if councils had decision-making scope, more taxing and spending powers and they had greater opportunities to participate between elections. It also found an information deficit, not least as a result of a reduction in local campaigning from the parties.

During the 2000 local elections there were some pilot schemes at the local level where it was found that easier postal voting had an impact on turnout. In 2002 there were many different experiments including electronic and Internet voting, all-postal voting, electronic counting and online registration. All postal ballots seemed to raise turnout significantly. In September 2002, the government invited councils to submit bids for further pilot projects for the 2003 elections so that there will be more experiments with Internet voting and voting by phone as well as by interactive television and by post.

How far the party system affects interest in local democracy is a moot point. In some areas there is very little party competition. However, in many parts of England competition is vigorous and Liberal Democrats, Greens and independents are able to secure representation in local

Table 11.2 *Council results Enland and Wales, 2002*

	Councillors	*Councils*
Conservative	7067	109
Labour	7576	122
Liberal Democrat	4223	27
Independent	2064	17
Plaid Cymru	207	3
No overall control	. . .	132
Total	21137	410

Source: Local Government Association (2002).

government. Indeed, of the total number of councillors in England and Wales, the combined totals of Liberal Democrats and Independents almost equal the number of Conservative councillors. And one of the most marked developments within local politics in recent years has been the growth in the number of councils with no overall party control – a larger number than councils controlled either by Labour or the Conservatives in 2002 (see Table 11.2).

Control of local government by central government

One of the causes most frequently given for lack of interest in local government is the sense that there is little genuinely *local* about the system in Britain where central government holds such strong powers in relation to finance, inspection and audit and setting policy priorities. Finance is at the heart of the central–local relationship and local authorities had very much hoped that after the Thatcher/ Major years a Labour government would loosen some of the controls on local authorities. But although there were a series of promises to review both the balance between central and local taxation and to reform some aspects of local government finance, change was slow in coming. Pressure groups such as the Local Government Association (LGA), while welcoming the government's proposals in relation to capital finance (which gave local authorities greater freedom to borrow), regretted that these had been balanced by provisions for additional financial management. These additional restrictions include new powers for the Secretary of State to specify the level of reserves for the local authority. Government proposals also involve new duties being imposed on finance officers to report on the adequacy of the authority's reserves, report on the robustness of budget figures and to monitor their budgets, all of which appeared to involve more regulation and the possibility of central intervention. The LGA is also unhappy with government proposals to merge business rates and the grant. But it welcomed the reforms scheduled for the council tax which provides about 20% of the average local authority budget. Although the council tax suffers from fewer defects than the poll tax or rates, it has been subject to extensive criticism because of its regressive nature and the banding structure which had been seriously affected by changes in property values. The government is now pledged to introduce a statutory revaluation and make the banding system more flexible. Although government no longer routinely sets a cap or ceiling for each council, central government has not given up its powers to cap council budgets. The Local Government Act of 1999 gave the government reserve powers if it thinks either tax or budgets have gone up too much. Moreover this is a more flexible power than before because central government can order cuts to take place in the following year as well as the current one.

Labour is also reviewing the way the government grant to local authorities is distributed, although the political implications of changes to the formula make radical change in this direction very unlikely. Grant is the major method of funding local authority services and amounts to about £47 billion per annum in England alone. The way the general grant is calculated is open to criticism because the formula takes into account past spending and therefore perpetuates inequalities. However any change in the formula (currently the Standard Spending Assessment) by which grant is assessed could create controversy by altering the extent to which such factors as deprivation are taken into account. What does seem likely to change is the management of ring-fenced grants (which currently amounts to about 14 per cent of council budgets). These grants are resented by councils because they are tightly targeted to particular services. Labour's reforms of ring-fence grants are however tied to a more general process of distinguishing between high-performing and poorly performing councils which perhaps more than any other aspect of its approach to local government reflects its approach to decentralization.

Inspection and audit

Any loosening of the reins of central control of finance (in so far as it has occurred) has been more than offset by the range of central government initiatives designed to give Whitehall greater powers of intervention. This provides central government with leverage over the local delivery of services and the operation of local councils generally. These initiatives aim to change the culture of local government, not least to make it more customer-focused. As such, they represent an ambitious and unprecedented attempt to reshape the structures, processes and strategic thinking of local government to bring them into line with central government's approach to public administration and management. These reforms have established increasingly exacting systems for improving the quality of locally delivered services and local authority performance. Prominent amongst these initiatives is Best Value, the replacement for the much disliked CCT. Best Value is the name of the regime that was established under the 1999 Local Government Act and introduced in April 2000. It has subsequently been reviewed and modified. This regime required all local authorities to develop a corporate strategy defining their overall goals and a programme of measuring performance for all local authority functions over a five-year period. In conducting these reviews, authorities and services were required to address what became known as the 'four C's': To *challenge* whether a service was necessary, to *compare* the performance of alternative providers, to consult local taxpayers, and to *compete* by demonstrating that the chosen method of service delivery was the most effective. It was a crucial part of this new regime that local authorities publish plans about how they would meet their targets for improving services. The legislation made services subject to inspection and made provision for direct central intervention where local authorities were failing to deliver adequate services. Part of Best Value's aims was to change the internal relationships *within* an authority, making them more flexible and encouraging both a clearer central strategy and the decentralization of authority to service officers. How far this has been achieved is open to doubt, though service officers themselves are more likely to perceive a change than top managers and members.

From 2002 local authorities are subject to a new framework of assessment, the Comprehensive Performance Assessment (CPA), which was outlined in *Strong Local Leadership – Quality Public Services*. CPA followed the publication of two documents on the need for a fuller audit regime to improve service delivery, *Changing Gear* (2001) and a report by Sir Ian Byatt and Sir Michael Lyons. The Audit Commission is now assuming an evolving role in the improvements in council performance across the board. This framework involves external assessment of *all* local authority services and the ranking of all single tier and county authorities in 'balanced scorecards' and 'league tables'. These tables for the first 150 councils were made public by the end of 2002. The CPA brings together judgments about core services (such as education, social services, housing and the environment), an assessment of the financial management of an authority, and grading of the council's leadership. Taken together these scores will enable an authority to be branded excellent, good, fair, weak and poor, a categorization which itself caused considerable hostility in councils. The use of league tables for councils is key to a new regime of central government intervention in local authority affairs, although it is an approach which is seen as heavy handed by many local authorities and their representatives.

How local authorities are ranked in the CPA will have an extensive impact on the freedoms and powers of the local authority, as well of course as having an impact on the council's image. Local authorities ranked 'excellent' will gain additional freedoms, be subject to fewer inspections and enjoy greater financial flexibility. In particular, it is envisaged that a local government bill (announced in the autumn of 2002) will give 'excellent' authorities greater freedoms in relation to ring-fenced grants, capital borrowing and the ability to set up trading groups. By contrast, where councils are rated poorly, there will be extensive central intervention and sanctions. As the government put it in its 2001 consultation paper, *Tackling Poor Performance in Local Government,* 'where a council or service is poor or failing we will expect councils to act to put things right and where necessary we will take decisive and tough action'. What this intervention could mean in practice could be anything from outsourcing of services, allowing one authority to run services for another or stricter central supervision. Central government intervention in council affairs is hardly novel: inspections, especially of education, police and social services, have long been a regular form of central control. But the expansion of inspection, the changing performance indicators and the emergence of new agencies of inspection and audit such as the Improvement and Development Agency have changed the character of the inspection process, and with it the relationship between central and local government. The Audit Commission has become a key player in the new world of local government, providing effective if uncomfortable scrutiny (and publicity) for weak councils such Hull and Walsall. It is as yet too early to assess fully the impact of these initiatives but certainly officers now see central government intervention as the primary force driving the modernizing agenda. However, for many officers costs associated with inspection outweigh the benefits because of the level of bureaucracy and regulation involved. Such burdens are likely to prove especially heavy for smaller councils.

Conclusion

There is little doubt that Labour has introduced a radical agenda of decentralization. Yet that agenda displays enormous contradictions and tensions. The tension between the urge to control policy outputs and to create vigorous new arenas of democratic activity or to breathe life into old ones runs through the approach to devolution, regional and local government. A new localism, at least as far as English local government is concerned is, is likely to prove more new than local and to remain highly regulated from the centre. Of course it may be that the population cares more about the quality of services than about democratic choice, and to that extent the government may be correct in placing such emphasis on performance. However, the weakness of genuine decentralization at the local level and of vigorous local democracy sets Britain apart from most of its European neighbours. Most particularly, however, it also places a question mark over claims that Britain has genuinely become a multilevel polity.

Chapter 12

Asymmetric Devolution: Toward a Quasi-Federal Constitution?

VERNON BOGDANOR

The four component parts of the United Kingdom are now governed in four different ways. Three of the component parts – Scotland, Wales and Northern Ireland – have devolved bodies, while England does not. Scotland, Wales and Northern Ireland, moreover, have devolved bodies of quite different types. Scotland enjoys a Parliament with legislative powers, but the National Assembly of Wales enjoys powers only over secondary and not primary legislation. Northern Ireland enjoys an Assembly with legislative powers, but the provisions of the Northern Ireland Act of 1998 require the executive to contain representatives of both of the two warring communities in the province, and the Assembly is to operate in a consociational rather than a majoritarian fashion. England, the largest component of the United Kingdom, containing around 85% of the population, has no devolved body to represent her interests, and calls for an English Parliament enjoy little resonance.

These variations between different parts of the United Kingdom have been defended as a justified response to dissimilar conditions in different parts of the country. Yet, the outcome is, as Douglas Hurd has pointed out, 'a system of amazing untidiness . . . a Kingdom of four parts, of three Secretaries of State, each with different powers, of two Assemblies and one Parliament, each different in composition and powers from the others, (Hurd 2001).

Devolution and the United Kingdom

Devolution poses two fundamental constitutional issues. The first, raised many years ago by Dicey (1959) is whether there is such a constitutional category at all, whether there can be a *via media* between the unitary state and separatism, other than federalism. Devolution, (or Home Rule, as it used to be known), would inevitably, so Dicey believed, lead to break-up. But, for the Blair government, the fundamental purpose of devolution was to avoid break-up and to hold the United Kingdom together, by containing the centrifugal forces of nationalism in Scotland and Wales, and providing a guaranteed role in government for the minority, nationalist, community in Northern Ireland. In Scotland, however, the nationalists welcomed devolution because they believed that it would encourage break-up rather than avert it; while, in Northern Ireland, Sinn Fein welcomed devolution as a step towards detaching the province from the rest of the United Kingdom. Opponents of devolution, therefore, maintained that it was a policy which, far from holding the kingdom together, would disrupt it by creating friction between London and Edinburgh, and a deadlocked form of government in Northern Ireland which, unable to operate effectively, would encourage the men of violence. The first issue then is whether devolution is a genuine *via media* between a unitary state and a federal one.

The second issue is whether asymmetrical devolution, a form of government which breaches the principle of equal rights for citizens living in different parts of the kingdom, is likely to prove stable; or whether it will prove a mere provocation to fresh demands. Already in Wales there is pressure for the Assembly to be given the same powers over primary legislation that the Scottish Parliament enjoys, and the Assembly has set up a Commission under the Labour peer, Lord Richard, to consider the reform of the Government of Wales Act. In the North of England there is pressure for a regional assembly which could compete with the Scottish Parliament in bidding for funds from central government. Thus, the second issue posed by devolution is whether an asymmetrical structure can yield a stable settlement.

Popular commentators and even some academics have not hesitated to rush to judgment on these matters, and, their judgments have been, on the whole, pessimistic. Indeed, they have tended to diagnose Britain as now in a state of terminal decline. Tom Nairn in his book, *After Britain*, insists that 'Britain has already broken up in spirit and the fact will soon follow', while Andrew Marr labels devolution as *The Day Britain Died*. Commentators from the right have been equally apocalyptic, with Peter Hitchens, for example, foreseeing *The Abolition of Britain*, while John Redwood, as befits a former Fellow of All Souls, shows a sense of scholarly caution in adding a question mark to the otherwise lurid title of his book, *The Death of Britain?* (Nairn 2000, Marr 2000, Hitchens 2000, Redwood 1999)

Those who believe that Britain will be no more are particularly afraid of an imbalance between a Scotland straining to burst the bounds of the devolution settlement and an England unable to express its nationalism for fear of disrupting the kingdom. The left tends to emphasize the first, the right the second. Perhaps the fears of both are exaggerated. They are certainly wildly premature. For the answer to the two questions posed above must be, in the words of the famous Chinese proverb, that it is far too early to tell.

In the second edition of his book, The English Constitution (*sic*), published in 1872, Walter Bagehot wisely remarked that it was

> too soon as yet to attempt to estimate the effect of the Reform Act in 1867. The people enfranchised under it do not yet know their own power . . . A new constitution does not produce its full effect as long as all its subjects were reared under an old constitution, as long as its statesmen were trained by that old constitution. It is not really tested till it comes to be worked by statesmen and among a people neither of whom are guided by a different experience. (Bagehot 1963).

It is perhaps natural to seek a verdict on whether devolution has 'worked' or not, just four years after the first Scottish Parliament and the first National Assembly of Wales were elected. Yet, any judgments as to the effectiveness or success of devolution can, at the present time, be no more than highly tentative. It would be very dangerous indeed to make rash generalizations about the workings of a new constitutional settlement, based on just four years' experience. For new institutions and organizational structures take at least ten years, and perhaps longer, to establish their own distinctive patterns. Thus any judgment of the consequences of the Great Reform Act of 1832 made in 1836, or the Government of Ireland Act of 1920 made in 1924, or the Life Peerages Act of 1958 made in 1962, would almost certainly have been falsified by later events.

Devolution, moreover, is more than a mere institutional or organizational change. It is a very radical constitutional reform, creating a form of government hitherto unknown in the United Kingdom, with the exception of the *de minimis* experiment in Northern Ireland between 1921 and 1972. The experience of Northern Ireland was of course deeply influenced by the religious-cum-tribal conflict in the province and by the electoral system, which allowed for the permanent dominance of one political party, the Unionists, who enjoyed an overall majority in the Parliament throughout its existence. Experience in Scotland and Wales is likely to be influenced by the evolution of party politics not only in Edinburgh and in Cardiff, but also at Westminster. From this point of a view, the relationship between Westminster and the devolved bodies since 1999 has been, in a sense, artificial in that a Labour government in London has been complemented by Labour/Liberal Democrat administrations in Edinburgh, and, since autumn 2000, in Cardiff also. No true test of whether devolution is 'working' or not will be possible until the majorities in Edinburgh and Cardiff find themselves in conflict with, rather than complementary to, the majority at Westminster.

Devolution and the Westminster Parliament

Devolution establishes new constitutional relationships between the different parts of the United Kingdom, relationships familiar perhaps in federal states, but wholly new in Britain, with the very limited exception of the 1921–72 Northern Ireland experience.

Devolution can of course be differentiated from federalism, in that it delegates sovereignty rather than dividing it. But this may be a difference of form rather than substance. Admittedly, the Blair government, in devolving power to Scotland, was anxious to stress that the sovereignty of Parliament was being retained at Westminster. The White Paper, *Scotland's Parliament*, declared in stern Diceyan tones in paragraph 42, that 'The United Kingdom Parliament is and will remain sovereign in all matters' (HMSO 1997). Section 28(7) of the *Scotland Act, 1998*, repeated this claim, declaring that, 'This section', which provided for the Scottish Parliament to make laws, 'does not affect the power of the Parliament of the United Kingdom to make laws for Scotland' (HMSO 1999).

In practice, however, it can already be seen that the sovereignty of Parliament has been limited by devolution. Westminster has agreed, by convention, that it will not normally legislate on matters devolved to Scotland without the consent of the Scottish Parliament. Scottish ministers at Westminster – the Secretary of State and her team – no longer accept questions on Scottish domestic affairs, since they are no longer responsible for them.

Even on Welsh matters, despite the fact that powers over only secondary and not primary legislation have been devolved to the National Assembly of Wales, ministers refused at the first Welsh question time after devolution, to accept questions on Welsh domestic affairs:

> In reply to a question on tourism, Peter Hain, Under-Secretary at the Welsh Office, replied, 'I had responsibility for this matter until 1 July.'

> The Speaker then interjected, 'If it is a devolved matter, we must pass on.'

Later, having been asked a question on the problems of the beef industry, Alun Michael, the Welsh Secretary, replied, 'This is a matter for the National Assembly for Wales.'

The Speaker interjected again. 'If the Minister announces that it is a matter for the National Assembly for Wales, I cannot allow the House to trespass on these responsibilities. [Interruption] If the Minister tells me that it is a matter for the Assembly, it cannot be a matter for the House, correct?'

Alun Michael: 'Correct.'

A question was then put to Welsh Office Under-Secretary, Jon Owen Jones, concerning abbatoirs in Wales. He replied, 'This is a matter for my Right Hon. Friend, the Minister of Agriculture, Fisheries and Food, or in Wales, for the National Assembly.'

The Speaker interjected yet again. 'Order. In that case, it is a matter for the Welsh Assembly. It cannot be the responsibility of both this House and the Assembly.' (*Hansard* 1999)

This was a remarkable decision, since the Government of Wales Act devolves to the National Assembly of Wales, not particular subject areas, as with the Scotland Act, but powers. Statutorily, every area of policy still remains with Westminster. It may be objected against the argument that Westminster has lost sovereignty, that ministers do not answer questions on matters which are the responsibility of local authorities, and yet it is not argued that Parliament is no longer sovereign over local authorities.

The Scottish Parliament and the National Assembly of Wales, however, are not local authorities, but bodies with powers to legislate over a wide range of domestic activity, and bodies which represent national feeling in Scotland and Wales. While it is normally a fairly easy matter for Parliament to assert its will over local authorities against their wishes, and even, as in 1985, to abolish a whole tier of local government – the metropolitan authorities and the GLC – that will hardly be the case with the devolved bodies. Admittedly, Westminster was able to prorogue, and in effect abolish, the Northern Ireland Parliament in 1972; but that, too, is hardly relevant, since the Northern Ireland Parliament was not set up to placate a centrifugal nationalism, but, on the contrary, to make it easier for ministers to cede a part of the United Kingdom for which they had no particular love. Political authority, moreover, depends upon its regular and continuous exercise; it must mean something more than the mere incursion of legislative authority during a pathological crisis. Moreover, the Scottish Parliament and the National Assembly of Wales, by contrast with the Northern Ireland Parliament set up in 1921, were established only after they had been validated by their respective electorates through referendums. It would not be easy to abolish them without securing approval for their abolition in further referendums.

It will not even be easy for Westminster unilaterally to alter the devolution settlement to Scotland's disadvantage. There is currently much discussion of revising the Barnett formula or the needs assessment formula determining the block grant going to Scotland, which is based on the Barnett formula. For, so it is alleged, these formulae are unduly favourable to Scotland. The White Paper, Scotland's Parliament declares, however, that

> Substantial revision [of the Barnett formula] would need to be preceded by an in depth study of relative spending requirements and would be the subject of full consultation between the Scottish Executive and the Government. (HMSO 1997).

It is not perhaps being too speculative to suppose that 'full consultation' will in practice mean that the Scottish Executive comes to enjoy a practical veto on proposals to revise the formulae to the disadvantage of the Scots. On such matters, therefore, the supreme body with the power to alter the provisions of the devolution settlement may well be, not Westminster alone, but Westminster together with the Scottish Parliament.

It is therefore difficult to resist the conclusion that Westminster is in practice no longer sovereign over the domestic affairs of Scotland and Wales; or that, at the very least, the sovereignty of Parliament means something very different in Scotland, and to some extent in Wales from what it means in England. In England, the sovereignty of the Westminster Parliament corresponds to a genuine supremacy over 'all persons, matters and things'. In Scotland, by contrast, it seems to mean little more than a vague right of supervision over the Scottish Parliament, together perhaps with a power in some pathological situation, such as afflicted Northern Ireland in 1972, to abolish that Parliament. Parliament's sovereignty over England still corresponds to a real power to make laws affecting every aspect of England's domestic affairs. In Scotland, by contrast, it no longer corresponds to such a real power, but to a power – fairly nebulous in practice, one may suspect – to supervise another legislative body which enjoys the real power to make laws over a wide area of public policy. Thus, except perhaps during periods of pathological crisis, the formal assertion of parliamentary supremacy will become empty since it will no longer be accompanied by a real political supremacy.

The term 'devolution', then, is highly misleading. It seems to imply a mere delegation of powers. But, in practice, it does far more than delegate powers. It divides the power to legislate for Scotland between Westminster and Edinburgh, creating a quasi-federal relationship between the two parliaments.

Perhaps the logic of devolution implies that, if it is to rest upon an enduring constitutional foundation, the distribution of powers should not be revocable at will by Westminster. At present, the Judicial Committee of the Privy Council can pronounce on the constitutionality of legislation emanating from the Scottish Parliament, but not upon Westminster legislation – although, in practice, were the Judicial Committee to pronounce that a particular statute deriving from the Scottish Parliament lay within its powers, it would be difficult for Westminster to override it. If that is the case, then Westminster would lose another of the characteristics of a supreme parliament, the power to make laws from which there is no appeal; for in practice both Westminster and the Scottish Parliament will have come to depend upon the decisions of a court for the protection of their sphere of action, a condition characteristic of a a federal system of government.

In his *Introduction to the Study of the Law of the Constitution*, Dicey detected 'three leading characteristics of completely developed federalism – the supremacy of the constitution – the distribution among bodies with limited and co-ordinate authority of the different powers of government – the authority of the courts to act as interpreters of the constitution' (Dicey 1959: 144). Were it ever to be recognized that devolution in fact implies an abdication of Westminster's ability to alter the settlement at will, and the transfer of powers to adjudicate the settlement to a court, then it will also have been recognized that the logic of devolution points to a constitution, a constitution, moreover that bears strong resemblances to the constitution of a federal state.

Already, however, devolution has introduced into Westminster a federal element, which has been absent from it throughout British history except, once again, for the de minimis exception of Northern Ireland between 1921 and 1972. With this exception, Westminster has always been characterized by the complete absence of the federal principle. Every Member of Parliament enjoyed similar rights and duties, and there were no territorial differences in the responsibilities of MPs from different parts of the United Kingdom, since every Member of Parliament was equally responsible for scrutinizing both the domestic and non-domestic affairs of every part of the United Kingdom. Since 1999, however, Members of Parliament have been able to play no part in legislating for the domestic affairs of Scotland or Northern Ireland, and no part in drawing up secondary legislation for the domestic affairs of Wales. Only with regard to England do Members of Parliament continue to enjoy the power which hitherto they have enjoyed for the whole of the United Kingdom, of scrutinizing both primary and secondary legislation. Thus, Westminster is no longer a Parliament for the domestic and non-domestic affairs of the whole of the United Kingdom. It has been transformed into a parliament for England, a federal parliament for Scotland and Northern Ireland, and a parliament for primary legislation for Wales. Westminster has become a quasi-federal parliament.

There is a further consequence, namely that MPs for Scotland and Northern Ireland have been deprived of most of their constituency duties. For most of the matters on which constituencies contact their Member of Parliament, matters such as housing and education, are now in the hands of the devolved bodies. MPs for Scotland and Northern Ireland are responsible primarily for foreign affairs, defence and macro-economic policy. There are thus MPs from England with constituency responsibilities and MPs from Scotland and Northern Ireland with no constituency responsibilities, and MPs from Wales with much reduced constituency responsibilities.

In June 1999, the Scottish Parliament proposed that reduced allowances be paid for 'additional' members elected under the list on the grounds that they had fewer constituency responsibilities than those elected in constituencies. In the Commons, shortly afterwards, a Conservative MP proposed a similar reduction in the allowances of MPs representing Scottish and Northern Ireland constituencies. To this request, the then Leader of the House, Margaret Beckett responded, 'I strongly hold the view . . . that there is not and should not be such a thing as two different kinds of Members of Parliament' (*Hansard* 1999a). Mrs Beckett thus turned a Nelsonian blind eye to the problem. Her answer had no basis in logic. For the first time in its history, with the exception of Northern Ireland between 1921 and 1972, there were in fact two kinds of Members of Parliament at Westminster – or three if the unique position of Welsh MPs were to be taken into account. So it was that, for the first time in British history, the general election of 2001 did not decide domestic policy for Scotland, Wales or Northern Ireland. Of New Labour's five policy pledges in 1997, at least two – the pledge to reduce class sizes and the pledge to reduce NHS waiting lists – now lay beyond the government's control outside England. The Scottish Parliament, indeed, could, if it so wished, abolish the National Health Service entirely. Thus, in England, voters were still electing a Parliament which would be responsible for their domestic affairs. In Scotland,

Wales and Northern Ireland, by contrast, the voters were electing a Parliament for a quasi-federal state.

Devolution for England?

England is of course the anomaly in the devolution settlement. It is by far the largest and most populous part of the United Kingdom, yet it is the only part of the United Kingdom without a Parliament or Assembly of its own. England indeed has always resisted federalism, but it has also resisted, in the twentieth century at least, the integration of the non-English parts of the United Kingdom, preferring a system of indirect rule, which allowed the indigenous institutions of the non-English parts of the United Kingdom to be preserved. Nor has English nationalism been a particularly strong force for much of the twentieth century. Part of the reason for this no doubt is that, with a characteristic lack of logic, many in England have failed to recognize the distinction between being English and being British, treating the two as interchangeable. In 1924, Stanley Baldwin, speaking at the annual dinner of the Royal Society of St George, was able to confess to 'a feeling of satisfaction and profound thankfulness that I may use the word 'England' without some fellow at the back of the room shouting out 'Britain' (quoted in Aughey 2001). Because so many used 'English' and 'British' as interchangeable terms, English nationalism found itself without any obviously recognizably patriotic symbols of its own.

If, however, the English were to seek to express their Englishness to the full, they could easily, as the dominant nation in the United Kingdom, threaten the unity of the country. Some commentators indeed, primarily on the right, such as the journalist, Simon Heffer, in his book, *Nor Shall my Sword: The Reinvention of England*, argue that devolution imposes such injustices upon the English that they should do precisely that (Heffer 1999). For it is, according to this viewpoint, no longer reasonable to expect the English to submerge their identity solely in order to hold the United Kingdom together. The English can become truly English only if they are willing to burst the bounds of union.

Survey evidence enables us to cast considerable light upon the reality of English attitudes, as opposed to the claims of the commentators as to what they are or ought to be. The options in Box 12.1 were put before English respondents for the Social Attitudes Survey in 1997 and 1999.

The same survey also showed that 65 per cent of the English believed that 'the government should do everything it can to keep all parts of Britain together in a single state', but that 54 per cent of the English believed that it would be in the long-term interests of Northern Ireland

Box 12.1   Social attitudes survey, 1997 and 1999

Scotland should have	*1997*	*1999*
Independence	14	24
Devolution, with some taxation powers	38	44
Devolution, with no taxation powers	17	10
No devolution	23	13

Wales should have	*1997*	*1999*
Independence	13	20
Devolution, with law-making and taxation powers	37	34
Devolution, with limited law-making powers, and no taxation powers	18	22
No devolution	25	15

England should have	*1999*
A Parliament	18
Regional assemblies	15
No change	62

Note: These results reflect the views of English respondents only (Curtice and Heath 2000: 162–6).

to join with the Irish Republic rather than remain within the United Kingdom. There has in fact been majority backing in England for Irish unity in opinion polls since the first British Election Survey in 1983 (Curtice and Heath, 2000).

The answers given to these survey questions seem to indicate that the English have come to accept devolution in Scotland and Wales. Indeed, there seems now to be a majority amongst English voters for devolution in Scotland and Wales. But the English do not want devolution for themselves. The late Donald Dewar, Scottish Secretary of State and then Scotland's First Minister, once said that devolution was the 'settled will' of the Scottish people. Devolution to Scotland and Wales, but not to England, now appears as the settled will of the English people too. The English have adjusted to the new status quo, but are uninterested in further constitutional change. They seek, not to become lions, but to remain ostriches, preferring, as Disraeli once put it, to be governed not by logic but by Parliament.

Perhaps there has been too much emphasis by political scientists upon the factors tending towards the break-up of the United Kingdom and too much historical discussion of the United Kingdom as an artificial construct, an 'invented nation', held together by essentially ephemeral factors (Colley 1992). The Scottish National Party (SNP), after all, achieved its highest vote in a general election, 30 per cent, over 27 years ago, in October 1974. Its vote in the most recent general election, in 2001, was 20 per cent. This means that 80 per cent of Scottish voters voted for unionist parties and that the SNP has lost one-third of its vote over the last quarter-century. There can be little comparison with the Irish situation in the nineteenth century where, outside Ulster, all but two of the Irish constituencies were won, after 1885, by the Home Rule party. If to be British is to wish to continue to be represented at Westminster, then there can be little doubt that there is a majority in each of the component parts of the United Kingdom for remaining British.

Perhaps there has been too little analysis of the factors which hold the United Kingdom together. In his somewhat underestimated book, *Understanding the United Kingdom*, Richard Rose suggested that too much had been written explaining what had not happened, i.e. the break-up of the United Kingdom, with the consequence that historians and political scientists had spent too little time analysing the factors which held Britain together (Rose 1982). Britain, Rose suggested, was united by functional issues and by common economic and social concerns. Paradoxically, the referendum in Scotland in 1997 which showed massive support for devolution, confirmed rather than refuted Rose's argument. For, the 'Yes' majority seems to have been founded primarily on instrumental reasons, rather than upon nationalism. Voters believed that a Scottish Parliament would improve the quality of public welfare, especially health and education. They regarded constitutional reform as a means rather than an end in itself. In the words of two psephologists who analysed the election, 'Most have expectations that [the Parliament] will make a difference to their lives in terms of the services they want it to provide. Those are the grounds on which its effectiveness is likely to be judged, rather than as an affective expression of nationhood' (Surridge and McCrone 1999: 52). If this view is correct, devolution will be seen to have renegotiated the Union between England and Scotland, rather than to have destroyed it.

England, however, does not seek a parliament of her own. When, during the 1997–2001 Parliament, William Hague, the Conservative leader, sought to put himself at the head of an English army by proposing one, he found himself bereft of followers. The Blair government, therefore, took the view that devolution in England should take the form, not of an English Parliament, but of devolution to the English regions. Such a policy is Gladstonian in nature. For, in 1879, during his

Midlothian campaign, Gladstone had declared, 'If we can make arrangements under which Ireland, Scotland, Wales, portions of England can deal with questions of local and special interest to themselves more efficiently than Parliament now can, that, I say, will be the attainment of a great national good' (Jenkins 1995: 432). It took nearly 120 years for a government of the Left to begin the fulfillment of this 'great national good'. By the millennium, however, Northern Ireland, Scotland and Wales enjoyed institutions through which they could 'deal with questions of local and special interest to themselves'. The unfinished business that remained concerned the 'portions of England' which alone lacked 'arrangements' by which they could deal with such questions.

In 1997, however, the government had established, as a first step towards devolution, regional development agencies and it had also provided for indirectly elected regional chambers to scrutinize them. In 2002, the government issued a White Paper, *Your Region, Your Choice: Revitalizing the United Kingdom*, (DLTR 2002), providing for, but not requiring, directly elected regional assemblies. The government's policy on English devolution, then, was permissive rather than mandatory.

The reason for this is of course that regional consciousness differs so greatly in intensity in different parts of England, being strong no doubt in the North, but weak or perhaps non-existent in the South East. The government proposed, therefore, that assemblies would be established only where favoured by a majority in a region in a referendum; and it would be for the government to gauge whether there was sufficient public interest in a particular region to justify holding such a referendum.

But there is a further difficulty with regional devolution. For, in England, devolution would add a third tier to sub-national government, since it would co-exist with a two-tier rather than, as in Scotland and Wales, with a one-tier system of local authorities. This is because local government had been reorganized into a system of unitary authorities in Scotland and Wales by John Major's administration in 1994, but no such reorganization had been completed in England. Thus the White Paper proposed that, in areas where a referendum was to be held, there would first be an independent review of local government structure by the Boundary Commission for England, which would recommend the most effective unitary structure for the region. A unitary system of local government would be a precondition for regional devolution in England. The problem of securing a unitary system of local government would, however, be less difficult in the three northern regions, since a substantial proportion of the population of the North East, North West and Yorkshire and Humberside already live under unitary authorities.

Elsewhere, however, the counties would almost certainly resist local government reorganization, since the county tier would probably be the one to be abolished.

The assemblies would be elected by the Additional Member System, already used for elections to the Scottish Parliament and the National Assembly of Wales. They would, like the National Assembly of Wales, enjoy no revenue-raising powers of their own, but would be funded primarily from a single government grant. They would, however, be able to raise additional funds through precepting the council tax, which would be collected on their behalf by local authorities in the region. This power would, however, be limited by arrangements comparable to the current local authority capping regime, and the assemblies would have no power to alter the non-domestic business rate. The assemblies would acquire powers from central government primarily over economic development, transport, land use and regional planning, and environmental protection and public health. They would not, however, enjoy powers over the politically sensitive areas of the National Health Service or education (except possibly further education). It is possible, of course, that the powers of the regional assemblies would be expanded in the long run and that devolution in England might become, as the former Welsh Secretary, Ron Davies, predicted would be the case in Wales, a process rather than an event.

Beyond the unitary state: devolution and its impacts

Devolution to the English regions would be a major step towards completing a radical constitutional reform which could, in the process of time, transform the United Kingdom, almost by stealth, from a unitary state into a quasi-federal one. The establishment of such a state would, however, threaten one fundamental principle which has lain at the basis of British politics from the time of the Attlee government, if not from the era of Lloyd George. It is that the benefits which the individual derives from the state, and the burdens imposed upon the him should depend, not upon geography, but upon need. Devolution, however, now allows the non-English parts of the kingdom to develop their own distinctive priorities in public policy. Yet the Welfare State was founded on the principle that the needs of citizens should be determined not locally but by central government, which alone could balance the requirements of different parts of the kingdom. The alternative would be what is now contemptuously called a postcode lottery. Perhaps it was for this reason that Neil Kinnock, then a rebellious backbencher, declared in 1976, that devolution 'could be an obituary notice for [the Labour] movement' (quoted in Taylor 2000: 180). For those Labour MPs, primarily but not wholly from the left of the party, who opposed devolution in the 1970s and 1990s were concerned less with the argument over sovereignty, that devolution would prove the slippery slope leading to the break-up of the kingdom, but, with a quite different argument, that from power, since they believed that with devolution, Westminster would lose the power to correct territorial disparities.

Devolution, then, threatens a fundamental principle of the welfare state and of social democracy. Already, after only four years, important divergencies have appeared in welfare benefits between Scotland and the rest of the United Kingdom. For the Scottish Parliament has decided to provide for the finance of university students, the salaries of teachers, and the needs of those in residential care, in a more generous way from that adopted by Westminster. As devolution progresses, it is likely that the non-English parts of the United Kingdom will continue to establish priorities of their own, distinct from those of Westminster. With devolution to the English regions, the discrepancies could become even larger. It is not clear how far that process can go within a single state. Perhaps a new definition of what social and economic rights are fundamental and should remain uniform throughout the kingdom would be helpful. What cannot be denied is that devolution threatens the power of the government of the United Kingdom to secure equal social and economic rights for all of its citizens. It is perhaps ironic that it has been a Labour government which has been so enthusiastic to promote devolution. For devolution conflicts profoundly with the traditional aim of social democrats, reiterated as recently as 1998 by Tony Blair in his Fabian pamphlet, *The Third Way*, as the promotion of 'social justice with the state as its main agent' (Blair 1998b). It is difficult to see how the state can promote social justice if it has been fragmented and cut into pieces by devolution.

Wherever a government is composed of more than one tier, whether it is federal in nature, or whether the lower tier is constitutionally subordinate, as in the United Kingdom, there needs to be communication between the various layers of government. The Blair government, in order to achieve, this, published in 1998 a *Memorandum of Understanding* (HMSO, 1999) and established a Joint Ministerial Committee comprising ministers of the Westminster government and the devolved administrations. Various concordats, which are not legally binding, but in the nature of statements of political intent, have also been issued to assist communication between the government and the devolved administrations. In addition, the Cabinet Office established a Constitution Secretariat in May 1997, in part no doubt to consider devolution issues.

These arrangements, experimental though they may be, are similar to, although of course they do not precisely mirror, those established in Canada, whose system of inter-governmental relations is perhaps the most highly developed and sophisticated amongst federal states. The dangers of these arrangements are also perhaps similar to those that have been noticed in Canada by many commentators.

The prime danger is that inter-governmental institutions create a third and unaccountable layer of government. The inter-governmental layer will in theory be accountable to Westminster and the devolved bodies, but in practice there is likely to be buck passing, with each side blaming the other for unpalatable decisions. Moreover, the public are, inevitably perhaps, excluded from this process of inter-governmental negotiations, which take place mainly in private. There are restrictions on the extent to which the information divulged in inter-governmental negotiations can be made available to the public. The *Memorandum of Understanding* proclaims that:

> Each administration will wish to ensure that the information it supplies to others is subject to appropriate safeguards in order to avoid prejudicing its interests ... Each administration can only expect to receive information if it treats such information with appropriate discretion. (HMSO 1999; cf. Rawlings 2000)

The danger, then, is that parliament and people will be presented with various *faits accomplis*, deals negotiated behind closed doors, which cannot be unpacked, and which reinforce the dominance of the executive both at Westminster and in Edinburgh and Cardiff. At a time when there are worries about parliamentary accountability and when electoral participation rates are declining, this exclusion of parliament and the public from the inter-governmental process must be a matter of some concern. Moreover, one of the aims of devolution was to lessen the load on central government and to relieve it of responsibilities. This purpose would be defeated if a new complex inter-governmental layer of government were introduced, with its accompanying bureaucratic load. There are perhaps no obvious ways of averting these dangers. It is possible, however, that accountability might be increased were the various legislatures and assemblies within the United Kingdom to become involved in the process in addition to their governments so that the views of the devolved bodies could be, as it were, built into the structures within which the key decisions are taken.

In my book, *Devolution in the United Kingdom*, I proposed that this be achieved by transforming the House of Lords into an indirectly elected chamber, modelled on the German Bundesrat, as a method of 'giving the devolved governments formal access to the legislative powers in a reformed second chamber' (Bogdanor 1999: 285).The central government would then need to secure the consent of representatives of the devolved bodies in the reformed second chamber. In Britain, such a chamber might, it was suggested, be composed of delegates from the devolved executives in Scotland, Wales and Northern Ireland, and from local authorities in England. The English representatives would be delegates from the London authority and the regional chambers, themselves elected in large part from local authorities. Were devolution to come about in the English regions, however, it would be natural to replace this form of representation with representation from the executives of the English regional authorities themselves.

Further reflection, however, and also consideration of the criticisms contained in the book by Ivor Richard, formerly Leader of the House of Lords, and Damien Welfare, *Unfinished Business* (1999), have served to convince me that the Bundesrat model cannot be applied to Britain. Part of the reason for this is that Britain has not yet become, as Germany already is, a federal state. Rather, devolution has so far created a form of asymmetric quasi-federalism in the United Kingdom. For the regional chambers in England do not as yet enjoy anything like the electoral legitimacy of the German Länder. They are non-statutory indirectly elected bodies, containing, in addition to local councillors, non-elected people such as business representatives. Thus, English representation in an indirectly elected second chamber would be a form of indirect election at two removes, by those originally elected to local authorities and then seconded to the regional chambers. Such supposed 'representatives' would hardly enjoy the legitimacy of those representing the directly elected devolved bodies in Scotland, Wales and Northern Ireland.

Moreover, in England, elections for local authorities would then become, in effect, invisible elections for the new second chamber. This would make it less likely that local elections would be decided by local issues, and more likely that they would come to depend upon the vicissitudes of national party politics. Instead of being asked to vote for a party pursuing policies in the interests of a locality, electors would be asked to vote for a party which would support or oppose the government in the new second chamber. Local elections would thus become bound more tightly into the Westminster system, and local and regional autonomy, far from being strengthened, might well come to be weakened.

The qualifications for local councillors would also alter. Instead of being chosen primarily for their ability to formulate policies for their locality, they would also need to be able to scrutinize the working of central government and to hold it to account in the new second chamber. That is a very different requirement, and it is by no means clear that one person could do both tasks effectively; nor that either of these tasks could be undertaken on a part-time basis. Most probably, some councillors would concentrate on the one task, and some on the other. This division of labour, however, could well weaken local government rather than strengthening it, by depriving it of a cadre of able councillors.

Moreover, in Scotland, Wales and Northern Ireland, an indirectly elected chamber, modelled on the Bundesrat, would have the effect of re-opening many of the contentious features of the devolution settlement. Scottish members of the second chamber, for example, would be able to scrutinize legislation emanating from the Scottish Parliament as well as government legislation (excluding financial legislation). This would give them a wider remit than is enjoyed by Scottish MPs, who, following devolution, are no longer in practice in a position to scrutinize Scottish domestic legislation emanating from the Scottish Parliament. Thus an indirectly elected second chamber would raise anew the West Lothian Question in a different and unpalatable form. Far from being the coping-stone to the devolution settlement, therefore, such a reformed second chamber could well re-open it, re-kindling English resentment at its inequity.

Britain as a multi-national state

The legislation providing for devolution to Scotland, Wales and Northern Ireland, establishes a new constitutional settlement amongst the nations comprizing the United Kingdom. Northern Ireland is, however, once again an exception since neither of the two communities in Northern Ireland see themselves as a nation; for the Unionists see themselves as part of the British nation, while the Nationalists see themselves as part of the Irish nation. Nevertheless, the United Kingdom is, as a result of devolution, in the process of becoming a new union of nations, each with its own identity and institutions – a multi-national state rather than, as the English have traditionally seen it, a homogeneous British nation containing a variety of people.

Moreover, it seems to have become implicitly accepted that the various nations comprizing the United Kingdom enjoy the right of self-determination, and that this includes the right of secession. Since the time of the Northern Ireland Constitution Act of 1973, it has become accepted that the constitutional status of Northern Ireland cannot be changed without the consent of the people of Northern Ireland; if, however, a majority in Northern Ireland seeks to leave the United

Kingdom and join with the Republic of Ireland, that wish will be accepted by the British government, which will indeed facilitate the transfer.

In Scotland in 1988, the Claim of Right, the foundation document of the Scottish Constitutional Convention, declared that 'We, gathered as the Scottish Constitutional Convention, do hereby acknowledge the sovereign right of the Scottish people to determine the form of Government suited to their needs'. On this view, sovereignty lay with the people of Scotland, not with Westminster, a claim implicitly accepted by the Blair government, which, in drawing up its proposals for devolution in Scotland followed closely the ideas of the Convention, and resisted departures from them on the grounds that they did not represent the wishes of the Scottish people. Significantly, the Claim of Right was ceremonially handed over to the Presiding Officer of the new Scottish Parliament just prior to its opening on 1 July 1999. So it is that, 'The legal doctrine of Westminster's sovereignty meets its limits in the assertion of popular sovereignty. Crucially, the source of the Scottish Constitution becomes rooted in the people as well as in the Westminster Parliament' (Hadfield, 2003). From this point of view, the Scotland Act represents a self-generated or autochthonous constitution, a constitution rooted, as it were, in Scottish soil, rather than, as the term 'devolution' implies, one imposed by Westminster (cf. Wheare 1960, Hadfield 2003). There can be little doubt that if, at some time in the future, it became the 'settled will' of the Scottish people to break the link with Westminster, the British government of the day would respect that wish, rather than, as it did in the 19th century in the case of Ireland, resist it. Thus, in both Northern Ireland and Scotland, it has come to be accepted that their constitutional status depends not only upon the decisions of a supposedly sovereign Parliament at Westminster but upon the wishes of their people.

The unitary British state was the expression of a belief that the non-English sections of the United Kingdom formed part of a single British nation. Devolution, by contrast, is the expression of a belief that the non-English parts represent separate nations which, nevertheless, choose to remain within the larger multi-national framework of the United Kingdom. But, as well as providing for a new constitutional settlement amongst the nations comprising the United Kingdom, the devolution legislation of 1998 establishes a constitutional settlement between the nations comprising the United Kingdom, and the other nation sharing these islands, namely the Irish nation – for the international treaty which gave legislative expression to the bulk of the Belfast Agreement, signed on Good Friday 1998, created a British–Irish Council whose role it would be, in the words of the

Belfast Agreement, 'to promote the harmonious and mutually beneficial development of the totality of relationships among the people of
these islands'.

The British-Irish Council was modelled in large part upon the Nordic
Council (Bogdanor, 1999). As with the Nordic Council, membership of
the British-Irish Council is not confined to nations. The members of the
Council will be Britain and Ireland, the devolved bodies in Scotland,
Wales and Northern Ireland, and, 'when established, and if appropriate,
elsewhere in the United Kingdom', but also representatives of three
British Crown dependencies which are not part of the United Kingdom,
the Isle of Man, Guernsey and Jersey. These dependencies do not of
course regard themselves as separate nations. The Council is to meet at
summit level, twice a year, and in specific sectoral formats, on a regular
basis, with each of the participants being represented by an appropriate
minister. It is primarily consultative and will consider such issues as
transport links, agriculture, environment and culture, health, education
and approaches to the European Union. It can agree upon common
policies, but has no power to bind individual members, who can choose
to opt out or not to participate in common policies.

Conclusion

The creation of devolved bodies in Scotland, Wales and Northern
Ireland, together with the British-Irish Council, not only transform a
unitary state into a quasi-federal one; they also provide for a confederal
link between the United Kingdom as a multinational state and the Irish
Republic. These arrangements constitute a remarkable attempt to realize the underlying theme of Gladstonian thinking, which implies recognition of the various and distinctive national identities of the peoples
living in these islands, and also of the close and complex links between
them. They offer a return to the Gladstonian conception of Home Rule
in a form suited to twentieth century conditions. It took indeed almost
the whole of the twentieth century for British politicians painfully to
rediscover the essential truth of the Gladstonian proposition that neither
the unitary state nor separation could yield solutions to the complex
problems posed by the multinational nature of the United Kingdom.
The devolution legislation and the British-Irish Council propose a solution which both recognizes and yet seeks to transcend nationalism
through institutions which express not only the separate national identities of the components making up the United Kingdom and the
Republic of Ireland, but also their underlying unity.

To give effect to and yet to seek to transcend nationalism may seem contradictory aims. Yet that, after all, is the logic of federalism, and also the logic of the peculiar quasi-federal system with confederal elements that makes up the new British constitution. The sociologist, Karl Mannheim once said that the British had 'a peculiar genius for working out in practice the correlation of principles which seem to be logically opposed to each other'. That genius will certainly be needed if the devolution settlement is to prove a success. The Russian painter, Wassily Kandinsky, predicted that the twentieth century would see the triumph of 'and' over 'either/or (quoted in Aughey 2001: 152–6). The history of the twentieth century refuted this prediction. It is just possible, however, that the evolution of the British state in the twenty-first century could prove him to have been right before his time.

Chapter 13

Ideas and Policy Agendas in Contemporary Politics

PAUL KELLY

Following the election victory of 1997, New Labour explicitly took up the idea of a Third Way between old-style social democracy and the neo-liberalism of Thatcher and Reagan as its preferred ideological agenda. This change of language was reinforced by Tony Blair's Fabian Pamphlet on The Third Way (Blair 1998b) and a series of seminars held with US President Bill Clinton. These occasions included the leading theorist of the Third Way, the sociologist Anthony Giddens, as well as academics such as Bill Galston and Benjamin Barber, who sought to provide a similar Third Way for the American 'new' Democrats (Barber, 2001). Clinton remains avowedly Third Way, and in a speech to the 2002 Labour Party Conference he drew strong links between the current Labour government and the Clinton administration as the two main pillars of Third Way politics (Clinton 2002). Giddens has become one of the most articulate and passionate advocates of Third Way politics, publishing three books on the subject over five years (Giddens 1998, 2000, 2001). His most recent Fabian/ Policy-Network pamphlet urged New Labour not to abandon the analysis and policy prescriptions of the Third Way in its second term in office, in particular by avoiding any returning to being a 'tax and spend' party (Giddens 2002). Giddens is not the only major theorist of the Third Way, but as his original book has been translated into 25 languages he remains the most prominent exponent of Third Way thinking in the world.

But while the language and policy agenda of the Third Way remain live, the New Labour government has become less inclined to speak in these terms. There are a number of reasons for this apparent change of heart. The most obvious is that in Britain the language of the Third Way was widely seen not as a renewal of social democracy but as an excuse and cover for its abandonment. Many traditional Labour supporters criticized the Third Way as either a betrayal of the core values and commitments of social democracy or as an attempt to incorporate a variant of neo-liberalism, with its preference for markets over government, into the heart of New Labour policy making (Heffernan 2001). This latter charge was easy to make because both Blair and Giddens are quite explicit about the role of market solutions within Third Way thinking and New Labour policy making.

A further significant problem for the advocates of the Third Way is that despite all the rhetoric around it, there does not seem to be much of a theory at its heart. In a political culture such as Britain's, which is traditionally unsympathetic to either 'theory' or intellectual gurus, it is hardly surprising that Third Way thinking has suffered from hostile criticism to the effect that it does not actually have a theoretical core. Unlike traditional democratic socialism with its various historical commitments to equality, public ownership and redistribution, or conservatism with its commitments to limited government, hostility to change and endorsement of social inequality, the Third Way can only offer an eclectic mix of policy suggestions that seems to borrow from rival ideological and philosophical traditions. Even those not unsympathetic to the New Labour project tended to see the whole approach as the elevation of political pragmatism to a philosophical theory.

Giddens' own approach seems to support this view since all of his Third Way books appear to concentrate on the minutiae of policy suggestions rather than the broad principles and distinctive values of a new ideological or philosophical tradition. Where major organizing concepts do feature in Third Way thinking they are usually ambiguous and indeterminate concepts such as responsibility, opportunity and community, rather than animating core values such as equality, freedom, social justice, nation or tradition. This has led one influential political theorist to describe the Third Way as not really a concept or a theory but a 'rhetorically defined space' (Lukes 1999), determined by values and policy instruments and strategies, such as a preference for the market over government control of industries. Yet this preference for markets is based on pragmatism and a judgment of what works, rather than an explicit endorsement of markets as part of a 'spontaneous order'. Inevitably, as Lukes acknowledges, this space is very expansive indeed, and this no doubt helps explain why so many critics see it as being without content.

In response to this charge sympathetic political theorists such as Stuart White have suggested that the language of the Third Way should be abandoned in order to liberate the ideas and theoretical aspirations that underpin it (White 2001). White's claim is that the language of the Third Way has become a liability, which obscures the fundamental analysis and ideological realignment that Third Way thinking was supposed to promise its defenders. This fact is perhaps illustrated best by Giddens' most recent pamphlet which continues to endorse his familiar analysis but revealingly does not use the phrase Third Way in its title (Giddens 2002).

Abandoning the headline discourse of the Third Way is helpful in clarifying precisely that the key theorists of the Third Way are primarily concerned with the substance and not the name of this new approach. At one level, Third Way discourse suggests a middle path between old-style social democracy with its commitments to demand management, deficit funding and the mixed economy, and neo-liberalism with its commitment to supply-side solutions in public policy and unlimited faith in markets as the best means of delivering higher living standards and economic growth. Somewhere between these two positions is the Third Way – one more ideological perspective to be contrasted with its discredited rivals. Yet when examined closely the Third Way prescriptions of Giddens or Blair tend to celebrate markets, entrepreneurship and all the other key phrases of neo-liberalism. Although Giddens and others have sometimes tended to characterize the Third Way in such terms, this is not the only or most important way of approaching it. Thinking of the Third Way as simply a further discrete ideology in competition with others is to misapprehend the fundamental point of Third Way thinking. But equally clearly the Third Way is not simply a feature of the morphology of traditional social democracy, for it does indeed incorporate ideas and strategies that have a place in neo-liberalism and which challenge some of the presumptions of European social democracy (Vandenbroucke 2001). This tendency appears to present the new policy language of the New Labour government as at best eclectic and plural and at worst opportunistic. But is that all there is to it? To answer that question we need to look deeper into what the theorists of the Third Way are saying about the nature of current politics and the language we use about it.

Ideological disaggregation and modern politics

There is a phenomenon, best described as ideological disaggregation, which lies at the heart of Third Way discourse. The language of policy making and justification used by Labour's leaders demonstrates some association between New Labour's progressive agenda and revisionist social democracy and post-Thatcherite neo-liberalism. Here, New Labour has sought to construct a new language for its progressive aspirations, in an effort to shape the ideological and theoretical agenda of British politics. Theorists of ideology give accounts of distinct ideologies in terms of the language of politics employed by recognizable social groups containing core and peripheral concepts and value terms (Freeden 1996, 1998). These groups are composed of theorists or philosophers, policy advocates and those who are motivated to act by them. What is important about ideologies (as opposed to academic or philosophical theories) is that they are not primarily concerned with issues of truth and right, but rather with mobilization and legitimation. This is not to deny that truth and right might be relevant to mobilizing and legitimating political actions and policy. But it is to place their significance in context alongside other ends. Consequently, it is the case that philosophical theories can be ideological at the same time. To describe a form of political discourse as ideological in this sense is to describe its function and not to play down its cognitive significance (Freeden, 1996). Is then the Third Way a new ideology to rank alongside social democracy or neo-liberalism? Or is it an eclectic mix of existing ideological forms, concepts and policies?

One of the hardest tasks for New Labour's theoreticians has been to provide a simple answer to both of these questions. White and Lukes suggest that New Labour's progressive agenda is not really a distinct new ideology to rank alongside traditional social democracy or neo-liberalism. But does that mean the Third Way, or however else we wish to identify New Labour's progressive agenda, is merely an eclectic mix and match of concepts and policies from other ideologies? The problem facing the theoreticians of New Labour's progressive agenda is that they deny that we are faced with this simple choice.

Why? Third Way thinkers such as Giddens have been important to renewing the theoretical agenda of progressive politics because they have set out to show that the changes in the world economy and the aspirations of citizens in modern democratic societies have significantly transformed the world in which our traditional ideological structures and traditions function. Unlike earlier social and political theorists of the 1950s and 1960s who preached the end of ideology (Bell 1962), or their later successors such as Francis Fukuyama (Fukuyama 1992) who preached the end of ideology because of the apparent triumph of a particular ideology, theorists of Third Way or progressive alternatives to existing ideologies have not claimed that social and political transformation has rendered ideology redundant. What they have suggested is that these broader social, political and economic changes have transformed the ideological discourse by challenging the priorities and targets of previous ideological discourse. Yet for such theorists politics continues to be 'ideas' driven, at least in the realm of policy making and legitimation. But the ideas that drive the new agendas and policy frameworks are derived not from the re-interpretation of traditional ideological forms but from the disaggregation of those traditions and the reintegration of fundamental ideas from these different theoretical discourses and political contexts.

This move involves a new emphasis on 'values' which are seen to be of continuing relevance, and which are claimed to be resilient to social and political changes, whilst some of the core features of institutional analysis are abandoned as outdated or redundant in the face of phenomena such as globalization (Held *et al.* 1999). In part the change here explains the prevalence of a moralized politics on the part of New Labour, which seeks to focus its agenda more on the 'goods' or 'ends' that policy should deliver than on the mechanism through which those 'goods' are distributed. As we will see later it also helps explain the near total indifference to traditional social democratic questions of ownership of sectors of the economy and civil society. But even where some basic values are retained in reconstructing the agenda of progressive politics, the contexts within which they are interpreted and used are themselves new.

Policy agendas and the language of progressive politics

The problem facing Third Way theorists is that they cannot simply rely on the received ideological traditions of either social democracy or neo-liberalism, as these no longer fit the changed circumstances within which New Labour must explain its progressive agenda. But these wider social and economic changes not only render existing ideological traditions redundant, they also place constraints on the way in which new discourses can be developed to replace them. Whereas all previous ideological forms have both pragmatic and utopian components in a continuous state of dynamic conflict, the transformations that Third Way thinkers identify in late modernity renders this utopian element deeply problematic. Progressive theorists therefore tend to cash-out the new directions for progressive politics in terms of specific policy measures and issues and reconfigurations of values, rather than in terms of some grand vision. It was the absence of a coherent grand vision that was claimed to undermine the Third Way as an appropriate discourse for progressive politics, yet it was precisely the inability to construct or sustain such grand visions that initiated the turn to Third Way thinking in the first instance. So whilst Stuart White might be right in suggesting that the language of the Third Way is no longer helpful in articulating New Labour's progressive vision (2001), the social and economic changes that underpin the turn to Third Way thinking in the first place rule out the possibility of constructing a grand vision or meta-narrative that does not have precisely the same features attributed to the Third Way.

Any progressive policy discourse will inevitably become a 'rhetorically defined space' that is filled by values and policy goals which have been disaggregated from single coherent ideological traditions and also separated from traditional understandings of the institutions through which they are pursued. But isn't there a danger that this is simply a complicated way of saying that New Labour's progressive agenda is pragmatism – or doing what works? To some degree those critics who claim that the Third Way is simply a cover for an unprincipled pragmatism are on to something. The more moralized conception of progressive politics that results from the disaggregation of traditional ideological forms and the final abandonment of utopianism as a source of policy vision and aspiration, inevitably entails a pragmatic approach, in that what matters is that various goods are achieved. In this the Third Way might seem merely to reflect the pragmatic revisionism of past Labour thinkers such as Anthony Crosland, who wished to detach the core values of democratic socialism from particular policies such as nationalization and state ownership (Crosland 1956). This theme is also picked up by commentators such as Raymond Plant who see New Labour as the heirs to the revisionist social democracy of Crosland and his followers (Plant 2001).

But this concession to pragmatism is not to say very much, since all viable policy agendas will have a pragmatic component. The progressive agenda of New Labour cannot be purely pragmatic because its exponents do not have a wholly free hand in deciding what its core values and commitments are, nor do they have a free hand in how it reintegrates those value commitments into public policy. Thus, while New Labour might well be able to abandon commitments to controlling the commanding heights of the economy, or conceptions of the welfare state and social provision that were developed in the 1940s and 1950s, it cannot abandon value concepts such as social justice, equality and citizenship. It is this fact that creates the ambiguity about how far New Labour offers a new politics (Fielding 2000).

The charge of narrow pragmatism depends upon a contrast with principled utopian aspirations. But, with the abandonment of the utopian component of traditional ideologies as a key feature of post-Third Way progressive thinking, this contrast is too simplistic. Instead we are left with a normative vision that is composed simply of values and principles in dynamic change, rather than some end-state, however far off that might be. To some degree all change in political discourse is a matter of degree. But the theorists of the Third Way and New Labour's progressive agenda would contend that there are times where the accumulation of small degrees of change constitutes qualitative change. The transformations of the global market and related changes to the global structure of politics represent one of those periods of qualitative change.

New Labour's progressive policy agenda is thus constrained in its eclecticism and pragmatism, but those constraints are not narrow. We can identify four features that shape the progressive agenda of New Labour and which reflect the role of ideas in the development of new policy frameworks:

- An emphasis on the inadequacy of received ideological frameworks to respond to significant changes in social, economic and political structure of modern politics, such as globalization, mass migration, mass communication and the information society and environmental change;
- The abandonment of utopian meta-narratives as the source of political inspiration;
- A greater reliance on basic values in the defence and legitimation of policy at the expense of a commitment to institutional practices and modes of delivery; and
- The combination of these core values with new mechanisms of delivery and new institutional contexts.

Policy agendas, think tanks and ideological entrepreneurs

The attempt to theorize a new progressive agenda for New Labour has not resulted in the discovery or construction of a new big idea. Neither have theorists and policy makers been able to congregate behind a distinctive policy, in the way in which Mrs Thatcher offered, say, privatization as the distinctive portal into her policy agenda. Instead the progressive agenda of the second New Labour term in office is characterized by the reinterpretation of core values in policy making. But those values are detached from institutional structures and commitments, and they are interpreted in new and distinctive ways. We can see this feature of the new progressive agenda in action in the character and agendas of new think tanks and policy entrepreneurs who move between these think tanks and government. Think tanks such as the Institute for Public Policy Research (IPPR) or Demos have been important players in the development of New Labour's progressive agenda. They set out to develop new progressive thinking that can shape and influence policy making. Although they are both close to New Labour, and identified in the public mind with Blairism, neither is formally connected to New Labour (unlike more traditional Labour think tanks such as the Fabian Society). Where Demos provides support for long term or 'blue sky' thinking with publications such as 'The Moral Universe' which explores the 'remoralization' of Western values following September 11th, the IPPR is more closely focused on developing the short and medium term contributions to New Labour policy making. In some cases these units act as a freelance policy research agency that can work closely with government in areas such as public–private partnerships, education policy and most recently on issues such as citizenship and social integration.

Both think tanks present themselves as modern and forward-looking and neither is weighed down by a historic attachment to the Labour movement, nor attached to any particular policy agenda or mode of policy delivery. Yet the efforts of both to provide a radical progressive agenda for the New Labour project are not merely fortuitous. Key people, such as the co-founder and first director of Demos, Geoff Mulgan, who subsequently moved to be first Director of the Performance and Innovation Unit in the Cabinet Office and then Director of the Prime Minister's Strategy Unit, are closely associated with the policy direction of New Labour at the most practical level. Similarly, the trustees of the IPPR combine New Labour figures and academic entrepreneurs such as Tony Giddens.

Yet what is most interesting about both think tanks and their key people is that their emphasis on new thinking is not merely an issue of style, but rather the institutional recognition of the need to develop ideas and a policy agenda beyond the boundaries of the traditional institutional commitments of the Labour movement. Both organizations contribute to policy debates in a context shaped by a recognition of the factors behind Third Way thinking, namely an acknowledgement of fundamental social and economic change, in the face of globalization, mass migration and new technology. But the think tanks' stance is also a recognition of ideological disaggregation or unlinking, a renewed interest in core values detached from their traditional institutional and policy commitments and finally a search for new mechanisms of delivery. By maintaining an independent status alongside a close commitment to the progressive agenda of New Labour, think tanks and policy entrepreneurs distance themselves from the more conservative and historically rooted policy agendas of other members of the Labour movement such as the trades unions. This enables them to pursue the agenda of progressive politics without bearing any substantial commitments to institutional structures and mechanisms of delivery.

This feature is clear in the mission statement '*A Progressive Future: IPPR's Agenda for a Better Society*' (IPPR 2002). This brief document sets out a broad agenda based on a range of values such as equality, community, diversity and pluralism, democracy and accountability, rather than focusing on a defining value or single organizing concept. The IPPR's broad range of core values is then pursued in a host of new policy initiatives and strategies that entail new forms of provision, institutional structure and regulation. Much is made of concepts such as civil society and community, rather than seeing the state as the main vehicle for delivering the progressive agenda.

This change does not simply concede provision of welfare and social justice to the market place, the course advocated by neo-liberals trying to influence the future direction of Conservative policy making. New Labour and Blairism have inevitably been criticized for adopting the neo-liberal strategy of privatizing public provision of welfare. The progressive agenda outlined in the IPPR policy document, echoing the language of Giddens' Third Way, is seeking to move the debate beyond the structures of provision. The defining feature of ideological debate that is being challenged is that progressive policy must inevitably be associated not merely with social provision but with state provision and public ownership. The whole thrust of the IPPR's mission statement is to reflect the direction of post-Third Way thinking in its rejection of the simple dichotomy between left and right as meaning public versus private provision. Against this we can see the strong emphasis on civil society as one way of trying to provide a space within which the pursuit of core values can be translated in varied and responsive policy programmes.

A further important consequence of the process of ideological disaggregation for the think tanks and entrepreneurs is that it allows access to a wide variety of social and political theories and theorists in the process of justification and legitimation. If the boundaries of old ideological structures have become redundant, as is suggested by Third Way progressives, then it becomes much easier to co-opt thinkers and ideas from outside of traditional ideological traditions to support, inform and help reinterpret the progressive policy agenda. One is just as likely to find the arguments of John Rawls, Ronald Dworkin, Bruce Ackerman or Phillipe Van Parijs as R. H. Tawney or Tony Crosland in discussions of social justice and equality. Many of these thinkers would previously have been thought of as beyond the boundaries of the social democratic tradition and therefore not legitimate contributors to the progressive policy agenda. But what is most important is that when they do appear in debates about policy, they are not used (as John Rawls was by some post-Croslandite social democrats, such as Roy Hattersley) to mark the latest statement and defence of a common ideological programme. Instead they appear as sources for particular arguments and perspectives that can be detached from their complete theories in order to bolster particular policy positions. This leaves us with a more eclectic and pluralist ideological context for policy making.

Third Way thinking in action: social justice

The influence of post-Third Way thinking and the impact of the new think tanks can be seen most clearly in the way that the policy agenda of New Labour has started to stabilize in a number of key areas. Much policy making in any government is reactive, but in certain areas the theoretical or philosophical context of policy making illustrates fundamentally the ideological direction of a government. Third Way thinking can be seen clearly in the most distinctive area of New Labour policy making, its traditional concern with social justice and redistribution. Throughout its long history, social justice has been a central goal of the Labour movement, initially closely tied to a class analysis of society and connected with the goal of social ownership, given its classic statement in the old Clause IV of the Labour Party constitution. Post-war revisionists such as Crosland sought to move the Labour Party away from this essentially class-based analysis, arguing that Labour needed to abandon the policy of nationalization and the connection of social justice with social ownership. Instead Crosland offered the idea of equality of status and what might be called (following the American philosopher John Rawls) fair equality of opportunity. Here everyone not only has legal access to opportunities of power and responsibility, but also the basic material conditions that make those opportunities genuinely open to all. New Labour policy making reflects traditionalist commitments to equality and redistribution, but it has reinterpreted these commitments in ways that have raised concerns even amongst Labour revisionists. Whilst many critics have suggested that New Labour has abandoned its commitment to equality, its defenders claim that it has merely applied and developed its core egalitarian commitments in new way.

Social exclusion and redistribution

One of the most striking features of New Labour's revised agenda for social justice has been its adoption of the language of social exclusion, together with the establishment of a Social Exclusion Unit close to the centre of power, and the recasting of areas of social policy in terms of the issue of social exclusion. First, this shows how New Labour has transformed its commitment to equality and social justice from one of simple redistribution of power and resources. Inequality of income in itself is not a major concern of the New Labour's policy agenda. Instead it has turned its attention to the sources of persistent disadvantage, or those aspects of policy which consign individuals and families to poverty and preclude them from gaining the benefits of economic growth and social co-operation. Within the 'social exclusion' label, the focus of policy has been with the factors that keep some people locked at the bottom end of the income scale rather than with the spread of the income scale itself. Second, however, this focus on social exclusion is used not to abandon a commitment to redistribution, but instead to focus on redistribution within the overall priorities of the welfare and education budgets. Furthermore, tackling social exclusion explains the government's focus on issues such as child poverty (where it has given a commitment to eradicate child poverty in a generation), educational opportunities, and the emphasis it places on measures and incentives to encourage welfare recipients to return to the labour market.

Many people see this policy as driven by the need to reduce the welfare budget, but other commentators see it not only as economically necessary in the long-term, but also as an aspect of a broader concern with social justice. The focus on social exclusion, and on labour market exclusion in particular, acknowledges the dignity of labour in terms of its contribution to personal self-respect and the social integration of families without a wage earner for long periods of time and unable to change their circumstances by small increases in income. The focus on labour market inclusion has also enabled the government to target the redistribution of resources within the constraints of its existing budget commitments through initiatives such as the national minimum wage, the Working Families Tax credit and lower tax rates and National Insurance contributions paid by the lowest paid. All of these changes took place within the very tight budget constraints of New Labour's first term when the government refused to consider raising personal taxation – a position that has only recently been relaxed with the increase in National Insurance contributions to fund increased health expenditure. That this broad policy direction was not simply dictated by the needs of the Treasury, but reflects a renewal of thinking about the nature of New Labour's commitment to equality and redistribution in new circumstances is reflected in the ideas and theories that underpin it.

Beyond universalism in social provision

Traditionally Labour's commitment to equality has been tied to the idea of universalism, two concepts which have been inextricably connected. The old Labour view was that equality of status, outcome or opportunity could only be achieved if they were to apply universally to all. This universalist idea was carried through in policy terms not simply for the pragmatic reason of tying the middle classes into support for the welfare state, but also at a more theoretical level as part of a strategy for under-mining inequalities of *status* (as well as income) between the poorest and the better off in society. This connection has been re-affirmed by some key figures, for instance, Gordon Brown's unwillingness to remove universal benefits such as Child Benefit. In other areas, however, the Chancellor has adopted a very different understanding of the demands of equality and social justice. This might be called 'egalitarianism as prioritarianism' and can be traced back to the writings of the American political philosopher, John Rawls. This Rawlsian aspect to Brown's social policy should not be a surprise because Brown has shown a considerable interest in the United States as a source for much of his social and political ideas. This interest is also shared by many of his key advisers who studied in the United States and are as just at home in post-Rawlsian political theory as they are in political economy and policy. This turn to the United States with its different political tradi-tions and history also offers an interesting example of ideological disag-gregation and realignment. New Labour has drawn on sources that have not been traditional for the party, such as American political liber-alism rather than European social democracy, to provide the interpreta-tion and development of core political values for Britain.

Whereas Rawlsian liberalism has been used in a broad sense to bolster the case for egalitarian redistribution by critics of New Labour such as Roy Hattersley, the New Labour turn to 'prioritarianism' is a much more selective use of Rawlsian ideas. In John Rawls' famous book *A Theory of Justice* (1971) he offers a general theory of egalitarian justice composed of two principles. The first is a liberal principle of equal basic liberties, but the second is the 'difference principle'. Its first part states that social and economic inequalities should be arranged to be of greatest expected benefit of the least advantaged. This approach is much closer to New Labour's vision of targeted egalitarianism. The significant part of this claim is that distribution and justifiable inequal-ities are tested against the claims of the worst off. New Labour's redis-tributionist strategy involves turning to the worst off, such as children, the lowest paid and the long-term unemployed, as the first claimants on social policy. It recognizes that the pursuit of social justice is not exhausted by a traditional focus on the structure of income distribution. At the level of ideology this turn to prioritarianism is interesting because it is not offered as an alternative to traditional egalitarianism. Instead the egalitarian perspective is broken down, or disaggregated, into components some of which are universalist, such as equal civil rights, and others which are more appropriately distributed in terms of prior-ity. Whilst Labour Governments have also had to focus much of their social policy on the claims of the poorest in society on grounds of urgency of need, New Labour connects that policy move with a renewed understanding of the claims of egalitarianism. The turn to social exclusion is therefore not intended as a substitute for social justice and redistribution, but as part of a new progressive agenda that seeks to understand these concerns in different ways.

Asset-based egalitarianism

Social exclusion and prioritarianism both focus on the primary recipients of social policy. but the expansion and development of the social justice agenda being pursued by New Labour, and by Gordon Brown in particular, can be seen in terms of the *objects* of distribution as well as the recipients. Again, following ideas being explored by American social and political theorists, we can see an interest in what the IPPR has advocated as asset-based egalitarianism. Contemporary advocates of asset-based egalitarianism include radical proposals, such as Bruce Ackerman and Anne Alstott's advocacy of a stakeholder or capital grant of $80,000 to all 18-year olds (Ackerman and Alstott 1999), or Phillippe Van Parij's call for a Citizen Income (Van Parijs 1995). These ideas are unlikely to be taken up by New Labour, but they do find echoes, however modest, in some schemes floated by the Chancellor's advisors.

The interesting thing about the asset-based approach is not simply that it focuses on the asset-poor, such as those without savings or access to credit. The asset approach also broadens concern from cash and financial resources to other kinds of assets such as educational opportunities and qualifications (which are increasingly an important currency for entering the labour market and therefore open access to many other kinds of goods). For progressive theorists this ties in with the attempt to look beyond income distribution in terms of achieving social justice and instead focus on the reasons why many of the poorest remain locked in a cycle of poverty. Thus high levels of employment – another preoccupation of New Labour and Gordon Brown – and better educational opportunities can all be linked together as part of a broad social justice agenda pursued across a variety of government departments. The key point for understanding the renewal of New Labour's policy agenda is its attempt to broaden the understanding of the remit of social justice from merely the overall profile of income distribution.

The focus on social exclusion, prioritarianism and asset-based egalitarianism shows how New Labour has tried to marshal new ideas and approaches to egalitarianism to broaden its traditional social justice agenda. However it has also opened up new problems that defenders of more traditional approaches to social justice have been keen to exploit. Labour critics such as those associated with the Catalyst Trust, and some Liberal Democrats have attacked what looks like an abandonment of a long held 'left' commitment to reduce income inequality across society. Many of the new approaches underlying social exclusion seem to be solely concerned with exclusion from the labour market, which is important but leaves aside the underlying increase in overall inequality between the poorest and the best off under New Labour. Tony Blair is on record as being indifferent to growing levels of income inequality, but it remains to be seen how indifferent New Labour can continue to be to this factor. Already since the 2001 election the Blair government seems to be reassessing its public indifference to the increase in income inequality. If income inequality continues to increase it will become increasingly harder to sustain the idea that giving priority to the worst-off such as children, unemployed youth and single mothers without jobs is really a way of pursuing social justice and egalitarianism. And without this possibility of ideological legitimation New Labour will merely be left with social policy targets, such as reducing youth unemployment, that might be better achieved by more coercive measures such as those pursued by recent Conservative administrations.

Disaggregation and new thinking: the Conservatives

For many British Conservatives the most pressing agenda is not ideological disaggregation, but avoiding their party's disintegration. Some of the features of policy debate and redefinition within the Conservative party reflect their need to address the same ideological context that led Labour towards the Third Way. Being in opposition forces the Conservatives to respond to the agenda set by the governing party. However, following two substantial electoral defeats, the party has also had to face up to providing a new analysis within which its own policy agenda can be developed. The redefinition of the Conservatives' policy agenda has become most apparent during and after the 2001 leadership election that brought Iain Duncan Smith to the Tory leadership. Much has been made in the press and popular commentary about the leadership contest and the subsequent redirection of policy, as a struggle between reformers and traditionalists, with Duncan Smith being on the side of the traditionalists.

Yet (as always) these categorizations are only partially helpful. What they obscure is the emergence of disaggregation within the ideological legacy left for her party by Margaret Thatcher. The debates within the party are no longer between right wing neo-liberals and left wing paternalist Tories. Thatcher effectively won those battles through her ideological redirection of the party, but also (more importantly) through the recreation of the party through successive waves of new MPs whose careers and ideological mind-sets have been formed under the long shadow of the Thatcher governments of the 1980s. In the light of Thatcher's success in recasting the party in her image it ought to be possible to reject the familiar view of the Conservatives as one party with two souls, a libertarian or small-state soul and a paternalist interventionist soul (Greenleaf 1983).

The neo-liberal turn in the Conservative party has been complete, but that turn has not rendered significant ideological debate about the future direction of the party redundant. Instead we can see the Conservatives also wrestling with the phenomena of disaggregation, in their efforts to make sense of the implications of neo-liberalism in the changing circumstances of globalization and the collapse of Soviet communism after 1989. The trajectory of these phenomena is different for Labour and the Conservatives but it would be a mistake to see this new context as merely something that affects New Labour. The simplicities of the neo-liberal agenda of the 1980s, with its commitment to rolling-back the state and privatization, have given way to a more complex appreciation of that legacy. What is beyond doubt is that the key debates about the future direction of the Conservatives involve reconstructing some version of the neo-liberal commitment to the primacy of liberty in the face of changing circumstances.

That said, some commentators previously associated with the Conservatives, such as political theorist John Gray, lament the embrace of neo-liberalism by the Conservative party. They argue that neo-liberalism exacerbates the globalization of the world economy which in turn undermines traditional forms of life and institutions, precisely the sorts of things that Conservatives are supposed to wish to conserve (Gray 1998). Gray's target is the equation of conservatism with the kind of market fundamentalism that is found on the right of the political spectrum in the United States. Somewhat ironically, Gray's anti-free market fundamentalism led him towards an equivocal relationship with New Labour as a potential bulwark against the excesses of global capitalism and because neo-liberal ideology is so powerful there is no possibility of a return to traditional conservatism (Gray 1998).

The ideological trajectory of the Conservatives has become more libertarian and less conservative, increasingly concerned with increasing personal freedom and reducing the role of the state. Whereas this was a distinct policy agenda against which paternalist Conservatives struggled, it is now much less distinctive, and this explains the shape of the current disputes between modernizers and traditionalists about the future direction of the party. Both camps within the party are undoubtedly libertarian, yet the significance of that commitment is deeply contested. On the one hand there are those who are committed to the retreat of the state and the adoption of a more robust economic, social and moral individualism. For these Conservatives the issue is simply one of individual or personal freedom. Drawn to Margaret Thatcher's claim that 'there is no such thing as society', they are therefore sceptical of practices designed to constrain and direct individual choices and oppose the role of state in directing economic choices. This kind of conservatism is driven by the ideological agenda of American libertarians such as Robert Nozick. For them there is no good ground for regulating private behaviour and sustaining conventional moral norms. These attitudes can be seen amongst modernizers who wish the party to be indifferent on issues of lifestyle choice, sexuality and marital status. In taking this stance they run up against traditional Tory views about morality, sexuality and the centrality of the family. Yet the important thing about their social liberalism is that it is defended as an extension of the ideas of personal responsibility that underlies the philosophy of market de-regulation and rolling back the state. The retreat from social authoritarianism is merely one further stage in the neo-liberal assault on the paternalism that used to characterize both the Conservative party and British society until it was put to the sword by Thatcher in the 1980s.

Against this sceptical libertarianism there is another libertarian strand in the Conservative party, which is more inclined to value conventional practices and institutions of social morality because these nurture and sustain civil society which is the ultimate bulwark of liberty against the state. This strand is also bolstered by ideological trends from the American right, but these trends are much less sceptical about the morality of social policy and more concerned about the role of sub-state institutions and associations as the key to policy delivery and the maintenance and protection of personal liberty against the overarching power of the state. For advocates of this view, such as the think tank Civitas (whose sub-title is 'The Institute for the Study of Civil Society') and social commentators such as Melanie Phillips, the issue is not one of the tyranny of conventional morality, but the threat posed to liberty and free associations by the power of the state. This conception of the neo-liberal agenda is similar to the 'compassionate conservatism' popularized by the Republican Party in the United States. It combines an assault on the structures of the welfare state with a commitment to local provision, freedom of association and moral authoritarianism. Defenders of this approach, whilst being supporters of the Thatcherite legacy for the economy, think that there is certainly more to society than individuals and their families. Where they remain neo-liberals is in their free-market ideology and their scepticism about the state usurping the role of civil society.

These strands of neo-liberalism in the modern Conservative party do not give rise to discrete political camps. There is an overlap between modernizers and traditionalists, but this overlap is not wholly benign since it explains the ambiguities in the direction of current Conservative thinking about the direction of policy. This thinking has still not been fully clarified by the proclaimed emergence of new Tory policy positions in late 2002. Yet the debates between advocates of both strands are often about emphasis until they involve fundamental questions about the family or sexuality, at which point the two perspectives start to coalesce into mutually antagonistic camps.

That neo-liberalism presents the Conservatives with an ambiguous legacy for future policy direction is also illustrated by the legacy of global free markets. Access to global free markets and international capital flows are an essential component of modern conservatism. But the consequences of those neo-liberal policies have been to transform the context of modern politics. The theorists of the Third Way have made a virtue of accommodating these changes into re-thinking progressive politics, but the Conservatives have been rather less confident about the consequences of their own policies. On issues like sovereignty and free movement of peoples the Conservatives have been more likely to rely on cautious and restrictionist policies. The problem of free-movement and economic migration has been addressed under the guise of restricting asylum seekers. In this respect, the Conservatives have followed both the trajectory of the European right generally and specific populist tendencies within New Labour, most forcefully articulated by David Blunkett as Home Secretary. Yet the challenges that globalization pose to the long-term viability of Conservative commitments to national sovereignty remain to be seen. Contemporary Conservatism has as yet been unable to combine its predilection for a small but strong state with its commitment to a conception of political economy that increasingly makes that conception of the state redundant. What is unclear is whether the Conservative response to global transformation will be the kind of libertarian retreat feared by traditionalists like John Gray, or the affirmation of a libertarian civil society approach. As the ideological agenda for the future development of Conservative policies is limited by the dominance of some variant of neo-liberalism, resolving the conflicting claims of the state and the global free market is unlikely to be a straightforward matter. It might well be the case that the libertarian civil society approach will provide the intellectual resources to construct a 'traditionalist' conservatism, of the sort many think is no longer possible, as a bulwark against the tendencies towards globalization which Third Way theorists emphasize. As yet, however, there is no clear sign of the emergence of any Conservative Third Way.

Conclusion

New Labour is in a precarious position in its second term in office. It has an opportunity to transform the ideological agenda of British politics and thus changing the terms of subsequent policy debate, but also faces the problem of providing a coherent new language of policy. The government is moving away from the language of the Third Way, but it retains important commitments that are derived from the analysis of Third Way thinkers, commitments not just relevant to New Labour but which also shape the context for the ideological redefinition of the Conservative party. It was always a central plank of Third Way thinking that it was a response to changed circumstances which rendered received concepts and values ineffective in responding to new challenges. Whilst New Labour has been most closely associated with responding to the changes of globalization, the demands of these new circumstances are as great for the other main parties as well.

New Labour's main break with the perspective of Old Labour is that it locates its analysis in terms of global transformations of the economy, rather than the failure of old style social democracy within the context of a national economy. It also claims that the Third Way is not merely the triumph of neo-liberalism, since it does not attach ideological preference to the market place, but seeks only to co-opt the market where this is best for its policy agenda. To provide the intellectual defence and justification of these changes post-Third Way progressive thinking has been keen to search beyond the familiar boundaries of ideological forms and political traditions, in order to construct new interpretations and defences of core values.

Here, ideas are trying to alter the policy agenda. The most striking feature of the dominant ideas that are presently generated is the abandonment of grand 'meta-narratives' or what in more traditional ideological terms we might describe as the utopian component – that is the vision of the desirable future society. This leaves post-Third Way thinkers and New Labour policy makers with a large problem. If they have nothing better than a pragmatic appeal to economic growth and increased social welfare, then they are subject to the constant threat of policy failure or the offer of new policies that are better placed to achieve these goals without a commitment to any role for public provision or regulation. Furthermore, they are also vulnerable to a revised and ideologically motivated neo-liberal Conservative party who 'really understand' the market and can propose serious measures to further liberalize it. Whilst the Conservatives continue to remain electorally weak, and the Liberal Democrats can be held at the margin, 'New

Labour' can continue to remain equivocal on its vision for a 'New Britain'. But once circumstances change that position becomes more problematic. What remains to be seen is whether the new ideological resources of post-Third Way progressive thinking are sufficient to help New Labour provide that vision.

Chapter 14

Economic Policy

WYN GRANT

Economic policy has been viewed for a long time as being at the centre of British politics. The objective of economic policy is 'getting and spending', raising taxes and then using them to achieve public policy objectives. The ways in which taxes are raised, and the effectiveness with which they are spent, can have a considerable impact on government popularity. More generally, governments are seen as being responsible for the performance of the British economy. British economic performance has improved considerably in the period since Britain left the European Exchange Rate Mechanism in September 1992. By 2002 unemployment had fallen to below one million and inflation was low and stable. The 'misery index', combining inflation and unemployment levels, has fallen over the decade (see Table 14.1) and the growth rate of

Table 14.1   *Unemployment and inflation, 1992–2001*

Year	Inflation (RPI) (%)	Unemployment (%)	Misery Index (%)
1992	3.7	9.2	12.9
1993	1.6	9.7	11.3
1994	2.4	8.8	12.2
1995	3.5	7.6	11.1
1996	2.4	7.0	9.4
1997	3.1	5.3	8.4
1998	3.4	4.5	7.9
1999	1.5	4.2	5.7
2000	3.0	3.6	6.6
2001	1.8	3.2	5.0
1980s mean	7.6	9.6	11.1

Note: Misery index is the sum of inflation and unemployment in any one year. Unemployment figure is based on claimant count.
Source: Data from HM Treasury

Table 14.2   *Relative labour productivity levels 1999*

Country	GDP per person employed	GDP per hours worked
United States	139	126
France	115	124
Germany	107	111
Japan	101	94

Note: UK = 100
Source: Extracted from Mahony and de Boer (2002: p. 7)

the economy compares favourably with competitor countries. After falling behind in the 1970s, living standards started to catch up with the main European economies from the mid 1980s onwards. By 2000 Gross Domestic Product (GDP) per capita, an approximate measure of living standards, was only slightly below the levels of France and Germany, although it remained one-third below the United States. (OECD 2000: 77).

Nevertheless, a continuing problem of poor productivity performance suggested that the British economy still had underlying structural weaknesses. 'UK productivity, however measured, lags behind that of other major industrialised countries'(HM Treasury 2001: p.1). Domestic output per worker is over a third higher in the American economy and 10 to 20 per cent better in France and in Germany (see Table 14.2).

Productivity growth has failed to break through the two per cent barrier in any year since Labour took office in 1997. This gap with the European countries appears to be largely explained in terms of lower levels of investment in the UK in both human and physical capital. The USA appears to have a more general lead in terms of total factor productivity, suggesting a more dynamic economy than that of the European countries. British workers continue to work longer hours than their counterparts elsewhere in Europe in an attempt to compensate for lower levels of performance. Continued prosperity has been dependent on sustained consumer spending supported by high levels of personal debt.

From Old to New Labour via Thatcherism

Economic policy was traditionally concerned with macroeconomics, the management of economic demand by government to influence economic aggregates such as inflation and unemployment. Microeconomics, the management of individual economic agents such as households and firms, was regarded as being of less importance. The principal mechanism used to secure desired economic outcomes was fiscal policy, concerned with taxation and government spending and monetary policy which relied on the manipulation of interest rates. 'Old' Labour governments of the 1940s, 1960s and 1970s are now a distant memory, and it is easy to construct an account of their economic policies that is tainted by the revisionism of Thatcherism and 'New' Labour. In general, however, such 'Old' Labour policies had the following three key features, unified by the existence of a highly politicized system of economic management: an emphasis on macroeconomic demand side management with full employment as the key objective; a belief in a mixed economy with state ownership of key industries, an element of economic planning and a range of industrial policies directed at the private sector, and the use of incomes policies to deal with the problem of inflation in a full employment economy, leading to a tripartite style of economic management involving the employers and the unions.

The direction and content of economic policy was substantially changed after the Conservatives under Mrs Thatcher came into office in 1979. Controlling inflation rather than reducing unemployment became the principal policy objective. By the time of the Major Government in 1990, this was expressed in the form of inflation targets, a device retained by Gordon Brown. The traditional relationship between macroeconomic and microeconomic policy was reversed. 'It is the conquest of inflation, and not the pursuit of growth of employment, which is . . . the objective of macroeconomic policy. And it is the creation of conditions conducive to growth and employment, and not the suppression of price rises, which is . . . the objective of microeconomic policy' (Lawson 1992: 414–15). The nationalized industries were privatized, the power of the trade unions was systematically weakened by a series of changes to industrial relations legislation, high unemployment and confrontations with key groups such as the miners, and incomes policies were no longer used as a policy instrument.

Not everything changed, however, and the overall level of taxation and public expenditure relative to the size of the economy was not very different when Mrs Thatcher left office than when she became Prime Minister. Tax was, however, collected in a somewhat different way, and there was a significant shift from direct to indirect taxation. This placed a greater burden on the poorer sections of the community, and the very high levels of taxation directed at the wealthiest sections of the population had disappeared. Having come to share the basic objectives of the

Thatcher and Major governments, the Blair government believes that sound money and the control of inflation were of prime importance. Direct forms of taxation, particularly the basic rate of income tax, had to be restrained. The re-nationalization of privatized industries, even the great public utilities like electricity, gas, water and rail, was abandoned, and further privatizations pursued where possible. Incomes policies were not to be reintroduced and there would be no close relationship with the trade unions or reversion to tripartism. Tony Blair's personal aspiration was to make Labour 'the natural party of business'.

The economic policy of the Blair Government was centred round 'two main strands: macro-economic stability and giving employment and economic opportunities to all by tackling supply-side barriers to growth' (Gamble and Kelly 2001: 173). The emphasis here, exemplified by the 'welfare to work' New Deal scheme, was on providing new opportunities for unemployed individuals to acquire the skills they needed to return to work, rather than government interventions to create jobs to deal with unemployment. Labour also introduced a minimum wage, a policy the Conservatives would not have followed, but one they now came to accept. The key economic policy innovation was the immediate decision to transfer responsibility for the control of interest rates to the Bank of England in May 1997. Granting operational independence to the Bank removed a key policy instrument from the control of government into the hands of decision makers more resistant to political pressures and enjoying greater credibility with the international financial markets. Above all else, however, 'Labour now affirmed more clearly than any. . .predecessor its support for an open world economy, renewing the strong Atlanticism of Labour governments and Labour leaders since the 1940s' (Gamble and Kelly 2001: 173). The belief that Labour had to work with rather than against international financial markets now lay at the heart of economic policy, something that was clearly evident in the Blair government's stance on globalization.

Globalization, regionalism and the European Union

A new political economy of economic policy has emerged which challenges the very possibility of an autonomous, politicized economic policy being followed at an exclusively national level. This challenge comes from the debate about globalization and regionalization. Globalization refers to the decreasing importance of national borders as impediments to the free movement of capital, goods and services, while barriers remain in the way of the free movement of labour. The formation of regional entities such as the European Union (EU) and the

North American Free Trade Area (NAFTA) is variously seen as a defensive response to globalization or as something that facilitates globalization by removing barriers to economic activity. The globalization debate is highly contested in both normative and analytical terms. Some analysts doubt whether there really has been any kind of step change in the international political economy and there is certainly no agreed definition of the term. (For a good overview of the debate, see Scholte 2000; for an essay that is close to the New Labour perspective, see Giddens 1998).

Three premises are most in evidence in this debate. First, it is assumed that there has been a step change in the organization of the international political economy, although it is not argued that this change is irreversible or cannot be politically contested. Particular importance is attached to the massive increases in flows across international financial markets and the potential created for the rapid transmission and magnification of what may have started as relatively small and localized economic events. There is also evidence of change in the character of global governance agencies, for example an authoritative disputes settlement mechanism by the World Trade Organization (WTO), the International Monetary Fund (IMF) and the World Bank, all of which can rule on domestic policies. Second, although globalization can take cultural and other forms, the emphasis is on economic globalization. Third, the assumed reality of globalization is an important part of Tony Blair's mental map of the world. Globalization is seen to present an opportunity and a challenge rather than a threat, and government has to respond positively, not negatively by withdrawing within its borders, or adopting protectionist measures.

The most important regional economic institution is the EU. Although the internal market is not fully operational, economic integration, the removal of trade and non-trade barriers to the movement of capital, labour, goods and services, has gone further within the EU than in any other regional entity. The EU also comes closer to being a protectionist trade bloc than any other regional arrangement. However, its position in relation to globalization is ambivalent. On the one hand, it facilitates globalization, particularly as the internal market, for example, makes it easier for multinational companies to organize their production to serve the European market. On the other, it makes a claim to mediate globalization, to protect EU member states against its worst effects. This is done, for example, by conferring certain social rights on European workers and by a rhetoric professing concern for socially excluded groups such as the long-term unemployed. Paradoxically, the EU has probably been most successful at creating a protected social space for European farmers, but at great expense in terms of expenditure costs, loss of economic efficiency and the creation of tensions in its relations with the United States.

This European ambivalence about globalization is reinforced by strong concern about the effects of globalization within particular member states, notably France. These concerns set the scene for tensions over the conduct of European economic policy between Britain and other member states. Britain is a strong supporter of the 'Lisbon process' agreed at the European Council in March 2000, which called for a series of measures to be taken in the face of globalization and the new knowledge-driven economy. Among the measures to be taken were an acceleration of the process of structural reform for competitiveness and innovation and a modernization of the European social model. Progress on the Lisbon process had been relatively slow by the summer of 2002, perhaps not surprisingly given that it was an election year for both France and Germany. The UK sees Europe's potential economic strength as residing in a flexible labour market. This is understood as one in which wages respond relatively easily to changes in supply and demand and where there are enhanced opportunities for workers to develop their skills. Trade unions are less able to operate as monopolies regulating entry to particular occupations and there are strong incentives to be in work rather than remain unemployed.

A flexible labour market is able to respond quickly and effectively to the challenges of globalization. In Britain the Thatcher and Major governments created this labour market, and it was predicated upon a substantial reduction in the bargaining power of the trade unions. Other EU member states have retained strong trade union movements and oppose any erosion of the levels of social protection provided to European workers. They see Labour's much vaunted 'Third Way' as a compromise between neo-liberalism and traditional social democracy, and one probably tilted towards neo-liberalism. Neo-liberalism favours a market driven economy in which individual agents can pursue their own interests with the minimum of restrictions imposed by government. Social democracy proposes a substantial role for government in managing and regulating the economy in the pursuit of social goals that are collectively defined rather than individually selected and pursued. These debates feed back into the discussion of policy at the British level, illustrating why it is increasingly difficult to maintain a distinctive focus on national economic policy under conditions of multi-level governance. The Blair government is sympathetic to American concerns that Europe's high levels of long-term unemployment reflect a rigid labour market in which excessive regulation places considerable transaction costs on employers. The Lisbon process was intended to move the

European economy closer to the British model before the United Kingdom would consider entering the Euro.

Explaining depoliticization

Even where the British government has retained considerable autonomy of action in the conduct of economic policy, there has been a shift towards a more rules-based economic policy that leaves less room for political discretion. There has been a shift of key policy instruments to other actors, notably the setting of interest rates by the Bank of England, and these developments are encapsulated by Burnham's depoliticization thesis. 'In essence, depoliticization as a governing strategy is the process of placing at one remove the political character of decision-making.' (Burnham 2001: 128). Economic policy becomes less overtly ideological 'in as much as debates centring on "Keynesianism" and "monetarism" have been replaced by a form of technocratic managerialism emphasising the constraints imposed by "global capital"' (ibid: 129). Burnham draws a distinction between politicized or discretion-based economic management that characterized the period between 1945 and 1976 (the year of the International Monetary Fund intervention in the UK economy) and a depoliticized rules-based form of economic management that has emerged since then. This approach may be traced back to the shift in economic policy that began with the abandonment of the commitment to full employment after 1976, but such a policy reached its full stage of development in the 1990s, at first under Thatcher and Major and then under Blair.

Under politicized management, the principal goal of policy was full employment. Governments accepted full political responsibility for the achievement of this goal, taking the risk that an economic crisis can quickly become a political crisis of the state. Government enjoyed reasonably effective national controls over capital movements, production and consumption, although incomes policies were a less effective way of trying to control inflationary pressures in conditions of full employment. There was little interlinking of fiscal and monetary policy although the Treasury was responsible for both.

In contrast, under depoliticized management, rates of unemployment are higher and labour markets more flexible. There is little effective national control over capital movements and increasingly integrated financial markets. In particular, governments see the need for 'expectation management', off-loading responsibility to others, principally the market, for the consequences of unpopular government policies. Tasks are reassigned elsewhere, new mechanisms are introduced to increase the external validation of policy, and there is an acceptance of binding 'rules' such as the European Exchange Rate Mechanism/European Economic and Monetary Union and the WTO Dispute Settlement Mechanism. As national controls are downgraded, it becomes more important to link fiscal and monetary policy with an ever more important exchange rate policy. As a result, there is a shift from international cooperation to regional integration.

It can also be argued that depoliticized management is associated with a reassertion of Treasury control over management of the economy. As the Keynesian management techniques of the immediate post-war era declined in efficacy, and in particular as public expenditure became more difficult to control, the Treasury suffered a loss of reputation in terms of its place at the heart of the core executive. The traditional coded language of understatement cannot conceal the note of quiet despair that often permeates the Treasury's own internal histories of the 1950s and the 1960s as the traditional Keynesian levers declined in effectiveness. Depoliticization offers the possibility of a reassertion of control by both doing less (but doing it better) and also doing more. Indeed, a strong Treasury may be regarded as a precondition of the success of the Blair Government:

> [The] concept of a strong Treasury can be seen as a shorthand for approaches at ministerial and official level which go much wider than the Treasury itself and permeate government as a whole. A strong Treasury in this sense ... was therefore a necessary condition if Labour wished to combine tight overall control of public expenditure with changed priorities and getting more out of available resources. (Deakin and Parry 2000: 198)

Depoliticization offers the possibility of a Treasury 'tool-kit' that would work on a number of levels: it would achieve specified goals; it would reinforce Treasury influence over the spending departments; and it would avoid political resistance.

It is possible, therefore, to identify a number of factors that have encouraged depoliticization. What is evident is that this is not some crude model in which globalization or liberalization simply permeates domestic policy decisions. Nevertheless, both factors exert some significant influence, although depoliticization itself is highly political, and is best seen 'as a governing strategy and, in that sense, remains highly political' (Burnham 2001: 130). Quite clearly, depoliticization involves governments making choices about preferred ends and the means of achieving them. Here, one key factor underlying the shift towards depoliticization is Labour's need to establish its competence to manage economic policy. By shifting key decisions such as interest rate setting to the Bank of England, the government has to manage a narrower range of policy instruments.

This argument is closely linked to the idea of credibility, which relates to the expectations of the market that government will actually adhere to its stated policies. It became widely believed that politicians were locked into a political business cycle that impelled them to boost the economy in the run up to an election. As the Treasury's own account of economic policy puts it, 'The mere fact that monetary policy decisions were made by politicians created the suspicion that they could be based on short-term political considerations, rather than the economy's long-run interests' (Balls and O'Donnell 2002: 17). Long-term interest rates tended to be higher than they would otherwise be because they contained a risk premium to reflect political impacts. More generally, the importance of short-term political pressures made public expenditure control difficult and tended to produce inflation. Independent central bankers, it was believed, could be better trusted to produce stable and consistent policies. Depoliticization also enables government to off-load responsibility for unpopular policies elsewhere. This tactic is not, of course, confined to economic policy. For example, the National Institute of Clinical Excellence (NICE) is used to convert difficult political decisions about the availability of new drugs to patients into apparently technical decisions taken by neutral experts.

Burnham refers to these developments as an attempt to 'capitalise on recent changes in the global political economy'(2001, p.137). His choice of the word 'capitalise' is fortuitous because the Blair Government's approach to economic policy was not merely driven by changes in the political economy. Instead it was based on a particular interpretation of those changes and their policy consequences. Globalization is an indirect cause of depoliticization, but it is also a convenient alibi that fitted in with the policy preferences of the Blair government.

Depoliticization is not irreversible, although it has occurred in a benign economic and political environment. As the IMF noted in its 2001 review of the UK economy:

The current nine-year expansion marks the longest period of sustained noninflationary growth of the UK economy in more than 30 years. Output has increased by an average of 3 per cent per year during 1993–2000, inflation has remained subdued, and unemployment is now at its lowest level for a quarter century. While activity has decelerated with the slowdown in world demand, this year the UK will grow faster than any G-7 country. (International Monetary Fund 2001)

The IMF report does also refer to some causes for concern, which include the weaker external demand environment, the persistent strength of sterling, the high level of private debt and the prolonged run in house prices. There is a sense in which the British economy is very consumer driven, dependent on consumer confidence that is in turn reliant on low interest rates and high house prices which give the appearance of wealth, something which might be described as a 'Britain shops while the world economy drops' phenomenon. Obviously, if economic performance declined, depoliticization might be threatened as citizens looked again to government to resolve the problems of an underperforming market. The danger that the world may be entering a period when deflation (falling prices) rather than inflation becomes the main economic problem again might change thinking about the role of government in the economy, as it did in the 1930s. Attitudes to tax, consumption, saving, pensions, and investment would all be transformed. The political strains of deflation might force a repoliticization of economic policy.

There are also areas of economic policy where depoliticization has been limited. Quite obviously, the question of whether Britain should join the euro remains a highly politicized question, despite the government's claims it is merely an economic choice. In addition, more rules have been introduced to guide the conduct of fiscal policy, because fiscal policy is always politicized to some extent, involving key decisions about 'who wins and who loses' in relation to the ways in which taxes are raised and money is spent.

Attempts to depoliticize fiscal policy

Fiscal policy lies at the very heart of the conduct of national economic policy and is defined by the Treasury as '[t]he combination of spending and tax policies which a government uses to achieve its objectives' (Balls and O'Donnell 2002: 365) National governments cannot escape responsibility for the consequences of its taxation and spending decisions. The Budget remains a major event in the economic and political calendar and public expenditure decisions attract considerable media interest. The political economy of fiscal policy is inherently difficult to manage for a government committed to sound money and prudent financial policies. Expectations management is extremely difficult in this area because of the state of public opinion, the demands of other political actors and the activities of interest groups.

There are a number of public misperceptions about taxation and expenditure and it is evident that there is a fairly widespread belief that British taxpayers are heavily taxed both absolutely and comparatively (Hedges and Bromley 2001: 13). In fact, Britain is just one percentage point ahead of Switzerland in terms of total tax as a percentage of GDP and was seven percentage points below the EU average in 1997. On the expenditure side, '[p]eople know in a general way that taxes are necessary to finance public services and works, but they feel they have no specific knowledge of what the money gets spent on, or how far it is spent wisely and productively'(ibid.: 47). For example, in relation to social security, the general expectation was that most of the money would go to unemployed people, perhaps as much as 70 per cent, when in fact the figure is 7 per cent. Public mistrust and misunderstanding about the way in which money is spent means that there is scepticism about whether increases in public expenditure will actually lead to better services.

The Labour government has tried to depoliticize fiscal policy as much as possible, and established a Code for Fiscal Stability in 1998 placing considerable emphasis on the maintenance of economic stability as the key to sustaining high levels of growth and employment. A credible framework for policy would lead economic actors to believe that the government would deliver its commitments. Two key fiscal rules were specified:

- The 'golden rule'. Over the economic cycle, the government would borrow only to invest, not to fund current spending. This would be achieved through a surplus on current budget over the economic cycle, but it should be noted that this implies levels of borrowing that are historically very low.
- The sustainable investment rule. Public sector net debt as a proportion of GDP would be held over the economic cycle at a stable and prudent level set by the government at 40 per cent.

In practice, the 'golden' rule may be somewhat tarnished because it is difficult to determine what constitutes current spending and investment. Should spending on physical capital be treated as investment and spending on human capital be treated as spending, even though human capital formation is seen as important in an increasingly knowledge based economy? In practice, current spending is defined as services consumed within one year, whereas spending producing a stream of services in excess of one year is defined as capital spending. Some items of spending that have many of the characteristics of investment – education – are thereby excluded. The Treasury claims that '[a]lthough education gives rise to a stream of benefits over time, the capital value of education and its depreciation rate is not something which can be estimated easily or reliably' (Balls and O'Donnell 2002: 167). It therefore becomes evident that the 'golden rule' is not a tablet of stone, but is susceptible to the political difficulty of defining and calculating what is and is not an investment.

Similarly, the sustainable investment rule set at 40 per cent appears to be somewhat arbitrary. The Treasury admits that '[n]either theory nor empirical evidence provide a definitive guide for policymakers' (ibid.: 177). In effect, the level selected represented a political judgment. Nevertheless, there is an argument for placing some limit on debt, and an arbitrarily chosen limit is better than no limit at all, even if many citizens are often surprised by the size of the share of government expenditure devoted to debt interest (Hedges and Bromley 2001).

The Labour government's approach to its fiscal policy rules is significantly affected by questions of intergenerational equity. It is argued that it is unfair for future generations to meet the cost of policies that primarily benefit the current generation, while the current generation should not have to pay for policies that will only benefit future generations. However, if one took too rigid a view of this principle, one would not be able to subsidize environmentally friendly forms of power generation on the grounds that global warming was a future problem. In any case, current spending may have differential benefits for citizens depending on their age. The Treasury argues that 'Firm fiscal rules also remove the tendency for fiscal policy to deviate from sound economic principles to provide short-term gains to certain interest groups' (Balls and O'Donnell 2002: 157). This seems to be a rather optimistic assumption, particularly as the number of interest groups, the sophistication of their operations and the intensity of their demands tend to rise over time, matched by a decline of more aggregative institutions such as political parties. There are many reasons for this trend, but one is the development of a more fragmented society in which citizens conceive their needs in more particularistic terms. There has been a shift towards a politics of collective consumption in which citizens are more likely to define themselves as consumers of public services.

Of course, the ultimate constraint on a government is the desire to remain in office. If economic principles come up against pressing political considerations, politics is likely to win. The decision to raise state pensions by only 75p in 2000 was said by Tony Blair to be the biggest mistake of the first term, disastrous in presentational terms and responsible for denting support for Labour among older voters. However, the decision was consistent with the rules for calculating state pension increases and it also reinforced the government's message that voters should not rely on the state pension as their means of support in their old age. In effect, fiscal rules are really only second-best solutions. They provide restrictions on behaviour, but also allow flexibility, allegedly only in relation to exceptional economic shocks, but in practice enabling a response to political developments as well. The rules may not be perfect, but the alternative is worse: 'it may well be the best economic response in a situation where the unconstrained political process produces outcomes that are even less desirable' (Balls and O'Donnell 2002: 157), but it is evident that the depoliticization of fiscal policy has been unsurprisingly partial at best.

Labour's first term restraint on expenditure

What was striking about the 1997 Parliament was the extent to which the Labour government constrained public expenditure growth. Excepting income taxes, taxes went up in real terms by an annual rate of two-and-a-half times as much as under the Conservatives, but at the same time spending increased at the same rate as under Thatcher and at a lower rate than under Major. Before its election Labour had pledged to follow the spending plans of the Conservatives for its first two years in office, even if, as the Conservative Chancellor, Kenneth Clarke, subsequently revealed, the Conservatives would have increased spending if they had returned to office. In fact, 'public spending in the first three years of the [1997] parliament was actually lower than the Conservatives' plans in real terms' (Institute of Fiscal Studies 2001: 35). In actual fact, Labour had provided a 'tax but don't spend' government; Increases in taxes was used to reduce the public debt and all of the additional real increase in taxes was used in this way up until 1999–2000. Public debt as a percentage of GDP declined from 43.7 per cent in 1996–7 to 31.2 per cent in 2000–1.

In recent years, government underspending has emerged as a key problem: 'In 1999–2000, public spending was supposed to increase as a proportion of GDP for the first time since 1923. Instead, the £9.4 billion underspend meant that once again public spending fell as a proportion of national income' (Institute of Fiscal Studies 2002: 15). Some underspend

Table 14.3   *Real average annual increase in taxation and spending as measured in percentage terms*

	Thatcher years	Major years	Conservatives 1979–97	New Labour to 2000–1
Total taxes	2.0	1.3	1.8	4.6
Total government spending	1.2	2.6	1.6	1.2
Education spending	1.2	2.1	1.5	3.6
NHS spending	3.0	3.3	3.1	4.7

Source: Extracted from Institute of Fiscal Studies (2001: 36)

was due to lower levels of spending on unemployment benefits and debt interest, but there were also shortfalls at key departments delivering public services in 2000–1, including the Department for Education and Employment (£1.4 billion) and the Department for the Environment, Transport and Regions (£0.9 billion). There appeared to be a number of reasons for these shortfalls, and, apart from defence expenditure, capital spending fell behind because the capacity of the public services to manage large projects had been undermined in the previous-quarter century of reduced capital spending. In particular, decentralization of purchasing following the privatization of the Property Services Agency by the Conservatives meant there was a lack of centralized procurement expertise. In addition, against a background of tight labour markets and discontent about salaries and working conditions, it was sometimes difficult to recruit public service workers.

Increases in spending, announced in the biannual Comprehensive Spending Reviews in 1998 and 2000, only raised public expenditure to a 39.2 per cent of GDP in 2001–2, still below the 41 per cent recorded in the last year of the Conservative government. However, spending was projected to rise at a faster rate over the second term of the Labour government, with total managed expenditure predicted to reach 41.8 per cent of GDP in 2005–6, compared with 42.6 per cent in 1995–6. Tax revenues are always more unpredictable than public expenditure and they were less buoyant because of the economic slowdown after the events of 11 September, and by April they were about £1 billion less than anticipated the preceding November. The government engaged in a major exercise in expectations management in the run up to the 2002 budget to prepare the electorate for a significant increase in taxation.

Getting and spending: the 2002 budget

Such was the general public disaffection about the standard of public services in the 2001 election, the government took this as a signal it had to increase spending on them. This had always been a government objective, but the main emphasis up to then had been on 'reform' of the public services, monies being tight thanks to the decision to abide by the Conservatives' spending plans. The messages that appeared to come from the government were confusing, alternating between criticizing the resistance of public service workers to change while praising their contribution to society. From a public sector union perspective, ministers' strategies appeared to be one of work intensification at a time of low morale and problems in recruitment. Salaries were made more attractive, but there was resentment about increasing workloads, which were often aggravated by the government's own performance indicators.

The dilemma ministers faced was whether increasing public spending on public services would actually lead to perceptible improvements in public services within the electoral life cycle. In this regard the 2002 budget was seen as a turning point in the development of the Blair government's economic policy. As a result, additional funding for the NHS should amount to £40 billion a year in cash terms, or £25 billion in real terms by 2007–8, a 43 per cent rise in real terms. The additional revenue required to meet this increase impacted less than expected on individuals because it was partly funded by a rise in the employers' national insurance contributions, although that hike in a payroll tax could have a longer-term impact on jobs and growth. In so far as the money was raised from individuals, the impact was greater on the better off with allowances frozen and the effective higher tax rate increased to 41 per cent. The impact of national insurance rises on middle-income households was reduced by a more generous child tax credit to come in force alongside the other changes in April 2003.

Although the budget showed a willingness to engage in what was termed 'investment' in public services, it was not a simple reversion to Old Labour 'tax and spend' policies. New measures were announced to monitor the effectiveness of NHS spending, although NHS employees might consider that substantial monitoring arrangements were already in place. The tax–GDP ratio will not increase very much, falling to 36.7 per cent in 2002–3, before increasing to 37.6 per cent in 2003–4. Even by 2005–6, however, tax levels as a proportion of GDP in Britain would still be at least 3 per cent lower than in France and Germany and the increases in tax and expenditure amounted to around less than 1 per cent of GDP over four years. As a result, levels of public expenditure as a share of national income should not be greatly out of line with the Thatcher period.

Britain and the single currency: the case for and against Euro membership

It is remarkable that the Treasury has chosen to produce its own mono-graph on economic policy (Balls and O'Donnell 2002), but even more remarkable that the discussion of UK membership of the single currency is confined to a single box containing a bald statement of the UK's position on membership. The most important economic policy decision the British government, parliament and people will have to take in the first decade of the twenty-first century is whether or not Britain should become part of the Eurozone. This is not only an important decision in itself, but it is one which will have profound consequences for the future of economic policy.

If Britain joins the Euro it will have to demonstrate that it can meet the following criteria set out in the Maastricht Treaty, although this should not prove too difficult given the recent performance of the British economy:

- The budget deficit should not exceed 3 per cent of GDP and accu-mulated debt should mot be more than 60 per cent of GDP. There is some room for manoeuvre on these criteria, but they are not a prob-lem for Britain.
- The inflation rate should not be more than 1.5 per cent higher than the level of the best three performing countries in the Eurozone. In 2002 Britain had the lowest inflation rate in Europe.
- Durability of convergence, measured in terms of long-term interest rates on government bonds, which should not be more than two percentage points above the three best performing EU members.
- The national currency must have been within the 'normal' fluctuation margins of the European Exchange Rate Mechanism (ERM) in the two years prior to membership. Britain left the ERM in 1992, so this might imply a two-year qualifying period.

Britain would also have to comply with the requirements of the Stability and Growth Pact, introduced in 1997 at the insistence of Germany to ensure that the stability of the Eurozone was not under-mined by 'irresponsible' economic policies. Countries are required to maintain broadly balanced national budgets over the economic cycle, something that is an objective of British policy in any case, although the European Commission has criticized plans to run a small budget deficit in coming years. Indeed, Germany itself has come close to violating the requirements of the pact and France and Italy have been in danger of doing so also. It has also been politically difficult to discipline smaller countries that have been in breach of the Stability and Growth Pact, such as Portugal which had a 2001 budget deficit equal to 4.1 per cent of GDP.

At the centre of the Euro system is the European Central Bank (ECB), which uses monetary policy to achieve the key stipulated objective of price stability. The ECB has a federal structure with the governors of all the National Central Banks represented on its board and constituting a majority. Key features of the ECB include 'the strength of its mandate and independence, the weakness of its accountability, and the assignment of monetary policy to price stability, derive from the German model of central banking' (Taylor, C 2000: 183). Membership of the ECB system implies transferring considerable authority to a weakly accountable group of central bankers whose independence is underwritten by an international treaty. It is therefore difficult to rapidly adjust the operation of the system in the way that happened when Britain transferred interest rate setting powers to the Bank of England.

Joining the Euro is a highly political project, and deciding whether or not to enter the Euro is a political decision. If the Labour government decides to recommend entry, it will no doubt try to present the argument in terms of economic benefits. The objectivity of the 'five economic tests' set by the Treasury that have to be met before Britain enters will be emphasized. These are:

- A sustainable convergence between the British and Eurozone economies. This is a key test: will Britain manage with a 'one size fits all' interest rate?
- Sufficient flexibility to cope with economic change;
- The effect on investment;
- The effect on the UK financial services industry; and
- Whether membership is good for employment and growth.

The Treasury will decide on political grounds whether the economic tests have been met, but the really difficult decision is the exchange rate at which Britain will enter. Analysts generally agree that the pound is overvalued against the Euro, although the National Institute of Economic and Social Research has argued that Britain could join at the rate of €1.61 to the pound prevailing in May 2002. Nevertheless, the rate at which Britain should join is a crucial and difficult question. If entry involved an effective devaluation, the authorities would then have the difficult task of managing that decline while minimizing economic and political costs. Parties associated with devaluation in Britain in the post-war period have always lost the following election:

Labour in 1951 (after clinging on to power in 1950) following devaluation in 1949, Labour again in 1970 after 1967, and the Conservatives in 1997 after the forced exit from the ERM in 1992. On the economic front, too rapid a devaluation would produce higher inflation.

The economic case for British membership of the Euro is quite finely balanced. Criticisms of the Eurozone have been made on the grounds that it does not represent an optimal currency area. Compared with the United States, wages are more rigid downwards, are less likely to be reduced in a response to a shift in the balance of supply and demand for labour, and there is less labour mobility. Hence, it is relatively difficult to make adjustments to economic shocks in the labour market and the burden might fall on higher unemployment. A 'one size fits all' interest rate is said to take insufficient account of the discrepancies within the European economy and the need to vary adjustment strategies accordingly. One response to this is that the Eurozone may not be an optimal currency area in terms of economic theory, but it is a feasible project that has nonetheless been successfully put into operation. In that sense, it is a prime example of politics, or more particularly the vision of a more integrated Europe, driving economics.

The economic arguments for joining the Euro have been well rehearsed. Transaction costs in terms of changing currency for individuals and firms would be reduced, although the impact would not be dramatic, probably generating savings of between 0.25 and 0.50 per cent of GDP. Price differentials between European countries would become more transparent and it would be difficult to justify higher prices charged for consumer goods such as cars in Britain. These benefits might, however, take some time to realize and there has been considerable media interest in the suggestion that the Euro had increased inflation in continental Europe. The statistical increase was small, but consumers were sensitive to the 'rounding up' of small everyday consumer items. It is also claimed that interest rates would tend to be lower. If Britain did not join, some foreign direct investors might be deterred from locating there in future. The City of London would benefit from participation in the Eurozone, although there is evidence to suggest that it could flourish outside it.

The economic arguments against entry centre on the claim that the structure of the British economy is different from that of continental European economies. Opponents of membership argue that 'Britain . . . resembles the United States in the extent of its high-tech industries such as biochemicals, aircraft, scientific instruments and telecommunications.'

(Eltis 2000: 188). Although most of Britain's trade is with Europe, the exchange rates against the yen and the dollar are important for key British companies and the general European rate might not be suitable for Britain. In addition, within the Eurozone, countries have less capacity to adjust to external economic shocks, known as asymmetric shocks if they affect countries differently. This is because member states' monetary policy is under control of the European Central Bank (ECB) and their fiscal policy is constrained by the Stability and Growth Pact. It is argued that the form and extent of Britain's integration with the global economy makes it particularly vulnerable to such shocks. Perhaps the most compelling argument relates to the impact of interest rates on the economy. Britain has high levels of home ownership by European standards, funded by mortgages with variable interest rates in most cases. Mortgages and other forms of borrowing are also used to fund the purchase of household durables. Britain is thus more sensitive to changes in short-term interest rates and euro membership could make the economy more volatile. One report suggested that the impact of an interest rate change in Britain on demand after two years is four times the EU average (ibid.: 186).

The most compelling arguments for membership are political rather than economic. The Euro is the central project of the EU and if Britain is not a participant, it will continue to punch below its weight in Europe. Britain is already formally excluded from some EU decisions and its informal influence would be reduced by a perception that it was not fully committed to the European project. The informal meeting of Eurozone ministers could assume a greater importance relative to the Council of Economic and Financial Ministers of which Britain is a member. Of course, membership of the single currency is not without its costs in terms of decision-making autonomy. Wilks argues that 'policy would take on a new pan-European character and there would no longer be an indigenous British macro-economic policy' (Wilks 1997: 697). Here, monetary policy would be transferred from the Bank of England to the ECB and '[n]ational central banks will simply become the regional agencies of the ECB, with no independent power to alter local monetary conditions' (Healey 2000: 32). Fiscal policy would be constrained by the Maastricht criteria and the Stability and Growth Pact.

The political opponents of membership of the single currency offer two alternative futures for Britain. The first would involve joining the North American Free Trade Area (NAFTA), which it is generally accepted would be incompatible with continued EU membership. Although there are structural and ideological similarities between the

British and American economies, Britain is much more integrated with Europe. It is by no means clear that the United States wants Britain within NAFTA because Britain is a more useful loyal ally within the EU that can usually be relied on to advance the American position. The second suggests that Britain is a big enough economy not to be part of any regional bloc. This revives post-imperialist dreams of Britain as a mediator between North America, Europe and the rest of the world, something that was not a very realistic proposition even fifty years ago. The proposition that Britain is the world's fourth largest economy never refers to GDP per capita or to the country's poor productivity record and its recent good growth record may not be sustainable in the long run outside the Eurozone. The response to globalization has been regionalization; autarky is no longer on the agenda. As result, Britain has to choose which regional bloc it wants to be in and Europe is the more feasible choice.

Can the government win a referendum on entering the Euro?

The Government has to convince the British people of these arguments in a referendum and at the time of writing it is by no means certain that a referendum would be called in the autumn of 2003, the last likely date in the lifetime of the 2001 Parliament. Opinion polls have consistently shown a majority against entry, but supporters of the Euro are optimistic on four grounds. First, most voters think Britain will eventually join. Second, support for entry increases once people are asked how they would vote if there was a positive recommendation from the government in favour. Third, it is hoped that the circulation of the Euro in notes and coins would have a positive impact, although the evidence from the experience of British citizens travelling in continental Europe in the summer of 2002 was that this had little effect on opinions. Fourth, there is some focus group evidence that voters are inclined to change their minds when they are given more information about the Euro, suggesting that a well run campaign could be effective. As a stylized fact, about a quarter of the electorate would probably vote against the Euro regardless of any arguments. They tend to be older voters who consider that British identity and autonomy is threatened by membership and they are probably more motivated to turn out than many lukewarm supporters. Inevitably, the result could be influenced by turnout and by the popularity of the government of the time as some voters might use it to register a protest against the government.

If Britain votes to join, British economic policy will have much less of a domestic focus. The consequences of a defeat could be far reaching because the economic policy credibility of the Labour government could be undermined, its chances of re-election diminished. In such a scenario, a Euro-sceptical Conservative government could then attempt to re-negotiate the EU treaties, presenting demands that other EU member states could not accept. That is indeed the hope of some opponents of the EU who would like Britain to withdraw. If that did happen, economic policy would once again become highly politicized. The decision to withdraw – or to make membership unworkable – would be highly contentious. If it did occur, difficult economic policy choices would have to be made in a turbulent environment. More likely outcomes are that Britain joins the Euro or that it will join a very successful single currency at a second attempt. By that time, however, Britain would have lost much of its potential for increased influence within the EU, one of the main arguments for membership. Whatever may transpire, it remains the case that at a period when economic policy has become depoliticized, Britain has now to take one of the most crucial economic policy choices it will face in the twenty-first century.

Conclusion

While depoliticization is the order of the day, economic policy could once again become repoliticized, particularly by the question of how to handle deflation if it takes hold, as well as by the question of whether Britain should join the Euro and the alternative futures that faces Britain if it does not. Despite much speculation on the subject after 11 September, globalization is unlikely to disappear as a phenomenon, although it may meet increasing political resistance. Even if it could be envisaged that Britain were to withdraw from the EU, Britain would still be exposed to globalization, probably more so. The rhetoric of economic policy insists that there is still space for autonomous government decisions, and this is certainly still the case in relation to fiscal policy, although membership of the euro would imply greater coordination with other European countries. Economic policy – specifically monetary policy – would then pass from the national to the regional level, leading Britain to cede sovereignty to Europe. Nevertheless, if globalization is seen as a neo-liberal force, it is likely to maintain the pressure for depoliticized and rules-based forms of economic management. The politics of economic policy may therefore continue to focus on 'getting and spending', but will do so within a policy framework that is constrained by international economic forces.

Chapter 15

Public Services

ANDREW DENHAM

Labour's manifesto at the 2001 general election had two main themes: maintaining a strong economy and reforming the public services. If the mission of its first term had been (as Tony Blair put it during the campaign) to 'sort out' the economy and 'begin the process' of increasing public service investment, Labour's declared aim in its second term was to pursue 'real and lasting' improvements in public services, particularly in health and education. To achieve this, ministers envisaged an increasing role for the private sector, a new approach that would refashion public services and the welfare state in line with the needs of the twenty-first century, redrawing what were deemed to be old-fashioned, outdated boundaries between the public and private sectors. This chapter examines developments under the Blair government in respect of health, education and welfare policy since 1997. It describes many of the key policy changes that have occurred since Labour came to power, but also seeks to explain the political and ideological context within which Labour's policies have been conceived and formulated.

In domestic politics, public service reform has become the key battleground of Labour's second term. The stakes could not be higher, since Labour is pledged to deliver improvements in public services that for the most part it failed to achieve in its first term, the benefits of which will be apparent to the British electorate. Labour is pursuing the agenda of using the state to modernize rather than privatize core public services such as education and health which was pioneered under the Conservatives. A sharp distinction is drawn between how services are funded and how they are delivered. Labour remains committed to state funding of public services, and plans to sharply increase the level of funding, but it also wants to introduce much greater involvement of the private sector in the delivery of public services, breaking up the public sector monopoly. Its 'Old Labour' critics such as John Edmonds and Dave Prentis in the trade unions argue that public services should be delivered through the public sector, and that the Government's plans threaten to produce two-tier systems in education and health. The

Government's response is that public sector solutions for delivering public services have not worked, and that if their plans do not succeed, the electorate will turn to the Conservative party which is beginning to consider options for privatizing both funding and delivery of public services.

A further political problem for the Government is whether the techniques for managing the public sector, which it inherited from the Conservatives and has developed further, emphasising targets and central monitoring of performance, can actually deliver improved performance. Critics argue that this will generate various kinds of wasteful and inefficient behaviour, at the same time destroying the ethos of public service. The alternative path of decentralizing public services and handing control to the service providers themselves runs the risk that the Government is left with little effective control over the quality of the services it is funding. It wants to be sure first that working practices have been modernized and the quality of services raised. Some experiments, for example the announcement of Foundation Hospitals, have begun, but it would be a radical government that set the whole public sector free. The Government appears split over the issue, with Gordon Brown and the Treasury preferring to retain central control, while Downing Street and some key ministers, including Alan Milburn at Health, favouring decentralization.

Labour has little time before the next election to persuade voters that beneficial change is occurring, and to convince the trade unions and the professions that they should co-operate with the Government's reforms. Public sector workers seeing the first major increases in real resources pledged to the public sector for almost thirty years are becoming increasingly militant and pursuing large wage claims, at a time when inflation is running below 2 per cent. The Government is seeking to stand firm against large public sector pay claims to prevent the extra resources it is providing being swallowed up by higher wages. At the same time the deterioration of the prospects for growth in the British economy threatens the ability of the Chancellor to deliver the higher spending on public services that has been promised without further increases in either taxation or borrowing.

The road to 1997

After Labour's defeat in 1992, senior party figures concluded that the process of 'modernization', which began under Neil Kinnock in 1983, had not gone far enough. Specifically, it was felt that further steps were needed to shake off the perception among key groups of target voters, particularly disillusioned Conservative supporters in marginal constituencies, that the party remained a by-word for 'tax and spend' and economic incompetence. For Labour, economic competence was measured by the management of the economy and by the provision of high quality, value for money public services.

Following the election of Tony Blair as leader in 1994, the process of reforming Labour's internal organization, reinventing its image, and reversing many of its policies continued and the pace of change accelerated. In terms of social policy, Blair insisted in May 1997 that 'we have reached the limits of the public's willingness simply to fund an unreformed welfare system through ever higher taxes and spending' (quoted in the *Guardian*, 4 May 1997: 13). Electoral calculation apart, other factors had encouraged Labour to rethink the party's traditional approach to social policy by 1997. The perceived pressures on welfare spending were of increasing concern to policy makers in all liberal democracies. Governing parties across the political spectrum were facing a series of challenges that threatened if not the very existence of the welfare state, then at least its capacity to adapt to a rapidly changing – and increasingly interdependent – world. The economic and social demands of globalization seemingly required governments the world over (and of whatever political complexion) to recast their welfare systems in order to foster economic competitiveness. In addition, the expectations citizens had of what the welfare state could ultimately provide were said to be increasingly excessive and unrealistic, as rising prosperity and advances in medical technology enabled them to live healthier and longer lives. Growing numbers of elderly people would need to be supported with cash benefits and care services beyond retirement. Health services for the elderly were inevitably more expensive than for people of working age. In short, the financial costs of welfare benefits and services were predicted to rise exponentially into the twenty-first century. Welfare states everywhere, it was claimed, would have to adapt to survive.

As it turned out, dire warnings about the long-term cost and sustainability of the welfare state were of limited relevance to Labour's reappraisal of its approach to social policy before 1997. Rumours of the welfare state's impending demise were much exaggerated and took no account of the British experience. In fact, Britain continued to spend a lower proportion of national income on social welfare than its neighbours in Western Europe, suggesting that – whatever other failings it might have – the financial costs of the British welfare state were (relatively) sustainable. Demographic fears of too few workers supporting the retirement incomes of a growing number of elderly people overlooked the probability that – whatever its size – the future workforce would be wealthier and therefore better able to bear the cost of state pensions. In addition, retrenchment under Conservative governments in the 1980s and 1990s had resulted in a projected rise in Britain's pensions bill far smaller than that in other countries, including the United States. Finally, the existence of a single funding stream under central government control meant that Britain continued to spend proportionately less of its national income on health care than other countries. Assuming it did not abandon the National Health Service (NHS), rising demand for health services would thus be easier for a Labour administration to contain than if it were governing a country (such as Germany or the United States) with a heavier reliance on private or social insurance.

Globalization and its perceived effects, however, were something Labour believed it could not ignore. Aside from efforts to persuade voters – and newspaper proprietors – who had backed the Conservatives in 1992 of the party's fitness to govern, Labour also set out to convince the business community and the financial markets it would be both 'prudent' and 'responsible' in its management of the British economy. The Labour leadership therefore embraced a neo-liberal macro-economic and fiscal strategy in the pursuit of economic stability, something it saw as enhancing its prospects of winning the election of 1997 and securing re-election in 2001. This meant a commitment to low inflation, low taxation and tight control of public spending. It also meant an activist policy of micro-economic intervention to 'free up' the 'supply side' of the economy to improve the competitiveness of British goods and services in domestic and overseas markets. All this implied promoting a different *kind* of welfare state, one that is dedicated to promoting investment in human and social capital and providing collective support for individual self-help.

In redefining its political image and identity before and after 1997, Labour sought to present its approach to public policy in different areas as a 'Third Way' between the 'free market' approach of the Conservatives and Labour's past commitment to redistribution and monopoly public services. In part, Labour's 'new' approach to social policy was anticipated by the report of the Commission on Social Justice set up by the late John Smith in the aftermath of the party's defeat in 1992. In its report, the Commission characterized three competing approaches to social policy:

- The first, that of the 'Old' Labour left, was to use public services and welfare benefits to redistribute resources from the rich to the poor;
- The second, that of the New Right, advocated free markets and deregulation; and

- The third, the one the Commission ultimately endorsed, was to use public resources to invest in opportunities for all in order to improve economic competitiveness. This attempt to characterize a 'Third Way' was later echoed by what Labour would say and do in government. As Gordon Brown put it, Labour stood for 'prudence with a purpose'.

Despite problems of definition, the Third Way served an important political purpose in Labour's first two years. It provided a slogan that emphasized the differences between New Labour and its political opponents and it portrayed both the Old Left and the New Right as ideologically-motivated, small 'c' conservatives, whose approaches to public service and welfare reform had become both simplistic and irrelevant. In contrast to the perceived rigidity of these approaches, the Third Way was flexible. If 'what matters is what works', this gave ministers some ideational room for manoeuvre in terms of policy development. In short, the Third Way was sufficiently broad (and vague) to justify whatever policy decisions were made. It made Labour look modern and innovative and it brought the Blair leadership time and political space to devise a longer-term strategy. In 1997, however, no such strategy had existed. Labour promised to cut class sizes in schools and reduce hospital waiting lists, but said little about how it proposed to reform education or the NHS. Significantly, however, the party did pledge there would be no increase in the basic or top rates of income tax during its first term and no overall increase in public spending in the Labour government's first two years. These pledges, considered vital to Labour's electoral prospects, were duly kept. The strategy of appealing to 'middle England' and appeasing the financial markets, apparently succeeded, but at a price. To the dismay of the party's traditionalist wing, the Blair government explicitly ruled out any increase in direct taxation to finance higher spending on health and education. Nor did it promise to raise the level of welfare benefits or other social services.

A further impediment to radical change in the immediate aftermath of Labour's landslide victory in 1997 was the legacy of reforms inherited from the Conservatives. These reforms, the most important being the introduction of 'quasi-markets' in health, education and social services and the stricter benefit codes for the unemployed, had taken the Conservatives a long time to introduce, but in each case had resulted in significant organizational and administrative upheaval by 1997. On assuming office, Labour was forced to recognize that, even for a radical government bolstered by a massive parliamentary majority, fundamental reform of the NHS or the social security system was politically impossible, at least in the short term. Thus the changes wrought by the

Conservatives over eighteen years could not be reversed overnight and the Labour leadership (for the reasons noted above) had no intention of trying to do so.

Accepting the Conservatives' aggregate spending plans for the first two years did not mean Labour's priorities were identical. Savings in defence and social security expenditures were used to finance additional spending on health, education and transport. Even so, the annual growth in health spending was lower (2.3 per cent) in Labour's first two years than the average for the previous twenty years (around 3 per cent). Spending on education was actually lower (4.7 per cent of national income) in 1997/8 than at any time since the early 1960s. The windfall levy, a tax on the privatized utilities which was exempt from the two-year moratorium, raised £5.2 billion, of which £3.6 billion was spent on the various 'New Deal' programmes between 1998 and 2002. The 1998 Budget saw significant increases in Child Benefit and Income Support for families and the introduction of a new Working Families Tax Credit to replace Family Credit (see later), although these changes did not come into effect until 1999.

Now in government, Labour briefly sought to promote a broader political and public debate about the long-term development of welfare policy, particularly within the area of social security. This was symbolized by the appointment of Frank Field as Minister for Welfare Reform, invited by Blair to 'think the unthinkable' but who instead soon left government altogether, following a reshuffle in 1998. In addition, a separate review of pensions was commissioned and appeared in December 1998 and a Royal Commission on long-term support for the elderly reported the following March. In each case, the Government's message was that significant policy change was required, but that this should be planned over the long term. This demonstrated Labour's willingness to engage with sensitive political issues, but did not commit the Government to anything concrete in the short term.

Reforming public services

Health

The 1997 General Election campaign gave little indication of what Labour had in store for the NHS, beyond pledges to keep and 'modernize' the service, reduce waiting lists and 'reverse' the changes introduced by the Conservatives. In government Labour reaffirmed the party's commitment to the founding principles of the NHS – equal access for equal need and universal coverage – and offered a guarantee of modernization, but did so on the basis of pragmatism, not ideology. Like their Conservative predecessors, Labour ministers identified lack of choice and convenience for patients as a major problem in the NHS. Their pledge to reduce waiting lists was in part a response to this but, unlike the Conservatives, Labour did not appear to have a 'big idea' to guide the process of reform. Its vision of the future – the promise of fast, convenient care, sensitive to individual need, delivered to a consistently high standard, using the best available modern facilities – was attractive, but Labour did not specify how such objectives would be achieved.

The record of the Labour government on health is best considered in two stages. The first two years were characterized by fiscal austerity and saw the publication of a key White Paper, *The New NHS: Modern, Dependable*. This contained three main themes: to abolish the 'internal market'; to mandate general practitioners (GPs) to establish Primary Care Groups (PCGs) to purchase services for their patients; and to improve the quality of clinical care, including plans to set and monitor national standards. In fact, the rhetoric of change disguised a significant degree of continuity. First, the Conservative 'internal market', based on (limited) competition, was replaced by (mandatory) collaboration between purchasers (health authorities and PCGs) and providers (NHS Trusts and local authorities) and annual contracts gave way to 'long-term' (three-year) service agreements. Thus, the 'internal market' introduced by the Conservatives was more superseded than 'abolished' and the 'purchaser–provider' split remained. Secondly, while the GP fund-holding scheme introduced by the Conservatives was technically 'abolished', in practice it was extended and made compulsory. Instead of individual practices opting to hold a limited budget, PCGs were required to hold large sums (averaging £60 million per year) from which to purchase a substantial range of hospital and other services for their patients.

To date, these changes have produced mixed results. Although thousands of general practices quickly formed themselves into 481 PCGs, successfully managing large budgets and securing long-term service agreements with local NHS Trusts (an impressive achievement, given the scale of change involved), there was little concrete evidence of any significant impact on patient care (Dixon 2001). In January 2000, concerned about adverse media coverage and frustrated by the slow pace of 'reform', Blair announced that NHS funding would be stepped up towards 'the European average'. In March, the Government announced that the percentage of GDP spent on health care would be increased from 7 per cent to 7.6 per cent by 2004 and that growth in real terms would double in each of the next five years. In July the Government published its NHS Plan, which was designed to shape the service to 2004 and beyond. This included more detail about how the extra cash would be used to boost capacity (for example, by recruiting 7,500 more consultants) and it unveiled an agreement that would allow the NHS to purchase more care provided in private hospitals. Overall, however, the Plan said more about ultimate ends than short-term means.

In 2001 the Labour manifesto promised 'a healthier nation with fast treatment, free at the point of use' by 2010 (Labour Party 2001: 3). Successful NHS hospitals would be allowed to take over 'failing' ones and, where it 'made sense' to do so, the Government would 'work with' the private sector to use spare capacity for the benefit of NHS patients. A new type of hospital – specially built surgical units, managed by the NHS or by the private sector – would be created to cut waiting times. More frontline staff would be recruited, including 20,000 more nurses and 10,000 more doctors, and there would be new powers for matrons, more control over budgets for ward sisters and a £500 million Performance Fund for doctors to spend on new patient services. In the 2002 Budget, the Chancellor, Gordon Brown, announced a £40 billion programme of investment in the NHS to bring health spending up to French and German levels within five years. This extra cash means that spending on the NHS in real terms is projected to double in the ten years between 1997 and 2007/8. By setting such an ambitious budget for health spending, Brown hoped to force the Conservatives onto the defensive, but the strategy here is a risky one, for two main reasons. First, it has put the Government's fate in the hands of people – doctors, nurses and NHS managers – whom ministers do not (and cannot) directly control. A stark reminder of this was provided in 2002 when hospital consultants voted by a large majority to reject the new NHS contracts which had taken two years to negotiate and were recommended by the BMA. Secondly, its success depends not only on the compliance of NHS professionals, but also on public perceptions. Public concerns about the state of the NHS remain high, and the Government is acutely aware of the need to deliver an improved service in this area. The political problem for Labour is that, according to opinion polls, the NHS remains the most urgent priority in the minds of the British people. More importantly, it has also become 'a major source of mistrust about official accounts of what is actually going on' (Young 2002). There are also considerable divisions within the Government over how far control of the NHS should be retained by central Government and how far it should be decentralized to the hospitals, doctors and nurses themselves, as in the plans for Foundation Hospitals. Significantly, Treasury ministers and officials, as well as trade union leaders and MPs remain very suspicious of the concept.

Primary and secondary education

As with the NHS, Labour inherited a legacy of significant organizational change from the Conservatives in regard to primary and secondary education, including Local Management of Schools (LMS), 'open enrolment' and Grant Maintained Schools (GMS). The new Government was not inclined to reverse these changes, Blair himself having taken advantage of open access policies to send one of his own children to a school outside his local area. For New Labour's supporters, such policies were anyway compatible with both the Third Way's emphasis on the accountability of public servants (teachers) to consumers (parents) and the necessary search for 'best value' in public services. In government since 1997, Labour has therefore embraced school league tables and the use of inspections as a means of maintaining public control over standards. Its desire to introduce 'performance-related pay' for teachers (on which its manifesto was silent in 1997) has (understandably) proved deeply unpopular with the teaching unions and other professional bodies.

Labour has made significant progress on its pre-1997 election agenda for education. Its promises here included:

- A guaranteed nursery place for all 4 year olds
- The reduction of class sizes for 5–7 year olds to 30 or fewer
- A literacy strategy and new standards of reading for 10–11 year olds
- Year-on-year targets for improving the performance of every school and Local Education Authority (LEA)
- A fresh start for 'failing' schools
- A home–school contract and minimum homework guidelines for every pupil
- Public–private partnerships to improve school buildings
- The creation of Educational Action Zones to tackle social disadvantage
- A General Teaching Council to represent the interests of, and raise standards in, the teaching profession
- A quick, fair system for removing teachers 'not up to the job'
- A 'fair and efficient' system of higher education funding
- A University for Industry to extend lifelong learning

On much of this 'transactional' agenda, Labour has proved to be 'substantially . . . as good as its word' (Brighouse 2001: 22). Conversely, however, the Government has conspicuously failed to deliver the promised change of mood that many teachers and lecturers had hoped for, if not expected. The initial retention of Chris Woodhead as Chief Inspector of Schools, for instance, and the 'naming and shaming' of 'failing' schools and universities were widely condemned by an increasingly vocal (and demoralized) teaching profession. That said, an additional benchmark against which Labour's performance can be assessed is the set of six 'guiding principles' outlined in its 1997 White Paper, *Excellence in Schools*:

- Education will be 'at the heart of government'
- Policies will be designed to benefit 'the many, not just the few'
- The focus will be on 'standards, not structures'
- Intervention will be 'in inverse proportion to success'
- There will be 'zero tolerance of under-performance'
- Government will work 'in partnership with all those committed to raising standards'

Since 1997, Labour has broadly adhered to these principles and the Government can also claim to have made progress on each of them. Through Education Development Plans and OfSTED/Audit inspections, Local Education Authorities (LEAs) have been required to focus on schools that are not performing well and on children with special educational needs. For Labour's critics, however, policies designed to benefit 'the many, not just the few' are wrong in principle and do not go far enough in practice. The preoccupation with pupils attaining (or not) five or more A*–C grades at GCSE – something which, because the examination is norm-referenced only 50 per cent of children can achieve – means that many school leavers inevitably fail to reach the 'much trumpeted standard for success in life' (Brighouse 2001: 24).

In its 2001 manifesto, Labour promised to increase education spending by more than 5 per cent in real terms each year for the next three years and to recruit 10,000 extra teachers (Labour Party 2001). A good quality nursery place would be provided for all 3 year olds and there would be more opportunities for primary school pupils to learn foreign languages, as well as higher standards of basic literacy and numeracy. Radical improvement was also planned in secondary education where schools would be required to develop a distinctive mission and the state sector would become more diverse, with the creation of new City Academies and expanding church (and other specialist) schools. There would be more 'freedom' for 'successful' schools and more money channelled directly to head teachers. Higher standards in mathematics, English, science and information technology at secondary level were also promised, and ministers set a target of 50 per cent of young adults entering higher education by 2010.

As in 1997 ('education, education, education', then being Blair's stated priorities in government), Labour's 2001 manifesto claimed that education remained the Government's 'top priority'. Primary school standards had been 'transformed', it claimed, thanks in part to smaller class sizes, with 'nearly half a million fewer primary pupils in classes of more than 30' (Labour Party 2001: 18). Significantly, there was no mention of the *increase* in class sizes for 8–11 year olds, which resulted from resources being redeployed to honour the 1997 pledge on class sizes for 5–7 year olds. In 1997, the manifesto recalled, Labour had promised to increase the share of national income devoted to education. Over the 1997 parliament this increased (albeit marginally) to 5 per cent and Labour pledged to raise it further to 5.3 per cent by 2003/4, but the initial *fall* in education spending as a proportion of GDP was ignored. The manifesto further pledged to 'increase the share of national income for education', but did not reveal how the extra cash would be found (Labour Party 2001: 18).

Whether or not education proves to be Labour's 'top priority' in its second term remains to be seen. In July 2002, the Government announced an extra £14.7 billion for education by 2006. Direct grants would rise by £50,000 to £165,000 per year for a typical secondary school and by £10,000 to £50,000 per year for a primary. This means that spending per pupil will have risen from £2,700 in 1997 to £4,500 by 2005/6. Some 1,400 schools in 'challenging circumstances' will receive £125,000 per year for three years, subject to demonstrating (on the basis of OfSTED reports and other data) that they are being 'properly run', but they can then spend the money as they choose. According to the most recent figures (from 1998/9), education spending is projected to rise as a proportion of national wealth from 5.1 to 5.6 per cent by 2005/6, rivalling the average in the EU and other industrialized countries. Head teachers welcomed the increase, but pointed out that the extra money Labour has put into education has always been tied to a particular initiative or scheme. They argue that unless ministers allow heads to decide for themselves what their schools need and then give them the money to deliver it, extra money alone will not result in the radically improved service they have promised. This is a tension that goes to the heart of Labour's programme of public service reform. Teachers, doctors and other public sector professionals are 'crying out for a free hand, but the Treasury wants to keep tabs on them – to make sure the taxpayer is getting value for money' (Freedland 2002).

The regime of targets and central control came in for strong criticism in 2002 due to the scandal over the alleged alteration of 'A' Level exam grades on the orders of the Government agency, the QCA, as well as over the prospect of top-up fees to provide greater funding for the universities. The Government appointed an inquiry into the grade-tampering allegations, under the former chief Inspector of OfSTED,

Mike Tomlinson, which concluded that the size of the problem was much smaller than some sections of the media had claimed. The political strain of this scandal, however, combined with alleged interference by the head of the Downing Street Policy Unit, Andrew Adonis, in the running of the Department, prompted Estelle Morris, the Secretary of State for Education, who had been in post for only eighteen months, to announce her resignation, on the unusual grounds that she did not feel up to the job. Her successor was Charles Clarke, a tough and independent minister, one of whose first tasks was to sort out Government policy on the funding of higher education. He had to balance the desire of the twenty or so leading research universities to increase tuition fees to enable them to compete with their American counterparts against Labour's commitment to expand the number of students going to university while protecting access to higher education for low income groups. All the available solutions of top-up fees, a graduate tax, and higher public spending had significant advantages, but also serious drawbacks, and within Government there appeared to be no consensus on the best way forward. The Government pledged in its 2001 manifesto not to introduce top-up fees in this Parliament, but ministers have now decided to introduce this in the next, Blair himself being widely committed in principle to such a change.

Welfare policy

Children and families

The Labour Government has introduced a number of measures designed to raise the incomes of low-paid families with children, including lone parents. A focus on children has emerged as a key priority, as evidenced by Labour's stated goal of ending child poverty within twenty years. In pursuit of this longer-term objective, ministers have significantly increased Child Benefit, raised the child additions to Income Support and introduced a Working Families Tax Credit, a Children's Tax Credit and (from April 2003) an Integrated Child Credit (see below). This strategy has combined a more selective targeting of support towards lower-income families with a commitment to raise universal benefits, notably Child Benefit (designed to ensure middle-class families retain a stake in the welfare state). Indeed, Child Benefit levels have risen faster than Labour promised or implied in 1997. In addition, by increasing child support additions to Income Support, the Government has enhanced the value of out-of-work benefits to families.

Even more central to Labour's strategy in respect of family policy, however, has been the targeting of support to those in low-paid jobs. In addition to the National Minimum Wage, the Working Families Tax Credit represents a more generous system of topping up the low incomes of working parents than its Conservative predecessor, Family Credit. As we shall see in more detail below, Labour's overriding welfare objective has been to 'make work pay'. The key element of this strategy has been to design appropriate policies along the 'crucial axis' between the benefits system and the labour market (McCormick 2001). As we have seen, the attack on child poverty has combined higher benefits, increased parental earnings and lower household (income) taxes. At the same time, Labour has spent substantial sums on increasing the financial incentive for non-working parents (and others) to move from 'welfare to work' (see later).

Labour's commitment to making income security for families with children a key priority is evidenced by its decision to replace the Married Couples Allowance with a Children's Tax Credit (CTC) and (from April 2003) an Integrated Child Credit (ICC). Both CTC and ICC are (or will be) paid to all parents, whether married or not, and at higher-income levels than in the past, but are then withdrawn before higher-rate taxpayers benefit. Although ministers have not spelt this out explicitly, Labour's underlying strategy of 'redistribution by stealth' has quietly taken shape. In some areas of welfare provision (including pensions), there is now greater reliance on means testing than in the past. At the same time, there is a growing emphasis on 'affluence testing', whereby higher-income groups receive less, while lower and middle-income households gain relatively more, roughly (if not exactly) in proportion to income (McCormick 2001).

In addition to these income-based approaches, Labour has also sought to improve the quality of other services for families with children. For example, it has overseen the introduction of a national childcare strategy, although serious questions have been raised about the affordability, quality and geographical coverage of provision. Lone parents participating in the New Deal have also received additional support towards the costs of childcare. Perhaps the most important development for vulnerable families, however, has been the Sure Start initiative. The focus here is on families with children under four years of age, living in areas of acute social deprivation. A key objective is to investigate how a more accessible range of services can be provided for families who need them. Although evaluations of the initiative are still at an early stage, there is a growing consensus among professionals who work with children that a more powerful set of policy instruments is needed to reduce the incidence of social deprivation.

The New Deal

A key policy commitment in the 1997 Labour manifesto was the 'New Deal'. This included features of New Labour thinking on welfare (notably the link between the rights and obligations of those in receipt of benefits), but also represented a continuation of the supply-side approach to employment policy developed by the Conservatives between 1979 and 1997. It offered training and work experience in the form of state subsidies paid to employers or other providers, such as voluntary organizations. The existence of these opportunities, Labour argued, would help individual citizens compete for and obtain the jobs being created through increasingly flexible labour markets. This, in turn, would help reduce wage pressures and increase output and employment in the economy, but without adding to inflation. Moving people from 'welfare to work' would also reduce the financial 'burden' of unemployment on the taxpayer and the public finances. As we have seen, a central part of Labour's strategy on welfare has been 'make work pay'. To this end, the New Deal has been supported by other measures designed to offer financial inducements to those in receipt of Income Support and other benefits to remain in or accept employment, even (or especially) in low-paid jobs. In addition, Labour has sought to make both the prospect and experience of employment more attractive by (among other things) embracing the EU Social Chapter and Working Time Directive and extending maternity and, latterly, paternity leave for working parents.

Labour's first 'welfare to work' budget in 1997 committed £3.6 billion of the proceeds of the windfall tax to various New Deal programmes between 1998 and 2002. Around £2.5 billion was specifically allocated to the 'flagship' New Deal for the young unemployed aged between 18 and 24. Other programmes were subsequently introduced for the long-term unemployed aged between 25 and 49, for the over 50s, for lone parents, for the disabled, for partners of the unemployed and for childcare. The programmes consist of a complex mix of mandatory advice, employment and training. Individuals who fail to take up a place or leave early without good cause have their benefit(s) reduced. Ministers accept this is tough, but insist it is fair. Sanctions, they insist, have affected only a small minority of claimants and are designed merely to remind 'jobseekers' of their obligations to the state and their fellow citizens.

Despite the fall in registered unemployment since 1997, and the attempts of ministers to claim that this 'proves' the success of the 'New Deal', there is no consensus on how effective the policy has been and the Government's approach has been criticized on a number of grounds.

First, 'welfare to work' can only succeed if jobs are actually available for all those who are able to work. In some regions of Britain there are many more 'jobseekers' than unfilled vacancies. As noted above, the New Deal is a supply-side approach to employment policy and the labour market. Without measures to activate and stimulate labour demand (especially in areas where there are relatively few jobs), it is unlikely to provide those out of work with a permanent escape route from poverty and other forms of disadvantage. Secondly, those who (for whatever reason) are simply unable to work still require support. Particularly in their early years of office, there were signs that the Government either failed to acknowledge this, or was failing to take steps to ensure that such support would be guaranteed. In 1999, for instance, legislation to 'reform' Incapacity Benefit (whereby new claimants became subject to both an 'affluence test' and a 'gateway' interview with advisors to establish their availability for work) resulted in cuts in benefit even for those who were unable to work.

In addition, some employment policy analysts have claimed that there is a large 'dead weight' element in the policy. The argument here is that many of those have recently entered (or re-entered) the labour market are beneficiaries not of the New Deal as such but of the fact that there will always be more jobs available in a buoyant and expanding economy. This point, it is argued, applies with particular force (and irony) to the young unemployed – the very group to which the Government has chosen to allocate the lion's share of the programme's resources. Conservatives have also criticized the cost (per successful outcome) of the voluntary parts of the programme (particularly for lone parents). For critics on the left, the New Deal for Lone Parents is inadequate (and belated) compensation for the cuts in lone parent benefit announced early in Labour's first term. There are also the (unresolved) questions of what happens to those who drop out of the New Deal and the benefits system altogether before completing their passage through the programme and of the future employment prospects of those who do succeed in making the transition from 'welfare to work'. Recent studies have confirmed that very few people who enter low-paid jobs (with the exception of students and trainee professionals) ever succeed in attaining even average earnings (Walker, R. 2002). Research on the New Deal itself has shown that most who have recently moved from 'welfare to work' continue to earn low wages, that many have subsequently returned to unemployment, while others have moved rapidly through a succession of low-paid jobs (Dickens 2002). Other studies have confirmed that the majority of New Dealers face the prospect of (in many cases, permanently) unstable employment. Young people, those working part-time, or with limited qualifications, or in poor health, have the most tenuous hold on the labour market and are at particular risk of losing their jobs within the first few weeks (Kellard 2002). On a more positive note, there is some evidence to show that the advice offered to New Deal clients by a network of personal advisers has improved the quality of service they receive and has given front-line staff a better insight into the particular difficulties they face (Millar 2000). Overall, however, and for the reasons identified above, it seems fair to conclude that there is still much to do if Labour is to achieve its (modest) target of 'full employment in every region' by 2010 (Labour Party 2001: 3).

Pensions

As with its approach to children and families, Labour's welfare policy in respect of people of retirement age has been characterized by a complex mix of (increased) selectivity and universalism. Labour's analysis of trends in the distribution of incomes and wealth in retirement over recent years has revealed a growing incidence of pensioner inequality over time, with the result that elderly people now tend to fall into one of three categories in respect of retirement income. Almost one third of pensioners continue to rely exclusively on state benefits. Another third have modest savings or second pensions (sufficient to push them above the Income Support and Housing Benefit thresholds, thereby losing them any entitlement to further assistance). The final third have sufficiently high incomes from second pensions, savings and other assets to pay income tax and to rely to a much lesser extent on state benefits.

Even before 1997, Labour was unwilling to countenance raising the Basic State Pension (BSP) above the rate of inflation and has since ignored calls to restore the link between the BSP and average earnings. Instead, its strategy has been to raise the incomes of the poorest pensioners in the form of a Minimum Income Guarantee (MIG). While this has significantly raised the incomes of some of Britain's poorest pensioners, the scheme has not been without its problems – or its critics. Specifically, MIG is not (despite its name) a *guarantee* of additional income. As a means-tested benefit, it has to be claimed in the same way as Housing Benefit or Income Support and the key to its success therefore lies in the level of take-up, which has proved (to say the least) disappointing. It has been estimated that as many as half a million pensioners entitled to MIG have not claimed it. Among the most likely reasons for this are 'poor communication and system complexity' (McCormick 2001: 93). An even more challenging political problem, however, concerns pensioners who continue to rely on the BSP (which means that they continue to fall behind the average living standards of the rest of the population) but who fail to qualify for any means-tested assistance at all. Among this group, there is (understandable) resentment that they have been 'penalized' for saving for their old age while others who could have afforded (but chose not) to do so are now being 'rewarded' with additional help from the state. The fact that MIG is also projected to grow in line with average earnings rather than prices (and thus at a faster rate than the BSP) has produced a sharp divide among pensioners in their response to it.

In April 2002, Gordon Brown announced plans to introduce a new Pension Credit in October 2003. The aim here is to guarantee a minimum income of £135 per week for a single pensioner and £200 per week for a pensioner couple. Approximately half of all pensioner households will qualify and the cost will amount to some £2 billion per year from 2004. Like the planned Integrated Child Credit (see earlier), the new credit will be paid to those on significantly higher earnings than in the past (up to around £20,000 per year), then withdrawn before it benefits the more affluent. As with the ICC, additional support will take the form of a tax cut rather than an across-the-board increase in benefits. In the interim, an above-inflation increase in the BSP is planned as a form of 'transitional' support. Even so, pensioners' groups remain (as yet) unconvinced. In April 2002, for instance, Help the Aged warned that, if the low take-up rate of the MIG were repeated, more than 1.5 million pensioners eligible for the new credit would not claim it (*Guardian*, 18 April 2002). Despite the promise of a major advertising campaign starting in April 2003, the introduction of the scheme is unlikely to diminish calls for the Government to restore the link between the BSP and average earnings.

In other respects, however, Labour's approach towards the welfare of people of retirement age shows a continuing commitment to universalism. Examples here include the winter fuel allowance and the decision to waive the television licence fee for pensioners over the age of 75. Designed to reflect the higher costs of basic household goods and services incurred by older people, these measures represent a clear and straightforward approach to policy making without the same obsession that the Government (and the Treasury in particular) has shown elsewhere for 'dead weight' and untargeted expenditure.

A growing problem for the Government was what to do about the number of companies which in 2001 and 2002 announced they were closing their final salary schemes, in part due to the increasingly difficult economic climate, and the resulting low returns on stock market investments. Since large numbers of workers in the private sector had been dependent on these schemes to assure them a decent pension, the political consequences were potentially explosive. It highlighted the difficulties of relying on the private sector to provide all citizens with a pension that would support them in retirement. The low rate of saving in the UK compounded the problem. In 2002 the Government was showing little desire to become involved, but events may force its hand.

The Private Finance Initiative

A key and (as we shall see) controversial component of Labour's attempts to modernize and improve public services is the Private Finance Initiative (PFI). The PFI was invented by the Conservatives in the early 1990s, when the Public Sector Borrowing Requirement (PSBR) was in danger of spiralling out of control, as a means of removing investment spending from the (then) Government's balance sheet. Although very few PFI projects had begun in earnest when Labour came to power, this did not stop the new Government from enthusiastically embracing the scheme. Having dropped the requirement that the PFI option be explored for every new public project (which became a further obstacle to building new schools and hospitals under the Conservatives), PFI was beginning to make an impact by 2000 as levels of public investment increased. According to the Treasury, PFI remains the only way to raise the new investment so desperately needed by Britain's threadbare public services. To abandon it, Gordon Brown warned the Labour Conference in October 2002, would endanger completion of the 550 new schools and 100 new hospitals Labour has started building since 1997.

PFI represents a significant break with the past in terms of both the organization and management of public services and how money is raised to pay for current and future investment in the public sector. The usual mode of public sector investment is for the state to procure new assets, such as schools, over which it then takes possession and owns. By contrast, a PFI project involves private contractors building and maintaining public assets and in some cases (such as prisons) running them. In addition, the two kinds of investment are financed by quite different means. Whereas public investment is normally financed 'up-front' by raising taxes or public borrowing, PFI projects are financed by private money, which is then repaid by the taxpayer, along with other services related to the contract, typically over a period of about 25 years. Whatever its other advantages, from the Government's own point of view PFI represents 'the ultimate buy now, pay later scheme' (*Guardian*, 3 October 2002: 24), something which keeps the Treasury's bills down by restricting current and capital expenditures.

Among the strongest opponents of PFI are public sector trade unions, whose chief complaint is that it represents a form of 'creeping privatization', whereby more and more public sector workers are transferred into private firms, resulting in a 'two-tier workforce'. The problem for the Government is that, despite having made some concessions to the unions on this issue, it is reluctant to guarantee identical rights to new workers recruited by the private contractors involved in PFI projects. Indeed, it has been suggested that the unions' grievance on this issue is actually a strong argument *for* PFI, in that many of the problems of the public services are a result of rigid employment practices. For example, it has been claimed that national pay scales with limited regional variation mean that teachers and nurses in London and the South-East of England are underpaid, leading to severe labour shortages (*The Economist*, 5 October 2002). A further criticism of PFI is that, contrary to one of its central objectives, it has failed to deliver better value for money for the British taxpayer, and has often been adopted regardless of whether or not it was the best-value option (IPPR 2001). Whereas PFI has delivered significant savings in regard to prisons, evidence of greater value for money in terms of schools and hospitals is much harder to find. The efficiency gains made in the prison sector may be due to the increased capacity of the private sector to make savings where it actually operates the facilities, rather than just designing and building them before leasing them back to the public sector. While this is so in the case of prisons, resistance to the idea of the private sector directly employing teachers and doctors has ensured that in health and education private operators only have control over ancillary staff. As a general rule, PFI contracts are estimated to save around 10 per cent of the cost of public investment procured by traditional means but, according to the Institute for Public Policy Research (IPPR), cost savings for schools and hospitals to date are typically as low as 3 per cent. According to the House of Commons Public Accounts Committee (PAC) almost 25 per cent of public sector organizations involved in PFI projects claim to be getting less value for money after completion of the initial construction work, in part because of the high prices charged for additional services (*The Economist*, 5 October 2002).

If such estimates are correct, and PFI is failing to deliver significant efficiency savings in key public services such as health and education, why is the government continuing to commission so many new projects? Why does it continue to defend the scheme in such robust terms? Part of the explanation may be that it hopes PFI will 'help to bring about the changes it needs to show taxpayers that the massive spending it is lavishing on the public sector is delivering results' (*Guardian*, 3 October 2002). From the Treasury's point of view, the PFI is not simply a different means of financing new investment in public services, but it is also a way of encouraging public sector managers to think about what they want out of their new facilities. The hope is that extending PFI will produce if not a 'cultural revolution' in what would otherwise remain 'monolithic' and uniform public services, than at least lead to significant improvements before the next general election. A further reason for the Government's continuing enthusiasm for PFI is one to which we have already referred: namely, that future rather than current taxpayers who will pick up the bill, even if this proves more expensive in the long term. In the meantime, PFI, for Labour as for the Conservatives, is an accountancy device that conceals from today's taxpayers the true cost of 'modernizing' public services, a device which allows the Treasury to 'balance' its books today.

Conclusion

Tony Blair claimed during the 2001 General Election campaign that the mission of Labour's first term had been to 'sort out' the British economy and to 'begin the process' of investing in and reforming public services. The primary tasks of Labour's second term, he argued, would be 'maintaining a strong economy' and securing 'real and lasting improvements' in key public services such as health and education. The fact that these statements were made in the heat of a General Election campaign means that they cannot (or should not) be taken at face value. It can be argued that the true 'mission' of Labour's first term was actually to maintain the strong economy (or at least favourable economic conditions) it inherited from the Conservatives. In particular, it is important to bear in mind that Labour inherited falling levels of unemployment in the context of making claims that the New Deal has helped to deliver at least the prospect of 'full' employment for the first time in a generation. Labour's critics could also interpret Blair's remarks as confirmation that the Government made little progress in 'reforming' public services in its first term, failing to 'invest' in them for the first two years and then only doing so to 'bribe' the British electorate with its own money. Whether or not Labour will have succeeded in delivering 'real and lasting' improvements in public services by the end of its second term remains to be seen. In some areas, including education, child poverty and employment, it will only be possible to assess whether or not the Government has met its targets at the end of a third term. What is clear is that Labour has an ambitious and wide-ranging agenda for the 'reform' of health, education and welfare, but has yet to persuade many of those who work in (let alone use) public services that the quality of those services is improving.

Chapter 16

Environmental Policy

MATHEW HUMPHREY

In his first speech on the environment for four years, Tony Blair claimed in October 2000 that 'no other British Government has put the environment at the heart of its policy making across the board – from foreign affairs to the national curriculum – in the way this government has' (Blair 2000). This claim highlights certain important aspects of environmental policy and raises a large question regarding the conduct of environmental policy under New Labour.

The argument that the environment has been at the heart of policy making 'across the board' poses the difficulty in isolating a specific aspect of government activity that can be called 'environmental policy making'. Whilst it is true that there are specific pieces of government legislation that are clearly focused on environmental issues, such as the Wildlife and Countryside Act of 1981, or the Countryside and Rights of Way Act 2000, in other aspects environmental policy cannot be easily disentangled from other policy areas. Policy in the fields of transport, agriculture, science and technology and energy, for example, has significant impact on the state of Britain's environment and possibly beyond. Thus whilst it may be true, as some commentators suggest, that the environment has declined in salience as a political issue, this does not necessarily imply that the environmental implications of policy in the areas listed above lack political salience. Indeed we shall see that the opposite is frequently the case.

The question raised by Tony Blair's claim is a simple one: has New Labour really succeeded in putting the environment 'at the heart' of its policy making? What, in policy terms, does New Labour claim it is trying to achieve? What environmental policy has been enacted and what forms of environmental governance have been put in place under Labour. What institutions has this government established to deliver environmental objectives? In terms of the environmental dimensions of particular policy areas, what does Labour's environmental record look like in the fields of transport, agriculture, waste management, and climate change?

The history of the environment as a policy issue

Although there have been environmental aspects to government policy making as long as there has been government policy making, 'the environment' as a distinct policy issue emerged with force during the 1970s. Concerns about particular environmental problems developed into a concern about the state of the global environment. This regard for environmental issues grew out of a literature that had begun with books such as Rachel Carson's *Silent Spring* (1962) which looked at the future of industrial society in the context of a set of key environmental variables such as pollution, human population, and natural resources, and which could foresee no future in which industrial society did not collapse as a result of the violation of at least one of these

---

Box 16.1 Key UK environmental policy since 1997

1998 Integrated Transport White Paper Promised new powers to local authorities for road use charging and levies on workplace parking. Also announced the creation of the Strategic Rail Authority and the Commission on Integrated Transport.

2000 Rural Affairs White Paper Contains a number of proposals for the 'rejuvenation' of rural life, including a 50 per cent rate cut for rural shops, pubs, and garages that offer benefits to the community, the discretion to local authorities to end the 50 per cent council tax discounts on second homes, and the building of 9,000 'affordable' new homes in rural areas each year.

2000 Transport Act Enabled some of the proposals of the 1998 White Paper, including the authority for local councils to implement road charging.

2000 Countryside and Rights of Way Act Strengthens protection for Sites of Special Scientific Interest and Areas of Outstanding Natural Beauty. Creates a statutory right of access on foot to certain types of open land.

2000 10-year Plan for Transport Promises £180bn investment in transport over the ten-year period. Aims at 50 per cent increase in passenger use of the railway, 100 new bypasses and 360 miles of motorway and trunk road widening, aims at 10 per cent growth in passenger use of buses, 'up to' 25 new light rail projects, lower emissions and better air quality. Heavily criticized by House of Commons Transport Committee for lacking the necessary mechanisms and resources to deliver on these aspirations.

environmental constraints. The Environment therefore became a political issue in its own right.

New Labour's approach to environmental policy has to be understood in the context of the legacy inherited from previous environmental regimes from the 1970s through to the 1990s. There are five notable factors in this period:

- In the 1980s, Britain went from being perceived by neighbouring countries as an environmental innovator to being seen as an environmental laggard, an obstinate force in preventing the development of effective European environmental policy – the 'Dirty Man of Europe'.
- Environmental policy-making has become increasingly Europeanized, to the extent that some four-fifths of British environmental policy emanates from the EU.
- A rising membership of environmental pressure groups and increasingly effective campaigning by these groups.
- Key pieces of legislation enacted under the previous government, in particular the *Wildlife and Countryside Act* of 1981 and the *Environment Act* of 1995 embedded the principle of a permissive, voluntary approach to environmental protection in Britain, with statutory regulation seen as something of a last resort.
- A structure of governance in which producer interests were well represented in certain departments that have an important environmental dimension to their activities, in particular agricultural producers in the Ministry of Agriculture, Fisheries and Food and the road haulage industry in the Department of Transport.

Thus New Labour inherited a situation in which, even if environmental concerns were well represented in the Department of the Environment (itself an open question), they were no more than weakly represented elsewhere in Whitehall; and there was little, if any, evidence of 'joined-up government' between the different departments whose remits included significant environmental factors. At the same time there was a rising tide of protest and direct action against government policies with important environmental impacts such as the road-building programme (for example at Twyford Down, Newbury and Glasgow) and intensive agriculture. Could New Labour's promise to put the environment 'at the heart' of government thinking be delivered? What institutional changes would be necessary in order to ensure that environmental concerns were not confined to a lead department and instead considered across Whitehall? Moreover, just how committed were New Labour to environmentalism in policy making?

New Labour and environmentalism

One central area through which environmental goals were to be achieved was transport, with the establishment of 'an integrated transport policy to fight congestion and pollution' (Labour Party 1997: 24). Beyond that proposal firm commitments on environmental goals are scarce in the 1997 document. There is a proposal to establish a parliamentary environmental audit committee (ibid), to reform the Common Agricultural Policy (ibid. p. 25), measures to offer 'greater protection for wildlife', although the only concrete policy proposal here is a free vote in Parliament on banning hunting with hounds (ibid.), and there is a proposed moratorium on large-scale disposals of Forestry Commission land (ibid.).

With regard to international environmental problems, the manifesto noted the threat of climate change, promised stronger co-operation in the EU on environmental issues and proposed a target of a 20 per cent reduction in UK CO_2 emissions by 2010. Domestically, Labour saw transport as one of the key areas through which environmental problems could be tackled. One of Labour's first moves here was to bring transport and the environment under a single ministerial brief through the creation of the Department of the Environment, Transport and the Regions, under the leadership of the Deputy Prime Minister, John Prescott. This change in the structure of the government was implemented, in part, to facilitate 'joined-up government' and to counter the perceived situation under previous regimes that the Department of the Environment and the Department of Transport were operating according to opposing policy agendas.

Despite this attempt to combine transport and the environment under one departmental roof, there were problems in delivering the promised integrated transport policy. This has been blamed in part on the sheer scale and complexity of this super-department, which employed 15,000 people, had an operating budget of £13bn, and which was responsible for not only transport and the environment but also local government in England.

The problems were also political, and go to the heart of the New Labour project. Labour strategists had long realized that the key to electoral success for their party lay in extending their appeal beyond their bedrock of traditional working-class support to the 'aspirational' working class and middle classes in England. A key theme here became 'modernization', showing that Labour had moved away from its 'old' concerns with such issues as nationalization, wealth redistribution through direct taxation, and links with trades unions. Third

Way politics sought to move beyond historical frictions between left and right towards the sunny uplands of a post-ideological politics: 'New Labour is a party of ideas and ideals, but not of outdated ideology' (Labour Party 1997: 1). The political problem with proposals for an integrated transport policy that prioritized pubic transport over private car use was that it seemed to strike at one of the core concerns of the median voter group New Labour had assiduously courted, the fabled 'Mondeo man'. Stories abounded in the press that the lack of progress on an integrated transport policy was due to Blair and his advisors blocking the proposals of Prescott's ministry. Above all Blair wanted to avoid being seen as 'anti-car', which would look more 'old' than 'new' Labour, and which was feared might play into the hands of the opposition.

In his speech on the environment made in October 2000, Tony Blair suggested, in true New Labour style, that old thinking about the environment, expressing a belief that there were trade-offs between progress and the environment, had been superseded: 'we can now see a way through' (Blair 2000). A combination of green consumerism, new technology, business flexibility and government incentives would allow Britain to be 'richer whilst being greener' (ibid). This discourse seeks to tie environmental concerns into New Labour's modernization agenda, something Michael Jacobs also seeks to do in his Fabian Society pamphlet *Environmental Modernization: the New Labour Agenda* (1999).

In Labour's 2001 manifesto, the environment does not appear as a discrete domestic policy issue (this could be said to reflect the stated belief that the environment is a cross-cutting issue across different policy areas), but does arise in the international context. The environment is cited a number of times in the section dealing with 'prosperity for all'. Integrated transport is mentioned but the environmental aspects of this are not highlighted this time and there is no mention of any desire to reduce car use. The environment features more prominently under energy policy, which proclaims a target of 10 per cent energy needs to be obtained from renewable sources by 2010 and the take-up of low-carbon technologies (Labour Party 2001). The environmental dimension of agricultural policy are highlighted, citing increased payments for conversion to organic farming, reform of the Common Agricultural Policy and the Common Fisheries Policy. Mention is also made of the creation of the first new National Parks in the UK since 1948 (South Downs and the New Forest), increased access to the countryside, the clean up of inland waterways and higher welfare standards for farm animals.

A more direct focus on the environment is given in the international section of the manifesto, 'Britain Strong in the World'. The party is 'convinced' of the scientific case for global warming and that 'now is the time to act' (Labour Party 2001: 40). The claim is made that in 2000 UK greenhouse gas emissions were below the levels of 1990 and that a 23 per cent cut in 1990 levels would be achieved by 2010. A target is also set to recycle 35 per cent of all household waste by 2015. As in Blair's 2000 speech, environmental protection and development needs are taken to go hand in hand, 'we cannot protect the environment without addressing the development needs of the poor' (ibid.: 41).

It is also worth noting that the government has moved away from purely quantitative output data such as GDP as a measure of national well-being, and has instead moved to a 'quality of life barometer'. This includes a basket of 15 (originally 13) different indicators, some of which have a clearly environmental intent, such as the size of the wild bird population, air quality, and the percentage of new homes being built on previously developed land. The aim of this approach, according to the government, is to allow for the measurement of 'clean growth' rather than just economic growth.

What does the above tell us about New Labour's approach to the environment? The party has a discourse that recognizes the way in which environmental issues cut across departmental policy boundaries, and acknowledges the corresponding need to place these issues on the agenda of every department and to co-ordinate government strategy on the environment across these departments. It is possible, however, to question whether the practice of New Labour has lived up to this rhetoric. John Prescott struggled to get his integrated transport bill before Parliament, showing the politically problematic nature of one of the key components of environmental policy in the 1997 manifesto. Blair has only made one speech on the environment since taking office, and in that speech said that he will 'make no apology for the priority we have given to education, health, and crime', indicating by its absence the status of the environment in New Labour thinking.

Internationally, the government has been rather more proactive, taking the lead on climate change discussions in Kyoto, Bonn, and The Hague, (and trying, but failing, to keep the United States on board) and promising a 23 per cent cut in CO_2 emissions on 1990 levels by 2010. New Labour thus seems more comfortable pursuing an environmental agenda in the international arena, perhaps because there are fewer electoral implications here.

The structure of environmental governance under Labour

To assess the environmental performance of the Labour government in practice, we will look at two broad areas. First, the structure of environmental governance under New Labour. Secondly, we will focus on four issue areas with important environmental implications – transport, agriculture, waste management and international problems such as climate change.

The Department of Environment, Transport and the Regions (DETR), set up in 1997, was frequently criticized for being too large to be workable, having to deal with everything from international negotiations on climate change to grant aid to local authorities. At this time agricultural and food issues were still the preserve of the Ministry of Agriculture, Fisheries and Food (MAFF).

Increasingly MAFF was seen to have a conflict of interest between its responsibility for agriculture and fisheries (and ties with producer groups) and its responsibility for food and consumer safety. It was also heavily criticized for having mishandled the Foot and Mouth crisis and BSE crisis before that. Both MAFF and the DETR were disbanded in June 2001. In their place was created a new Department of the Environment, Food, and Rural Affairs (DEFRA); and the DETR, minus the environmental remit, became the Department of Local Government, Transport, and the Regions (DLTR) (later reformed again in May 2002). DEFRA was intended to move away from the producer orientation of MAFF and to spearhead a major new drive on green issues and the countryside. There were concerns about the new department's ability to pursue its environmental remit at the time of its creation, particularly so as the break-up of the DETR separated direct responsibility for the environment from transport and planning, both of which had been seen by New Labour as key environmental policy areas. There were also concerns that rather than MAFF and its sectoral corporatism being swept aside, Defra would merely be 'MAFF plus' with the environmental remit added to its existing responsibilities.

A survey of DEFRA by the Green Alliance concluded that the new department had made a difference to environmental policy, but that the government remained 'woefully cautious' in its environmental policy. DEFRA was praised by the RSPB for bringing in a wider range of stakeholders to decision making than had been the case under MAFF, although the campaign group Transport 2000 lamented the direction in which transport policy had gone (i.e. that it was more pro-car) since the environmental and transport remits had once again been separated.

Box 16.2 UK institutions of environmental governance

Department of the Environment, Food, and Rural Affairs (DEFRA) Established in 2001, taking in the remit of the old Ministry of Agriculture, Fisheries and Food along with the Environment portfolio from the Department of the Environment, Transport and the Regions.

Environment Agency Created as a result of the Environment Act of 1995, which merged the National Rivers Authority with Her Majesty's Inspectorate of Pollution. Responsible for environmental protection and improvement in England and Wales with regard to pollution standards and management of rivers.

English Nature Established by the Environment Protection Act 1990 to work on the conservation of wildlife and habitats. Scottish Natural Heritage and the Countryside Council for Wales are the equivalent bodies in these two countries. Collective activity is undertaken by the Joint Nature Conservation Committee.

Countryside Agency Created through the merger of the Countryside Commission and the Rural Development Commission. The Countryside Agency is a statutory body charged with 'conserving and enhancing' rural areas and working for social equity and economic opportunities for rural dwellers.

House of Commons Environment, Food, and Rural Affairs Committee Shadows and reports upon the activities of DEFRA.

House of Commons Environmental Audit Committee Created to monitor the extent to which government departments and non-departmental public bodies contribute to environmental protection and sustainable development.

Royal Commission on Environmental Pollution An independent standing body created in 1970 to advise government on policy in the field of environmental pollution. Labour began its period in office by creating an environmental 'super-ministry' incorporating transport, the environment, and local government under one ministerial remit in an attempt to co-ordinate strategy across these closely interlinked policy areas.

Indeed, in 2002, following a series of calamitous failures of policy, Transport was recreated as a stand-alone ministry, with local government issues returning to the Deputy Prime Minister.

A report on DEFRA by the government's Rural Advocate appointed in 2001, Ewen Cameron, claimed that government departments were not, as had been promised in the 1998 Rural White Paper, taking rural concerns into account when drawing up policy (so called 'rural proofing'). In this regard DEFRA came equal bottom on the Rural Advocate's ranking along with the DTI and the Home Office. Cameron, who is Chair of the Countryside Agency, claimed that there had been 'little sign of a shift in departmental policies' and 'no measurable difference across rural England' as a result of the provisions in the White Paper (*Observer*, 5 May 2002).

As with other areas of environmental policy, New Labour's success at achieving its declared aims seems patchy. DEFRA has been praised for opening up the environmental policy-making process to a wider array of groups; but it is also criticized for failing to act upon its own policies. The separation of environment, transport, and planning responsibilities seems to make the achievement of integrated government in this area more difficult, rather than less.

New Labour's record on key environmental issues

Transport

Transport has been a controversial area for the New Labour government. The 1997 manifesto holds that an integrated transport policy is a direct requirement for environmental sustainability. The key issue here is the balance between private car use and public transport. In June 1997 John Prescott famously declared 'I will have failed if, in five years time, there are not many more people using public transport and far fewer journeys by car. It's a tall order, but I urge you to hold me to it.' (quoted in Prescott 2002). There were to be two policy aspects to achieving this goal, the carrot of an improved public transport system and cycleways, and the stick of increasingly expensive motoring costs through the use of such mechanisms as congestion charging and a workplace parking levy.

In its early years in office the Labour government did massively reduce the road-building programme, ending the 'predict and provide' approach to road building of the old Department of Transport. There had been fierce opposition to a number of road-building projects in the latter period of the Conservative administration, and so this was seen as something of a 'soft target' for a Treasury keen to make savings in public expenditure. In June 1998 John Prescott's much heralded White Paper on Transport was published and this was developed in 2000 into 'Transport 2010: the 10-Year Plan'. This plan proposes a £180 billion investment package over the ten-year period, consisting of £60 billion each on road, rail, and local transport, with a roughly two-thirds–one-third split between public and private finance.

Politically, there are two important points to make about the ten-year plan. First, it leaves New Labour exposed to accusations of carrying out a U-turn with respect to road transport policy. If we really were to judge John Prescott on his 1997 pledge, it is unlikely that we would be impressed. The real costs of car use have come down during this five-year period, and correspondingly car use has continued to grow, at the same time we have one of the most expensive and fragmented public transport systems in Europe. The 10-year plan includes provision for 100 new bypasses and 360 miles of trunk road and motorway widening. Even if the plan is implemented in full, a further 17 per cent growth in road traffic is predicted by 2010. Second, the original White Paper was criticized by the House of Commons Transport Select Committee, partly because there was no mechanism in the plan for achieving integrated transport, and much responsibility was being placed with local authorities 'ill-prepared' to carry out such tasks. Furthermore the additional funds announced were held by the Committee to be insufficient to meet the objectives and the Committee observed that different government departments were still pursuing diverse goals, frequently at odds with the aims set out in the plan – and hardly an example of 'joined-up government'.

Congestion charging will become a reality in London from 17 February 2003 (a minor scheme is already in place in Durham). This policy has not, however, been introduced by the government but by the London Mayor, Ken Livingstone. The £5 charge will apply inside the inner ring road from 7.00 a.m. to 6.30 p.m. on weekdays. Most vehicles (all bar those exempt or entitled to a discount) will have to pay the charge, and the scheme will be policed by traffic cameras that will record number plate details and fines will be levied on all non-payers. The scheme is expected to raise £130m per annum, which will be put towards improving transport in London – the average speed of rush hour traffic in inner London is currently down to three miles per hour. Interestingly, some people oppose the charge, claiming that it was not road taxing, but road pricing. The complaint here is that road pricing has to be distinguished from congestion charging. Congestion charges are specifically targeted to reduce congestion in certain areas at peak times, whereas road pricing is a more general approach to altering the relative costs of different modes of transport and raising revenue. However, complaints that the tax penalizes the poor driver at the expense of the rich, who can still congest the city even if they can pay, do miss an important point. Revenue raised can be used to transfer resources towards transport systems for the lowest income groups who are far more reliant on public transport than wealthier cohorts.

Overall the environmental credentials of this government in relation to transport policy are mixed. There are clear aspirations to improve and increase the uptake of public transport, and a desire to see a more integrated transport system. On the other hand there does not appear to be the political will to increase the real costs of motoring, and there does appear to have been a policy U-turn on car use, with one Transport Minister, Lord Macdonald, claiming the priority was to reduce congestion and pollution rather than car use. The policy sphere for transport has been overwhelmingly domestic, focusing on British road and rail transport. There is of course a European dimension to transport policy, with the creation of the European motorway network and EU imposed targets for air quality being two examples, but these issues have not had such a high degree of political salience as domestic transport.

Agriculture

The issue that has dominated the environmental aspect of agricultural policy is the development and commercialization of genetically modified (GM) crops, although other important agricultural issues such as the foot and mouth crisis, the Common Agricultural Policy and access to the countryside have also had environmental consequences. It is, however, around GM crops that environmental pressure groups have been most active. The issue gained political salience through 1998–9 as it became clear that GM and non-GM soya were being mixed in the United States and imported to Europe, GM soya, for instance, arriving unlabelled. Greenpeace launched direct action campaigns against grain ships bringing the soya into UK ports. In addition, scientific work demonstrating possible harmful effects of GM crops received much publicity. A study in the US appeared to show that insects were adversely affected by GM pollen, and there were suggestions in the UK that rats fed on GM potatoes suffered damage to their immune systems.

Both studies were controversial, but the effect on consumer demand was palpable, and one by one the major supermarkets withdrew GM products from their shelves in response to consumer pressure. Initially the government continued to give strong support to the biotechnology industry, which was seen as an area in which Britain was one of the most advanced nations. The government repeatedly insisted that GM food was safe, and ruled out a moratorium on the introduction of GM crops in Britain. The government ran into political trouble, however, as news came to light of regular meetings between biotech companies and government officials, the provision of inducements for international biotech companies to expand their UK operations, and that the science minister Lord Sainsbury owned the rights to a genetic enhancer intended to boost the productivity of GM crops. Eventually, in the face of intense public and media pressure, the government did prevent the commercial plantation of GM crops until a series of farm-scale trials assessed the effect of GM crop cultivation on surrounding farms and wildlife. Subsequently, two separate enquiries were announced, one into the viability of GM crops, and the other examining the implications of GM cultivation for the UK's organic farming sector, enquiries to be led by the government's Chief Scientific Adviser and the Chief Scientific Adviser to DEFRA. The GM debate had implications beyond the domestic policy sphere, with public scepticism in Europe with regard to GM crops threatening US–Europe trade relations, already strained by disputes over banana imports and US steel tariffs. The United States is likely to consider the demand for labelling GM crops in Europe as a restraint on international trade and is likely to refer the matter to the World Trade Organization.

In addition to GM crops, another difficult agricultural issue for the government was the outbreak of foot and mouth disease in 2001. Ministers rejected vaccination as a possible policy response and instead opted for mass slaughter, which resulted in the destruction of some seven million farm animals, a £1.3 billion compensation package, and a total cost to the economy of around £8 billion. This reaction has been criticized on a number of grounds, in particular the failure to bring in the army at an early stage despite the recommendations of an official enquiry into the 1967 outbreak. In 2001 there was persistent pressure from the National Farmers' Union against a vaccination programme, but the government has stated that vaccination would be a part of the containment programme for any future outbreak.

More generally, agriculture has a strong European dimension and EU agricultural policy, exemplified in the Common Agricultural Policy (CAP), has been seen as productivist and geared to the needs of producer groups, inimical to environmental concerns. There has been consistent pressure from countries including Britain for reform to the CAP, which consumes a large proportion of the EU's budget. There is also concern that EU expansion to include countries with large agricultural sectors without substantial reform will make the CAP prohibitively expensive. Agenda 2000 negotiations in Berlin in March 1999 had two important outcomes for agricultural policy: a shift in the structure of agricultural support away from price support towards direct payments to producers and the creation of an EU Rural Development Policy. This is intended to shift the focus of EU agricultural policy away from producer interests towards environmental and rural economy concerns. In June 2002 the EU Farm Commissioner, Franz Fischler, announced proposals to peg farming subsidies to environmental criteria rather than production. It remains to be seen how these proposals fare with the EU Council of Ministers.

Waste management

The 2001 Labour manifesto set a target of 35 per cent of UK household waste being recycled by 2015, although there are no details of how this policy objective is to be achieved. Indeed this is another area of environmental policy where the government stands accused of espousing aspirations but failing to back these up with an implementation strategy; something exemplified in 2002 by the so-called 'fridge crisis'. The 'fridge crisis' also demonstrates the need for coordination between the European and domestic levels of policy making, and illustrates what can go wrong if this is not achieved.

   Policy innovation with regard to recycling has, as far as Britain is concerned, come almost exclusively from the EU. In recent years there have been specific EU directives on the recycling of cars, fridges, and tyres, and the European Parliament has recently passed new legislation setting targets for the recycling of all electrical household goods.

   The EU End of Life Vehicle Directive, covering the disposal of cars, became effective in April 2002. The directive demands that 85 per cent of the elements of a car are recycled by 2006, rising to 95 per cent by 2015. In the initial period it applies only to cars made in 2001 onwards, but from 2007 it will apply to all cars. Furthermore, by 2006 there are targets of 75 per cent recycling on cars made before 1980. Currently the UK achieves about 74 per cent recycling by weight from all of the 2 million cars disposed of each year. With the recycling cost estimated at anything between £40 and £125 per unit if the EU targets are to be met, there has inevitably been an argument over who should bear the cost of appropriate disposal. The EU directive clearly targets the original manufacturer as the relevant party to bear the costs of recycling the product. However, producer groups such as the UK Society of Motor Manufacturers and Traders claimed that everyone who benefited from a car should pay for its recycling at the end of its life. In effect this means that the final owner of the vehicle is expected by the manufacturers to pay at least part of the bill for disposal. The British government appears to be moving towards a policy position of forcing the last owner to pay a levy towards disposal costs. The problem here is that final owners tend to be the least affluent class of motorist, and the levy may well encourage an increase in on-street dumping of old motor vehicles, a phenomenon that is already on the increase.

In the case of fridges, an EU directive took effect at midnight on 31 December 2001. It prevented the disposal of old fridges until all of the chlorofluorocarbons (CFCs) present in the fridge are removed. This prohibition covers CFCs stored in the foam lining of the fridges. The problem is that there is no plant in Britain equipped to remove CFCs that are present in this form, a deficiency which suggests inadequate preparation by a government over the implementation of a directive agreed two years before it became effective. As over two million fridges are disposed of in Britain each year, the storage problem has escalated rapidly and retailers have ceased offering a collection service on the delivery of new fridges. By mid-2002 around one million old fridges were being stockpiled at local authority dumps.

The House of Commons Environment, Food, and Rural Affairs Select Committee criticized the government for not acting before the directive came into effect to ensure the capacity existed to deal with discarded fridges. For its part, the government claimed (alone among the 15 member states) that the relevant EU directive was 'unclear' and that there was 'considerable doubt' about the practicality of the legislation. More recently still, in April 2002, the European Parliament voted for legislation that would force firms to cover the expense of recycling all domestic electrical goods. Between 1998 and 2002 the EU produced more than 6 million tons of electrical waste, and output of this waste is rising by some 5 per cent per year (*Guardian*, 9 April 2002). Only 10 per cent of this waste is currently recycled, with most of the remainder going to landfill or incineration. Again, there is already dispute over who will foot the bill for this, although the European Parliament is keen to promote the 'polluter pays' principle by forcing manufacturers to pay the costs of collection, recycling, and disposal.

On recycling, as with other areas of environmental policy, New Labour might be accused of setting ambitious targets, but of lacking the political will to introduce the necessary policy instruments needed to achieve them. Environment minister Michael Meacher has described the 9 per cent recycling level achieved in Britain as 'pathetically low' (Meacher, 2000). It is proposed that landfill use will drop from 85 per cent of all rubbish to 35 per cent by 2016. One of the main problems with achieving recycling targets is the question of how to distribute the burdens associated with it. Landfill, at least in the short term, is cheap, and it allows the cost of disposal to be externalized onto the environment and communities living near dumps. Recycling requires an internalization of the costs of waste disposal, and this must be borne by someone, be it the government, the final user or the manufacturer. Placing the onus on the final user tends to lead to increases in fly-tipping, whilst the EU's preferred option, charging the manufacturer under the 'polluter pays' principle, has led to strong opposition from manufacturing industry. Britain has at times, such as on fridge recycling, appeared out of step with EU legislation, leaving it ill-prepared to implement EU policy directives. When this happens, political problems arise for the government, when what might have constituted no more than routine administration of EU directives is picked up by the media and a discourse of 'crisis' is developed along with images of the British countryside littered with waste products.

New Labour, international governance and the environment

There are various international and European-level environmental agreements and directives that impact upon the environmental policy choices of the British government. It is in the area of policy on climate change that the international dimension of environment policy is most fully illustrated. Labour declares itself 'convinced' by the science of climate change, convinced both that global warming is happening and that human activities are responsible for it. The 2001 manifesto commitments on tackling global warming in the light of this belief are clear: a 23 per cent cut in the emission of greenhouse gases by 2010 on 1990 levels, and the establishment of an internal CO_2 trading system. Cuts achieved so far in British levels of CO_2 emissions have mainly come about through changes in energy generation policy, switching from coal to the less-polluting gas-fired power stations. In April 2001 the government launched the 'Carbon Trust', a not-for-profit company with an annual budget of £50m, charged with encouraging the development of low-carbon technologies and ensuring that targets for reductions in carbon emissions were met.

Internationally the Labour government has adopted a high profile at the climate conferences in Kyoto, and at the follow up meetings in The Hague, Bonn, and Marrakech. The Kyoto agreement binds participating nations to a reduction of 5.2 per cent on 1990 CO_2 emission levels by 2012. Following the election of George W. Bush the United States has unilaterally withdrawn from ratification of the Kyoto agreement, claiming that it would cause disproportionate harm to the United States economy. Interestingly, Environment Minister Michael Meacher has publicly refuted this claim, stating that the United States' economy would 'grow by something of the order of 30 per cent [by 2010] and the proportion of the amount by which adherence to the Kyoto protocol will reduce American GDP is about 0.01 per cent, so we are talking about one three-hundredths of the game. Now that is not a serious argument and we have said this very clearly to the Americans.' (Meacher, 2002)). Given that the United States produces 24 per cent of global carbon dioxide emissions, its non-participation represents a serious handicap to any international agreements to counter climate change. The British government has protested 'at the highest level' to President Bush about the United States policy on climate change. (*Guardian*, 4 March 2002).

The EU now plays a key role in determining EU environmental policy. EU environmental directives are developed by the European Commission (specifically Directorate-General XI) and passed by the Council of Ministers. As we have seen, the severe problems Britain is currently experiencing in the area of recycling waste goods have developed directly from a failure to respond in good time to European legislation. Many of the current standards for environmental goods such as drinking water, air quality, beaches and bathing water, wildlife habitat and vehicle emissions emanate from the EU. The application of common standards in many of these fields stems in large part from the requirements of a single European market, and the prevention of member states of the EU gaining either a competitive advantage through lower standards or erecting barriers to trade though higher standards. It has been a concern of environmental groups that membership of the WTO may lead to pressure on EU countries to lower environmental standards or themselves be found to be in restraint of trade at the global level.

The critique of New Labour

Criticism of New Labour's track record on environmental policy has come from both within and without the government. In August 2002 the Environment Minister Michael Meacher caused a stir in an interview in the Sunday Times in which he described himself as a 'lone voice in the wilderness' on environmental concerns. This was taken to mean a 'lone voice' in government, and Meacher's media profile is certainly as the 'greenest' member of the government. Meacher also said, 'I don't think the government as a whole is yet ready to take the magnitude of decisions I think are necessary' (Meacher, 2002). In response, Deputy Prime Minister John Prescott played down the appearance of splits over environmental policy within government. He described the *Sunday Times* version of the interview as a 'terrible distortion of the truth', claiming that when Michael Meacher had used the 'lone voice' expression, he had not 'necessarily' been referring to within government, but to discussions with other governments (Prescott 2002). A study of the transcript of the interview (Meacher 2002) is inconclusive on this, partly because part of the interviewer's question is claimed to be 'inaudible' and therefore is not transcribed. In the previous passage Meacher has stressed the magnitude of the importance of the Johannesburg Summit on the Environment, and claims that 'very, very, very, very few people understand that' (ibid). The last three word of the interviewer's next question (the only ones transcribed) are 'the Prime Minister', and it is in response to this that Meacher talks of being 'like a lone voice in the wilderness' (ibid). It appears, then, that Meacher was talking of his relationship with other members of government, although one cannot rule out the possibility that he is also referring to the international scene. Rumours have consistently circulated that Meacher, despite being the Environment Minister, was dropped from the government team due to attend the Johannesburg Summit as a result of this criticism, and was only reinstated at the last minute as a result of pressure from environmental campaigners.

Criticism of Labour's environmental policy has also come from without, including, unsurprisingly, the campaigning groups that make up the green lobby. One voice here that does seem to have the government's ear more than most is that of Jonathon Porritt, one time Director of Friends of the Earth and now Chair of the UK Sustainable Development Commission, in which role he acts as an advisor to the government. Porritt criticized the Prime Minister for not giving leadership on environmental issues and for showing a 'naive adulation' for business people, which is 'bad for democracy' (Porritt 2002). He also criticized the government for lacking a coherent overall strategy for dealing with environmental issues across the various policy areas upon which they impact, and for making 'no progress at all' on transport and waste management.

It has to be said that the government is also, of course, under pressure from organizations with an at least non-and frequently anti-environmental agenda. For all of Tony Blair's Third Way discourse on overcoming antagonisms between the objectives of growth and environmental policy, the politics of the environment still involve direct clashes between environmentalists and groups representing industries such as transport, agriculture, biotechnology and manufacturing. One interesting but complex example of this was the fuel duty protests of September 2000. These were direct-action protests by hauliers and farmers protesting at the level of British fuel duty, a tax which had been justified in the past as an environmentally friendly form of taxation, aimed at containing the growth of travel by road. The protests, mainly involving a blockade of fuel depots, had a massive impact, causing panic buying of fuel and leading to nationwide shortages, before ending with a 60-day ultimatum to government to reduce fuel taxes'. The degree to which these protests could be seen as anti-environmental is not clear, and here the farmers' concerns (part of a wider set of issues concerning the rural economy) have to be separated from the hauliers' (self-interest being clearer in the latter case). People did not necessarily see fuel duty as an environmental tax, seeing it more as part of a general shift away from taxes on income to taxes on consumption. Furthermore the government did not oppose the fuel protests on environmental grounds, but on the grounds that these taxes helped to pay for schools and hospitals. In addition, whilst some green pressure groups opposed the action, others looked for common ground with farmers, focusing on questions such as the close-to-monopoly power of supermarkets.

Conclusion

Delivery has become one of the mantras of Labour's second term, reflecting the belief that the policy platforms are in place for success in education, health and the environment, and that the emphasis now has to be in the implementation of these policies. It is certainly a contention of their environmentalist critics that Labour have been rather longer on environmental commitments than they have on environmental achievements. Tony Blair's 2000 speech to the Green Alliance made it clear that the government's priorities were the economy, education, and health, and these are clearly the issue areas that the government saw as crucial for its prospects for re-election (Blair, 2000). The environment comes some unspecified distance behind these other policy areas in terms of priority, reflected in a lack of political will in the environmental arena. Nonetheless there have been undoubted environmental achievements under Labour as well, and we need to reach a balanced view of this government's environmental policy record.

What, then, has driven development in environmental policy under this government? There has been a combination of both strategic policy innovation aimed at addressing long-term environmental problems, and short-term reactive policy adaptation. At times policy failure has been due to immediate political imperatives. The most vociferous and legitimate claim is that Labour has committed a policy U-turn on transport. In its 1997 incarnation Labour was clear that an integrated transport system was an essential plank of environmental policy and that a reduction in car use (not just a reduction in the rate of growth of car use, as John Prescott now claims) was an environmental desideratum, alongside improvements in public transport. This thinking was clearly reflected in the combination of environment and transport under one ministry in the DETR. In practice, transport has proved intractably problematic. Labour inherited a fragmented, inchoate rail system, which had suffered from chronic under-investment for many years. In addition, allowing the government to be seen as 'anti-car' was considered by many around the Prime Minister to be politically suicidal. Five years later, however, transport stands once again as a independent government department: road-building is back on the agenda and the declared aim is to reduce the negative externalities involved in car use rather than car use itself.

Nonetheless, the Government did eventually publish a White Paper on Integrated Transport and there does appear to be a genuine commitment to improving public transport, although plans to refurbish the London Underground on a 'public–private partnership' basis have been opposed by the Mayor of London and dogged by controversy. There has also been a White Paper on Rural Affairs and the 2000 Countryside and Rights of Way Act. At the same time, however, the government stands accused of undermining EU efforts to protect the habitats of endangered species.

Policy failure seems starkest in the field of waste management, where (despite the 1999 DETR strategy document 'A Way With Waste', setting out a 20-year programme in waste management) the government appears to have no clear policy mechanism for achieving recycling targets, and where integration between British and EU levels of governance has been lacking. Overall, these mixed results seem to reflect the status of environmental policy under Labour. Positive environmental outcomes are valued, but at a lower level than success in education and health care, and will not be pursued at the expense of continued economic prosperity. Declared ambition is then often not matched by policy achievement.

Chapter 17

Britain in the International Arena

CAROLINE KENNEDY PIPE and RHIANNON VICKERS

The events of 11 September 2001, or, as the Americans have termed it, 9/11, became a terrible but potent symbol of international affairs at the beginning of the twenty-first century. The loss of human life following the collapse of the Twin Towers and the damage to the Pentagon caused shockwaves around the globe, initiating a period of reflection on the contemporary nature of international affairs and prompting military action against those believed to be guilty of perpetrating acts of terrorism. In the aftermath of 9/11, the British Government has shown itself to be a staunch ally of the United States in the 'war on terror'. While the Bush Administration is willing to act unilaterally both in the fight against terrorism and in international affairs, the British Government favours a multilateral approach, one based on the idea that in a rapidly globalizing world the international community and international institutions are key pillars to stability and peace. However, as military action in Iraq demonstrates, Britian is prepared to act in concert with the US to deal with perceived threats from 'rogue states' should multilateral agencies such as the UN fail to do so.

Clear and present dangers

Immediately after the assaults on New York and Washington DC by the Osama bin Laden-led al-Qaeda network the United States declared war on terrorism and those regimes which harboured and nurtured terrorist groups. The 'Bush Doctrine' justifies a new assertiveness abroad in a manner unprecedented since the early years of the Cold War. It has redefined US foreign policy and been used to isolate states such as Iraq, Iran and North Korea, participants all in a so-called 'axis of evil'. The new strategy committed the United States to the eradication of the al-Qaeda network and to the downfall of the Taliban Regime in Afghanistan which had allowed the terrorist group to operate from bases in its territory from where it orchestrated the attacks of 9/11. It also prompted war with Iraq in March 2003. The ongoing continuing threat of international terrorism has reinforced the determination of both the White House and Downing Street to work to eradicate all terrorist networks and to deal with rogue states such as Iraq.

Tony Blair was an early advocate of the use of military force in Afghanistan should the ruling Taliban regime fail to hand over the al-Qaeda leader Osama bin Laden. In a speech shortly after the attacks on New York and Washington, he posed the choice facing the Taliban starkly: to 'surrender the terrorists or surrender power' (*Guardian*, 2 November 2002). Blair justified the support of his government for war in Afghanistan though a sophisticated rubric, combining a rationale for war against terrorism with a powerful case for regime change in Kabul. Alongside the duty of principled nations to act against terrorism, he had earlier highlighted the primitivism of al-Qaeda and the Taliban, arguing there was a moral imperative that the 'modern' world act against those in Afghanistan who were 'the sworn enemies of everything the civilized world stands for' (*Guardian*, 3 October 2001).

The failure by the Taliban to hand over the terrorist leaders led to war. Coalition forces engaged on battlefields supporting the opponents of the Taliban, the Northern Alliance, in the successful bid to retake the Afghanistan capital Kabul. Special Forces mounted a major military expedition to capture the leaders of the terrorist organization but failed to find and capture Osama bin Laden. Concerns were expressed at the prospect of British military casualties, but the bombing campaign waged against the Taliban regime proved most controversial among opponents of the war. Opposition was expressed both among backbench Labour MPs and by a range of groups and individuals opposed to war. Particular objections were made to the use of cluster bombs dropped from high altitude and their impacts on civilian casualties, objections which were to surface again in the run up to war with Iraq in early 2003. Labour Ministers robustly defended government policy, condemning opposition to the conflict in Afghanistan and likening the contemporary terrorist threat to that which had been posed by Nazism (*Guardian*, 22 October 2001).

Government critics were momentarily undermined by the unexpected capitulation of the Taliban regime in November 2001. It appeared that intervention, if not the bombing campaign itself, had brought about regime change. Ministers argued that military action had been both necessary and justified and that there had been a duty to act against the Taliban. In Tony Blair's words, the moral stance of Britain had to be projected into the international arena: 'We are a principled nation and this is a principled cause' (*Daily Telegraph*, 30 October 2001). Although the war against the Taliban was successful (in spite of forecasts that the military campaign would likely fail), Osama bin Laden was not captured (and presumably remains at large), but the al-Queda network was dealt a considerable blow, having been ousted from its territorial stronghold.

The threat posed by terrorist groups and the economic and human consequences of terrorism prompted the British government to espouse the need to apply firm moral principles in the international arena. Blair himself propounded an optimistic message, arguing that good could come from the evil of 9/11, that globalization not isolation could solve the problems dogging contemporary international affairs, reiterating his belief that Britain had to both face down threats and engage with the positive challenges that resulted from multiplying global forces (Blair 2002).

The consequences of the ongoing war on terror allowed Britain to restate its confidence in the idea of the international community and in international institutions. During the post 9/11 crisis, Blair made much of the power of the international community to act together for global good, arguing that 'around the world, 11 September is bringing governments and people to reflect, consider and change . . . There is a coming together. The power of community is asserting itself. We are realizing how fragile are our frontiers in the face of the world's new challenges' (quoted in Toynbee 2002). Indeed, in the aftermath of 9/11, Tony Blair tried to further advance a new foreign policy agenda based on the notion that by multilateral means the international community can defend human rights and support the rule of law. This approach has had to engage with the instincts of the United States to use unilateral means to deal with security threats posed by international terrorism and so-called rogue states, such as Iraq and others. It was to be severely tested in 2003 as Britain backed the US-led war in Iraq to disarm Saddam's weapons of mass destruction (WMDs), while other states, notably France, Germany and Russia, opposed the war and withheld UN support for it. Since the end of the Gulf War in 1991, Iraq has persistently flouted the UN's right to order the destruction or removal of its WMDs, interfering with the work of UN weapons inspectors on numerous occasions. The events of 9/11 exacerbated the continuing crisis between Iraq on one hand and the United States and Britain on the other. The United States condemned Iraq for breaching the UN inspection regime and for having links with many of the terrorist networks which have targeted America and its service personnel abroad. As such, in March 2003 the Bush Administration, having failed to secure UN support, launched pre-emptive military action against Iraq, not just to prevent it retaining or obtaining WMDs, but in order to secure a regime change in Iraq through the ousting of Saddam.

Applying the logic of the war in Afghanistan, the British government sent British troops to support the US-led campaign to remove Saddam. Although Blair initially claimed that Iraqi disarmament, not regime change, would be the reason for military action against Iraq, he has also admitted that he feels that 'Iraq would be a much better place without Saddam' (*Guardian*, 15 October 2002): 'Because terrorism and weapons of mass destruction threaten us. . .the response will have to involve military action and regime change' (ibid). This posture proved controversial, provoking debate both within Britain and the wider international community, with several voices suggesting that every option short of war should be explored. The Liberal Democrat leader, Charles Kennedy, while calling for definitive evidence linking Iraq with al-Qaeda and 9/11, raised concerns over the possibility of regime change, arguing it does not fall to the USA (or the UN) to decide what government should be installed within which state (Kennedy 2002). Similar questions have been raised from the Labour backbenches, where there has been considerable unease at the thought of a war with Iraq and the possibility that military action might provoke anger and retaliation within the Muslim world.

Both before and after 9/11 Tony Blair has spoken of the special bond between the United States and Britain, and the global importance of their close cooperation within the international community. Some commentators had been impressed by the close relationship which developed between the Labour government and the Clinton Administration. So close was Blair and Clinton's relationship, Bill Clinton attended a meeting of the Cabinet in 1997 and, even having left office, was invited to the Labour Party Conference of 2002 in Blackpool. The fact that Blair has remained close to the White House after the election of the Republican George Bush is testament to the importance that Britain places on the transatlantic partnership. While there is a tension between Blair's undoubted loyalty to Washington and his commitment to multilateral institutions such as the UN, the Prime Minister is keen to square the circle. He feels it is right to stand by the United States, but wants America to act through the international community in a concerted and decisive manner. Britain was one of the few states in Europe to endorse the Bush Administration's first initiative in the international arena, the revival of the so-called Star Wars project. While Blair has at times been undoubtedly frustrated by the unilateral instincts of the Bush White House, something articulated by the US Strategic Defence Review, which signalled a clear desire for unilateral American action and a distrust of international organizations, Britain has always sought to work with, not against, the United States. Hence Blair's support for action against Iraq – through the UN if possible, but outside the UN because it proved necessary. Yet, unilateralism has proved somewhat difficult for the British Government, and there is little doubt it has undermined Blair's ambition to coalition-build, although he has pushed America to engage in a Middle East peace process to help calm Arab fears over the direction of policy towards Israel and Palestine.

That said, current tensions between the United States and Europe should be placed in a historical context within which there have been a number of transatlantic disputes. Most recently, controversy arose in the 1980s over the stationing of American Intermediate Nuclear Forces in Europe and differences over Israel date back over two decades. Policy disagreements are not a novel features of Euro–American relations. Yet, while America and Britain continue to work closely together, particularly in dealing with the ongoing war on terrorism and the problem of Iraq, the US-led war with Iraq proved a serious area of contention for many European leaders. Bush and Blair were very disappointed with the manner in which some European leaders, notably Jacques Chirac and Gerhard Schroder, stymied UN action over Iraq.

The special relationship between the United States and Britain remains central to Blair's foreign policy, and Britain has sought to protect and promote the relationship with Washington. Naturally, there have been differences between the two, particularly on trade, issues of colonialism, and over the direction of the European project. In the case of the EU Britain had previously feared that integration within Europe would harm the 'special relationship' with America, although US diplomats have often expressed impatience at Britain's difficulty to see itself as part of Europe. The decision, finally enacted in the early 1970s, that Britain should become an active and engaged European, was controversial because Britain remained close to the United States in so many ways (Young 1997). Yet, by the end of the Cold War, although it had undoubtedly declined in terms of its relative greatness, Britain retained considerable international influence, certainly across the Atlantic, in the Commonwealth and within what was the G7, now the G8. Now, as a result of 9/11 and the prevailing international climate, Tony Blair is perceived in Washington as being a central actor shaping the international political agenda, and, differences on Iraq notwithstanding, specifically within Europe.

In the war against terror, while the sheer economic, political and military strength of the United States enables it to think and sometimes act in a unilateral manner, Britain still has a substantial and useful defence network. Its imperial legacy means Britain, having access to strategic bases in the Indian Ocean and throughout the Commonwealth, exercises influence in places where America has found it difficult to establish political relationships of any substance. In addition, Blair has the objective, often stated, of Britain being a 'bridge' between the United States and Europe, able to explain European concerns to Washington and present American objectives in Europe. In this capacity, particularly since 9/11 and during the Iraq crisis, Blair has engaged in a great deal of shuttle diplomacy, trying to persuade a range of foreign leaders to back the war on terrorism and act against Iraq. He has tried to encourage direct contacts between France and the United States, each traditionally suspicious of the other. Most recently, however, the French have reacted with an outburst of what may be described as 'Gaullism', and relations between Mr Blair and Mr Chirac, already uneasy over intra-EU differences, particularly on reform of the Common Agricultural Policy, have been marred by disputes over strategy towards Iraq. Although the Anglo–American strategy of moving to disarm Iraq gained momentum when the UN Security Council voted to require Saddam to accept a new weapons regime, France, Germany and Russia ultimately opposed the use of force. As Blair phrased it, while 'conflict was not inevitable, disarmament is; defy the UN's will and we will disarm you by force' (*Guardian*, 9 November 2002). The unanimous vote by the Security Council in November 2002 to (again) call for Iraqi disarmament strengthened the bottom line of the United States: that the USA will take military action, alone or in concert with others, if Iraq did not comply with UN demands and meet the new inspection regime through verifiable disarmament of its WMDs. However, in March 2003, the UN Security Council refused to support military action against Saddam, France leading the way in calling for more inspections and the continuation of a containment strategy. As a result, the USA and Britain, backed by thirty other countries, unilaterally waged war on Iraq to disarm Saddam by force.

Thus, while Tony Blair may be fulfilling what Henry Kissinger once described as the best British role in foreign policy – to act as an arm of the US administration (Kissinger, 2001) – this characterization gains little favour in some European capitals. Blair has been criticized within the Labour Party for his closeness to the Bush Administration, and for weakening positive relationships within Britain and its EU partners, as demonstrated by the huge backbench Commons revolt, which saw 139 Labour MPs vote against launching a war on Iraq. Nevertheless, the British government insists on the importance of maintaining a close and harmonious relationship with America. For Blair, recent terrorist attacks in Bali and Moscow, together with the prospect of further 9/11-style attacks on the United States and Britain, demonstrate that 'what Bali shows is that if you don't deal with problems they will come back and hit you. The same applies to Iraq. It's not either or, it's both' (*Guardian*, 15 October 2002). Military action against Iraq is therefore bolstered, in this view, not compromised, by the ongoing war on terrorism. Being engaged in a conflict of global proportions against 'evil fanatics' has led Britain, in alliance with the USA, to use military force to disarm Iraq and prosecute the war on terrorism. Such force, if not deployed through a multilateral agency such as the UN, must be deployed by a 'coalition of the willing' led by the USA. In this regard, it is prepared to stand shoulder to shoulder with the United States, and to do so in spite of UN opposition. While continuing public support for this stance is hard to predict, what is not in question is the determination of the British Government to continue to act against terrorist groups and dangerous rogue states, and to do so hand in glove with its oldest and closest ally.

Globalization and internationalization

It remains to be seen which way Britain will jump should there be a conflict between its own multilateral preferences and the United States' unilateral instincts, but the US–British special relationship remains at the core of British foreign policy, something not remotely likely to change in any foreseeable future. Should public opinion permit, Blair may well prioritize the relationship over all other geo-political considerations. It is therefore worth considering exactly how the pursuit of multilateralism in international affairs, something we might term *internationalization*, has developed as a policy since the election of the Labour government in 1997.

Labour claims it has pursued a distinct agenda in foreign policy, one linked to the idea of a Third Way. While the Third Way has been explained in a variety of domestic forums since 1998, predominantly as a modernized version of democratic socialism, Tony Blair has emphasized the importance of the Third Way in the international arena. In January 1999, during a speech in South Africa, he suggested that in the international context the Third Way was about how a state would perceive its own place in the world. It expressed the idea of acting well in the international arena and making a commitment to 'internationalism', defined as recognizing a duty to act and intervene in favour of human rights, international stability and the global environment (Blair 1999). On occasion, this might include an imperative to act on grounds of humanitarian intervention, but the duty to act should, ideally, be a multilateral one and not rest on unilateral action. Hence the importance Labour seemingly places on international organizations and international law. One state or nation cannot easily act alone, not least because we live in a globalized world.

For Tony Blair, the Third Way, as applied in external policy, seems to be about appreciating the transformations to society and national economies brought about by the processes of globalization (Giddens 1998). By globalization, Blair refers to the way relations between states have become part of a global network and are intimately connected together. Events in one part of the world increasingly have effects on peoples and societies far away (Baylis and Smith 2001), and, because states (and markets) are therefore linked together in a common destiny, both have a communal stake in solving international problems that affect all.

The defining moment in the articulation of Labour's foreign policy came with a speech delivered by Tony Blair in Chicago on 22 April 1999. The 'Chicago' speech, as it became known, proposed a 'new internationalism', something Blair described as 'The Doctrine of the International Community'. Here the Prime Minister emphasized the dual process of globalization and increasing interdependence, both of which meant that all states and peoples now 'live in a world where isolationism has ceased to have a reason to exist. We are all internationalists now, whether we like it or not' (Blair 1999a).

As a result, the principle of 'non-interference' in the affairs of other states had now to be qualified in several respects. In particular, 'acts of genocide can never be a purely internal matter' (ibid). Speaking in defence of the NATO campaign then being waged in Kosovo against Serbia in defence of Bosnian Muslims, Blair asserted that NATO's actions had 'shifted the balance between human rights and state sovereignty' (ibid), challenging the traditional and pragmatic conventions of state behaviour which warned against intervention. Where Bismarck had claimed that the Balkans were not worth the bones of a single Pomeranian grenadier, Bismarck, according to Blair, had been wrong (Ignatieff 2000). In the course of his speech Blair laid out a framework for testing the principle of intervention. These were:

- First, are we sure of our case?
- Second, have we exhausted all diplomatic options?
- Third, are there military operations we can sensibly and prudently undertake?
- Fourth, are we prepared for the long term?
- Finally, do we have national interests involved?

While the fifth point might be taken as a frank admission that, despite the rhetoric, a realist state-centred approach remained crucial to foreign policy, Blair created his own version of a 'just war' theory. He argued that, should the above five questions be answered in the affirmative, the international community had the duty to intervene, and if necessary, by military force, and this had been proved by the West's response to the Kosovan crisis. Hence, Blair's 2003 determination to act against Iraq, even if this imperative should conflict with his multilateral preferences.

The conflict in Kosovo was rooted deep in the complexities of Balkan history (Judah, 2000) but the most immediate cause of war was the failure of the talks held at Rambouillet (chaired by the then British Foreign Secretary Robin Cook) which had been, at least according to NATO, originally designed to ensure the security of the ethnic Albanian population in Kosovo, a region of Serbia. The Serb leader, Slobodan Milosevic, had refused to allow NATO forces to maintain peace in the province, perceiving the Kosovo Liberation Army (KLA) as terrorists. In 1999 Kosovo was stripped of its autonomy and a policy of repression against the Albanian majority began. Albanians responded through non-violent resistance and began building separate political, economic and social institutions in the province. Once it became apparent that Serbian forces were engaged in ethnic cleansing against the Albanian community, the UN condemned the use of force by Serbia and imposed a comprehensive arms ban on Yugoslavia. Unlike the previous war in Bosnia, however, NATO, not the UN, then intervened militarily, claiming it launched a war against Serbia mainly for humanitarian purposes (Booth 2001).

NATO's strategy was to bomb key targets within Serbia in a bid to remove Milosevic from power and halt Serbian military engagement in Kosovo. The bombing campaign, which lasted nearly 80 days, proved controversial, especially when NATO missiles mistakenly hit civilian targets (Booth 2001).

Yet Blair adopted the hardest line against the Serbian leader Milosevic and he led the debate over whether NATO should send ground troops into Kosovo. While European unity had held throughout the duration of the bombing, there were evident contradictions between member states. In particular, Germany wished to terminate the bombing, but Britain was the most outspoken proponent of continuing the war, using NATO ground forces if necessary. President Clinton, aware of the American aversion to casualties in foreign fields, particularly after the 1993 intervention in Somalia which had claimed 18 US military lives, was a less forceful and ardent proponent of the use of ground forces. While it has been argued that Britain's Kosovo policy did not emerge as a deliberate set of measures driven by ethical concerns (and that it helped create the postwar refugee crisis), Blair himself remained convinced that the humanitarian credentials of the war were intact and did not waver in his determination that military action ended the ethnic cleansing and removed the threat of a wider war (Blair 1999a).

Blair's Chicago speech inspired a debate on both the morality and legality of the NATO intervention (Booth 2001). When Robin Cook, then Foreign Secretary, appeared before the House of Commons Foreign Affairs Committee in April 1999 to explain the legal basis for NATO's actions in Kosovo, he argued that states had the right to use force in the case of overwhelming humanitarian necessity. Most importantly, Blair proved that he did not eschew changing traditional Labour policy which had supported the integrity of Tito's Yugoslavia. Perhaps most telling of all was that even many on the left of the party, committed to anti-militarism, supported the use of force for the protection of human rights against a regime Blair described as dictatorial.

The issue of human rights has become an important part of the Labour agenda for action in the international arena. This commitment to internationalism, which was demonstrated militarily, as well as politically, in the conflict in Kosovo, can also be seen in the commitment to international institutions. Britain strongly supports the establishment of an International Criminal Court, the International War Crimes Tribunal on the former Yugoslavia, and has incorporated the European Convention on Human Rights into UK law in the form of the Human Rights Act. Here again, however, there was a gap between the British endorsement of international law and an American response which was far less enthusiastic and wholly dismissive of the International Criminal Court.

The international moralism of New Labour: arms sales to Indonesia, Sierra Leone and Zimbabwe

In 1997, Labour adopted an optimistic interpretation of existing historical conditions. Upon election to office, Tony Blair embarked on a sustained effort to reformulate Britain's role in the world. Part of this meant creating alternative sources for thinking about foreign policy, and one example of this was the 1998 establishment of the new think tank 'The Foreign Policy Centre' as an alternative source of information (http://fpc.org.uk/main). It was claimed that Labour's attempt to modernize foreign policy would find new ways to get people involved in rethinking Britain's foreign policy goals through public debate. Panel 2000, for example, was set up to stimulate debate on how Britain's identity would be projected abroad, and while the idea of 'Cool

Britannia' proved something of an embarrassment, the government remained committed to rebranding Britain's – and Labour's – external image.

Underpinning Britain's new thinking on foreign policy was the idea that collaboration could replace confrontation, although, as we have seen, there has been no rejection of military force should its use be deemed necessary. Here, it was argued that challenges to global stability such as climate changes, poverty and ethnic conflict could be tackled through international cooperation. The Labour government emphasizes the centrality of a sound moral leadership though which Britain would exercise influence. Part of Labour's original mission statement was to implement a new foreign policy, and the Labour Party Manifesto of 1997 had argued the government would 'make the protection promotion of human rights a central part of our foreign policy' (Labour Party 1997).

The Labour government's human rights objectives had been set out in numerous statements made before and after the election, but it was the then Foreign Secretary Robin Cook's very public launch of his Foreign and Commonwealth Office Mission Statement in May 1997 that caught the media's attention. Labour, Cook declared, would implement an 'ethical foreign policy', one that 'recognized that the national interest cannot and should not be defined only by narrow realpolitik' (Cook 1997). Although the 'ethical dimension' was soon played down by ministers (and, some say, soon abandoned as an embarrassment) this did mark an important break with the British tradition of pragmatism in foreign policy. The pragmatic, what some termed the realist, vision of foreign policy sees the national interest, sovereignty and anarchy as the reality of the international environment within which states operate. Here states pursue selfish interests, and cooperation between states is a rarity, not a norm. This approach to foreign policy was challenged by Labour's declaration that it wishes 'to make Britain once again a force for good in the world' (Cook 2000). This ambition fitted well with what may be described as the 'internationalist' strand within the Labour Party, one which had always emphasized a 'moral component' in the making of foreign policy. However, the Labour government almost immediately encountered the problem of how this ethical dimension would fare in relation to the commercial dimensions of British foreign policy. This was most notable in the issue of arms sales to third-world regimes. Britain has a robust arms industry and is second only to the United States in arms exports. Such business is worth more than £5 billion to Britain a year. Britain is the second largest arms exporter in the world, securing some 25 per cent of the world market in defence equipment; and the arms industry within the UK represents a powerful domestic lobby group. However, in the run up to the General Election of 1997, Labour did make a number of promises to regulate the arms trade, particularly by establishing a new criterion for granting arms export licences. Part of this criterion fitted with the idea of the promotion and protection of human rights. Accordingly, it was promised that an export licence of armaments and munitions would not be issued if there was a clearly identifiable risk that any such export would be used for internal repression by the purchasing state.

While the intent of this policy was clear in theory, the dilemma ministers faced (indeed, the severe challenge) was how to regulate the arms trade without also damaging British commercial interests or further weakening Britain's already vulnerable industrial base (Cook 1997). In this regard, the first challenge for Robin Cook was whether Britain should proceed with the sale of Hawk fighter jets to the ruling regime in Indonesia. As a Labour MP, Cook had himself opposed British arms sales to repressive regimes (Kampfner 1998) and he had singled out the sale of British Hawks to the third world as especially dishonourable to the conduct of foreign policy. He therefore had some sympathy with those who campaigned on the issue of human rights in East Timor. Opponents of the arms sales argued that the aircraft, alongside the proposed sale of water cannons and Alvis riot-control vehicles, would be used by the Indonesian government to subdue domestic discontent. While denying the claims of the campaigners as to how the jets would be used, the Foreign Office did turn down four arms licences to Indonesia while granting twenty-two. In doing so, it acceded to pressure from the Department of Trade and Industry (DTI) requiring existing commercial contracts to be honoured. Although Cook had grave misgivings over the sales, he was obliged to regard their continuation as the result of commercial pressures, and the decision to honour existing arms contracts led to allegations that the much-vaunted ethical dimension in Labour foreign policy was little more than rhetoric (Wheeler and Dunne 1998). The issue of arms to Indonesia therefore proved an embarrassment to the notion of an ethical dimension in foreign policy, even as the publication of a report on British arms sales did herald an era of new openness and accountability in foreign affairs.

If the issue of 'arms to Indonesia' proved difficult for Labour, so too did the issue of 'arms to Africa', and specifically the sale of arms to Sierra Leone, a former British colony (Reno, 1997). In 1998, the democratically elected leader of Sierra Leone, President Kabbakh, had been overthrown in a military coup. Although all international organizations, including the UN through Resolution 1132, had vowed to return

Kabbakh to power, the international community was slow to provide resources to support the restoration of the President. Indeed, both the United States and the EU saw Sierra Leone as essentially an area of British interest, and being the former colonial power Britain took the lead in mustering international support for Kabbakh, maintaining his government in exile and encouraging forces loyal to him. The British position was complicated by the Labour government's refusal to provide support to the regional body, the Economic Community of West Africa Monitoring Group (ECOMOG), as long as the Nigerian Sani Abacha headed the organization. At the 1995 Commonwealth Conference in New Zealand Britain played a leading role in passing strong condemnation of Abacha's human rights regime within Nigeria. The Foreign Office had insisted on a total ban on assistance to Nigeria (Hirsch 2000) and the UN Security Council did act to invoke sanctions, so by 1998 Britain was actually operating an arms embargo on seventeen countries including the one affecting Sierra Leone.

The government, and specifically Robin Cook and the Foreign Office, were therefore embarrassed by revelations that a British company, Sandline International, had been acting as military consultants in a bid to provide weapons and advisers in support of President Kabbakh. In late 1997 the Director of Sandline, Tim Spicer, had held meetings with Kabbakh and ECOMOG officials to discuss military plans to restore the President and vanquish the rebel forces. So successful was the subsequent military operation that Kabbakh was returned to power in Sierra Leone. In London controversy erupted over the role of the Foreign Office in the shipment of arms and the role of advisers made by Sandline. Of particular embarrassment was the allegation widely touted in the press that the Foreign Office had known of Sandline's intentions to violate the UN arms embargo, and allegations were made that the Foreign Office had actually known and approved of the activities of Sandline. Cook was accused of mismanaging the Foreign Office, but was exonerated in the final report of the House of Commons into the affair.

In May 2000, under the pretext of evacuating British nationals from the country, a British military force was dispatched to the capital city, Freetown, in a bid to deter the anti-government rebel forces of the RUF from destabilizing the government. The primary task of the British force was to act as a deterrent, but a second mission was to restore security in and around the capital and to shore up the peacekeeping forces of the UN. Paratroops were deployed and the Royal Navy provided the logistical support and air-combat capability in the largest military deployment force since the Falklands war some twenty years before. British soldiers in the country were also engaged in an exercise to train the somewhat unprofessional Sierra Leone army. However a crisis ensued when British soldiers were captured and held hostage by a rebel group, the so-called 'West Side boys'. The British Government took the decision to send British Special Forces (the SAS and the Parachute Regiment) to rescue the men. In this instance the Prime Minister refused to negotiate for the return of the soldiers, and although one serviceman lost his life the outcome of the mission was successful (Shawcross 2001). The initial deployment of British troops into Sierra Leone was in line with the Blair philosophy on humanitarian intervention to save lives in circumstances of chaos. It also answered some of Blair's critics on the Labour backbench that he had chosen to avoid responsibility for either the Commonwealth or Britain's imperial past. Imperialism and its many legacies have proved to be a particularly challenging issue for the Labour Government. Whilst the phrase 'liberal imperialism' was coined to describe military interventions undertaken by the Labour Government in areas such as Sierra Leone, some ministers have declared themselves troubled by Britain's past colonial role and attempts to resuscitate imperialism in however positive a manner. Cook's successor as Foreign Secretary, Jack Straw, argued in 2002 that Britain must accept responsibility for some of the world's most enduring regional problems, among them relations between India and Pakistan (*Times*, 12 November 2002).

Within the Commonwealth the most complex challenge to the British government has been the deterioration of political stability within Zimbabwe. For Labour, the issue of arms for export to Zimbabwe promised to be as embarrassing as the row over arms to Indonesia. Despite intense engagement by Zimbabwe in the bloody Congolese Civil War and its deployment of some 11,000 troops in defence of President Kabila, Tony Blair permitted the exports of spare parts for the British jets which had been sold to Harare during the early 1980s. The Prime Minister's announcement in early 2000, that Britain would indeed allow the sales to proceed, provoked widespread condemnation. Critics argued that these sales not only breached the EU code of conduct on arms sales but also demonstrated that Labour was not serious about humanitarian concerns. There had also been fierce criticism over the sales of arms from within the Cabinet, principally from Robin Cook and Clare Short, the International Development Secretary, but their objections appear to have been overruled by Tony Blair and Trade and Industry ministers. Commercial and contractual reasons were given as the principle for the decision, although the government did say that it would 'tighten' protocols dealing with arms exports to Zimbabwe.

In the spring of 2000, Zimbabwe's political stability degenerated into violence when the Mugabe Government backed the illegal occupation of farms owned by white settlers. As so-called 'war veterans' attempted to take land from the white farmers using violence and intimidation, the British Government urged Mugabe to restore the rule of law, threatening to suspend Zimbabwe from the Commonwealth and freeze the British-held foreign assets of the ruling elite. Both Australia and New Zealand supported Britain in this stance. These states argued for the immediate suspension of Zimbabwe from the Commonwealth, but this suggestion met with stiff resistance from African states. Although the crisis in Zimbabwe deepened through 2001, with Mugabe's internal opponents demanding free and fair elections, the British, Australian and New Zealand governments failed to persuade the African states to operate a framework of sanctions. In the spring of 2002, Britain distanced itself from a Commonwealth compromise on Zimbabwe which had deferred the issue of sanctions. Britain remains locked in dispute with Mugabe, and Jack Straw himself has been criticized for the sympathy he has espoused over the land issue and the consequences of early colonization.

Conclusion: a presidential foreign policy?

By January 2001, the then Europe Minister, Peter Hain, argued that Foreign Ministries across the world were in the process of becoming Departments of Global Affairs, charged with dealing with a world in which 'there is no such place as abroad' (Hain 2001). Globalization and its impacts seemingly weigh heavily on the minds of Labour Ministers, none more so that the Prime Minister, Tony Blair. During the first period of Labour's tenure in office it might be argued that Britain was seeking to steer a course through a period of post-cold war uncertainty. Yet, despite some criticisms at home of Blair's closeness to the United States, what emerged during the close of the twentieth century and the beginning of the new millennium is a greater confidence in Britain's role in global politics. Blair has 'resolved' some of what might be regarded as the traditional dilemmas in British foreign policy. He has eschewed a choice between Europe and the United States, seeing little contradiction between membership of the EU and having a close relationship with the United States. The Blair/ Bush personal relationship has been central to the post 9/11 pursuit of the war on terror, and more than any other postwar British leader Blair has attempted, at times with great difficulty, to provide a bridge in maintaining Euro–Atlantic relations.

During Labour's second period in office much of the making of foreign policy has been personally attributed to Tony Blair rather than the Foreign Secretary, Jack Straw. Some commentators say Blair is his own Foreign Secretary, and have argued that he feels most at ease with 'high politics' because foreign affairs and the international element enable him to act decisively in a way that often eludes him in the domestic realm. The Prime Minister can act in international crises in a bolder manner than he might be permitted in, say, the politics of health care or public service reform. Over Kosovo it might be argued that Blair, whose credentials in the international arena had not been tested before, had to demonstrate that as Prime Minister he could act as robustly on defence and national security as some of his Conservative predecessors, most particularly Margaret Thatcher. In her conduct of her office (if not the policies she espoused) Blair has in the past expressed his admiration for Lady Thatcher. The conduct of the wars in Afghanistan and Iraq proved beyond doubt that Blair was willing to dispatch British troops into action abroad when necessary. While the legacies of imperialism have proved troubling for many within the Labour Party, Labour is seemingly eager to embrace a 'new moralism', one based on powerful states intervening, should it prove necessary, in pursuit of human rights, international stability, and genuine international and national interests. In such terms, notably the notion of freeing the Iraqi people from Saddam, did Blair justify the use of force against Iraq in 2003.

It would be a mistake, however, to see British foreign policy as solely arising from Tony Blair's preferences. Although there is little doubt that the Prime Minister was keen to see the development of an ethical dimension in the making of foreign policy, the idea had wide support within Labour more generally, and many Labour MPs remain critical of the way in which commercial arms transfers appear to override principle. Despite the large parliamentary majorities Labour won in 1997 and 2001, Blair failed to carry one in three of his parliamentary party in support of war on Iraq, and many Labour MPs remain critical of military action in general.

That said, there is a feature of policy that might be termed a Blair doctrine. The current Labour Government is committed to a new humanitarianism abroad, as demonstrated during the crises in Kosovo in 1999 and Sierra Leone in 2000. There is a commitment to act morally within the international environment and a greater emphasis placed upon human rights. This strand in Labour thinking has been reinforced by the events of 9/11, and while it is the case that the government does not always succeed in persuading the United States to think in positive terms about international organizations, it is the case that in being a candid, but loyal, steadfast friend the British government and the Prime Minister exert some influence on the Bush Administration. In this regard, through the deepening United States–British special relationship and in becoming a committed European, Britain, to use a somewhat worn phrase, having lost an empire, hopes to define a clear role for itself in the troubled and complicated international politics of the early twenty-first century.

Chapter 18

Analysing Political Power

PATRICK DUNLEAVY

with Ian Byrne and Bernard Steunenberg

Power denotes a capability on the part of its holder to get other people to change their behaviour in ways they would have preferred not to do, had they not been subject to power. To have power is a 'dispositional' thing: it describes a potential that has not yet been realized but which will come about under normal circumstance. Dispositional qualities like this are famously elusive and tricky to grasp in research terms. Many past political analysts have argued that the only way to spot power is to see it being implemented, and they have hence equated power with its exercise. But if I say 'This Ming vase is fragile', I do not mean that the vase is already broken or that it is certain ever to break – only that it has a disposition to break under certain circumstance (Morriss, 2002). And so it is with power – it is a much more hypothetical and counter-factual concept than some one actor or some group getting their way by stamping roughshod over another actor or group.

An actor has power *over* others *to* bring certain things about. At its broadest, the concept includes both the ability to change others' behaviour, and the ability to achieve certain outcomes. This capability to achieve outcomes may be based upon the actor's own resources, or the resources of other people whom I can influence or constrain to do what I want. Key resources are a position controlling key decision-making points, a reputation for influence, the loyalty or support of other people, possession of key information, or controlling large wealth and income. But simply having resources is also not the same as having power. Actors can expend resources unskillfully, in ways that create more enemies or resistance instead of achieving the actor's goals. Nor is power to be equated with being successful or getting what you want. Often people are 'lucky' because they get what they want without having to take any action to influence others, and without having to mobilize or expend resources (Dowding 1991). For their own reasons, other powerful actors or groups may bring about an outcome favourable for me without my having to try. Just because someone or

338

some group is successful in benefiting from decisions does not establish that they brought those decisions about, or that they could have done so if they wanted to. Perhaps they were just lucky, in the right place at the right time with the right interests to benefit from others' actions. Equally sometimes, in a 'no win' situation, everyone loses and nobody benefits – but there can still be power relations between these 'losing' actors in terms of distributing relative costs among themselves, or unequally sharing the pain (Dowding 1996).

Determining who has power is a tricky exercise. Simply asking people involved in decision-making situations whether they have power or not is of little use in advancing well-based political science knowledge. Most people in relatively senior positions like to think that they are their own person, and not a creature of someone else's will, so that those subject to power may under-report the fact. At the same time powerful people themselves rarely admit that they are able to influence or control others, lest it become a focus for resentment or detract from their public image. People or groups who are in conflict with each other behind closed doors inside government may also go to extraordinary lengths to keep their disagreements secret and to represent the internal political debates as more balanced, collegial and well-tempered than they actually are. Senior people in government usually believe that their side or their generation is running the shop better than their predecessors or adversaries. And when problems or crises occur, people inside government blame external factors or the flow of adverse events far more than the opposition parties or external observers, who blame the internal dispositions of governmental actors far more for mistakes.

But equally it is little use to forswear knowledge derived from studying decision-making situations, and to retreat instead into inferring power from people's outward resources or their public reputations for influence. In 1998–9 UK newspapers and TV channels sponsored elaborate 'power list' exercises in which panels of 'experts' (mostly members of 'the great and good') were asked to rank 'who has power in Britain', spanning across the worlds of politics, public administration, business, entertainment, and social life. In both years Tony Blair was ranked first, but with the second slot occupied by overseas businessmen, Rupert Murdoch in 1998 and Bill Gates in 1999. Gordon Brown was rated fifth and then fourth, (this change precipitated by the sudden disappearance from the cabinet of Peter Mandelson, previously ranked second in power terms). Soap stars and celebrities ranked above many members of the cabinet in both lists. The pluralist objection to all such exercises is that they confuse public reputations for wealth, status or influence with political power itself. For pluralists the presence of Gates or Murdoch in high positions under different lists in one year but not the next might reflect little more than their being talked about a lot as successful, whereas the fact that holders of the government posts ranked top or near top even in this method suggests a consistent importance of office-holders – their undisputed involvement in making salient decisions.

Of course, the eclectism and variability of the power lists capture the shifting influence of wider contexts and circles of influence in shaping what the British polity can achieve. Gates and Murdoch may soar or fall back in particular year's rankings but the influence of financial markets and major business figures or corporations in structuring government policy is fairly clear. Equally a struggle for influence between United States, European and wider world governments and actors to influence public policy and political elites has been a recurring feature of British politics. Normally these linkages are rather remote and general influences, but on occasions (like the 1996 Westland affair) the disputes within the heart of British government arguably reflect or parallel the wider struggles of corporations and blocs of nations (Dunleavy 1995b). The context of power is also strongly influenced by changes in the external context, such as changes in the world economy and alterations in Britain's relative economic and trade positions *vis-à-vis* other countries.

Few of these qualifications or subtleties ever appear in empirical discussions of the allocation of political power in contemporary Britain. Instead most journalistic and historical discussion focuses down on a long-established and largely rhetorical controversy about 'Cabinet government' versus Prime Ministerial 'control'. Protagonists in these ritual debates normally offer only generalized 'evidence' about the resources of the Prime Minister, Cabinet colleagues, top civil servants and Whitehall departments, plus multiple anecdotes about the 'exercise of power' and the triumph of this person over that on such and such an occasion. Sweeping statements are the norm, simple summaries of complex situations, such as the growth of a 'British Presidency' (Foley 2000). In this literature 'power' is seen as unproblematic and is commonly never even defined. Judgments about the distribution of power typically proliferate in many directions, often phrased in rather broad-brush ways that create as many problems as they seem to resolve. For instance, Margaret Thatcher is conventionally portrayed as a powerful Prime Minister who easily dominated her Cabinet and Parliamentary Party. But she (eventually) was forced out of office and into effective retirement in autumn 1990 by a revolt of her own Cabinet and MPs against her continuing premiership (Jones 1995, Smith 1995). That is, Thatcher's demise resulted from a simple withdrawal of support by the very people whom she was supposed to have so cowed and subordinated. The fragility of power is also well illustrated by Peter Mandelson's roller-coaster career. These cases highlight the dangers of assigning power or influence too unconditionally or too broadly. Carefully analysed, even the power of a dictator may be seen as based on maintaining winning coalitions, although the dictator often has the ability to continually shift the composition of the winning coalition to suit their own purposes (Dowding 1991).

In the New Labour governments the difficulties in assigning power to actors at the heart of government stem from the fact that both the Prime Minister Tony Blair and the Chancellor of the Exchequer Gordon Brown are widely seen as simultaneously exercising high levels of influence over government policy. A specific trigger for this speculation has been the by now reasonably well-attested story that in the early summer of 1994 Gordon Brown agreed not to run against Tony Blair for the post of Labour leader in return for a pledge that Brown would become and remain Chancellor in a Blair-led government. This part of the deal is acknowledged, but less established is the supposed 'secret clause' that Brown would in due course inherit the leadership mantle from Blair when he stepped down, after perhaps two terms in office (Naughtie 2002). This Blair-Brown pact is widely seen as explaining the special pre-eminence of Gordon Brown, his evident status as far more than just another (potentially dispensable) senior cabinet minister within new Labour's ranks. His prominence also underpins the rise of the Treasury under his leadership to something like an alternate power centre to 10 Downing Street within British government. The Chancellor's perceived success in handling the economy, and his steady pursuit of a distinctive constituency of support within the Cabinet, the Parliamentary Labour Party and the trades union movement have given added currency to the notion that he is politically untouchable as heir apparent to Blair.

The Blair-Brown axis raises important problems. There have been almost continuous tensions between the top three positions in British government (Prime Minister, Chancellor and Foreign Secretary) stretching back to the middle 1980s and encompassing, amongst other incidents, the forced resignation of Margaret Thatcher, two Chancellors (Nigel Lawson in 1989, and Norman Lamont forced out in 1993) and two Foreign Secretaries (Geoffrey Howe, reshuffled in 1989 and finally forced out of a 'Deputy PM' role a year later, and Robin Cook, reshuffled in 2001). This history of conflict makes the Blair-Brown axis seem inherently tension-prone and unstable. How can these two key actors both be powerful at once? Surely one must be down if the other is up, on a simple 'see-saw' model of power? Or if one has a larger slice of the cake of policy influence, must that not necessarily imply that a smaller slice remains for the other?

In fact because the determination of public policy is always multi-causal, there is ample scope for both Brown and Blair to accrete influence at the same time. They could jointly claw power away from other actors in the political system, such as Cabinet ministers, civil service departments, or other tiers of government, in order to centralize influence within 10 Downing Street and the Treasury. And power is not necessarily a fixed sum or cake to be divided. Blair and Brown might simultaneously accumulate power if their government is run more successfully than previous administrations, if the capability of the government machine as a whole is expanding through New Labour's greater skill in governing and making choices. Finally they might just be beneficiaries of a more favourable (lucky) world economic and political environment, which enhances the apparent effectiveness of British government. For instance the transition to a low-inflation regime in the late 1990s across most advanced industrial economies after decades of acute inflationary pressure substantially eased some of the 'governability' problems that had plagued their predecessors.

To illuminate these and other issues of ascribing power in contemporary Britain I consider two topics in more detail: power and institutional positions, specifically within the Cabinet Committee system, widely seen as critical for governmental co-ordination and priority-setting; and some recent rational choice models which show why there will be limits on either the Prime Minister's (or the Chancellor's) abilities to shape policy in line with their preferences.

Power in the Cabinet Committee system

If it is not to run erratically from one problem or policy extreme to another, every system of government must have some internal sifting and balancing mechanisms – some ways of bringing together and comparing different considerations so as to reach a resolution of priorities. Any successful national leadership must be able to adjudicate between different sectors of government and their attendant political and social interests. In presidential systems like the United States an elected chief executive colonizes the central administration with political appointees and answers to a separately elected legislature with real control over the budgetary purse strings and the legislative timetable. American public policy thus emerges out of public compromises between multiple actors (Cameron 2000). In European parliamentary systems, by contrast, the executive emerges from the legislatures, so no separate majorities could seem feasible. However, with elections conducted by proportional representation no one party can usually command a majority on its own, and hence processes of majority coalition formation and maintenance between parties determine who is to be in government and what policies are to be followed (Tsebelis 2002: ch. 4).

In Britain there is no equivalent either to the American separation of powers or the European inter-party negotiations for balancing out policy. Whatever sorting and sifting of options occurs, and whatever adjusting of policy to meet different interests is achieved, must typically be orchestrated within a single-party government. This task is made pretty difficult because the executive normally commands a clear House of Commons majority, dominates all the budgetary and legislative levers, and operates with a reasonably strong and distinctive partisan ideology and history of governing. Meetings of the full Cabinet were historically important as the primary focus for internal balancing in the nineteenth century, a role that persisted through to the inter-war period of the twentieth century. Today these weekly Cabinet sessions perhaps remain important in concerting ministers' behaviour, securing a measure of unity and coherence in policy making at senior level, and in co-ordinating a response to periodic major governmental crises. But in the post-1945 period a system of formally constituted Cabinet Committees, which had emerged earlier, became much more important in determining how virtually all detailed public policy is made. In 1992 the then Prime Minister John Major finally acknowledged the committees' importance officially. He got rid of complete secrecy which had previously surrounded their operations, and instead began publishing a full list of the committees and their ministerial members and chairs (Dunleavy 1995a).

This change lifted a tiny part of the veil of official secrecy, which surrounds so much central policy making in Britain. It allows us to generate some hard data which are relevant for analysing the distribution of positional power. Policy making inside government is like a lottery process in one small respect – you have to be in it to win it. Where the institutional channels for making certain decisions are carefully specified and designated for people holding particular positions, we can be reasonably confident that people not holding those positions are out of the loop. Looking at which ministers sit on which Cabinet Committees can generate potentially important insights into who has the capability to influence policy, and who does not. Not all those holding positions relevant for decision X may actually mobilize resources to try and influence its outcome on issue X. And even amongst those who do mobilize, some may be more skilled and resourceful than others, and these actors will win while others lose. So knowledge of who holds what positions cannot tell us who is powerful within the involved group. But it can tell us a much more limited thing: we can be reasonably certain that people *not* holding any of the relevant ministerial and committee positions, *not* sitting around the relevant table for issue X, will also not be powerful in that area. Notice too that this claim does not imply that committees are the *only* venues in which discussions can take place. Of course, many prior discussions take place before Cabinet Committees meet – such as discussions between the key departments, 'bi-laterals' on spending issues between the Treasury and spending departments, and interventions by Downing Street. But at some stage all the threads of these diverse forms of discussions have to run together in a Cabinet Committee decision. A Cabinet Committee place is thus a passport to involvement not just in the committee meeting itself but to the preparatory work which leads up to it.

It is for this reason that Prime Ministers spend so much time thinking about the personnel permutations open to them for staffing different kinds of ministerial posts and installing people on committees. There are two key kinds of people on Cabinet Committees: ministers from relevant departments, whose presence is essentially mandatory because their brief falls within the committee's purview; and non-departmental ministers chosen by the Prime Minister to balance the committee and to look after his or her interests there, sometimes seen as 'fixers' and often including the committee chair. The main roles here are positions like the Chancellor of the Duchy of Lancaster (an empty title disguising a co-ordinating role fixed by the Prime Minister) and in the past 'Minister Without Portfolio'; plus people the Prime Minister uses to co-ordinate the government's legislative programme and organize Parliamentary business, such as the Leader of the House of Commons, Chief Whip and leader in the Lords. Occasionally departmental ministers whose briefs are fairly peripheral to a committee may nonetheless be drafted onto it to give more weight to some position that the Prime Minister favours.

Figure 18.1 shows that there are three main types of committees. (i) *Full committees* stand out because they are just below the cabinet in importance and all or virtually all their members are ministers in the cabinet. Very few if any members are junior ministers. The top-level full committees are chaired by the Prime Minister and have very few members (less than eight). The more normal full committees are chaired by the Prime Minister or other senior ministers and have a wide range of departmental or functional ministers attending and are much larger, with between 12 and 20 members. (ii) *Sub-committees* pre-process issues for the full committees. They all report to a full committee, which may modify or overturn their positions before they get to Cabinet. Sub-committees may involve junior ministers who are not of Cabinet rank, usually people called 'ministers of state' or 'parliamentary under-secretary'. Sub-committees are generally fairly flexible bodies, with new ones forming more rapidly than changes in full committees occur, to reflect

Figure 18.1   *The Cabinet Committee System in May 2001*

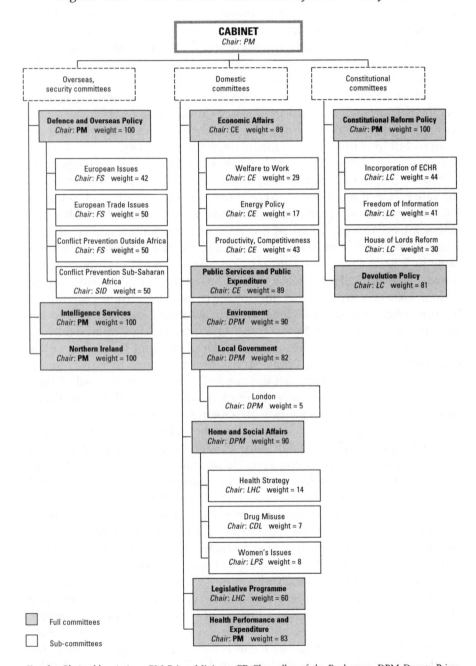

Key for Chair abbreviations: PM Prime Minister, CE Chancellor of the Exchequer; DPM Deputy Prime Minister; FS Foreign Secretary; LC Lord Chancellor; LHC Leader of the House of Commons; SID Secretary of State for International Development; CDL Chancellor of the Duchy of Lancaster; LPS Lord Privy Seal.

new issues. Older sub-committees may drift on for some time without meeting very often before being terminated. (iii) *'Symbolic' sub-committees* may be semi-permanent, addressing an issue which Whitehall's departmental structure may otherwise tend to fragment, but not very often or very vigorously. The fewer the number of Cabinet rank ministers who sit on a sub-committee, and hence the more its membership consists of junior ministers, the lower its status and the more remote it usually is from the key political issues of the day. The three sub-committees of the Home Affairs committee and the London sub-committee seem to fall into this third and least important category.

Comparing across May 1992, when John Major first published the Cabinet Committee lists and May 2001, Tony Blair's system just before the general election, allows us to see how much the set-up of committees had changed in ten years. Blair operated with considerably fewer full Cabinet Committees, 12 to Major's 16, but the same number of sub-committees, 14 in both years. Two-thirds of the full committees were the same in 2001 as nine years earlier. Some 1992 bodies disappeared, for instance, covering Hong Kong which has since been handed over to China. Others were merged, for instance, two legislation committees became one, and the previous nuclear weapons committee was re-absorbed into the wider Defence and Overseas Policy Committee. And some committees were split – the 1992 Domestic and Economic Policy Committee chaired by the Prime Minister was replaced by two committees covering Economic Affairs and Public Services and Public Expenditure (PSX), both now chaired by the Chancellor. The Prime Minister's committee places (all of which are chair positions) greatly reduced, from nine under Major to just five under Blair, chiefly because Blair had John Prescott as Deputy Leader of the Labour Party and Deputy Prime Minister to consider. He allocated Prescott three Cabinet Committees and one sub-committee to chair, all relevant to his brief covering environment and local government. But Blair also used as chairs of committees or sub-committees the Lord Chancellor, the Foreign Secretary, the Leader of the Commons, the Secretary for International Development, the Chancellor of the Duchy of Lancaster, and the Lord Privy Seal (see Figure 18.1). Chairing was quite a widely distributed role then, with eight people in the Cabinet of 23 having this experience.

The most important aspect of these changes, however, is how they affected the standing of senior ministers within the Cabinet Committee system. Here we need to be able to control for the varying importance of the different committees and sub-committees. A basic method for assigning differing weights to them was developed by Dunleavy (1994, 1995a). Committees are assigned a starting weight of 100 and sub-committees a starting weight of 50 points, and this score is then reduced in proportion to the presence of junior members on the committee. The total weight for each committee is divided evenly amongst its members, with an extra share being assigned to the chair. Figure 18.1 includes the resulting weights for each committee and sub-committee.

To see how these scores were derived, and the implications for ministers' positional power rankings, consider four examples. The Defence and Overseas Policy Committee in 2001 scored 100 points, each of its seven Cabinet members receiving 12.5 points and the Prime Minister (as chair) 25 points. The Local Government committee included a few junior ministers and so scored 82 points: each of its 17 members receiving 4.3 points and the Deputy PM (as chair) 8.6 points. The European Issues Sub-Committee started at 50 points, but with three junior ministers out of its 19 members scored 42 points; each member got 2.1 points, with a double ration for the Foreign Secretary as chair. The least important sub-committee was that for London. Again it started at 50 points, but with 10 junior ministers and only one Cabinet-rank member (the Deputy PM in the chair), its final score was just 5; each ordinary member thus attracted a weight of only 0.4 points. This approach uses the limited information we have about Cabinet Committees to control for the fact that some are clearly much more salient than others. It is the simplest feasible scheme, has a clear rationale and when applied in a consistent way it can be used to compare how the system has operated over time.

Looking across the scores which ministers received from all their committee positions, Figure 18.2 shows their relative positional influence on two dimensions:

- what proportion of all Cabinet Committee system point weights each minister controlled; and
- what each minister's average point weight was on the committees where they sat.

When the first results for 1992 under the weighting scheme above were published, they were quite controversial (Dunleavy, 1994, 1995a). They suggested that the Prime Minister accounted for less than 15 per cent of the scores in the committee system as a whole, although well ahead of his nearest rival, the Foreign Secretary on 9 per cent of all scores, and the Chancellor in fourth place on less than 7 per cent. However, the analysis also showed the PM had an average of 28 points for all committees where he sat, more than three times greater than the levels for any other Cabinet minister, so that he was clearly far and away the most influential person in Cabinet.

Applying the same method in 2001 Figure 18.2 shows that there was a

Figure 18.2   *Two measures of Cabinet ministers' positional influence in May 2001, and changes in the positions of major Cabinet posts, 1992–2001*

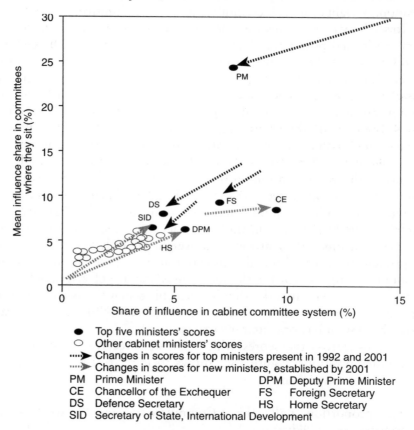

- ● Top five ministers' scores
- ○ Other cabinet ministers' scores
- ┄┄▶ Changes in scores for top ministers present in 1992 and 2001
- ┄┄▶ Changes in scores for new ministers, established by 2001

PM Prime Minister	DPM Deputy Prime Minister
CE Chancellor of the Exchequer	FS Foreign Secretary
DS Defence Secretary	HS Home Secretary
SID Secretary of State, International Development	

dramatic change in the pattern of scores under Labour. Tony Blair's share of the points across the whole Cabinet Committee system shrank dramatically to less than 9 per cent. At the same time Gordon Brown's share of total points rose dramatically, giving him the largest personal share of any Cabinet minister. The Prime Minister still remains much more influential on those committees where he sits than anyone else, but in terms of presence across the committee system as a whole he is clearly ranked number 2 to the Chancellor, who chairs two new and powerful committees. The arrows in Figure 18.2 show how the Prime Minister's and the Chancellor's positions under Labour differ from those of nine years' earlier. They seem to offer striking confirmation of the importance of the Blair-Brown pact and of the extent to which Brown's status rose as a result. Nor is that all – for the other three ministers in the Cabinet's top five ranks under Major (the Foreign Secretary, Defence Secretary and Home Secretary) also posted significant declines in their shares of Cabinet Committee system points in 2001, further enhancing the Chancellor's new prominence. In addition, the Treasury second-in-command, the Chief Secretary, was in the 2001 Cabinet. In fact, he moved into the top ten ministers in terms of shares of points across the committee system as a whole, giving the Treasury far more prominence than before, and more than one in seven of the available committee points.

But looking a little closer also shows some changes which reflect different Labour priorities in government. Other shifts suggest a sophisticated Blair style of Cabinet management which perhaps hoodwinks the Chancellor by appearing to give away more influence than it actually does. Historically, Labour assigns less of a priority to defence than have the Tories. And some part of the declines recorded for the Prime Minister, Foreign Secretary and Defence Secretary reflects the arrival on the Defence and Overseas Policy committee and its sub-committees of Clare Short, heading the Department for International Development, set up by Blair in 1997 to reflect Labour's stronger emphasis upon overseas aid to developing countries. John Prescott's role as Deputy Prime Minister also accounts for much of the remaining changes, as he became the fourth member of the Cabinet in terms of sharing points across the committee system. It might be debated to what extent Blair can rely on Prescott for unswerving or unconditional support, although in practice he has seemed very close to Blair on most issues.

But Blair also clearly took steps to give himself eyes and ears on the domestic committees and sub-committees where he did not sit. The new junior post of Minister of State in the Cabinet Office was created for Lord Falconer, a close personal friend of Blair, who moved straight into ninth rank across all ministers, despite being outside the Cabinet. The Prime Minister could also rely on the Chancellor of the Duchy of Lancaster. Table 18.1 shows that the effect of Blair's jugglings was to reduce considerably the loss of positional influence apparently implied in Figure 18.2. Indeed, if it is legitimate to count the Deputy Prime Minister as squarely in the Blair camp, then the Prime Minister's bloc's share of the points across the cabinet system as whole did not shrink but slightly grew under Labour. Elsewhere, the Lord Chancellor (Lord Irvine, a close career and personal friend of Blair's) and the Chief Whip moved up the rankings of ministers appreciably, to eleventh and twelfth places in the rankings, putting their normally low salience posts above all the major departmental ministers. Adding them in as well would take the Prime Minister bloc's share to over a quarter of all Cabinet Committee system points in 2001, up considerably on 1992. Of course Major had allies in his Cabinet, but amongst ministers who had their own independent personal and political basis for being there, and who seemed much less dependent on him for their positions chairing

Table 18.1 *How the PM's and the Chancellor's blocs matched up in 1992 and 2001*

	% of all points in the cabinet committee system		
	1992	*2001*	*Change 1992 to 2001*
Chancellor alone	6.4	9.5	+3.1
All Treasury ministers	10.7	13.8	+3.1
PM alone	14.9	7.6	−7.3
PM bloc (includes CDL in 1997, and MSCO + CDL in 2001)	19.3	14.5	−4.8
PM bloc + Deputy PM	19.3	20.2	+0.7
PM bloc + DPM + LC +CW	24.2	26.9	+2.7

Notes: MSCO is the Minister of State, Cabinet Office; CDL is the Chancellor of the Duchy of Lancaster; LC is the Lord Chancellor; CW is the Chief Whip.

committees. The Chief Whip under Major was also less prominent in terms of his position. On this basis, the Prime Minister's personal involvement has declined, but the presence of his wider 'bloc' is not much changed. Blair wields his influence more at one remove, where Major seemed to have felt more that he needed to be present in person at committees.

Apart from Prescott, the heads of most major Whitehall departments lost ground somewhat under Blair, because the top positions in the cabinet committee system were carved up between the Prime Minister's allies (including the parliamentary/legislative ministers) and the Treasury. The Trade and Industry Secretary moved downwards sharply, falling from eight in importance in 1997 to fifteenth in 2001. An exception was the Secretary of State for Social Security, who acquired some new prominence (again reflecting a pattern typical of previous Labour governments changing over from the Tories, for whom this welfare state role was less important). The biggest loser in the new cabinet structures was the Secretary of State for Scotland, whose rank plunged from tenth in 1992 to twentieth in 2001 on the weighting system used here. This change reflecting the Scottish Office's much reduced role because of legislative devolution to Scotland. By contrast, the Welsh Secretary actually acquired more points share in 2001, although moving down the ranking of ministers slightly.

Of course, this analysis provides only a starting point for discussion. The precise scores given here can easily be varied by changing the starting weights assigned to committee or sub-committees, and by assigning a greater or less weight to committee chairs *vis-à-vis* ordinary committee members. But notice that the *patterns* shown here are very, very resistant to change. If you want to increase the positional power of the Prime Minister you have to weight full committees as more than twice as important as sub-committees and also increase the weight of committee chairs to more than twice that of ordinary members. But these same changes will benefit all the other top five ministers as well as the Prime Minister, and strengthen the power of the Chancellor in 2001 and his increase in influence relative to the Prime Minister. Similarly, it is possible to pick on any particular minister's ranking in positional terms and dispute it. But however you score these positions the scope for changing any minister's relative position against others is really quite small.

In sum, the Cabinet Committee data give an important insight into Blair's leadership style. They unequivocally show him conceding a far greater role to his Chancellor on domestic policy issues than his Conservative predecessor. Blair restricted his own committee system activity in 2001 to three key committees with tiny memberships that he must chair (Defence and Overseas Policy, the Intelligence Services, Northern Ireland) and two others: Constitutional Reform Policy, and a special case committee on Health Performance and Expenditure, carved out of the Chancellor's public expenditure domain in 2000 because of its central political significance for Labour's election pledges. For the rest Blair seems to rely more than Major did on trusted allies and agents to chair and to nudge policy in the 'right' direction, and to give a committee presence to his influential Downing Street special advisors and larger Number 10 staff.

The data on committee allocations are not much help if we want to go further, and to understand how influence is distributed amongst those clearly involved in decision-making. To understand these wider aspects we can turn to what we know about the core executive's internal operations in a general way, and consider how rational actor models may help us shed more systematic light on what is going on.

Thinking about power using rational choice models

Why does the Prime Minister not decide every contentious issue in government? Since they appoint and can dismiss every minister, why are their preferences not just simply decisive, sweeping through and overriding the views of other ministers? Of course the Prime Minister's involvement may be limited for logistical reasons. There are only so many hours in a day to master information and decide upon policy options, and there are multiple competing demands upon his or her time, especially in the fields of foreign affairs and overseas summitry. But with the burgeoning Number 10 staff to assist him, why should

Blair not have been able to extend his competence ever more widely, using them to pre-process issues for his attention and then to police what ministers and Whitehall departments do about implementing a wide range of decisions he wants to see go through?

One obvious constraining possibility is the rivalry between PM and Chancellor. Perhaps Blair has been thwarted in his efforts by the growth of Treasury influence? Public expenditure control requires Treasury involvement in almost all major policy choices and the Blair-Brown pact has given the Chancellor an unassailable political position. But if Brown has in fact been guaranteed a 'reserved area' of mainly domestic policy to influence, then the same questions apply equally to him. Why are there limits on Treasury control? Why cannot his officials simply refuse to fund any scheme with which Brown disagrees, keeping the money tap turned off until departmental ministers come round to his way of seeing things?

To understand some of the limits on Prime Ministerial and Treasury power some simple rational choice models can help. At their foundation is the idea that decision making entails 'transactions costs' for those who take part. To launch an issue or try to change or defend their policies, any minister or actor must take risks of failing, losing reputation and incurring penalties (such as seeming weak and ineffective, or even risking losing office altogether). Win or lose, those senior actors who decide to get involved in any given policy scrap must also immediately run up costs in marshalling information, trying to justify more funding, writing policy documents, and lobbying potential allies in Whitehall, the Cabinet and the parliamentary party. None of these activities comes cheap in terms of information, time, reputation and other political resources. The longer an issue drags on, the more these downside cost factors and political risks will rise.

In fact the whole British policy system is structured to take advantage of this feature of rising transactions costs over time. Issues or initiatives start off in departmental or inter-departmental working groups of officials before they migrate from the network of 'official' committees into the cabinet committee system involving ministers. No department can manage this transition without the agreement and active support of their departmental minister. Since most major and many quite minor policy initiatives require public spending or changes in the law, departments are also rarely in a position to change things on their own. They have to take their case and make it work before a sceptical Treasury anxious to curtail the growth of the department's spending, or make cutbacks, or at the least secure important efficiency improvements in return for more funding. Often too the department and its minister must argue for parliamentary time and priority with an even more sceptical set of ministers managing the government's legislative and parliamentary processes.

Behind all these interactions lies 'the shadow of the Prime Minister', as Albert Breton (1998) describes the Prime Minister's role in the Westminster systems as the ultimate core executive tie-breaker, the person who can knock together the heads of recalcitrant parties, enforcing a final deal on everyone.

Yet despite the strong concentration of resources in the Prime Minister's hands described in detail in institutional accounts, there are significant limits on the premier's ability to get their way because other actors are 'first movers', and they can perhaps settle issues early on before they ever get bid up to the Prime Minister. Perhaps the most important and pervasive policy scrutiny process in British government is that where departments seek budgetary approval for new or existing programmes from the Treasury. Both sides know that if they cannot reach agreement between themselves in bilateral discussions, then the unresolved issues will have to be referred up to the Public Services and Public Expenditure (PSX) committee of the cabinet, which is chaired by the Chancellor and mostly includes non-departmental ministers. Issues that PSX in turn cannot determine will generally go to the Prime Minister to resolve. (There is a notional recourse to a full cabinet vote as well, but the Prime Minister very rarely allows this option to be activated). However, bidding up issues from bilateral discussions between the Treasury and the department to the PSX committee or to the Prime Minister carries transactions costs for both sides, in terms of extra preparation, disapproval from top government personnel if trivial issues are added to their workload unnecessarily, and risks that the policy decision will go off in directions that the department or Treasury may not like.

We can look at this process in stages using some simple diagrams. Figure 18.3 shows the opening stage of the budgetary process. Both the department and the Treasury define their ideal positions on a dimension running from high to low levels of spending. We can assume that the department officials are generally keen to spend more and the Treasury to spend less on a programme. The civil servants in the department are limited in what they can propose by the attitude of their minister, whose

Figure 18.3 *The UK core executive budget process 1*

The department and the Treasury try to resolve their disagreements in bilateral bargaining

agreement is essential before the issue can go into the budgetary or cabinet systems for processing. We show the minister's optimum position here as next to the department's, but to the right and hence a bit closer to the Treasury position. (Of course, different situations could easily arise). A large gulf still separate the minister's proposal from the Treasury's ideal point however. In negotiations they will almost certainly split the difference between them if they can. But whereabouts exactly?

To formulate a realistic position both the minister and the Treasury will try to anticipate what will happen if they do not reach an agreement but instead the issue gets bid up to a higher level in the Cabinet Committee system. Figure 18.4 shows that at stage 2 their divergent views would go to the PSX committee to resolve, which as drawn here has a more centrist ideal point between the minister's and the Treasury's positions, but more towards the Treasury end of the dimension. (This position would actually be that of the crucial deciding member of the committee – which might be the Chancellor who is chairing it, or of the member of the committee most in the middle in this controversy, but we need not go into such complications here). Given his or her position is a long way from the PSX point, the department minister clearly has to compromise, to try and offer the PSX committee a settlement that they will find just a little bit better than the Treasury's position. A rational minister will pitch her or his case to the committee just to the right of the PSX (T) position, a very important location which has a special name. It is the committee's 'reflection point' for the Treasury, defined as being the same distance to the left of the committee's ideal point as the Treasury's demand is to the right of it. Remember that the PSX committee wants to get as close as it can to its ideal point. A bid just to the right of the PSX

Figure 18.4   *The UK core executive budget process 2*

The issue is bid up to the PSX committee in stage 2

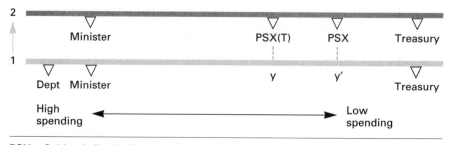

PSX = Cabinet's Public Services and Public Expenditure Committee
PSX(T) = PSX's reflection point for Treasury position

(T) reflection point would still involve more spending than the committee really wants to approve. But the committee will prefer this outcome to making the deep cuts which the Treasury are holding out for. Notice too that in negotiating to the right of PSX (T), the departmental minister can also know that the worst outcome they can finish up with is a settlement at the committee's ideal point PSX. The minister will never risk getting an outcome at the Treasury's position so long they are willing to compromise. The Treasury may try to combat departmental concessions, by moving its own position closer to the PSX ideal point. If both the departmental minister and the Treasury can successfully anticipate where the PSX committee stands they will realize that they should settle within the range y to y' shown on the lower scale.

Perhaps the Treasury could force the issue even higher, however, beyond the PSX committee and up to the Prime Minister to decide. To justify this risky step, and to get the Prime Minister's attention, the issue would have to be a significant one in expenditure terms or one with considerable political implications. But if the Treasury knows that the Prime Minister's ideal point is closer to their position than the committee's is then they might be prepared to bear the costs of this course. Figure 18.5 shows a situation where the Prime Minister is indeed keener to hold down spending than the PSX committee. So the departmental minister will have to make more concessions, pitching his or her bid at a point closer to the Prime Minister's optimum than the Treasury's position. So the final proposal from the minister would be to the right of the Prime Minister's reflection point for the Treasury, somewhere between the point PM (T)

Figure 18.5   *The UK core executive budget process 3*

The issue is bid up to the Prime Minister by Treasury in stage 3

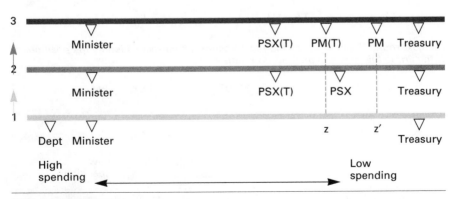

PM = Prime Minister
PSX(T) = PSX's reflection point for Treasury position
PM(T) = PM's reflection point for Treasury position

and the Prime Minister's optimum on the stage 3 dimension line. Again the Treasury could only counter this move by converging its own position towards the Prime Minister's optimum point. If the departmental minister and the Treasury had both been able to anticipate that the issue would be bid up all the way to the Prime Minister, and to accurately identify where the Prime Minister stood on the issue, they would have negotiated between them within the range z to z' shown on the original bargaining line at the bottom of Figure 18.5.

There are good reasons to believe that the elite actors in the cabinet and in Whitehall will be able to anticipate pretty well how the PSX committee and the Prime Minister are likely to react on any spending issue. Cabinet colleagues will know the Prime Minister and other PSX committee members well at a personal level and have ample opportunity to study their views and reactions. The civil servants in the department and Treasury will also know in detail what is the balance of political and social or economic benefits and costs in each issue area. So if all the actors involved hold the positions diagrammed here, then right from the earliest stages of bilateral bargaining between the minister and the Treasury both sides will know that the range of potentially viable solutions is that shown as y to z' in Figure 18.6. In other words if actors behave rationally, and prefer to get the closest possible outcomes to their position, then the range of feasible solutions runs from the PSX (T) point at the high-spending end to the Prime Minister's position at the low-spending end.

Notice where this leaves the Prime Minister though – occupying an 'extreme' position within the feasible range, which is highly unlikely to be reached. The Prime Minister will not get exactly what he or she wants on this issue unless the Treasury insist on bidding the issue all the way up the

Figure 18.6   *The UK core executive budget process 4*

The next round if departments and the Treasury can correctly identify the positions of the Prime Minister and the PSX committee

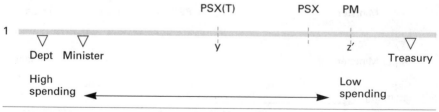

PM = Prime Minister
PSX(T) = PSX's reflection point for Treasury position
PM(T) = Prime Minister's reflection point for Treasury position

cabinet committee hierarchy. Until the last possible moment the Treasury must be determined to defeat and humiliate the departmental minister, whatever the transaction costs and other risks involved. Such a protracted struggle is unlikely to occur frequently. Far more commonly the departmental minister and the Treasury will do a deal somewhere in the range from y to z′ in their early bilateral discussions, so that the decision will become a fait accompli, never to trouble the Prime Minister's busy agenda. Because other actors have strong 'first mover' advantages, the Prime Minister may get something of what they want some of the time. But they will very rarely exercise the unfettered and detailed ability to fix policy claimed by the exponents of 'Prime Ministerial dominance' arguments.

This point could be firmed up further, and generalized beyond the budgetary process to apply to all kinds of policy discussions and debates within the core executive, for example by looking at situations where the Prime Minister's influence may be cut out altogether or severely reduced). The cases considered so far assume that ministers adopt positions close to those of their departmental civil servants. But what if they do not? If the Prime Minister appoints the 'wrong' person to head up a Whitehall department, someone out of sympathy with its basic mission, the results can be disastrous for the government. Where the wrong person is picked, the normal weak checks and balances of the Cabinet Committee system can be completely short-circuited. In the early 1980s Margaret Thatcher put her ideological mentor, Sir Keith Joseph, in charge of the Department of Industry for two years, even though he opposed all state intervention in the economy and kept holding seminars with his civil servants on whether to close down the department. His stance did not prevent policy interventions from occurring as the economy sagged and unemployment soared, but it did rob departmental policy of much of its coherence. Later on in the decade Thatcher repeated the mistake when Nicholas Ridley was made Secretary of State for the Environment and made no secret of his disdain for green issues, and eventually left the Cabinet after a separate row over his anti-EU remarks.

A second main source of difficulty for Prime Ministers arises from the multi-dimensionality of politics, the fact that most policy problems are not just about one thing, but instead involve several connected aspects (see Dunleavy 1995b for a case study). The paradox for a Prime Minister is that the more influence she has on where policy is fixed, the less difference she can make by intervening personally to decide anything. A Prime Minister confronting such problems, and able to find out what they were, will try to fight being pushed to the sidelines in various ways. For instance, a Prime Minister could do what Blair has done, developing a strong staff in 10 Downing Street, and trying to make the perennially useless (or perennially constrained) Cabinet Office better at shaping policy options and generating strategies or implementation ideas. Like Blair too, he or she could appoint trusted colleagues to sit on Cabinet Committees as their eyes and ears and tied votes, and use patronage or other incentives they control to persuade ministers to move policy closer to the premier's ideal point. We might think that an intelligent and middle-of-the-road premier like Blair, instinctively inclined to Third Way solutions and able to grasp a lot of policy information, might have more personal influence in changing policy formation than someone who adopts cruder or more extreme positions, like Margaret Thatcher. But no such effect is obvious empirically. And even if we could reliably establish such variation in the capabilities of individual premiers, it might not make a huge impact. There are only so many issues that a Prime Minister can intervene on, and they can never be more than a fraction of the flow of business through the Cabinet Committee system, forcing him or her to radically prioritize his or her time and effort.

It is also no accident that so much of this section has focused on budgetary issues. Any Prime Minister struggling to get their policy preferences enacted against a Chancellor of the Exchequer with different views will face an uphill struggle in the Cabinet Committee system, even in finding out what ministers and departments have agreed with the Treasury. But on issues where he disagrees with Gordon Brown, Blair must face a very substantial extra burden because he has conceded so much additional positional advantage to his rival, so much extra weight within the committee places and rankings. The Chancellor also derives immense reputational advantage from the widespread talk about the Blair-Brown pact, which makes him seem politically invulnerable, as no doubt his supporters hope. Departmental ministers have stronger incentives to get on well with Brown since they know that he will be there for the long run, and perhaps will inherit the premier's mantle at the end of his chancellorship. So this theoretical analysis in terms of rational choice models provides strong circumstantial reasons for believing that perhaps the empirical changes captured in Figure 18.2 above are real ones. These changes almost seem to signal a 'split premiership', with Brown in control of much domestic policy and Blair confined to foreign affairs and the few domestic policy issues which he can take directly under his wing, such as aspects of health service modernization, and educational policy change.

The Prime Minister has a last power which can be used *in extremis* to enforce their will, but again not without costs. This source of influence is their veto-power, their capacity to intervene late on to stop progress towards an outcome they oppose, a capability much discussed for other chief executives like the United States President (Camero, 2000). Even if Number 10 and the Prime Minister have not been extensively involved in an issue early on, they may still be able to halt initiatives they find objectionable, spotting and stopping deals which have already been done between the department and the Treasury, or between the department and the guardians of the legislative programme. This 'last mover' competence seems dramatic. But it also entails costs for the Prime Minister to intervene to scrap the progress made on a new spending programme or new legislation, and instead send the issue back to the drawing board. Often the government *has* to do something about pressing issues that will not go away and cannot be delayed, so it will face political costs if it does nothing (Thompson 1995, Keliher 1995). And other actors may easily anticipate the threat of a Prime Ministerial veto by placing their proposals just within the bounds of acceptability – for example, choosing an outcome that is just better for the PM than the policy status quo. A premier who then aborts progress has to live with an even less satisfactory status quo. So even the veto power may be a more limited resource for the Prime Minister than institutional accounts normally acknowledge.

Conclusion

Writing just after the English civil war in the mid-seventeenth century, the philosopher Thomas Hobbes argued that a powerful person needs friends and servants, wealth to buy friendship and service, a reputation for being powerful to attract the adherence of people needing protection, and success to seem lucky or wise (either of which will tend to make opponents back off from open conflicts with them). In the more settled institutional context of contemporary British government, presence on the right committees and agenda control over their business are current corollaries, along with relevant ministerial roles. Both Blair and Brown can use institutional and political resources to 'buy' friends and maintain thriving factions in partial tension and conflict across the Labour government and the wider Labour movement. The importance of allies within the heart of government arises from the detailed budgetary and policy-making arrangements within the core executive. We have shown that important mechanisms are in place which inherently limit the influence of any given position to control policy making at different levels or different sectors of the overall decision-making system. On their own the Prime Minister and Chancellor control only narrow strategic bridgeheads within the committee system. But with organized blocs they may operate a controlling duopoly for now, and muster resources for a possible future showdown, a polite undercover civil war between the 'royalist' Blair and the 'puritan' Brown for the soul of the Labour movement.

Guide to Further Reading

Chapter 2   Remaking the Constitution

An indispensable source on how the constitutional reform programme is unfolding is the Constitution Unit, especially their Monitor which appears four times a year. Their website is www.ucl.ac.uk/constitution-unit. For arguments on all sides of the constitutional argument see Johnson (1999), Hutton (1995), Heffer (1999), Freedland (1998) Bogdanor (1997) and Barnett (1997). Parliament is well covered by Riddell (1998) and the Monarchy by Bogdanor (1995). See also the Fabian Society (2003). The constitutional implications of the European Union are analysed in Siedentop (2000). For an account of the rise of Charter 88 see Evans (1995).

Chapter 3   The Europeanization of British Politics

The history of Britain's relationship with the EU is covered by George (1998) and Young (1999), while Baker and Seawright (1998) offer detailed issue driven analyses. Good introductory accounts of the EU include George and Bache (2001) and McCormick (2002). More detailed and advanced discussion of EU institutions and policy-making dynamics can be found in Richardson (2001) and Wallace and Wallace (2000). The concept of Europeanization is variously covered by Bomberg and Peterson (2000), Börzel (2002), Knill (1998, 2001), Knill and Lehmkuhl (1999), Ladrech (2001) and Radaelli (2000). Specific analyses of Europeanization in Britain can be found in Annesley (2001), Bulmer and Burch (2001) and George (2001). A very good analysis of Britain and EMU is Gamble and Kelly (2002). The principal source of information about the EU on the internet is http://europa.eu.int while information on the European Convention can be found at http://european-convention.eu.int. The European Commission's representation in Britain is at http://www.cec.org.uk while information about British public opinion and European integration can be accessed from http://www.data-archive.ac.uk/findingData/euroBarometer.asp.

Chapter 4   The Core Executive and the Modernization of Central Government

For the recent debate on the Prime Minister and Cabinet see Hennessy (2001) and Foley (2000). The Core Executive framework is developed in Rhodes and Dunleavy (1995) and Smith (1999). For a recent and useful account of developments in Number 10 see Kavanagh and Seldon (1999). For the role of the Cabinet Office see Lee, Jones and Burnham (1998) and for an examination of the impact of the EU see Bulmer and Burch (1998). On joined-up government Perri 6 *et al.* (2002) give a good account of the key issues. For recent developments at the centre see the webpages at Number 10 and the Cabinet Office which are available through www.ukonline.gov.uk. For an examination of the wider context, and the impact of Europeanization and glob-alization, in which changes are occurring see Richards and Smith (2002) and Rose (2001).

Chapter 5   Political Culture and Voting Participation

The best work on recent trends in political participation and political percep-tions in Britain can be found in the British Social Attitudes series: Bromley and Curtice (2002). Bromley, Curtice and Seyd, B. (2001) present a large amount of evidence covering a vast range of issues in an informative manner. A longer time series is provided by Heath and Taylor (1999), who also examine issues of theory. Comparative perspectives on turnout are provided by Franklin (2001) while Norris (2002) covers cross-national themes in other forms of political participation. Those interested in young people's political participation will find White, Bruce and Ritchie, (2000) a useful source of information. Park (1999) provides a good introduction to evidence and issues and Plutzer (2002) presents advanced analysis with a more theoretical emphasis. Websites are plen-tiful: www.edemocracy.gov.uk presents the proposals in the Government's consultation on e-democracy and www.electoralcommission.org.uk contains useful reports a range of issues.

Chapter 6   Changing Voting Systems

Good recent accounts of the broader comparative literature on alternative voting systems are given in Bingham Powell (2000) and Colomer (2001). On electoral systems in general, see Dummett (1997) and Farrell (2001). The Jenkins Report (1988) remains essential reading for the future, and on recent electoral reform in Britain see Dunleavy and Margetts (2001). Lijphart (1994) and (1999) provides analysis of electoral system impacts on democratic processes.

Chapter 7   Political Parties and the Party System

Useful up-to-date recent histories of the major parties are provided by Seyd (2002), Norton (2002) and Denver (2002) while King (2002) and Butler and Kavanagh (2002) contain studies of the 2001 election and brief histories of the parties in the 1997 Parliament. Webb (2000) remains the best introductory text on British parties and the party system, and both Ware (1996) and Maor (1997) apply theoretical approaches to British party politics. Dalton and Wattenberg (2002) contains an excellent collection of essays on the comparative study of parties, which illuminates study of the British case. This is well complemented by Gunther, Montero and Linz (2002) and Muller and Strom (1999). Hay (1999), Heffernan (2001), Ludlam and Smith (2001) and Driver and Martell (2002) discuss the changing nature of the Labour Party, and Norris (1997a) and Denver (2002a) provide an overview of the changing electoral environment within which British parties are located, as does Sanders (2002).

Chapter 8   The Media and Politics

On the general idea of public relations politics see Davis (2002), which examines the expansion of professional public relations and its impact on the media and political process in contemporary Britain. Manning (2001) provides an excellent analysis of the relationship between sources and news media within a broadly political–economic framework, while Barnett and Gaber (2001) examine the interdependence between politicians and media with an emphasis on political journalism and its practitioners. Writing from the perspective of a BBC political correspondent, Jones (1993; 1999; 2002) provides an informative and stimulating insider account of politicians' attempts to manage the news. For an academic analysis of the relationship between the Blair government and the media see Scammell (2001). Finally, Blumler and Gurevitch (1995), Franklin (1997) McNair (2000) and Norris (2000) examine from different perspectives the notion of a 'crisis' in public communication, covering issues such as the professionalization of communication techniques by political actors, adversarial journalism, the alleged 'dumbing-down' of news and the possible consequences for audiences in terms of voters' civic knowledge and attitudes to political participation.

Chapter 9   Politics in Scotland

There is vast and growing literature on Scottish politics and for reviews of these see McGarvey (2001) and Mitchell (2001). Useful studies on voting behaviour and public opinion include those by Brown *et al.* eds (1999) (2000), and a short historical overview of political parties in Scotland is provided by Hutchison (2001). Of the numerous works on devolution, the best legal overview is Burrows (2000) and Wright (2000) makes some interesting contributions on the politics of devolution, including good work on policy making under devolution. The current affairs journal Scottish Affairs is a lively forum for debates at a level of high journalism, and carries some important updates on research of Scottish politics.

Chapter 10   Politics in Northern Ireland

Dixon (2001) offers an illuminating account of how much of the peace process was choreographed by the British, Irish and American governments, assisted by the political parties. Tonge (2002b) argues that the peace process was constructed because of the changed political agenda of republicans. Hennessey (2002) offers a detailed guide to the negotiations leading to the Good Friday Agreement and Wilford (2001) and O'Leary (1999) provide thoughtful analyses of the consociational basis of the Good Friday Agreement and the precarious institutions created by the deal. Maloney (2002) offers one of the most authoritative works yet produced on the IRA and a comprehensive and intellectually rigorous pre-Good Friday Agreement analysis of the basis of the Northern Ireland problem is provided by McGarry and O'Leary (1995).

Chapter 11   Politics in England and Wales

There is a growing literature on the working of devolution including the regions. Especially useful are Hazell (2001) and Trench (2001) and Wales is well covered in Chaney, Hall and Pithouse (2001). Regional and decentralized government is explored in Pierre (1995). London government is well covered in Travers and Jones (1997) and Pimlott and Rao (2002). On local government more generally Rao (2000) and Pratchett (2000) offer an excellent discussion of the issues surrounding local democracy and the modern local government agenda. Stewart (2000) and Wilson and Game (2002) offer a thorough overview of all aspects of local government. Stoker (2000) provides an overview of the new politics of local government and management issues. Jones (2002) looks at local government finance. Jones and Stewart (2003) look at central control. Websites are an essential tool for keeping up to date in these fields. Particularly useful are the Constitution Unit website http://www.ucl.ac.uk/constitution-unit/ which monitors developments in the various parts of the United Kingdom and the Office of the Deputy Prime Minister website (www.odpm.gov.uk). The Local Government Association website (www.lga.gov.uk) and NLGN (www.nlgn.org.uk) website are also a source of much useful material.

Chapter 12   Asymmetric Devolution: Toward a Quasi-Federal Constitution?

Pilkington (2002) provides a basic introductory discussion of devolution and its impacts, while Bogdanor (2001) is the best text on the subject published so far. The Constitutional Unit based at University College, London has produced two useful texts on post-1997 constitutional reform in the UK, edited by Hazell (2000) and Tench (2001). It also produces a quarterly bulletin, The Monitor, which provides an update on constitutional developments, http://www.ucl.ac.uk/constitution-unit/reports/monitor.htm and has an useful ancillary webpage, Nations and Regions: The Dynamics of Devolution, at http://www.ucl.ac.uk/constitution-unit/leverh/index.htm. Aughey (2001) is worth consulting on the nationalist challenge devolution poses to the British state, as is Nairn (2002) Elcock and Keating (1998) and Bulmer et al (2002) consider the wider impacts devolution has on politics and public policy. The House of Commons fact sheet, Scottish and Welsh Business (2000), is also worth consulting at http://www.parliament.uk/commons/lib/fs65.pdf

Chapter 13   Ideas and Policy Agendas in Contemporary Politics

The best introduction to the concept of ideology remains Freeden (1996). The idea of the Third Way has had an extensive discussion but the best place to start remains Giddens (1998 and 2000) and the collection of essays edited by Giddens (2001). The Third Way as an ideological form is discussed by Lukes (1999) White (2001) and Plant (2001). For a polemical critique of the Third Way as a new direction for social democracy see Callinicos (2001). On social and political changes that underpin the turn to Third Way thinking such as globalization see Held and McGrew (1999). The literature on the political theory of equality is vast, new approaches focusing on basic income, stakeholding and asset based eqalitarianism can be found in Van Parijs (1995) and Ackerman and Alstott (1999), see also the IPPR website as www.ippr.org. For a source of ideas that is increasingly being taken up in Conservative policy making see www.civitas.org The Conservative party website remains a good source of recent speeches www.conservative-party.org.uk and Tony Blair's speeches can be accessed at the Downing Street website.

Chapter 14   Economic Policy

Grant (2002) and Middleton (2000) provides an introduction to British economic policy and performance since 1945. Heffernan (2001) analyses the intellectual links between the Thatcherite settlement and New Labour. Scholte (2000) offers a comprehensive survey of the globalization debate and Deakin and Parry (2000) provide excellent insights into the role of the Treasury under New Labour. A journalistic but nevertheless useful account of the pivotal relationship between Gordon Brown and Tony Blair can be found in Naughtie (2002). Balls and O'Donnell (2002), is an interesting attempt by the Treasury to provide its own textbook account of current economic policy.

Chapter 15   Public Services

For an audit of New Labour's performance in regard to health, education and welfare policy during its first term, see Dixon (2001), Brighouse (2001) and

McCormick (2001). Toynbee and Walker (2001) provide an audit of the Labour government's successes and failures across a range of public policy fields. For further analysis of public–private partnerships, PFI and the future of public services, see Institute of Public Policy Research (2001) and the following websites:
http://www.society.guardian.co.uk/privatefinance
http://www.society.guardian.co.uk/futureforpublicservices

Chapter 16   Environmental Policy

For a recent and very thorough treatment of environmental politics in its policy, theoretical, and party and pressure group dimensions see Carter (2001). For works more specific to UK environmental politics and policy in its European and global context see Garner (2000) Gray (1995) and Lowe and Ward (1998).

Chapter 17   Britain in the International Arena

Hershberg and Moore (2002) provide analysis of 11 September and its impacts across the world and Hirsh (2002) presents a useful analysis of the foreign policy of the Bush Administration and the United States' sense of its place in the world, both before and after 11 September. A good general introduction to the foreign policy of the Labour government (and of New Labour's sense of international politics) is the edited collection by Little and Wickham-Jones (2000). Vickers (2000) and (2003b) looks at Labour's external policy in the 1997 Parliament, and Wheeler and Dunne (1998) critically examine its ideological underpinnings.

Chapter 18   Analysing Political Power

Two good short books analysing the concept of power are those by Dowding (1996) (1991). Morriss (2002) provides a longer and wordier account and makes mistakes later on, but chapters 2 to 11 are helpful. The best empirical coverage of where power lies within the core executive can be found in Rhodes and Dunleavy (1995) which includes several useful case studies of limits on the PM's power, especially Jones (1995), Keliher (1995), Thompson (1995) and Dunleavy (1995b). It also has a chapter on how to measure influence in Cabinet Committees, Dunleavy (1995a); or alternatively see Dunleavy (1994). The best coverage of more conventional literature on who has 'power' in Britain, none of which even seems to define 'power' before starting, is given in Weir and Beetham (1999), chapters 6 to 8. For rational choice approaches there is currently no UK work, but Breton (1998) is a Canadian's analysis which applies to Britain and Cameron (2000) uses a similar approach to that here to look at US Presidents' influence over Congress.

Bibliography

Ackerman, B. and Alstott, A. (1999) *The Stakeholder Society*, New Haven, CT, Yale University Press.

Aldrich, J. H. (1993) 'Rational Choice and Turnout', *American Journal of Political Science*, 37, pp. 246–78.

Allen, G. (2001) *The Last Prime Minister: Being Honest About the UK Presidency*, London, Politicos.

Almond, G. and Verba, S. (1963) *The Civic Culture: Political Attitudes and Democracy in Five Nations*, Princeton, NJ, Princeton University Press.

Anderson, P. and Mann, N. (1997) *Safety First: The Making of New Labour*, London, Granta Books.

Anderson, P. J. and Weymouth, A. (1999) *Insulting the Public? The British Press and the European Union*, London, Longman.

Annesley, C. (2001) 'UK Social Policy: Between Europeanisation and Americanisation', http://www.york.ac.uk/depts/poli/juc/2001/capaper.htm

Ashdown, P. (2000) *The Ashdown Diaries Volume 1: 1988–1997*, London, Allen Lane.

Aughey, A. (2001) *Nationalism, Devolution and the Challenge to the United Kingdom State*, London, Pluto Press.

Bache, I. (1998) *The Politics of European Union Regional Policy: Multilevel Governance or Flexible Gatekeeping?* Sheffield, Sheffield Academic Press/UACES.

Bache, I. (1999) 'The Extended Gatekeeper: Central Government and the Implementation of EU Regional Policy in the UK', *Journal of European Public Policy*, 6(1), pp. 28–45.

Bagehot, W. (1963) *The English Constitution* London, Fontana.

Baker, D. and Seawright, D. (eds) (1998) *Britain for and Against Europe: British Politics and the Question of European Integration* Oxford, Oxford University Press.

Baker, D., Gamble, A. and Ludlam, S. (1994) 'The Parliamentary Siege of Maastricht', *Parliamentary Affairs*, 47(1), pp. 37–60.

Ballinger, C. (2002) 'The Local Battle, the Cyber Battle', in Butler, D. and Kavanagh, D. (eds), *The British General Election of 2001*, Basingstoke, Palgrave.

Balls, E. and O'Donnell, G. (eds) (2002) *Reforming Britain's Economic and Financial Policy*, Basingstoke, Palgrave.

Bambridge, M., Whyman, P. and Burkitt, B. (eds) (1998) *The Impact of the Euro: Debating Britain's Future*, London, Macmillan.

Bara, J. and Budge, I. (2001) 'Party Policy and Ideology: Still New Labour?' in Norris, P. (ed.), *Britain Votes 2001*, special issue of *Parliamentary Affairs*, 54, pp. 590–606.

Barber, B. (2001) *Speaking Truth to Power*, New York, W. W. Norton.

Barnett, A. (1997) *This Time: Our Constitutional Revolution*, London, Vintage.

Barnett, S. and Gaber, I. (2001) *Westminster Tales: The Twenty-First-Century Crisis in Political Journalism*, London, Continuum.

Baylis, J. and Smith, S. (2002) *The Globalization of World Politics. An Introduction to International Relations*, 2nd edn., Oxford, Oxford University Press.

Bell, D. (1962) *The End of Ideology: On the Exhaustion of Political Ideas in the Fifties*, New York, Free Press.

Bingham Powell, G. (2000) *Elections as Instruments of Democracy: Majoritarian and Proportional Visions*, New Haven, CT, Yale University Press.

Blackburn, R. and Plant, R. (eds) (1999) *Institutional Return: The Labour Government's Constitutional Reform Agenda*, London, Longman.

Blair, T. (1995) Speech to Rupert Murdoch's News Corporation Leadership Conference, Labour Party Press Release.

Blair, T. (1998a) *Leading the Way: A New Vision for Local Government*, London, Institute of Public Policy Research.

Blair, T. (1998b) *The Third Way: New Politics for the New Century*, London, Fabian Society.

Blair, T. (1999a) 'Doctrine of the International Community: The Chicago Speech', Downing Street Press Release, 22 April.

Blair, T. (1999b) Prime Minister Reports on First Night of Operation 'Allied Force'. [online] [Edited transcript of doorstep interview by the PM. Berlin]. Available from: http://www.fco.gov.uk/news/newstextaspP?2149 [Accessed 15 November 2002].

Blair, T. (2000) Speech to CBI/ Green Alliance, 24 October. http://www.number-10.gov.uk/output/page1255.asp.

Blair, T. (2001), Speech to the Welsh Assembly Available from: http://www.number-10.gov.uk/output/page3723.asp [Accessed 14 November 2002].

Blair, T. (2002) Prime Minister's Speech at the George Bush Senior Presidential Library. Available from: http://www.number-10.gov.uk/output/Page4756.asp [Accessed 14 November 2002].

Blais, A. and Dobrzynska, A. (1990) 'Turnout in Electoral Democracies', *European Journal of Political Research*, 33, pp. 239–261.

Blake, R. (1976) *Report of the Hansard Society Commission on Electoral Reform*, London, Hansard Society for Parliamentary Government.

Blumler, J. G. and Gurevitch, M. (1995) *The Crisis of Public Communication*, London, Routledge.

Bogdanor, V. (ed.) (1985) *Representatives of the People? Parliamentarians and Constituents in Western Democracies*, Aldershot, Gower.

Bogdanor, V. (1995) *The Monarchy and the Constitution*, Oxford, Clarendon.

Bogdanor, V. (1997) *Power and the People: A Guide to Constitutional Reform*, London, Gollancz.

Bogdanor, V. (1999) The British-Irish Council and Devolution, *Government and Opposition*, 34(3).

Bogdanor, V. (2001) *Devolution in the UK*, Oxford, Oxford University Press.

Bomberg, E. and Peterson, J. (2000) 'Policy Transfer and Europeanization: Passing the Heineken Test?', Queen's Papers on Europeanization No. 2/2000 http://www.qub.ac.uk/ies/onlinepapers/poe2.pdf

Booth, K. (1999) NATO's Republic: Warning from Kosovo, *Civil Wars*, 2(3), pp. 89–95.

Booth, K. (ed.) (2001) *The Kosovo Tragedy: The Human Right Dimension*, London, Frank Cass.

Börzel, T. A. (2002) 'Pace-Setting, Foot Dragging, and Fence-Sitting: Member State Responses to Europeanization', *Journal of Common Market Studies*, 40(2), pp. 193–214.

Brady, H. (1993) 'Political participation', in Robinson, J. P., Shaver, P. R. and Wrightsman, L. S. (eds) *Measures of Political Attitudes*, London, Academic Press.

Brand, J., Mitchell, J. and Surridge, P. (1994) 'Will Scotland Come to the Aid of the Party?' in Heath, A., Jowell, R. and Curtice, J. (eds), *Labour's Last Chance? The 1992 Election and Beyond*, Aldershot, Dartmouth.

Breton, A. (1998) *Competitive Governments: An Economic Theory of Politics and Finance*, Cambridge, Cambridge University Press.

Briefing Book on: The Bush Administration's Strategic Defense Review (May 2000) [online] Available from: http://www.foreignpolicy-infocus.org/media/0105briefingbook/index_body.html [Accessed 15th November 2002].

Brighouse, T. (2001) 'New Labour on Education: Could Do Better', *Political Quarterly*, 72(1): pp. 19–29.

Bromley, C. and Curtice, J. (2002) 'Where Have All the Voters Gone?' , in A. Park *et al.*, (eds) *British Social Attitudes: the 19th. report*, London, Sage.

Bromley, C., Curtice, J. and Seyd, B. (2001) 'Political Engagement, Trust and Constitutional Reform', in Park, A., Curtice, J., Thomson, K., Jarvis, L. and Bromley, C. (eds), *British Social Attitudes: the 18th report (Public Policy, Social Ties)*, London, Sage.

Brown, A., Curtice, J., Hinds, K., McCrone, D., Park, A., Paterson, L. and Surridge, P. (2001) *New Scotland, New Politics*, Edinburgh, Edinburgh University Press.

Brown, A. (2000) 'Scottish Politics After the Election: Towards a Scottish Political System?', in Wright, A. (ed.), *Scotland: the Challenge of Devolution*, Aldershot, Ashgate.

Brown, A., McCrone, D., Paterson, L. and Surridge, P. (1999) *The Scottish Electorate*, London, Macmillan.

Bruce, S. (1986) *God Save Ulster! The Religion and Politics of Paisleyism*, Oxford, Oxford University Press.

Bruce-Gardyne, J. and Lawson, N. (1976) *The Power Game*, London, Macmillan.

Budge, I. (1999) 'Party Policy and Ideology: Reversing the 1950s?', in Evans, G. and Norris, P. (eds), *Critical Elections: British Parties and Voters in Long-term Perspective*. London, Sage.

Buller, J. (1995) 'Britain As An Awkward Partner: Reassessing Britain's Relationship with the EU', *Politics*, 15(1).

Buller, J. and Smith, M. J. (1998) Civil Service Attitudes Towards the European Union in Baker, D. and Seawright, D. (eds) *Britain For and Against Europe: British Politics and the Question of European Integration*, Oxford, Clarendon Press.

Bulmer S. and Burch, M. (1998) 'Organizing for Europe: Whitehall, the British State and the European Union', *Public Administration*, 76, pp. 601–28.

Bulmer, S. and Burch, M. (2001) The 'Europeanisation' of Central Government: the UK and Germany in Historical Institutionalist Perspective', in Schneider, G. and Aspinwall, M. (eds), *The Rules of Integration: Institutionalist Approaches to the Study Europe*, (Manchester, Manchester University Press.

Bulmer, S., Burch, M., Carter, C., Hogwood, P. and Scott, A. (2002) *Devolution and European Policy Making: Transforming Britain into Multi-Levelled Governance*, Basingstoke, Palgrave.

Bulpitt, J. (1983) *Territory and Power in the United Kingdom*, Manchester, Manchester University Press.

Burch, M. and Holliday, I. (1996) *The British Cabinet System*, Hemel Hempstead, Prentice Hall.

Burnham, P. (2001) 'New Labour and the Politics of Depoliticisation', *The British Journal of Politics and International Relations*, 2, pp. 127–49.

Burrows, N. (2000) *Devolution*, London, Sweet & Maxwell.

Butler, D. and Kavanagh, D. (2002) *The British General Election of 2001*, Basingstoke, Palgrave.

Butler, D and Stokes, D. (1974) *Political Change in Britain*, London, Macmillan.

Cabinet Office (2002) 'Briefing on the Performance and Innovation Unit and Prime Minister's Forward Strategy Unit', London, Cabinet Office.

Callinicos, A. (2001) *Against the Third Way*, Cambridge, Polity Press.

Cameron, C. (2000) *Veto Bargaining: Presidents and the Politics of Negative Power*, Cambridge, Cambridge University Press.

Campbell, A., Converse, P., Miller, W. E. and Stokes, D. (1960) *The American Voter*, New York, Wiley.

Campbell, C. and Wilson, G. (1995) *The End of Whitehall: Death of a Paradigm*, Oxford, Blackwell.

Campbell, J. (1993) *Edward Heath: A Biography*, London, Cape.

Carey, J. and Shugart, M. (1992) *Presidents and Assemblies: Constitutional Design of Electoral Dynamics*, Cambridge, Cambridge University Press.

Carson, R. (1962) *Silent Spring*, Boston, MA, Riverside Press.

Carter, I. (2001) *The Politics of the Environment*, Cambridge, Cambridge University Press.

Cerny, P. (1997) 'Paradoxes of the Competition State: The Dynamics of Political Globalization', *Government and Opposition*, 32(2), pp. 251–74.

Chalaby, J. K. (2002) *The de Gaulle Presidency and the Media*, Basingstoke, Palgrave.

Chaney, P., Hall, T. and Pithouse, A. (eds) (2001) *New Governance: New Democracy? Post-Devolution Wales*, Cardiff, University of Wales Press.

Chomsky, N. (1999) *The New Military Humanism: Lessons from Kosovo*, New York, Pluto Press.

Clarke, H., Sanders, D., Stewart, M., and Whitely, P. (2002) 'Turnout in the 2001 British Elections', paper presented at the American Political Science Association Annual Meeting, Boston, 28 August–1 September.

Clinton, Bill, (2002) Speech to the Labour Party Conference in Blackpool, http://politics.guardian.co.uk/labour2002/story/0,12294,8003564,00.html

Cockerell, M. (2000) 'Lifting the lid off spin', *British Journalism Review*, 11(3) pp. 6–15.

Coleman, S. (2001) 'Online Campaigning', *Parliamentary Affairs*, 54, pp. 679–88.

Colley, L. (1992) *Britons: Forging the Nation, 1707–1837*, New Haven, CT, Yale University Press.

Colomer, J. M. (2001) *Political Institutions: Democracy and Social Choice* Oxford, Oxford University Press.

Commission of the European Communities (1993) *White Paper on Competitiveness, Growth and Employment: The Challenges and Ways Forward into the 21st Century* (93) 700 final http://europa.eu.int/en/record/white/c93700/contents.html

Commission of the European Communities (2000) *Proposal for a Decision of the European Parliament and of the Council Establishing a Programme of Community Action to Encourage Cooperation between Member States to Combat Social Exclusion*, Com(2000) 368 finalhttp://europa.eu.int/comm/employment_social/soc-prot/soc-incl/calprop00157/0157_en.pdf

Commission for Local Democracy (1995) *Taking Charge: The Rebirth of Local Democracy*, London, Municipal Journal Books.

Commission on Local Government Electoral Arrangements in Wales (Sunderland Commission) (2002) *Improving Local Democracy in Wales*, Cardiff, Welsh Assembly.

Constitution Unit (2000) Monitor 12, September, London, Constitution Unit http://www.ucl.ac.uk/constitution-unit/reports/monitor.htm

Constitution Unit (2001) Monitor 16, September, London, Constitution Unit http://www.ucl.ac.uk/constitution-unit/reports/monitor.htm

Coogan, T. (1995) *The Troubles: Ireland's Ordeal 1966–1995 and the Search for Peace*, London, Hutchinson.

Cook, R. (2003) 'A Modern Parliament in a Modern Democracy', *Political Quarterly* 74:1.

Cook, R. (1997) *Mission Statement for the Foreign and Commonwealth Office* London, Foreign and Commonwealth Office.

Cook, R. (1999) Message to Serb People from Britain's Foreign Secretary Available from: http://www.fas.org/man/dod-101/ops/docs99/99040102_tlt.htm [Accessed 14 November 2002].

Cook, R. (2000) *The Ethical Dimension to Foreign Policy*. Available from: http://news.bbc.co.uk/1/hi/uk/830604.stm [Accessed 14 November 2002].

Coulter, C. (1999) *Contemporary Northern Irish Society*, London, Pluto.

Cowley, P. (2001) *Revolts and Rebellions*, London, Politicos.

Cowley, P. and Norton, P. (1999) 'Rebels and Rebellions: Conservative MPs in the 1992 Parliament', *British Journal of Politics and International Relations* 1(1), pp. 84–105.

Cox, M. (2000) 'Northern Ireland after the Cold War', in Cox, M., Guelke, A. and Stephen, F. (eds) *A Farewell to Arms? From 'Long War' to Long Peace in Northern Ireland*, Manchester, Manchester University Press.

Cracknell, R. and Hicks, J. (2000) *The Local Elections and Elections for London Mayor and Assembly*, House of Commons Research Paper 00/53, London, House of Commons Library.

Cram, L. (2001a) 'Imagining the Union: A Case of Banal Europeanism?', in Wallace, H. (ed.) *Interlocking Dimensions of European Integration*, Basingstoke, Palgrave.

Cram, L. (2001b) Governance 'to Go': Domestic Actors, Institutions and the Boundaries of the Possible, *Journal of Common Market Studies*, 39(4), pp. 595–618.

Crewe, I. and Thomson, K. (1999) 'Party Loyalties: Dealignment or Realignment?' in Evans, G. and Norris. P. (eds), *Critical Elections: British Parties and Voters in Long-Term Perspective*, London, Sage.

Crewe, I., Gosschalk, B. and Bartle, J. (eds) (1998) *Political Communications: Why Labour Won the General Election of 1997*, London, Frank Cass.

Crosland, C. A. R. (1956) *The Future of Socialism*, London, Cape.

Crow, B. and Rix, M. (2002) 'Give us our party back', *Guardian*, 1 May.

Curtice, J. (1999) *The Crisis of Local Democracy in Britain*, CREST Working Paper No 77, London and Oxford, Centre for Research into Elections and Social Trends.

Curtice, J. (2001) 'Hopes Dashed and Fears Assuaged? What The Public Makes Of It So Far', in Trench, A. (ed.), *The State of the Nations 2001*, London, Imprint.

Curtice, J. (2001) 'The Electoral System: Biased to Blair?', in Norris, P. (ed.), *Britain Votes 2001*, Oxford, Oxford University Press.

Curtice, J. (2002). Talk given at the House of Commons, 13 February, 2002.

Curtice, J. and Heath, J. (2000) 'Is the English Lion About to Roar?' in Jowell, R (*et al* eds) *British Social Attitudes: The 17th Report: Focusing on Diversity*, London, Sage.

Curtice, J. and Jowell, R. (1995) 'The Sceptical Electorate', in Jowell, R., Curtice, J., Park, A., Brook, L., and Ahrendt, D. (eds), *British Social Attitudes: the 12th Report*, Aldershot, Dartmouth.

Curtice, J., and Jowell, R. (1997) 'Trust in the Political System', in Jowell, R., Curtice, J., Park, A., Brook, L., Thomson, K., and Bryson, C. (eds), *British Social Attitudes: the 14th Report – The End of Conservative Values?*, Aldershot, Ashgate.

Curtice, J. and Steed, M. (2000) 'And Now for the Commons? Lessons from Britain's First Experience with Proportional Representation, *British Elections and Parties Review*, 10, London, Frank Cass.

Curtice, J., and Steed, M. (2001) 'Appendix 2: The Results Analysed', in Butler, D. and Kavanagh, D. (eds) *The British General Election of 2001*, Basingstoke, Palgrave.

Curtice, J., Seyd, B. and Thomson, K. (2001) *Devolution to the Centre: Lessons from London's First Mayoral Elections*, CREST Working Paper No.90, London and Oxford, Centre for Research into Elections and Social Trends.

Curtice, J., Seyd, B., Park, A. and Thomson, K. (eds) (2002) *Wise After the Event? Attitudes to Voting Reform after the 1999 Scottish and Welsh Elections*, London, Constitution Unit.

Dalton, R., (2002a) 'The Decline of Party Identifications', in Dalton R., and Wattenburg, M. (eds) *Parties Without Partisans: Political Change in Advanced Industrial Democracies*, Oxford, Oxford University Press.

Dalton, R., (2002b) *Citizen Politics*, New York, Chatham House.

Dalton, R. J. (1999) 'Political Support in Advanced Industrial Democracies', in Norris, P., (ed.) *Critical Citizens: Global Support for Democratic Governance*, Oxford, Oxford University Press.

Dalton, R. J. and Wattenberg, M. (eds) (2002) *Parties Without Partisans*, Oxford, Oxford University Press.

Davis, A. (2000) 'Public Relations, News Production and Changing Patterns of Source Access in the British National Press', *Media, Culture & Society*, 22(1), pp. 33–59.

Davis, A. (2002) *Public Relations Democracy: Public Relations, Politics and the Mass Media in Britain*, Manchester, Manchester University Press.

Deacon, D., Golding, P. and Billig, M. (2001) 'Press and Broadcasting: "Real Issues" and Real Coverage', *Parliamentary Affairs*, 54, pp. 666–78.

Deakin, N. and Parry, R. (2000) *The Treasury and Social Policy*, Basingstoke, Palgrave.

Denver, D. (2000a) *Elections and Voters in Britain*, Basingstoke, Palgrave.

Denver, D. (2002b) 'The Liberal Democrats in Constructive Opposition', in King, A. (ed) *Britain at the Polls 2001*, New York, Chatham House.

Denver, D. and Hands, G. (1997) 'Turnout', in Norris, P. and Gavin, N. (eds), *Britain Votes 1997*, Oxford, Oxford University Press.

DETR (1998) *Modern Local Government in Touch with the People*, London, HMSO.

Dicey, A. V. (1959) *Introduction to the Study of the Law of the Constitution*, 10th edn, London, Macmillan.

Dickens, R. (2002) 'Is Welfare to Work Sustainable?', *Benefits*, 10(2), pp. 87–92.

Dixon, P. (2001a) *Northern Ireland: The Politics of War and Peace*, Basingstoke, Palgrave.

Dixon, J. (2001b) 'Health Care: Modernising the Leviathan', *Political Quarterly*, 72(1), pp. 30–8.

DLTR (2002) *Your Region Your Choice: Revitalising the English Regions*, London, HMSO.

Dowding, K. (1991) *Rational Choice and Political Power*, Aldershot, Edward Elgar.

Dowding, K. (1996) *Power*, Buckingham, Open University Press.

Downs, A. (1957) *An Economic Theory of Democracy*, Chicago, Brown.

Driver, S. and Martell, L. (2002) *Blair's Britain*, Cambridge, Polity Press.

Dumez, H. and Jeunemaître, A. (1996) 'The Convergence of Competition Policies in Europe: Internal Dynamics and External Imposition', in Berger, S. and Dore, R. (eds) *National Diversity and Global Capitalism*, Ithaca, NY, Cornell University Press.

Dummett, M (1997) *Principals of Electoral Reform*, Oxford, Oxford University Press.

Dunleavy, P. (1994) 'Estimating the Distribution of Influence in Cabinet Committees under Major', in Dunleavy, P. and Stanyer, J. (eds) *Contemporary Political Studies 1994*, Belfast, Political Studies Association.

Dunleavy, P. (1995a) 'Estimating the Distribution of Positional Influence in Cabinet Committees under Major', in Rhodes, R. A. W. and Dunleavy, P. (eds) *Prime Minister, Cabinet and Core Executive*, London, Macmillan, pp. 298–321.

Dunleavy, P. (1995b) 'Reinterpreting the Westland Affair: Theories of the State and Core Executive Decision-Making', in Rhodes, R. A. W. and Dunleavy, P. (eds) *Prime Minister, Cabinet and Core Executive*, London, Macmillan.

Dunleavy, P. and Margetts, H. (2001) 'From Majoritarian to Pluralist Democracy? Electoral Reform in Britain Since 1997', *Journal of Theoretical Politics*, 13(3), pp. 295–319.

Dyson, K. (1980) *The State Tradition in Western Europe: A Study of an Idea and an Institution*, Oxford, Martin Robertson.

Eckstein, H. (1988) 'A Culturalist Theory of Political Change', *American Political Science Review*, 82, pp. 789–804.

Elcock, H. and Keating, M. (1998) *Remaking the Union: Devolution and British Politics in the 1990s*, London, Frank Cass.

Electoral Commission (2001) *Election 2001: The Official Results*, London, Politicos.

Electoral Commission (2002) *Modernising Local Elections: A Strategic Evaluation of the 2002 Electoral Pilot Schemes*, London, Electoral Commission.

Electoral Commission/NOP (2002) *Public Opinion and the 2002 Local Elections*, October.

Eltis, W. (2000) *Britain, Europe and EMU*, Basingstoke, Palgrave.

Evans, G. (2000) 'The Working Class and New Labour: A Parting of the Ways?' in Jowell, R., Curtice, J., Park, A., Thomson, K., Bromley, C., Jarvis, L. and Stratford, N. (eds) *British Social Attitudes, the 17th Report: Focusing on Diversity*. London, Sage.

Evans, G. (2002) 'European Integration, Party Politics and Voting in the 2001 Election', *British Elections and Parties Review*, 12, London, Frank Cass.

Evans, G. and Letki, N. (2003). 'Social Capital and Political Disaffection in the New Post-Communist Democracies', in Montero, R. and Torcal, M. (eds) *Political Disaffection in European Democracies* (forthcoming).

Evans, G. and Norris, P. (1999) *Critical Elections: British Parties and Voters in Long Term Perspective*, London, Sage.

Evans, G. Heath, A. and Payne, P. (1999) 'Class: Labour as a Catch-All Party?' in Evans, G. and Norris, P. (eds) *Critical Elections: British Parties and Voters in Long-term Perspective*, London, Sage.

Evans, J. and Tonge, J. (2001) 'Northern Ireland's Third Tradition(s): the Alliance Party Surveyed', in Tonge, J., Bennie, L., Denver, D. and Harrison, L. (eds) *British Elections and Parties Review, 11*, London, Frank Cass.

Evans, M. (1995) *Charter 88: A Successful Challenge to the British Political Tradition?*, Aldershot, Dartmouth.

Evans, M. (1997) 'Political Participation', in Dunleavy, P., Gamble, A., Hollliday, I. and Peele, G. (eds) *Developments in British Politics, 5*, London, Macmillan.

Fabian Society (2000) *The Commission on Taxation and Citizenship*, London, Fabian Society.

Fabian Society (2003) *Report of the Fabian Commission on the Future of the Monarchy*, London, Fabian Society.

Farrell, D. (2001) *Electoral Systems: A Comparative Introduction*, Basingstoke, Palgrave.

Farrell, D. and Webb, P. (2002) 'Political Parties as Campaign Organisations', in Dalton, R. and Wattenburg, M. (eds) *Parties Without Partisans: Political Change in Advanced Industrial Democracies*, Oxford, Oxford University Press.

Fielding, S. (2000) 'A New Politics', in Dunleavy, P., Gamble, A., Heffernan, R., Holliday, I. and Peele, G. (eds) *Developments in British Politics 6*, Basingstoke, Palgrave.

Flynn, P (1999) *Dragons Led by Poodles: The Inside Story of a Labour Stitch Up*, London, Politicos.

Foley, M. (2000) *The British Presidency*, Manchester, Manchester University Press.

Foster, C. D. (2001) 'The Civil Service Under Stress: The Fall in Civil Service Power and Authority', *Public Administration*, 79, pp. 725–49.

Franklin, B. (1997) *Newszak and News Media*, London, Arnold.

Franklin, M. (1996) 'Electoral Participation', in LeDuc, L., Niemi, R. and Norris, P. (eds), *Comparing Democracies: Elections and Voting in Global Perspective*, Thousand Oaks, CA, Sage.

Franklin, M. (2001) 'The Dynamics of Electoral Participation', in Leduc, L., Niemi, R. and Norris, P. (eds) *Comparing Democracies 2: Elections and Voting in Global Perspective*, Thousand Oaks, CA, Sage.

Freeden, M. (1996) *Ideologies and Political Theory: A Conceptual Approach*, Oxford, Clarendon Press.

Freeden, M (1998) 'The Ideology of New Labour', *The Political Quarterly*, 69.

Freedland, J. (1998) *Bring Home the Revolution: How Britain Can Live the American Dream*, London, Fourth Estate.

Freedland, J. (2002) 'Thanks for the money, now set us free', *Guardian*, 16 July.

Fuchs, D. and Klingemann, H. D. (1995), 'Citizens and the State: A Changing Relationship?', in Klingemann, H. D., and Fuchs, D., *Citizens and the State*, Oxford, Oxford University Press.

Fukuyama, F. (1992) *The End of History and the Last Man*, New York, Free Press.

Gamble, A. (1974) *The Conservative Nation*, London, Routledge & Kegan Paul.

Gamble, A. (1998) 'The European Issue in British Politics', in Baker, D. and Seawright, D. (eds) *Britain For and Against Europe: British Politics and the Question of European Integration*, Oxford, Clarendon Press.

Gamble, A. and Kelly, G. (2001) 'Labour's New Economics' in Ludlam, S. and Smith, M. J. (eds) *New Labour in Government*, Basingstoke, Palgrave.

Gamble, A. and Kelly, G. (2002) 'Britain and EMU', in Dyson, K. (ed.) *European States and the Euro: Europeanization, Variation and Convergence*, Oxford, Oxford University Press.

Gamble, A. and Wright, T. (2002) 'Commentary: Is The Party Over?' *Political Quarterly*, 73(2), pp. 123–4.

Garner, R. (2000) *Environmental Politics: Britain, Europe, and the Global Environment*, Basingstoke, Palgrave.

Geddes, A. and Tonge, J. (eds) (2002) *Labour's Second Landslide: The British General Election 2001*, Manchester, Manchester University Press.

George, S. (1995) 'A Reply to Buller', *Politics*, 15(1).

George, S. (1998) *An Awkward Partner: Britain in the European Community*, Oxford, Oxford University Press.

George, S. and Bache, I. (2001) *Politics in the European Union*, Oxford, Oxford University Press.

George, S. (2001) 'The Europeanisation of UK Politics and Policy-Making: the Effect of European Integration on the UK', *Queen's Papers on Europeanization*, 8/2001. http://www.qub.ac.uk/ies/onlinepapers/poe8-01.pdf

Giddens, A. (1998) *The Third Way: The Renewal of Social Democracy*, Cambridge, Polity Press.

Giddens, A. (2000) *The Third Way and its Critics*, Cambridge, Polity Press.

Giddens, A. (2001) *The Global Third Way Debate*, Cambridge, Polity Press.

Giddens, A. (2002) *Where Now for New Labour?*, Cambridge, Polity Press.

Glyn, A. and Wood, S. (2001) 'Economic Policy Under New Labour: How Social Democratic is the Blair Government', *Political Quarterly*, 72(1) pp. 50–66.

Grant, W. (2002) *Economic Policy in Britain*, Basingstoke, Palgrave.

Gray, J. (1995) *Enlightenment's Wake*, London, Routledge.

Gray, J (1998) *False Dawn: The Illusions of Global Capitalism*, London, Granta.

Gray, M. and Caul, M. (2000) 'Declining Voter Turnout in Advanced Industrialized Democracies, 1950 to 1997,' *Comparative Political Studies*, 33, pp. 1091–122.

Gray, T. (1995) *UK Environmental Policy in the 1990s*, London, Macmillan.

Greater London Assembly (2002) *Is the Mayor Listening? Report of the London Assembly's Investigating Committee on the Mayor's Consultations with Londoners*, London, The Greater London Assembly.

Greenleaf, W. H. (1983) *The British Political Tradition Vol. 2, The Ideological Heritage*, London, Methuen.

Guardian (2002) *Special Report: Chechnya* [online] Available from: http://www.guardian.co.uk/chechnya/0,2759,180787,00.html [Accessed 16 November 2002].

Gunther, R., Montero, J. R. and Linz, J. J. (eds) (2002) *Political Parties: Old Concepts as New Challenges*, Oxford, Oxford University Press.

Hadfield, B. (2003) 'The United Kingdom as a Territorial State' in Bogdanor, V. (ed) *The British Constitution in the Twentieth Century*, Oxford, Oxford University Press.

Hain, P. (2001) *Globalisation: The End of Foreign Policy?* [online] Available from: http://news.bbc.co.uk/hi/english/static/in_depth/uk_politics/2001/open_politics/foreign_policy/globalisation.stm [Accessed 16 November 2002].

Hansard (1999a) *House of Commons Debates*, 6th Series, vol. 332, col. 795, 10 June.

Hansard (1999b) *House of Commons Debates*, 6th Series, vol. 334, cols 1013–5, 7 July.

Hansard (2000), *House of Commons Debates*, 6th Series, vol. 342, col. 468, 12 December.

Harrison, M. (2002) 'Politics on the Air', in Butler, D. and Kavanagh, D. (eds), *The British General Election of 2001*, Basingstoke: Palgrave.

Haverland, M. (2000) 'National Adaptation to European Integration: The Importance of Institutional Veto Points', *Journal of Public Policy*, 20(1), pp. 83–103.

Hay, C. (1999) *The Political Economy of New Labour: Labouring Under False Pretences*, Manchester, Manchester University Press.

Hay, C. and Rosamond, B. (2002) 'Globalization, European Integration and the Discursive Construction of Economic Imperatives', *Journal of European Public Policy*, 9(2), pp. 147–67.

Hayes, B. and McAllister, I. (2000) 'Sowing Dragon's Teeth. Public Support for Political Violence and Paramilitarism in Northern Ireland', Paper presented to the Political Studies Association of the United Kingdom's Annual Conference, LSE, April 2000.

Hazell, R (ed) (2001a) *The State and the Nations: The First Year Devolution in the UK*, Exeter: Academic Imprint.

Hazell, R. (2001b) 'Reforming the Constitution', *Political Quarterly*, 72:1, pp. 39–49.

Headey, B. (1974) *British Cabinet Ministers*, London, Allen & Unwin.

Healey, N. M. (1998) 'The Case for European Monetary Union' in Bainbridge, M., Whyman, P. and Burkitt, B. (eds) *The Impact of the Euro*, London, Macmillan.

Heath, A. and Taylor, B. (1999), 'New Sources of Abstention?', in Evans, G. and Norris, P. (eds), *Critical Elections: British Parties and Voters in Long-Term Perspective*, London, Sage.

Hedges, A. and Bromley, C. (2001) *Public Attitudes towards Taxation*, London, Fabian Society.

Heffer, S. (1999) *Nor Shall My Sword: The Reinvention of England*, London, Weidenfeld & Nicolson.

Heffernan, R. (2001) *New Labour and Thatcherism*, Basingstoke, Palgrave.

Heffernan, R. (2002) 'The "Possible as the Art of Politics": Understanding Consensus Politics', *Political Studies*, 50, pp. 742–60.

Heffernan, R. and Stanyer, J. (1998) 'The Enhancement of Leadership Power: The Labour Party and the Impact of Political Communications', in Denver,

D. *et al.* (eds), *British Elections and Parties Review*, Vol. 7, London, Frank Cass.

Held, D., McGrew, A., Goldblatt, D. and Perraton, J. (1999) *Global Transformations*, Cambridge, Polity Press.

Held, D. and McGrew, A. (2000) 'The Great Globalization Debate', in Held and McGrew (eds) *The Global Transformations Reader*, Cambridge, Polity Press.

Henn, M., Weinstein, M., and Wring, D. 2002. 'A Generation Apart: Youth and Political Participation in Britain', *British Journal of Politics and International Relations*, 4, pp. 167–92.

Hennessey, T. (2002) *The Northern Ireland Peace Process: Ending the Troubles?* Dublin, Gill & Macmillan.

Hennessy, P. (2001) *The Prime Minister: The Office and its Holders Since 1945*, London, Penguin.

Hershberg, E. and Moore, K. W. (eds) (2002) *Critical Views of September 11: Analyses From Around the World*, New York, Social Sciences Research Council.

Heseltine, M. (2000), *Life in the Jungle: My Autobiography*, London, Hodder & Stoughton.

Hirsch, J. L. (2000) *Sierra Leone: Diamonds and the Struggle for Democracy.* An International Peace Academy Occasional Paper.

Hirsh, M. (2002) 'Bush and the World', *Foreign Affairs*, 81(5), pp. 18–44.

Hitchens, P. (1999) *The Abolition of Britain*, London, Quartet.

HM Treasury (1996) 'European Union Stability Pact', News Release 169/96, 22 November http://archive.treasury.gov.uk/pub/text/press96/p169_96.txt

HM Treasury (2001) *Productivity in the UK: Enterprise and the Productivity Challenge*, London, HM Treasury and Department of Trade and Industry.

HM Treasury (2001a) *Fifth Report on Euro Preparations* (London, HM Treasury) http://www.hm-treasury.gov.uk/mediastore/otherfiles/euro_5th_report.pdf

HM Treasury (2001b) *Maintaining Economic Stability: Convergence Programme for the United Kingdom. Submitted in Line with the Stability and Growth Pact*, London, HM Treasury http://www.hm-treasury.gov.uk/mediastore/otherfiles/2001%20UK%20Convergence%20Programme.pdf

HM Treasury (2001c) *Preliminary and Technical Work to Prepare for the Assessment of the Five Tests for UK Membership of the Single Currency*, London, HM Treasury http://www.hm-treasury.gov.uk/mediastore/otherfiles/Preliminary%20and%20Technical%20work.pdf

HMSO (1997) *The White Paper: Scotland's Parliament*, Cm 3658, London, HMSO.

HMSO (1998) *The Scotland Act*, London, HMSO.

HMSO (1999) *Memorandum of Understanding and Supplementary Agreements*, London, HMSO.

Holliday, I. (2002) 'Executives and Administrations', in Dunleavy, P., Gamble, A., Heffernan, R. and Peele, G. (eds) *Developments in British Politics 6*, Basingstoke, Palgrave.

Holme, R. and Elliott, M. (eds) (1988) *1688–1988: Time for a New Constitution*, London, Macmillan.

Home Office (1999), *Review of the European Parliamentary Elections 1999*, London, Home Office.

Hooghe, L. and Marks, G. (2001) *Multi-Level Governance and European Integration*, Lanham, MD, Rowman and Littlefield.

Horowitz, D. (2001) The Northern Ireland Agreement: Clear, Consociational and Risky', in McGarry, J. (ed.) *Northern Ireland and the Divided World*, Oxford, Oxford University Press.

House of Commons (1999) The Defence, Foreign Affairs, International Development and Trade and Industry Committees Special Report (1999) *Committee's Inquiry into the 1997 and 1998 Annual Reports on Strategic Export Controls* HC 540, London, HMSO.

House of Commons (2000) *Shifting the Balance: Select Committees and the Executive* HC 300 2 March. London, HMSO.

Hurd, D. (2001) *On from the Elective Dictatorship*, First Hailsham Lecture to the Society of Conservative Lawyers.

Hutchison, I. G. C. (2001) *Scottish Politics in the Twentieth Century*, Basingstoke, Palgrave.

Hutton, W. (1995) *The State We're In*, London, Cape.

Hutton, W. (2002) *The World We're In*, London, Little, Brown.

Ignatieff, M. (2000) *Virtual War. Kosovo and Beyond*, London, Chatto & Windus.

Improvement and Development Agency and Employers Association for Local Government (2001) *National Census on Councillors*.

Inglehart, I. (1990) *Culture Shifts in Advanced Industrial Society*, Princeton, Princeton University Press.

Institute of Fiscal Studies (2001) *The IFS Green Budget: January 2001* (edited by A. Dilnot, C. Emmerson and H. Simpson) London, Institute of Fiscal Studies.

Institute of Fiscal Studies (2002) *The IFS Green Budget: January 2002* (edited by A. Dilnot, C. Emmerson and H. Simpson) London, Institute of Fiscal Studies.

Institute of Public Policy Research (2002) *A Progressive Future: IPPR's Agenda for a Better Society*, London, Institute of Public Policy Research.

Institute of Public Policy Research (2001) *Building Better Partnerships*, London, Institute of Public Policy Research.

International Monetary Fund (2001) *Report on UK Economic Performance*, Washington, DC, IMF.

Jackman, R. (1987). 'Political Institutions and Voter Turnout in the Industrial Democracies', *American Political Science Review*, 81, pp. 405–23.

Jackman, R. and Miller, R.A. (1995) 'Voter Turnout in the Industrial Democracies During the 1980s', *Comparative Political Studies*, 27, pp. 467–92.

Jacobs, M. (1999) *Environmental Modernisation: the New Labour Agenda*, London, Fabian Society.

Jenkins, R. (1998) *The Report of the Independent Commission on the Voting System*, London, Stationery Office.

Jenkins, R. (1995) *Gladstone*, London, Macmillan.

Johnson, J. (1999) 'Second Most Powerful Man in Britain?', *British Journalism Review*, 10(4), pp. 67–71.

Johnson, N. (1999) 'The Constitution', in Holliday, I. Gamble, A. and Parry, G., (eds) *Fundamentals in British Politics*, London, Macmillan.

Jones, G. W. and Stewart, J. (2003) 'Central Local Relations Since the Layfield Report' in Carmichael, P. and Midwinter, A. (eds) *Regulating Local Authorities: Emerging Patterns of Central Control*, London, Frank Cass.

Jones, G. W. (1995) 'The Downfall of Margaret Thatcher', in Rhodes, R. A. W. and Dunleavy, P. (eds) *Prime Minister, Cabinet and Core Executive*, Basingstoke: Macmillan.

Jones, N. (1993) *Soundbites and Spin Doctors*, London, Gollancz.

Jones, N. (1999) *Sultans of Spin*, London, Gollancz.

Jones, N. (2002) *The Control Freaks*, London, Politicos.

Jospin. L. (2002) *My Vision of Europe and Globalization*, Cambridge, Polity.

Jowell, R. and Park, A. (1998) *Young People, Politics and Citizenship: A Disengaged Generation?*, London, Citizenship Foundation.

Judah, T. (2000) *Kosovo: War and Revenge*, New Haven, CT and London, Yale University Press.

Judge, D. (1993) *The Parliamentary State*, London, Sage.

Kampfner, J. (1998) *Robin Cook: The Biography*, London, Weidenfeld & Nicolson.

Katz, R. (1997) *Democracy and Elections*, New York, Oxford University Press.

Katz, R. and Mair, P. (1995) 'Changing Models of Party Organisation and Party Democracy: The Emergence of the Cartel Party', *Party Politics*, 1, pp. 5–28.

Katz, R. and Mair, P. (2002) 'The Ascendancy of the Party in Public Office: Party Organisational Change in Twentieth Century Democracies', in Gunther, R., Montero, J. R. and Linz, J. (eds) *Political Parties: Old Concepts and New Challenges*, Oxford, Oxford University Press.

Kavanagh, D. (1995) *Election Campaigning: The New Marketing of Politics*, Oxford, Blackwell.

Kavanagh, D. and Seldon, A. (1999) *The Powers Behind the Prime Minister*, London, HarperCollins.

Keating, M. and Midwinter, A. (1981), 'The Scottish Office in the United Kingdom Policy Network', *Studies in Public Policy No.96*, Glasgow, University of Strathclyde, Centre for the Study of Public Policy.

Keating, M. and Midwinter, A. (1983), *The Government of Scotland*, Edinburgh, Mainstream.

Keliher, L. (1995) 'Core Executive Decision Making in High Technology Issues: The Case of the Alvey Project', in Rhodes, R. A. W. and Dunleavy, P. (eds) *Prime Minister, Cabinet and Core Executive*, London, Macmillan.

Kellard, K. (2002) 'Job Retention and Advancement in the UK: A Developing Agenda', *Benefits*, 10(2): pp. 93–98.

Kellas, J. (1973) *The Scottish Political System*, 1st edn, Cambridge, Cambridge University Press.

Kellas, J. (1984) *The Scottish Political System*, 3rd edn, Cambridge, Cambridge University Press.

Kennedy, C. (2002) *Statement on Iraq*. Available from: http://www.libdems.org.uk/index.cfm/page.news/section.conference/article.3410 [Accessed 14 November 2002].

Kenny, M. and Smith M. J. (2001) 'Interpreting New Labour: Constraints, Dilemmas and Political Agency', in Ludlam, S. and Smith, M. J. (eds) (2001), *New Labour in Government*, Basingstoke, Palgrave.

King, A. (1992) 'Over the Shoulder Politics', in King, A. (ed.) *Britain at the Polls 1992*, New York, Chatham House.

King A. (ed.) (2002) *Britain at the Polls 2001*, New York: Chatham House.

King, D. and Wickham-Jones, M. (1999) 'From Clinton to Blair: The Democratic (Party) Origins of Welfare to Work', *Political Quarterly*, 70(1), pp. 62–74.

Kissinger, H. (2002) *Toward a Diplomacy For The Twenty-First Century. Does America Need a Foreign Policy?*, London, Simon & Schuster.

Klein, N. (2000) *No Logo*, London, Flamingo.

Klingemann, H. (1999) 'Mapping Political Support in the 1990s: A Global Analysis', in Norris, P. (ed.), *Critical Citizens: Global Support for Democratic Governance*, Oxford, Oxford University Press.

Knill, C. (1998) 'European Policies: The Impact of National Administrative Traditions', *Journal of Public Policy*, 18(1), pp. 1–28.

Knill, C. (2001) *The Europeanisation of National Administrations: Patterns of Institutional Change and Persistence*, Cambridge, Cambridge University Press.

Knill, C. and Lehmkuhl, D. (1999) 'How Europe Matters: Different Mechanisms of Europeanization', *European Integration Online Papers* 3(7), http://eiop.or.at/eiop/texte/1998–007a.htm

Kohler-Koch, B. (1999) 'The Evolution and Transformation of European Governance', in B. Kohler-Koch and R. Eising (eds) (1999) *The Transformation of European Governance*, London, Routledge.

Koole, R. (1996) 'Cadre, Catch-all or Cartel? A Comment on the Notion of Cartel Parties', *Party Politics*, 2, pp. 507-23.

Kuhn, R. (2002) 'The First Blair Government and Political Journalism' in Kuhn, R. and Neveu, E. (eds), *Political Journalism: New Challenges, New Practices*, London, Routledge.

Labour Party (1997a) *Labour into Power: A Framework for Partnership*, London, Labour Party.

Labour Party (1997b) *New Labour: Because Britain Deserves Better: Manifesto 1997*, London, Labour Party.

Labour Party (2001) *Ambitions for Britain: Labour's Manifesto 2001*, London, Labour Party.

Ladrech, R (2001) 'Europeanisation and Political Parties: Towards a Framework for Analysis', *Queen's Papers on Europeanisation* No. 2/2001 http://www.qub.ac.uk/ies/onlinepapers/poe2–01.pdf.

Laver, M. (2000) 'Coalitions in Northern Ireland: Preliminary Thoughts', *Programme for Government Conference*, Belfast.

Lawson, N. (1992) *The View from No.11*, London, Bantam.

LeDuc, L., Niemi, R. and Norris, P. (eds) (1996) *Comparing Democracies: Elections and Voting in Global Perspective*, Thousand Oaks, Ca., Sage.

Lee, J., Jones G.W. and Burnham, J. (1998) *At the Centre of Whitehall*, London, Macmillan.

Lees-Marshment, J. (2001) *Political Marketing and British Political Parties: The Party's just Begun*, Manchester, Manchester University Press.

Leys, C. (1996) 'The Labour Party's Transition from Socialism to Capitalism', in Panitch, L. (ed.) *The Socialist Register*, London, Merlin Press.

Liaison Committee (2002) 'Minutes of Evidence' http://www.publications. parliament . . . select/cmliason/1065/106501.htm 16 July,

Liebfried, S. and Pierson, P. (2000) 'Social Policy' in Wallace, H. and Wallace, W. (eds) *Policy-Making in the European Union*, 4th edn, Oxford, Oxford University Press.

Lijphart, A. (1994) *Electoral Systems and Party Systems: A Study of Twenty-Seven Democracies, 1945–1990*, Oxford, Oxford University Press.

Lijphart, A. (1999) *Patterns of Democracy: Government Forms and Performance in Thirty Six Countries*, New Haven, Yale University Press.

Little, R. and Wickham-Jones, M. (eds) (2000) *New Labour's Foreign Policy. A New Moral Crusade*, Manchester, Manchester United Press.

Lovenduski, J. (2001). 'Women in Politics: Minority Representation or Critical Mass?', *Parliamentary Affairs*, pp. 54, 743–58.

Lowe, P. and Ward, S. (1998) *British Environmental Policy and Europe*, London, Routledge.

Ludlam, S. and Smith, M. J. (eds) (2001) *New Labour in Government*, Basingstoke, Palgrave.

Lukes, S. (1999) 'The Last Word on the Third Way' *The Review*, London, Social Market Foundation.

Macintyre, D. (2000) *Peter Mandelson and the Making of New Labour*, London, HarperCollins

Mahony, M. and de Boer, W. (2002) 'Britain's relative productivity performance updated to 1999' http://www.niesr.ac.uk/research/research.htm

Majone, G. (1996) *Regulating Europe*, London, Routledge.

Major, J. (1999) *The Autobiography*, London, HarperCollins.

Mallie, E. and McKittrick, D. (1996) *The Fight for Peace: the Secret Story behind the Irish Peace Process*, London, Heinemann.

Maloney, E. (2002) *A Secret History of the IRA*, London, Penguin.

Maor, M. (1997) *Political Parties and Party Systems: Comparative Approaches and the British Experience*, London, Routledge.

Manning, P. (2001) *News and News Sources: A Critical Introduction*, London, Sage.

Margetts, H. (2002) 'Political Participation and Protest' in Dunleavy, P., Gamble, A. Heffernan, R., Hollliday, I. and Peele, G. (eds) *Developments in British Politics, 6*, Basingstoke, Palgrave.

Marks, G. (1993) 'Structural Policy and Multilevel Governance in the EC', in Cafruny, A. and Rosenthal, G. (eds) *The State of the European Community, Vol 2: The Maastricht Debates and Beyond*, New York, Lynne Rienner.

Marks, G., Hooghe, L. and Blank, K. (1996) 'European Integration from the 1980, Statecentre *v.* Multilevel Governance', *Journal of Common Market Studies*, 34(3).

Marks, G., Nielsen, F., Ray, L. and Salk, J. (1996) 'Competencies, Cracks and Conflicts: Regional Mobilization in the European Union', in Marks, G., Scharpf, F. W., Schmitter, P. C. and Streeck, W., *Governance in the European Union*, London, Sage, pp. 40–63.

Marquand, D. (1988) *The Unprincipled Society: New Demands and Old Politics*, London, Cape.

Marr, A. (2000) *The Day Britain Died*, London, Profile Books.

Marsh, D, Smith, M. J. and Richards, D. (2000) 'Bureaucrats, Politicians and Reform in Whitehall: Analyising the Bureau-shaping Model', *British Journal of Political Science*, 30, pp. 461–82.

Marsh, D., Richards, D. and Smith, M. J. (2001) *Changing Patterns of Governance in the United Kingdom*, Basingstoke, Palgrave.

May, J. D. (1973) 'Opinion Structures of Political Parties: The Special Law of Curvilinear Disparity', *Political Studies*, 21, pp. 135–51.

McAllister, I. (2001) 'Electoral Participation and its Political Consequences: The 2001 British General Election', paper presented at the American Political Science Association Annual Meeting, San Francisco, 30 August–2 September.

McCormick, J. (2001) 'Welfare and Well-Being', *Political Quarterly*, 72(1), pp. 86–96.

McCormick, J. (2002) *Understanding the European Union*, Basingstoke, Palgrave.

McGarny, J. and O'Leary, B. (1995) *Explaining Northern Ireland*, Oxford, Basil Blackwell.

McGarvey, N. (2001) 'New Scottish Politics, New Texts Required' *The British Journal of Politics and International Relations*, 3(3), pp. 427–44.

McGowan, F. (2000) 'Competition Policy: The Limits of the European Regulatory State', in Wallace, H. and Wallace, W. (eds) *Policy-Making in the European Union*, 4th edn., Oxford, Oxford University Press.

McIntyre, A. (2001) 'Modern Irish Republicanism and the Belfast Agreement: Chickens Coming Home to Roost, or Turkeys Celebrating Christmas?' in Wilford, R. (ed.), *Aspects of the Belfast Agreement*, Oxford, Oxford University Press, pp. 202–22.

McKenzie, R. T. (1964) *British Political Parties*, London, Heinemann.

McLean, I. and Smith, J. (1994) 'The Poll Tax, the Electoral Register, and the 1991 Census: An Update', in D. Broughton, D. Farrell, D. Denver and C. Rallings (eds). *British Elections and Parties Yearbook*, London, Frank Cass.

McNair, B. (2000) *Journalism and Democracy*, London, Routledge.

Meacher, M. (2000) 'UK recycling levels "pathetic" – Meacher' http://news.bbc.co.uk/1/hi/uk_politics/763402.stm accessed 25/10/02.

Meacher, M. (2002) Transcript of Interview with *The Sunday Times* http://www.odpm.gov.uk/about/pdf/transcript.pdf accessed 25 October 2002.

Middleton, R. (2000) *The British Economy Since 1945*, Basingstoke, Palgrave.

Millar, J. (2000, *Keeping Track of Welfare Reform: The New Deal Programmes*, York, Joseph Rowntree Foundation.

Milward, A.S. (1999) *The European Rescue of the Nation-State*, 2nd edn, London, Routledge.

Mitchell, J (1998), 'The Evolution of Devolution: Labour's Home Rule Strategy in Opposition', *Government and Opposition*, 33(4), pp. 479–96.

Mitchell, J (2001) 'The Study of Scottish Politics Post-Devolution: New Evidence, New Analysis and New Methods?', *West European Politics*, 24, pp. 216–23.

Mitchell, P. (2001) 'Transcending an ethnic party system?', in Wilford, R. (ed.), *Aspects of the Belfast Agreement*, Oxford, Oxford University Press.

Moore, C. and Booth, S. (1989) *Managing Competition: Meso-Corporatism, Pluralism and the Negotiated Order in Scotland*, Oxford, Oxford University Press.

Moravcsik, A. (1993) 'Preferences and Power in the European Community: A Liberal Intergovernmentalist Approach', *Journal of Common Market Studies*, 31(4), pp. 473–524.

Moravcsik, A. (1998) *The Choice for Europe: Social Purpose and State Power from Messina to Maastricht*, London, UCL Press.

Morriss, P. (2002) *Power: A Philosophical Analysis*, 2nd edn, Manchester, Manchester University Press.

Mount, F. (1992) *The British Constitution Now*, London, Heinemann.

Mowlam, M. (2002) *Momentum: The Struggle for Peace, Politics and the People*, London, Hodder & Stoughton.

Mulgan, G. (2001) 'Joined-up Government: Past, Present and Future', paper presented at British Academy Conference on Joined Up Government', 30 October.

Mulgan, G. and Wilkinson, H. (1997), 'Freedom's children and the rise of generational politics', in Mulgan, G. (ed.), *Life after Politics: New Thinking for the Twenty-First Century*, London, Fontana.

Mullard, M. (2001) "New Labour, New Public Expenditure: The Case of Cake Tomorrow', *Political Quarterly*, 72(3), pp. 310–21.

Müller, W. and Strøm, K. (1999) *Policy, Office or Votes? How Political Parties in Western Europe Make Hard Decisions*, Cambridge, Cambridge University Press.

Murray, G. (1998) *John Hume's SDLP*, Dublin, Irish Academic Press.

Murray, G. and Tonge, J. (2003) *The SDLP and Sinn Fein 1970–2001: From Alienation to Participation*, London, Hurst.

Nairn, T. (2000) *After Britain: New Labour and the Return of Scotland*, London, Granta.

Nairn, T. (2002) *Pariah: Misfortunes of the British Kingdom*, London, Verso.

Naughtie, J. (2002) *The Rivals: The Intimate Story of a Political Marriage*, London, Fourth Estate.

New Local Government Network (2001) *Your Mayor, Your Choice*, www.nlgn.org.uk

Newton, K. and Brynin, M. (2001) 'The National Press and Party Voting in the UK', *Political Studies*, 49, pp. 265–84.

Norris, P. (1997a) *Electoral Change in Britain Since 1945*, Oxford, Basil Blackwell.

Norris, P. (1997b) 'Political Communications', in Dunleavy, P., Gamble, A., Holliday, I., and Peele, G. (eds), *Developments in British Politics 5*, London, Macmillan.

Norris, P. (2000) *A Virtuous Circle: Political Communications in Postindustrial Societies*, Cambridge, Cambridge University Press.

Norris, P. (2002) *Democratic Phoenix: Reinventing Political Activism*, New York, Cambridge University Press.

Norris, P., Curtice, J., Sanders, D., Scammell, M. and Semetko, H. (1999) *On Message: Communicating the Campaign*, London, Sage.

Norton, P. (1992) 'In Defence of the Constitution: A Riposte to the Radicals' in Philip Norton (ed.) *New Directions in British Politics*, Aldershot, Edward Elgar.

Norton, P. (1995) 'Parliamentary Behaviour since 1945', *Talking Politics*, vol. 8, no. 2.

Norton, P. (2002) 'The Conservative Party: Is Anyone Out There?, in King, a. (ed.), *Britain at the Polls, 2001*, New York, Chatham House.

Norton, P, and Wood, B. (1994) 'Do Candidates Matter? Constituency-Specific Vote Changes for Incumbent MPs, 1983–87', *Political Studies*, 42: pp. 469–79.

Oborne, P. (1999) *Alastair Campbell: New Labour and the Rise of the Media Class*, London, Aurum.

OECD (2000) *OECD Economic Surveys: United Kingdom*, Paris, Organisation for Economic Co-operation and Development.

O'Leary, B. (1999) 'The Nature of the British-Irish Agreement', *New Left Review*, 233, pp. 66–96.

O'Shaughnessy, N. J. (1990) *The Phenomenon of Political Marketing*, London, Macmillan.

Panebianco, A. (1988) *Political Parties: Organisation and Power*, Cambridge, Cambridge University Press.

Panitch, L. and Leys, C. (1997) *The End of Parliamentary Socialism: From New Left to New Labour*, London, Verso.

Park, A. (1999) 'Young People and Political Apathy', in Jowell, R., Curtice, J., Park, A., and Thomson, K. (eds), *British Social Attitudes: the 16th Report – Who Shares New Labour Values?*, London, Sage.

Parry, G., Moiser, G., and Day, N. (1992) *Political Participation and Democracy in Britain*, Cambridge, Cambridge University Press.

Pattie, C. and Johnston, R. (1998) 'Voter Turnout at the British General Election of 1992: Rational Choice, Social Standing or Political Efficacy?', *European Journal of Political Research*, 33, pp. 263–83.

Pattie, C. and Johnston, R. (2001) 'A Low Turnout Landslide: Abstention at the British General Election of 1997', *Political Studies*, 49, pp. 286–305.

Perri 6, Leat. D., Seltzer, K. and Stoker, G. (2002) *Towards Holistic Governance: the New Reform Agenda*, Basingstoke, Palgrave.

Pharr, S. and Putnam, R. D. (eds) (2000) *Disaffected Democracies: What's Troubling the Trilateral Countries?* Princeton, Princeton University Press.

Pierre, J. (ed.) (1995) *Urban and Regional Policy*, Aldershot, Edward Elgar.

Pilkington, C. (2002) *Devolution in Britain Today*, Manchester, Manchester University Press.

Pimlott, B. and Rao, N. (2002), *Governing London*, Oxford, Oxford University Press.

Plant, R. (1991) *The Plant Report: A Working Party on Electoral Reform*, London, The Guardian.

Plant, R. (2001) 'Blair and Ideology' in Seldon, A. (ed.) *The Blair Effect*, London, Little, Brown.

Plutzer, E. (2002) 'Becoming a Habitual Voter: Inertia, Resources and Growth in Young Adulthood', *American Political Science Review*, 96: pp. 41–56.

Porritt, J. (2002) quoted in BBC, 'Blair's green record condemned, 26 August 2002 http://news.bbc.co.uk/1/hi/uk_politics/2214821.stm [Accessed 25 October 2002].

Porter, N. (1996) *Rethinking Unionism. An Alternative Vision for Northern Ireland*, Belfast, Blackstaff.

Pratchett, L. (ed.) (2000) *Reviewing Local Democracy? The Modernization Agenda is British Local Government*, London, Frank Cass.

Prescott, J. (2001) quoted in BBC, 12/4/01, 'Public Transport vs. the Car' http://news.bbc.co.uk/vote2001/hi/english/main_issues/sections/facts/newsid_1203000/1203475.stm [Accessed 25 October 2002]

Prescott, J. (2002) quoted in BBC 'Prescott "proud" of green record' 14 August 2002 http://news.bbc.co.uk/1/hi/uk_politics/2192174.stm [Accessed 25 October 2002]

Prochashka, F. (1995) *Royal Bounty: The Rise of the Welfare Monarchy*, Newhaven, CT, Yale University Press.

Public Administration Committee (2001) '*Public Administration – Minutes of Evidence*', http://www.publications.parliament.uk/pa/cm200102/cmselect/cmpupadmin, 18 March.

Public Administration Committee (2002) *The Second Chamber: Continuing the Reform*, London, HMSO.

Radaelli, C. (2000) 'Whither Europeanization? Concept stretching and substantive change', *European Integration On-line Papers*, 4(8) http://eiop.or.at/eiop/texte/2000–008a.htm

Rawlings, R. (2000) Concordats of the Constitution', *Law Quarterly Review*, 116, pp. 257–86.

Rao, N. (2000) *Reviving Local Democracy: New Labour, New Politics*, London, Policy Press.

Rawls, J. (1971) *A Theory of Justice*, Harvard, Harvard University Press.

Rawnsley, A. (2001) *Servants of the People: The Inside Story of New Labour*, London, Penguin.

Redwood, J. (1999) *The Death of Britain? The United Kingdom's Constitutional Crisis*, London, Macmillan.

Reef, M. J. and Knoke, D. (1999). 'Political Alienation and Efficacy', in Robinson, J. P., Shaver, P. R. and Wrightsman, L. S. (eds) *Measures of Political Attitudes*, London, Academic Press, pp. 413–64.

Reno, W. (1997) *Warlord Politics*, Boulder, CO, Lynne Rienner.

Rhodes, R. A. W. (1995) 'From Prime Ministeral Power to CoRE Executive' in Rhodes and Dunleavy (eds), *Prime Minister, Cabinet and Case Executive*, London, Macmillan.

Rhodes, R. A. W. and Dunleavy, P. (1995) *Prime Minister, Cabinet and Core Executive*, London, Macmillan.

Richard, I. and Welfare, D. (1999) *Unfinished Business*, London, Vintage.

Richards, D. (1997) *The Civil Service Under the Conservatives 1979–97: Whitehall's Political Poodles*, Brighton, Sussex Academic Press.

Richards, D. and Smith, M. J., (2002) *Governance and Public Policy in the UK*, Oxford, Oxford University Press.

Richardson, J. (ed.) (2001) *European Union: Power and Policy Making*, London, Routledge.

Riddell, P. (1998) *Parliament Under Pressure*, London, Gollancz.

Rosamond, B. (2001) 'Functions, Levels and European Governance', in Wallace, H. (ed.) *Interlocking Dimensions of European Integration*, Basingstoke, Palgrave.

Rosamond, B. (2002) 'Britain's European Future', in Hay, C. (ed.) *British Politics Today* Cambridge, Polity.

Rose, R. (1982) *The Territorial Dimension in Government: Understanding the United Kingdom*, Chatham, NJ, Chatham House.

Rose, R. (2001) *The Prime Minister in a Shrinking World*, Cambridge, Polity.

Rose, R. and McAllister, I. (1986) *Voters Begin to Choose: From Closed-Class to Open Elections in Britain*, London, Sage.

Ryan, M. (1994) *War and Peace in Ireland: Britain and the IRA in the New World Order*, London, Pluto.

Saarlvik, B. and Crewe, I. (1983) *Decade of Dealignment: The Conservative Victory of 1979 and Electoral Trends in the 1970s*, Cambridge, Cambridge University Press.

Sabato, L. J. (1991) *Feeding Frenzy: How Attack Journalism Has Transformed American Politics*, New York, Free Press.

Saggar, S. (2001) 'The Race Card Again?, in *Britain Votes 2001*, Special Issue of *Parliamentary Affairs*, Oxford, Oxford University Press.

Sanders, D. (2002) in King, A. (ed.), *Britain at the Polls 2001*, New York, Chatham House.

Scammell, M (1995) *Designer Politics*, London, Macmillan.

Scammell, M. (2001) 'The Media and Media Management' in Seldon, A. (ed.), *The Blair Effect: The Blair Government 1997–2001*, London, Little, Brown.

Scammell, M. and Harrop, M. (2002) 'The Press Disarmed', in Butler, D. and Kavanagh, D. (eds), *The British General Election of 2001*, Basingstoke, Palgrave.

Schlesinger, P. (1990) 'Rethinking the Sociology of Journalism: Source Strategies and the Limits of Media-Centrism', in Ferguson, M. (ed.), *Public Communication: The New Imperatives*, London, Sage.

Schmidt, V. A. (1997) 'Discourse and (Dis)Integration in Europe: the Cases of France, Germany and Great Britain', *Daedalus*, 126(3), pp. 167–99.

Schmidt, V.A. (2001) 'The Politics of Economic Adjustment in Britain and France: When Does Discourse Matter?', *Journal of European Public Policy*, 8(2), pp. 247–64.

Scholte, J. A. (2000) *Globalization: a Critical Introduction*, Basingstoke, Palgrave.

Scott, Paul (2002), *A Twentieth Century Life*, Glendaruel, Argyll Publishing.

Scruton, R. (2000) *England: An Elegy*, London, Chatto & Windus.

Seawright, D. (1999) *An Important matter of Principle: The Decline of the Scottish Conservative and Unionist Party*, Aldershot, Ashgate.

Seldon, A. (1997) *Major: A Political Life*, London, Weidenfeld & Nicolson.

Seligson, M. (2002). 'the renaissance of political culture or the renaissance of the ecological fallacy?', *Comparative Politics*, 34, pp. 273–92.

Seyd, P. (2002) 'Labour Government-Party Relationships: Maturity or Marginalisation?', in King, A. (ed.), *Britain at the Polls 2001*, New York, Chatham House.

Seymour-Ure, C. (1998) 'Are the Broadsheets becoming Unhinged?', in Seaton, J. (ed.), *Politics and the Media: Harlots and Prerogatives at the Turn of the Millennium*, Oxford, Blackwell.

Shaw, E. (1994), *The Labour Party Since 1979: Crisis and Transformation*, London, Routledge.

Shawcross, W. (2001) *Deliver Us from Evil. Warlords and Peacekeepers in a World of Endless Conflict*, London, Bloomsbury.

Shugart, M. and Wattenberg, M. (eds) (2001) *Mixed-Member Electoral Systems: The Best of Both Worlds?* Oxford, Oxford University Press.

Siedentop, L. (2000) *Democracy in Europe*, London, Allen Lane.

Silcock, R. (2001) 'What is e-Government?', *Parliamentary Affairs*, 54, pp. 88–101.

Smith, M. J. (1999) *The Core Executive in Britain*: London, Macmillan.

Smith, M. (1995) 'Interpreting the Rise and Fall of Margaret Thatcher: Power Dependence and the Core Executive', in Rhodes, R. A. W. and Dunleavy, P. (eds) *Prime Minister, Cabinet and Core Executive*, London, Macmillan, pp. 108–24.

Spear, J. (2002) 'Foreign and Defence Policy', in Dunleavy, P., Gamble, A., Heffernan, R., Holliday, I. and Peele, G. (eds) *Developments in British Politics*, Basingstoke, Palgrave.

Steel, D. (2001) 'A dozen differences of devolution', Speech to Oxford Union, 5 June, http://www.scottish.parliament.uk/whats_happening/news-01/pa01–031.htm

Stewart, J. (2000) *The Nature of British Local Government*, Basingstoke, Palgrave.

Stoker, G. (ed.) (2000) *The New Politics of British Local Governance*, Basingstoke, Palgrave.

Straw, J. (2001) *Military Action Was The Only Way*. Available from: http://www.observer.co.uk/afghanistan/story/0,1501,596984,00.html [Accessed 14 November 2002].

Surridge, P. and McCrone, D. (1999) 'The 1997 Scottish Referendum Vote' in Taylor, B. and Thomson, K. (eds) *Scotland and Wales: Nations Again?* Cardiff, University of Wales Press.

Sutherland, K. (ed.) (2000) *The Rape of the Constitution?* London, Imprint Academic.

Swaddle, K. and Heath, A. (1989), 'Official and Reported Turnout in the British General Election of 1987', *British Journal of Political Science*, 19, pp. 537–70.

Swanson, D. and Mancini, P. (eds) (1996) *Politics, Media, and Modern Democracy*, Westport, CT, Praeger.

Taylor, C. (2000) 'The Role and Status of the European Central Bank: Some Proposals for Accountability and Cooperation', in Crouch, C. (ed.) *After the Euro*, Oxford, Oxford University Press.

Taylor, M. (2000) Labour and the Constitution' in Tanner, D., Thane, P. and Tiratsoo, N. (eds) *Labour's First Century*, Cambridge, University Press.

Teixeira, R. (1992) *The Disappearing American Voter*, Washington, DC, Brookings Institute.

Thompson. H. (1995) 'Joining the ERM: Analysing a Core Executive Policy Disaster', in R. A. W. Rhodes and P. Dunleavy (eds) *Prime Minister, Cabinet and Core Executive*, London, Macmillan.

Tomlinson, M. (1995) 'Can Britain leave Ireland? The Political Economy of War and Peace', *Race and Class*, 37(1), pp. 1–22.

Tonge, J. (2002a) *Britain Needs to Clean Up its Export Controls to Help Conflict Prevention in Africa* [online]. Available from: http://www.jenny-tonge.org.uk/ [Accessed 16 November 2002].

Tonge, J. (2002b) *Northern Ireland: Conflict and Change*, London, Pearson.

Tonge, J. and Evans, J. (2001) 'Faultlines in Unionism: Division and Dissent Within the Ulster Unionist Council', *Irish Political Studies*, 16, pp. 111–32.

Toynbee, P. (2002), *A World of Bullies*. Available from: http://www.guardian.co.uk/Print/0,3858,4491232,00.html [Accessed 14 November 2002].

Toynbee, P. and Walker, D. (2001) *Did Things Get Better? An Audit of Labour's Successes and Failures*, London, Penguin.

Trench, A. (2001) *The State of the Nation, 2001: The Second Year of Devolution in the United Kingdom*, Exeter, Imprint Academic.

Travers, T. and Jones, G.W. (1997) *The New Government of London*, London, Joseph Rowntree Foundation.

Tsebelis, G. (2002) *Veto Players: How Political Institutions Work*, Princeton, NJ, Princeton University Press.

Tumber, H. (ed.) (1999) *News: A Reader*, Oxford, Oxford University Press.

Tunstall, J. (1971) *Journalists at Work*, London, Constable.

Van der Eijk, C., Franklin, M. *et al.* (1996) *Choosing Europe? The European Electorate and National Politics in the Face of Union*, Ann Arbor, MI, University of Michigan Press.

Van Parijs, P. (1995) *Real Freedom For All*, Oxford, Clarendon Press.

Vandenbroucke, F. (2001) 'European Social Democracy and the Third Way: Convergence, Divisions and shared Questions', in White, S. (ed.) *New Labour: The Progessive Future?*, Basingstoke, Palgrave.

Verba, S. and Nie, N. (1972) *Participation in America: Political Democracy and Social Equality*, New York, Harper & Row.

Verba, S., Nie, N. and Kim, J. (1978) *Participation and Political Equality: A Seven Nation Comparison*, New York, Cambridge University Press.

Verba, S., K. Schlozman and Brady, H. (1995) *Voice And Equality: Civic Voluntarism in American Politics*, Cambridge, MA, Harvard University Press.

Vickers, R. (2000) 'Blair's Kosovo Campaign: Political Communications, the Battle for Public Opinion and Foreign Policy', *Civil Wars*, 3(1), pp. 54–70.

Vickers, R. (2003a) *Labour and the World. The Evolution of the Labour Party's Foreign Policy since 1900*, Vol. 1, Manchester, Manchester University Press.

Vickers, R. (2003b) 'Robin Cook', in Theakston, K. (ed.), *Foreign Secretaries Since 1974*, London, Frank Cass.

Vowles, J. (2001) 'If PR Enhances Turnout, why not in New Zealand: The Puzzle of the 1999 Election', Paper delivered at the American Political Science Association Annual Meeting, San Francisco, 30 August–2 September.

Walker, D (2002) 'E-Democracy's eleventh hour', *Guardian*, 18 July.

Walker, R. (2002) 'Work after Welfare, Employment after Benefits', *Benefits*, 10(2), pp. 83–5.

Warleigh, A. (2002) *Understanding European Union Institutions*, London, Routledge.

Wallace, H. and Wallace, W. (eds) *Policy Making In the European Union*, Oxford, Oxford University Press.

Ware, A. (1996) *Political Parties and Party Systems*, Oxford, Oxford University Press.

Weakliem, D. and Heath, A. (1999) 'The Secret Life of Class Voting: Britain, France, and the United States Since the 1930s', in Evans, G. (ed.) *The End of Class Politics? Class Voting in Comparative Context*, Oxford, Oxford University Press.

Webb, P. (2000) *The Modern British Party System*, London, Sage.

Weir, S. and Beetham, D. (1999) *Political Power and Democratic Control in Britain: The Democratic Audit of the United Kingdom*, London, Routledge.

Wheare, K. C. (1960) *The Constitutional Structure of the Commonwealth*, Oxford, Oxford University Press.

Wheeler, N. and Dunne, T. (1998) 'Good International Citizenship: A Third Way for British Foreign Policy', *International Affairs*, 74(4), pp. 847–70.

White, C., Bruce, S., and Ritchie, J. (2000) *Young People's Politics: Political Interest and Engagement Amongst 14–24 Year-Olds*, York, Joseph Rowntree Foundation.

White, S. (2001) 'The Ambiguities of the Third Way', in White, S. (ed.) *New Labour: The Progressive Future?*, Basingstoke, Palgrave.

Whiteley, P. (2002) 'An Electoral Earthquake', *Guardian*, 14 November.

Whiteley, P., Clarke, H., Sanders, D., and Stewart, M. (2001) 'Turnout', *Parliamentary Affairs*, 54, pp. 775–88.

Wilford, R. (2001a) 'The Assembly and the Executive', in Wilford, R. (ed.), *Aspects of the Belfast Agreement*, Oxford, Oxford University Press.

Wilford, R. (2001b) 'The Assembly and the Executive: A Discursive Appraisal', *Irish Political Studies*, 16, pp. 233–44.

Wilks, S. (1996) 'Britain and Europe: An Awkward Partner or An Awkward State', *Politics*, 16(3).

Wilkes, G. and Wring, D. (1998) 'The British Press and European Integration: 1948 to 1996', in Baker, D. and Seawright, D. (eds), *Britain For and Against*

Europe: British Politics and the Question of European Integration, Oxford, Clarendon Press.

Wilks, S. (1997) 'Conservative Governments and the Economy, 1979–97', *Political Studies*, 45, pp. 689–703.

Wilson, D. and Game, C. (2002) *Local Government in the United Kingdom*, Basingstoke, Palgrave.

Wincott, D. (2001) 'The Court of Justice and the European Policy Process', in Richardson, J. (ed.) *European Union: Power and Policy-Making*, London, Routledge.

Wolinetz, S. (2002) 'Beyond the Catch-All Party: Approaches to the Study of Parties and Party Organisations in Contemporary Democracies', in Gunther, R., Montero, J. R. and Linz, J. (eds) *Political Parties: Old Concepts and New Challenges*, Oxford, Oxford University Press.

Womack, S. (2002) 'Teenagers shun "boring, lying" MPs', *Independent*, 4 July.

Wright, A. (2000) *Scotland: The Challenge of Devolution*, Aldershot, Ashgate.

Wring, D. (1996) 'Political Marketing and Party Development in Britain', *European Journal of Marketing*, 30, pp. 100–11.

Wrong, D. (1988) *Power*, Oxford, Blackwell.

Young, A. and Wallace, H. (2000) 'The Single Market: A New Approach to Policy', in Wallace, H. and Wallace, W. (eds) *Policy-Making in the European Union*, 4th edn, Oxford, Oxford University Press.

Young, H. (1999) *This Blessed Plot: Britain and Europe from Churchill to Blair*, London, Macmillan.

Young, H. (2002), 'Exposing nerves, testing intellectual muscle', *Guardian*, 18 April.

Young, J. W. (1997) *Britain and the World in the Twentieth Century*, London, Edward Arnold.

Index

'A' level exam scandal   292–3
Abacha, Sani   333
accountability   22, 34–6
Adams, Gerry   193–4, 196
adaptation, national   45, 50–2, 55
Additional Member System (AMS)
    101–2, 107, 108, 117, 124, 171–2,
    177
advisers, special   60–1, 66, 72, 73, 145
Afghanistan   321–3, 336
agriculture   306, 312–14
alienation   85–6
Alliance Party of Northern Ireland (APNI)
    183, 192
al-Qaeda network   321–3
Alternative Vote Plus system   102, 115
Alternative Vote system (AV)   102, 103
Ancram, Michael   132
Anderson, Donald   26
Appointments Commission   29, 30
arms sales   330–5
Ashcroft, Michael   128
Ashdown, Paddy   137
asset-based egalitarianism   254–5
asymmetric shocks   279
attack journalism   156–7
audit   218–20
Audit Commission   219, 220
authority   64–5

backbench rebellions   25
Baldwin, Stanley   230
Balls, Ed   73
banal Europeanism   54
Bank of England   35, 73–4, 264, 269
'basic law'   23
Beckett, Margaret   229
behavioural political participation   83
Best Value   219
bin Laden, Osama   321, 322, 323
Bingham, Lord   35
Blair, Tony   4, 6–7, 11, 112, 123, 235,
    242
    business friendly image   127–8
    constitutional reforms   18, 19, 27
    core executive   60, 61, 65–9 passim, 81;
        limits of power 76–80 passim
    devolution in Scotland   171, 172
    directly elected mayors   214
    environment   302, 305, 306, 307, 319
    euro   8
    income inequality   255

international arena   8–9, 330–1, 335–7;
    arms sales 334, 335; internationalism
    327–30; relationship with US 324–5;
    security threats 322–7 passim
    and media   145–7, 149, 158
    mission of first and second terms   282,
        301
    Northern Ireland   190, 194
    party leadership   128, 132, 135, 136
    PFI   13
    power   339, 351–2, 358; cabinet
        committee system 346, 348–51
    relationship with Brown   16–17, 78,
        133, 341–2, 352, 358
    social policy   284
    state pensions   273
Blunkett, David   74, 132
Boateng, Paul   91
Boulton, Adam   158
British Energy   14–15
British–Irish Council   186, 239–40
British–Irish Intergovernmental Conference
    186
Brown, Gordon   6–7, 12, 98, 132, 283
    advisers   73
    Bank of England independence   73–4
    euro 8; five economic tests   7, 54
    Pension Credit   298
    PFI   13–14
    power   339, 358; cabinet committees
        348–51
    relationship with Blair   16–17, 78, 133,
        341–2, 352, 358
    social justice   253
Brown, Nick   150
Budget   150
    2002   275–6
budgetary process   353–7
Bundesrat model   236–8
Bush, George W.   324, 325
Byers, Stephen   16, 72, 151, 157, 206, 335

Cabinet   60, 61, 343
Cabinet Committee system   342–51
Cabinet Office   145
Cabinet Secretary   66, 67
Cameron, Ewen   309–10
Campaign for the English Regions (CFER)
    207
Campbell, Alastair   73, 145, 152–3, 158
Canavan, Dennis   117, 177
carbon dioxide emissions   307, 316–17

Carbon Trust   306, 316
cars
    recycling   314–15
    transport   310–12
central government   60–81
    control of local government   217–20
    modernization of Whitehall   69–76
    from personalism to institutionalism
        65–9
Central Office of Information   145
Chamberlain, Neville   133
Charles, Prince of Wales   31, 32
Child Benefit   293
children   293–4
Children's Tax Credit   293, 294
Chirac, Jacques   325, 326
Churchill, Winston   132
civic duty to vote   86–7, 88–9
civil servants   63, 64
    relations with ministers   69–76
Clarke, Charles   157, 293
Clarke, Kenneth   17, 126, 132, 133, 273
climate change   307, 316–17
Clinton, B.   242, 324, 330
coalitions   113
codified constitution   23, 24
Commission on Social Justice   285–6
Common Agricultural Policy   (CAP)
    313–14
Commons, House of   11, 24–8
Commons Liaison Committee   26, 27
competition policy   56–7
Comprehensive Performance Assessment
    (CPA)   219–20
Comprehensive Spending Review (CSR)
    78
congestion charging   311–12
Conservative Party   1–2, 4–5, 16, 17
    and core executive   69–70
    economic policy   263–4, 274
    House of Lords reform   29, 30
    leadership race 2001   126, 132–3
    party system   119–39 *passim*
    policy agendas   255–8
    Scotland   167–8, 169, 170–1, 177
    voting patterns and electoral systems
        105–6, 109–15, 116–17
consociationalism   182–7, 188–9, 200–2
constitution   18–38
    judiciary   34–6
    Monarchy   31–3
    nature of   21–4
    Parliament   24–30
constitutional modernizers   20
constitutional radicals   20–1
constitutional traditionalists   21
convergence criteria   48, 49, 53, 276
Cook, Robin   42, 132, 157, 341
    constitutional reforms   26–7, 30

Foreign Secretary   329, 330, 331, 332,
    333, 335
core executive   60–81
    budget process   353–7
    limits of prime ministerial power   76–80
    personalism and institutionalism   65–9
    power within   72–6
    relations between ministers and civil
        servants   69–76
    understanding   62–5
council tax   218
councillors, local   212–13, 237–8
Crosland, Anthony   247, 250, 251

Dalyell, Tam   179
Davies, Ron   234
Davis, David   17, 132, 133
decentralization   203–21
    control of local government by central
        government   217–20
    and devolution   203–5
    local democracy   215–17
    local government   210–15
    London   208–10
    regionalism   205–8
Delivery Unit   68–9, 71
Delors, Jacques   57
democracy
    consociational   182–7, 200–2
    crisis of   94–5
Democratic Unionist Party (DUP)   183,
    186, 188, 189, 191–2, 197–9, 200, 201
Demos   248–9
Department of the Environment, Food and
    Rural Affairs (DEFRA)   72, 308–10
Department of the Environment, Transport
    and the Regions (DETR)   305, 308
departments   65–6, 79
    core executive budget process   353–7
depoliticization   267–70
devolution   9–10, 222–41
    Britain as a multi-national state   238–40
    and decentralization   203–5
    for England   230–4
    and its impacts   234–8
    and the UK   222–5
    and the Westminster Parliament   35,
        225–30
Dewar, Donald   175, 231
difference principle   253
directly-elected mayors   113–15, 214–15
disaggregation, ideological   244–6, 255–8
Dobson, Frank   151–2
Downing Street Declaration 1993   182,
    194
Duncan Smith, Iain   1–2, 17, 97, 128–9,
    131, 147, 255
    leadership race 2001   126, 132–3
Dunwoody, Gwyneth   26

e-Democracy website   141
economic growth   12, 269–70
economic and monetary union (EMU)
    48–9, 52–4
    see also Euro
economic policy   48, 261–81, 285
    depoliticization   267–70
    fiscal policy   270–6
    globalization, regionalism and EU
        264–7
    Old Labour, New Labour and
        Thatcherism   262–4
    single currency   276–81
education   16, 162, 175, 287, 290–3
Educational Institute of Scotland (EIS)   167
egalitarianism   252–4
    asset-based   254–5
elderly, care for   175–6
elections   108–15
    general   *see* general elections
    local   215–17
    mayoral   113–15, 214–15
    Northern Ireland   188–9
    turnout   *see* turnout
    see also voting
electoral systems   37, 100–18
    level and quality of electoral participation
        103–8
    political parties and   123–5
    representation   115–18
    role of elections   108–15
    varieties of   101–3
electorates of belonging   122
electrical goods   315
employment   58–9
enforced Europeanization   47–9
England, devolution for   230–4
environmental policy   302–20
    critique of New Labour   317–19
    history of environment as policy issue
        303–4
    international governance and   316–17
    New Labour and environmentalism
        305–7
    New Labour's record   310–16
    structure of environmental governance
        308–10
ethical foreign policy   330–5
Euro   8, 17, 39, 276–81
    case for and against membership
        278–80
    possibility of winning referendum
        280–1
    see also economic and monetary union
European Central Bank (ECB)   277, 279
European Convention   8, 36, 40
European Parliament   113, 114, 124
European Union (EU)   7, 35–6, 80, 154,
    325

British debates about   41–4
economic policy and   264–7
enlargement   7–8, 40
environmental policy   313–14, 314–15,
    316, 317
Europeanization   7, 39–59
    enforced   47–9
    as feedback   46–7, 54–9
    of governance   44–7
    ideational   46, 52–4, 55
    and national adaptation   45, 50–2, 55
expenditure teams   78

Falconer, Lord   349
federalism   228–30, 234–8
feedback   46–7, 54–9
Field, Frank   287
fiscal policy   270–6
    attempts to depoliticize   271–3
    Labour's first term restraint on
        expenditure   15, 273–4
    2002 budget   275–6
five economic tests   54, 277
Fischer, Joschka   36
Foot, Michael   132
foot and mouth epidemic   75, 152, 313
foreign policy   *see* international arena
Foreign Policy Centre, The   331
Forsyth, Michael   172
Forward Strategy Unit (FSU)   68, 71
fragmentation of party system   120–5
fridges, disposal of   314, 315
fuel duty protests   152, 319
full committees   344, 345
Fundamental Expenditure Reviews (FER)
    70

general elections
    devaluations and   277–8
    1997   16
    parties and electoral system   123–4
    Scotland   168, 169, 177
    turnout   *see* turnout
    2001   1, 2–7, 82, 89–94, 177; campaign
        143–4, 145–6
    voting patterns and electoral systems
        109–12, 116–17
genetically modified (GM) crops   312–13
Giddens, Anthony   242, 243–4
Giscard d'Estaing, Valéry   8, 36, 40
Gladstone, W.E.   232–3
globalization   7, 258
    economic policy   264–7
    internationalism and   327–30
'golden' rule   271–2
Good Friday Agreement   181, 182–91,
    197, 239–40
    consociational democracy   182–7, 200–2

Good Friday Agreement (*cont.*)
  practical and intellectual problems
    187–91
Gould, Philip   148
governance
  Europeanization of   44–7
  international   316–17
Government Information and
    Communication Service   144
Gray, John   256
Greater London Authority (GLA)   208–10
Greenpeace   15, 148, 312

Hague, William   4, 131, 132, 146, 147,
    206, 232
health   16, 78, 275, 287, 287–9
Heath, Edward   65, 133, 169
hereditary principle   28, 32, 33
Heseltine, Michael   133, 214
Hinduja affair   156–7
hollowed out state   79–80
Howard, Michael   74
Howe, Geoffrey   77, 341
human rights   330, 331
Human Rights Act 1998   34–5
Hume, John   193–4, 195

ideas   242–60
  ideological disaggregation   244–6,
    255–8
  ideological entrepreneurs   248–50
ideational Europeanization   46, 52–4, 55
Improvement and Development Agency
    220
Income Support   293
indirectly elected second chamber   236–8
individualism   257
Indonesia   332–3
Ingram, Adam   322
Institute for Public Policy Research (IPPR)
    248–50
institutions
  institutional change and participation   84
  institutionalism in central government
    65–9
  Scotland: after devolution   173–6;
    pre-devolution 164–7
Integrated Child Credit (ICC)   293, 294,
    298
integrated transport policy   303, 305–6,
    307, 310–12, 320
Inter-Departmental Committees   72–3
interest groups   174–5
interest in politics   86–7, 88–9
international arena   7–9, 321–37
  arms sales and ethical foreign policy
    330–5
  globalization and internationalism
    327–30

presidential foreign policy   335–7
  security threats   321–7
international governance   316–17
internationalism   327–30
Iraq   8–9, 323–4, 325, 326–7
Irish Republic Army (IRA)   182, 188, 190,
    192–3, 194, 195
Irvine, Derry   29, 349

joined-up government   71
Joint Ministerial Committee   235
Jones, Iuean Wyn   205
Joseph, Keith   135, 357
journalism   *see* media
judiciary   34–6

Kabbakh, President   333
Kavanagh, Trevor   154, 158
Kennedy, Charles   128–9, 137, 146, 324
Kinnock, Neil   136, 234–5, 283
Kosovo   328–30, 336
Kyoto Protocol   316–17

labour market   266–7
Labour Party   1, 16–17, 58
  and constitutional reform   18–19, 29, 30
  economic policy   262–4, 274
  and electoral system   37, 100
  and environmentalism   305–7; critique
    of New Labour 317–19
  and media   144–8; news management
    149–59
  party system   119–39 *passim*
  public services   283–7
  Scotland   168, 169, 171–2, 177
  threats to public policy   12–16
  transition from Old to New Labour
    135–6
  2001 general election   3–7, 90
  voting pattens   89–90, 92, 105, 106,
    109–15, 116
Lamont, Norman   13, 78, 341
Law Lords   34
Lawson, Nigel   77, 341
leadership, party   128–9, 130, 145–7
  leadership predominance   131–4
league tables   219–20
Liberal Democrats   1, 4–5, 17, 118
  constitutional reform   29, 30
  party system   119–39 *passim*
  Scotland   171, 172, 177, 180
  voting patterns   89, 92, 108, 109–15
Lilley, Peter   74
Lisbon process   266–7
Livingstone, Ken   15, 113, 117, 131, 152,
    208–10, 311
lobby briefings   152–3, 157–8
local government   210–20, 233–4, 237–8
  central government control   217–20

elections 215–17
internal structures 213–15
local councillors 212–13, 237–8
role 211–12
Local Government Association (LGA)
217, 218
London 208–10
mayoral election 113–15
transport 15, 208–9, 311
Lord Chancellor 34, 349
Lord Chief Justice 34
Lords, House of 28–30
as indirectly elected chamber 236–8
loyalists 181, 183, 191, 197–9

Maastricht Treaty 48, 49, 53, 57, 276
Major, John 77, 78, 112, 123, 132, 133,
134, 182
cabinet committee system 343, 349
departments 65
devolution 171
leadership style 66
Mandelson, Peter 16, 132, 151, 156–7,
158, 339, 341
marginality of seats 105–6
mass parties 125
mayoral elections 113–15, 214–15
McConnell, Jack 172
McLeish, Henry 176
media 140–60, 166
Labour and news management 149–59
political communications media 140–3
public relations politics 143–9
Meacher, Michael 317, 317–18
Michael, Alun 131, 204, 205
Milburn, Alan 283
Milosevic, Slobodan 329
Minimum Income Guarantee (MIG)
297–8
Ministry of Agriculture, Fisheries and Food
(MAFF) 75, 308
misery index 261
Modernization Committee 26
modernization of Whitehall 69–76
Monarchy 31–3
Moore, Jo 149, 157
Morgan, Rhodri 204, 205
Morris, Estelle 1, 16, 293
Mugabe, Robert 335
Mulgan, Geoff 249
multilateralism 327–30
multilevel governance (MLG) 44–5
multi-national state 238–40
Murdoch, Rupert 154, 339

national adaptation 45, 50–2, 55
National Air Traffic Control Service 14
National Health Service (NHS) 16, 78,
275, 287, 287–9

nationalists 181, 183–4, 192–3, 193–6
NATO 328–30
neo-liberalism 255–8
New Deal 294, 295–7
New Zealand 98
news management 149–59
newspapers 140–1, 142, 156–7
partisanship 153–4
Nice, Treaty of 42
Nolan Committee on Standards in Public
Life 34
North American Free Trade Area (NAFTA)
279–80
North–South Council 186
Northern Ireland 9–10, 181–202
devolution 222, 223, 224, 238–9,
239–40; and Westminster Parliament
225–30
Good Friday Agreement *see* Good
Friday Agreement
nationalist and republican politics
193–6
party system 191–3
unionist and loyalist politics 197–9
Northern Ireland Assembly 182–4, 185,
190, 192
Northern Ireland Women's Coalition
(NIWC) 183, 192
Norton Commission 26–7

Office of Public Service Reform 69
Omagh bombing 195
online voting 98
Orange Order 191, 192, 198–9
Orde, Hugh 190

Packaging Waste Directive 50–1
Panel 2000 331
paramilitary organizations 182, 183–4,
190, 191
Parliament 11–12, 24–30, 37
devolution and 35, 225–30
House of Commons 11, 24–8
House of Lords 11–12, 28–30
parliamentary sovereignty 23–4, 52
participation 82–99
comparative perspective 94–7
declining culture of 85–7
level and quality of electoral participation
103–8
participatory culture and (non)-voting
87–9
and political culture 83
social inclusion 91–4
voting and party competition 89–91
ways to increase electoral participation
98
party list systems 102–3, 117–18
party in public office 128–34

party system   *see* political parties
Patten, Chris   150
Patten Commission on policing   189–90
Pension Credit   298
pensions   273, 284–5, 297–9
people, sovereignty of   31–2, 238–9
Performance and Innovation Unit (PIU)
    68, 75
personal voting   116–17
Plaid Cymru   112, 136
pluralism   162–3
plurality rule   37, 100, 101
policing   189–90
policy activism   74
policy agendas   242–60
    Conservative Party   255–8
    language of progressive politics   246–8
    social justice   251–5
    think tanks and ideological entrepreneurs
        248–50
Policy Directorate (formerly Policy Unit)
    66, 68, 77
policy making
    core executive and   68–9, 70–6
    Scotland: after devolution   173–6;
        pre-devolution 164–7
policy transfer   74
political advisers   60–1, 66, 72, 73, 145
political collegiality   131–4
political culture   83
    see also participation
political efficacy   86
political parties   1, 119–39
    fragmentation of party system   120–5
    funding   127–8
    intra-party politics   128–30
    leadership   128–9, 130, 131–4;
        leadership predominance and political
        collegiality 131–4
    local elections   216–17
    membership   126–7, 129–30
    Northern Ireland   183–4, 185, 191–9;
        party system   191–3
    organizational change   125–8
    party conferences   130
    party identification   87, 88, 88–9,
        122–3
    political realignment within party system
        134–8
    rationality   95
    Scotland: after devolution   176–8;
        pre-devolution 167–8
    voting and party competition   89–91
    voting patterns and electoral systems
        108–15
    see also under individual parties
political realignment   134–8
political system   9–12
    Scottish   162–4

poll tax   84
Porritt, Jonathon   318
Portillo, Michael   17, 132, 133
postal voting   98
Powell, Jonathan   73
power   338–59
    Cabinet Committee system   342–51
    limits of prime ministerial power
        76–80
    rational choice models   351–9
    within core executive   72–6
Prescott, John   16, 132, 214, 305, 318,
        346, 349
    regionalism   206–7
    transport policy   307, 310
primary care groups (PCGs)   288
Prime Minister   33
    and core executive   60–9, 75–6, 81;
        limits of power 76–80
    power: Cabinet Committee system
        346–51; rational choice models 351–2,
        355–9
    press conferences   158
Private Finance Initiative (PFI)   13–14,
        130, 299–301
privatization   14–15
process journalism   155–6
Progressive Unionist Party (PUP)   183,
        199
proportional representation (PR)   37, 98,
        104, 106–8, 116, 124
    role of elections   108–15
    see also under individual systems
protest   83, 96, 97
Public Administration Committee   29–30
public expenditure   287
    education   287, 291, 292
    fiscal policy   270–6
    health   287, 288, 289
    Labour's first term restraint   15, 273–4
    Scotland   165–6
public opinion   4–7
    Scotland: after devolution   176–8;
        pre-devolution 167–8
public–private partnership (PPP)   15, 208
public relations politics   143–9
Public Service Agreements (PSAs)   69
public service ethos   32–3
public services   12–16, 282–301
    development of Labour policy   283–7
    education   16, 162, 175, 287, 290–3
    health   16, 78, 275, 287, 287–9
    PFI   13–14, 130, 299–301
    welfare policy   234–5, 284–5, 287,
        293–9
Public Services and Public Expenditure
        (PSX) Committee   353, 354–7

qualified majority voting (QMV)   42

Railtrack 14
rational choice
    models and power 351–9
    and voting 89–91
rationality 95
Rawls, John 250, 251, 253
Real IRA (RIRA) 184, 195
realignment, political 134–8
referendums 169, 172–3, 185, 187, 280–1
regional assemblies 207–8, 233–4
Regional Development Agencies (RDAs) 206, 233
regionalism 205–8, 232–4
    globalization, EU and 264–7
regulation 50, 56–7
Reid, John 199
representation
    local government 212–13
    voting systems and 109, 115–18
Republican Sinn Fein 194
republicans 181,183–4, 191, 193–6
Richard Commission 204, 223
Ridley, Nicholas 357
road transport 310–12
Ross, Willie 166
rule of law 23–4

Saddam Hussein 8, 323–4, 327
Sainsbury, Lord 128, 313
Sandline International 333
Schroder, Gerhard 325
Scotland 161–80, 239
    devolution 9–10, 161–2, 222, 223, 224–5, 232; rationale for 168–73; and Westminster Parliament 225–30
    institutions and policies: after devolution 173–6; pre-devolution 164–7
    political system 162–4
    public opinion and parties: after devolution 176–8; pre-devolution 167–8
    voting systems 107–8, 113, 114, 124
Scottish National Party (SNP) 136, 168, 169, 172, 177, 179, 180, 232
Scottish Office 164–6
Scottish Parliament 9, 32, 124, 171–2, 173–6, 178–9, 222
Scottish Socialist Party 177, 180
Scottish Unionist Party 167
Select Committees 25–6, 27
September 11 terrorist attacks 76, 142, 321
Serbia 328–30
Sheridan, Tommy 177
Short, Clare 335, 349
Sierra Leone 333–4, 336
simple plurality voting 37, 100, 101
Single Member Plurality System (SMPS) 12, 101–2, 104, 107–8, 123

representation 115–18
role of elections 108–15
Single Transferable Vote (STV) 100, 103, 205
Sinn Fein (SF) 182, 183, 188–9, 190, 192–3, 193–6, 200, 201
small parties 112
Smith, John 18, 136
Smyth, Reverend Martin 198
Social Democratic and Labour Party (SDLP) 184, 189, 192, 193–6
Social Exclusion Unit 71, 74–5, 251
social inclusion/exclusion 91–4, 251–2
social justice 251–5
social policy 57–9
Socialist Alliance 136
special advisers 60–1, 66, 72, 73, 145
specialist units 74–5
spin 155
    as problem 157–9
Stability and Growth Pact 48–9, 276–7, 279
state pensions 273, 284–5, 297–8
Steel, David 174
Strategic Communications Unit 144
Straw, Jack 40, 334, 335
sub-committees 344–6
Sun, The 154
Sunderland Commission 204–5
Sunningdale Agreement 1974 185–6
Supplementary Vote (SV) 102, 113–15
Sure Start 294
sustainable investment rule 271–2

tactical voting 107–8
Taliban regime 321–3
task forces 74
taxation 263–4
    fiscal policy 270–6
television 140, 142
10 Downing Street 68–9, 77
    organizational structure 66, 67
    website 141
territorial politics 164
terrorism 8–9, 321–3, 325–6, 326–7
Thatcher, Margaret 11, 48, 79, 123, 132, 133
    administrative reforms 50, 65
    and devolution 169, 170
    and the EU 57
    ideology 248, 255–6, 257
    leadership 66, 76–7; disagreement with ministers 77; poor ministerial appointments 357
    media and 154
    removal from office 340–1
    Thatcherist economic policy 263–4
think tanks 248–50

Third Way
  foreign policy   327–8
  public services   285–6
  social justice   251–5
Tomlinson, Mike   292–3
trade policy   47
trade unions   13–14, 127, 128
transport   303, 305–6, 307, 310–12, 320
Treasury   268, 341
  changing role   77–8
  power and core executive budget process
    353–7
Treaty on European Union (TEU)   48, 49,
    53, 57, 276
Trimble, David   184, 197–8
trust   85–6, 88, 97
tuition fees   175, 293
Turnbull, Andrew   66
turnout
  electoral systems and   104–6
  general elections   90–1, 92–5; decline
    2–4, 89–94, 94–5
  local elections   215–16
two-party-plus system   121, 125
two-party system   120–1

Ulster Defence Association (UDA)   183,
    191, 199
Ulster Democratic Party   199
Ulster Freedom Fighters (UFF)   183, 199
Ulster Unionist Party (UUP)   183, 188,
    189, 190, 191–2, 197–9
unionists   181, 183, 193, 197–9
United Nations (UN)   326, 329
United States (US)   57, 342
  British foreign policy and   321–7
  Kyoto agreement   317
  war on terrorism   8–9, 321–3, 325–6

voting   82–99
  comparative perspective   94–7
  declining culture of participation
    85–7
  participatory culture and   87–9
  and party competition   89–91
  and seat share   123–4
  social inclusion   91–4
  systems   *see* electoral systems
  turnout   *see* turnout

Wakeham Commission   29, 30
Wales   107, 113, 114, 124
  devolution   9–10, 203–5, 222, 223,
    224–5; and Westminster Parliament
    225–30
waste management   307, 314–16, 320
weapons decommissioning   190
weapons of mass destruction (WMDs)
    323–4, 326
welfare policy   234–5, 284–5
  reform   287, 293–9
Welsh Assembly   9, 124, 203, 204, 205,
    222, 223
Westminster model   10–11, 19–20
Whelan, Charlie   153
Wilson, Harold   66
Wilson, Richard   61, 73
Women's Institute   149
Women's Unit   75
Woolf, Lord   35
working class   91–2, 93–4
Working Families Tax Credit   293–4

Zimbabwe   334–5